Key Thinkers in Linguistics and the Philosophy of Language

For Caitlin Esther

Key Thinkers in Linguistics and the Philosophy of Language

Edited by

Siobhan Chapman and Christopher Routledge

Edinburgh University Press

© in this edition Edinburgh University Press, 2005
© in the individual contributions is retained by the authors

Edinburgh University Press Ltd
22 George Square, Edinburgh

Typeset in 9/11pt and prelims 10/12pt Sabon
by TechBooks, Delhi, India, and
printed and bound in Great Britain
by The Cromwell Press, Trowbridge, Wilts

A CIP record for this book is available from the British Library

ISBN 0 7486 1757 4 (hardback)
ISBN 0 7486 1758 2 (paperback)

The right of the contributors
to be identified as authors of this work
has been asserted in accordance with
the Copyright, Designs and Patents Act 1988.

Contents

CONTENTS

CONTENTS

Preface

The entries in this book describe the work of thinkers from antiquity to the present day and, although most of them concern linguists or philosophers, they also include discussions of psychologists, anthropologists, cognitive scientists, critical theorists and mathematicians. What these subjects all have in common is that each has made an important contribution to the description or the theory of language: contributions that can be traced in twenty-first-century thinking about language in the disciplines of linguistics and the philosophy of language. They are also all selected from the Western tradition of thought. This is not of course to deny that thinkers from other parts of the world have had, and continue to have, things to say about language that are just as interesting and important. However, it would simply not be possible to do justice in a volume of this scale to these many other traditions. The perhaps artificial restriction to Europeans and Americans reflects the names that most frequently recur in discussions of the Western tradition in linguistics and philosophy of language.

Each entry offers an overview of the work of a particular thinker and a closer analysis of one or more aspects of that work. The emphasis is on what makes the thinker important to the study of language, and as a result the aspects highlighted may not always be his or her best-known or more generally significant ideas. An interesting side effect of this is often to shed new or unexpected light on an otherwise well-known figure. The main focus of each entry is on the development of ideas, but some biographical information is included where this is relevant to illuminating the character of the thinker or explaining his or her career and ideas in their historical and cultural context. The introductory material to each entry includes the names of other related key thinkers (listed after 'see also'), further contextualising the subject. The list may include people who worked with the subject, those who have been significant in similar areas of thought, those who influenced or were influenced by the subject, or those whose work offers a significant contrast. In addition, other key thinkers who have their own entries are indicated with an asterisk when first mentioned in an entry. These two types of cross-referencing allow influences, commonalities and continuities in thinking to be traced to other contemporary work, and across the history of ideas.

Entries include an indication of the nature and significance of the subject's influence, but they offer a summary of the work rather than a critique or novel interpretation. Above all, they are intended to promote further interest, providing an introduction to the key thinkers represented here in the hope that readers will be encouraged to explore the ideas described in more detail. For this reason, each entry concludes with some suggestions for primary reading and, where possible, for further reading. The former indicate those of the key thinker's own writings that are particularly salient in their impact on language study, while the latter cite some of the most important discussions of the relevant ideas.

Notes on Contributors

Annalisa Baicchi. Department of Linguistics, University of Pavia, Italy.

Jennifer A. Baldwin. Software developer, USA.

Philip Carr. Professor of Linguistics, Department of English, University Paul Valery, Montpelier, France.

Siobhan Chapman. University of Liverpool, UK.

Billy Clark. Senior Lecturer in Communication and English Language Studies, Middlesex University, UK.

Claire Cowie. Lecturer in English Language and Linguistics, University of Sheffield, UK.

Iris Einheuser. Visiting Assistant Professor, Wellesley College, USA.

Yousif Elhindi. Associate Professor of Linguistics, Department of English, East Tennessee State University, USA.

Iván García-Álvarez. Department of Linguistics, Stanford University, USA.

Agustinus Gianto. Pontifical Biblical Institute, Rome, Italy.

Hans Götzsche. Associate Professor and Director, Centre for Linguistics, Aalborg University, Denmark.

Eva Herrmann-Kaliner. Computational linguist, Germany.

Patrick Honeybone. University of Edinburgh, UK.

Asa Kasher. Laura Schwarz-Kipp Professor of Professional Ethics and Philosophy of Practice, Tel-Aviv University, Israel.

Alan S. Kaye. Professor of Linguistics and Director, Phonetics Research Laboratory, California State University, Fullerton, USA.

Stavroula-Thaleia Kousta. Research Centre for English and Applied Linguistics, University of Cambridge, UK.

Anthony Newman. Department of Philosophy, Tufts University, USA.

Ahti-Veikko Pietarinen. Post-Doctoral Fellow of the Academy of Finland, Department of Philosophy, University of Helsinki, Finland.

Ingrid Piller. University of Sydney, Australia.

Geoffrey Poole. Lecturer in English Language and Linguistics, University of Newcastle, Newcastle upon Tyne, UK.

Professor Kanavillil Rajagopalan. State University at Campinas (UNICAMP), Brazil.

Christopher Routledge. Freelance writer and editor, Lancashire, UK.

Mike Scott. School of English, University of Liverpool, UK.

Marie Šafářová. Department of Philosophy, University of Amsterdam, the Netherlands.

Jürg Strässler. Senior Lecturer, Universities of Berne and Zurich, Switzerland.

Geoff Thompson. Senior Lecturer in Applied Linguistics, University of Liverpool, UK.

NOTES ON CONTRIBUTORS

Dominic Watt. Lecturer in Sociolinguistics, Centre for Linguistic Research, School of Language and Literature, University of Aberdeen, UK.

Klaas Willems. Supervisor, Advanced Studies in Linguistics, Universities of Gent, Louvain, Antwerp and Brussels, Belgium.

John Williams. Literacy consultant, UK.

David V. Witkosky. Auburn University, Montgomery, USA.

ARISTOTLE

Aristotle (*b.* 384 BC, *d.* 322 BC; Greek), philosopher who produced an 'empirical' account of knowledge and language. According to Aristotle reality is anchored in particular entities, rather than in the universal world of ideas. In other words, knowing things means being aware of their causes. Aristotle's distinctions between particular and universal, substance and accidence, and matter and form give birth to the traditional analysis of language elements. He maintains that there is a natural correspondence between object and mental image conventionally represented by arbitrary signs of both spoken and written forms. (*See also* Plato; Putnam, Hilary; Locke, John; Leibniz, Gottfried Wilhelm.)

Aristotle was born in Stagira in eastern Macedonia in 384 BC. His father, Nicomachus, was a physician of the Macedonian king and his profession helps explain Aristotle's interest in biology and other experimental knowledge. At the age of 17 Aristotle went to Athens to attend *Plato's Academy. When his master died in 347 BC Aristotle left for Atarneus, on the coast of Asia Minor. The king of this place, whose niece Aristotle was to marry, gave him the town of Assos to live in and set up a circle of intellectuals. Later he moved to Mytilene, on the island of Lesbos, where he did zoological research and met Theophrastus, who later became his intellectual heir. In 334 BC Philip II, king of Macedonia, invited Aristotle back to Pella to become tutor of his son, Alexander (later known as Alexander the Great). Aristotle returned to Athens in 335 BC and started a school of his own, known as the Lyceum. In 323 BC he retired to Chalcis, on the island of Euboea, and died the following year. His writings, both extant or otherwise known from ancient sources, represent a vast array of subjects: ethics, metaphysics, politics, economics, logic, rhetoric, psychology, natural sciences. His pupil Theophrastus succeeded him as head of the Lyceum. He also brought to completion some projects Aristotle himself did not finish.

By joining Plato's circle in Athens Aristotle gained access to the most prestigious and stimulating company of intellectuals in the Western world. Like Plato, Aristotle was very much immersed in questions about the nature of knowledge and in what way knowledge represents truth. But more than his master Aristotle introduced a systematic account of knowledge that was to exercise great influence in philosophy for almost a millennium and a half after his death. Some scholars think that when he moved out of Athens in 347 BC Aristotle also began to distance himself from the Platonic school of thought. It is true that in fundamental issues like the ontological status of particulars and in what constitutes the good life Aristotle differs greatly from Plato. Yet a closer scrutiny of Aristotle's works suggests that he never completely abandoned Platonism. Nor do Aristotle's works show an all-embracing empiricism as is often thought. His originality lies in offering a new philosophical synthesis that can account for empirical knowledge.

The collection of essays known as *Metaphysics* begins with a statement that human beings have a natural desire for knowledge. Aristotle thus claims, on the basis of experience, that the desire to satisfy curiosity is part of the nature of human beings. This desire for knowledge is first of all a search to find out what individual things have in common. Aristotle explains that for particular entities to make sense they must share a complex of qualities with other entities. This complex of qualities is what constitutes the universal properties. Unlike Plato, who believed that such universal properties build the essence of reality, Aristotle maintained that it is the particulars that constitute reality. His concern was to show the 'one throughout the many' rather than Plato's 'one apart from the many'.

For Aristotle, knowing something means being able to give a satisfactory explanation for the changes in the nature of things. For this he elaborated a theory of four causes of change: material (the stone that is to become a statue), efficient (the sculptor), formal (the shape of the statue) and final cause (to commemorate the individual). Together these causes give a complete analysis of the necessary conditions of all existing things. More importantly they also constitute the principle for their intelligibility. Thus for Aristotle any given things necessarily have their material, designer, design and purpose. The doctrine of the four causes improves on earlier similar efforts. Philosophers like Thales, Anaximander and Anaximenes (sixth

century BC) gave inadequate explanations simply because they considered material causes only. The Pythagoreans (sixth century BC) too, because of their sole interest in formal causes such as number and proportion, failed to give a more satisfactory account. Even Plato did not succeed in giving a complete account of things simply because he was too concerned with material and formal causes only.

Aristotle did not write a special treatise on language and was not interested in language in its own right. None the less it is possible to reconstruct what he thought about language. Though scattered in different writings, most of his views about language are found in *Categories* 1–9, *De Interpretatione* 1–4, *Poetics* 20–1 and *Rhetoric*, book III. Before tracing his more detailed view about language, it is useful to deduce from his general ideas about the cognitive faculties found in *De Anima* that according to Aristotle there is no specific organ for language, though different organs work together for the production and reception of language. This leads to the idea that language is inseparably connected with perceptions. For that reason it is necessary to study perceptions in order to arrive at language. Language is seen in terms of its observable manifestations, which are the sounds produced by speech organs. For Aristotle, language is a potential whose realisation occurs in the act of speaking. But this act indispensably requires the vocal organs, which belong to the world of matter. This makes language intrinsically bound to the world of matter. Of all the objects in the observable world, matter is the least accessible to knowledge. Therefore the best one can hope, according to Aristotle, is to acquire a practical knowledge of it. This knowledge is worth pursuing because it teaches a lot about an instrument which itself is necessary to achieve knowledge of things and to feel about them. Aristotle maintained that even if language cannot reveal lasting truth it plays an indispensable role in achieving practical goals. For him, language is an instrument that is useful in pursuing higher ends such as the knowledge of truths.

According to Aristotle, intellectual activities are based on the ability to characterise something, hence saying that something belongs to something else. The ability to group different things under the same heading or categories is the basis of human reasoning. These categories furthermore represent the different modes of being. According to Aristotle there are ten different categories which determine the meaning of the predication: substance (man, horse), quantity (two cubits long), quality (white, grammatical), relation (half, double, bigger), location (in the marketplace, in the Lyceum), time (yesterday, last year), position (is lying, is sitting), possession (is shod, is armed), doing (cuts, burns), undergoing (is cut, is burned). It is clear from these categories that the substance is what stays in the individual things when the accidental properties are taken out. Therefore the category of substance is fundamentally different from the rest, which are accidental categories. Aristotle's theory of categories has a double bearing on traditional grammar given that language is both the object of study and the instrument for analysis.

Aristotle also assumed that words signify things according to their modes of being, namely as substances or as accidents. This correspondence is what gives intelligibility of things to the human mind. There is congruence between the categories of beings, of meanings, and of understanding, which explain why philosophy, grammar and logic in the Aristotelian traditions are closely associated with each other. Thus nouns are understood as words which refer to substance, and adjectives as qualities, verbs as activities or doing something. The classification into parts of speech reflects the categories established to classify different modes of being.

The difference between substance and accidental properties also explains the analysis of propositions as consisting of a subject that is particular and a predicate that is universal. Proper names are the most individual and the most substantival, and thus represent something definite of which something universal can be predicated. Abstract nouns, verbs, adjectives and adverbs belong to the universal or general, since they do not refer to individual substances.

Aristotle also worked out a system of major grammatical classes of words on the basis of the then common view originating with Plato. For Plato, words belong either to the class of nouns (*onomata*) or that of verbs (*rhemata*). This is primarily meant to explain the constituents of a proposition. The first are words that can function as subject in any predication and the second include all words that function as action or quality predicated. In *Poetics* 20, while maintaining this distinction, Aristotle added

3

a third category of words: conjunctions (*syndesmoi*). This class contains all words that are not nouns or verbs. Such a classification was later taken over by medieval Arab grammarians with their tripartite categories of words: nouns, verbs and particles. Aristotle's *onomata* and *rhemata* are later expanded in traditional grammar as major parts of speech, and *syndesmoi* as minor parts of speech. The major-against-minor distinction is in fact analogous to the matter–form distinction. For Aristotle, every existing thing consists of matter and of form, which give its individuating reality. Applied to language, this distinction leads to the observation that only the major parts of speech, such as nouns, adjectives, verbs and adverbs, have referents, and because of that they provide the subject matter of sentences. Other parts of speech, like conjunctions, prepositions and other particles, serve to give a form to the total meaning of discourse.

With this general overview of his understanding of the elements of language, it is possible to explore Aristotle's views on semantics. The beginning of *De Interpretatione* contains a succinct synthesis of Aristotle's view about linguistic meaning: 'Spoken words are symbols of affections in the soul, and written letters are symbols of spoken words. And just as written letters are not the same for all humankind, neither are spoken words. But what these are in the first place signs of – the affections (*pathemata*) of the soul – are the same for all, and what these affections are likenesses of (*homoiomata*) – actual things (*pragmata*) – are also the same' (1, 16a3–8). Aristotle noted two relations here: first, between a sound and some mental state, and second, between this mental state and the external object. The first is conventional, the second is natural.

The background to Aristotle's thoughts on language is Plato's fundamental disagreement with two contrasting philosophical theories of language in *Cratylus*, namely, either that words are conventional signs and have arbitrary meanings, or that they are natural signs, as smoke signals fire. For Plato, the fact that language breaks up reality into knowable real objects suggests the natural connection between language and reality. However, Plato rejects naturalism on the grounds that the meaning of a sequence of sounds uttered by a speaker is agreed upon by all speakers. Aristotle's idea of sign as having two relations, one natural and the other arbitrary, resolves the conflicting views. The sign itself therefore is not sufficient to settle the question of truth or falsehood, which will happen only when the sign is employed in a proposition, thus where something is said about something else in a predication. This is different from Plato's objection to both conventionalism and naturalism.

The double relation above gives grounds for the existence of four components in Aristotle's theory of meaning: real-world objects; their natural impressions in the mind; spoken signs, which conventionally represent these impressions; and finally, written signs, which stand for spoken words. The relation between written language and spoken words is also conventional, as is the relation between spoken words and the mental states that function as carriers of meaning.

Different languages can identify different sounds with the same things, and conversely the same sounds can correlate to different things. But the relation between the mental state and the thing in the real world has to be natural, since it is the same for all people and languages. There is thus, using a twenty-first-century terminology, a prototypical resemblance in all. This universal validity of laws of thought remained unchallenged until the end of the nineteenth century.

Aristotle's view that mental states resemble objects in the real world gives a foundation to a realist epistemology. These mental states, generated by the senses and thought, correspond to objects in the real world and are in fact likenesses of these objects. This means that sensing allows perceptions about real objects. These perceptions are shaped by the real objects and bear resemblance to them. Memory retains these perceptions for comparison with future perceptions. On the basis of this experience, generalisations and predictions are possible: this is the basis of knowledge. Thus knowing things means having a concept of things in the form of a likeness of them, and language performs this function. Since the objects in the real world are stable, the senses of the words also have stability. In other words, reference is established by sense so that anyone who is capable of using language is also capable of referring to and describing objects in the real world.

According to Aristotle forms exist in the empirical world and are accessible to human minds. Thus meanings find their intelligible essence in the real world. More comprehensive treatises like *Metaphysics* can justifiably be used to elucidate and systematise various seminal insights developed in an earlier work like *De Interpretatione*. The cognitive ability to use sensory contents to represent objects through mental images (*phantasmata*) is called imagination (*phantasia*). As a mode of sensory representation *phantasia* is well placed to secure the reference of a common noun such as tree or man. Indeed simple names, including proper names and common nouns, are the basis of Aristotle's theory of language. When used in single affirmations these are likened by the thought to substances existing in the real world, namely the individuals or objects named so. But thought can only do this if it has imagination. An image derived from the perception of a tree or man resembles other trees or men. The extension of Aristotle's theory of meaning to include scientific definition, however, is not without problems. At best the image of a tree seems to convey minimal information about the essence of a tree. Furthermore, the conceptualisation of such images constitutes meanings. Thus, the cognitive process of thinking and perceiving relates to external objects and shares the same structures. Aristotle's belief that the mental state (*pathema*) reflects external objects gives grounds for the relation between cognition and meaning.

For Aristotle, verbal definition of an object gives an ostensive definition of its form (*eidos*); he considers that the meaning of words lies in their capacity to indicate objects. This ostensive definition of meaning is in conformity with Aristotle's view that knowledge in sciences, namely metaphysics, physics and mathematics, is a representation of the physical objects or their properties in the mind. The criterion of truth or falsehood of this knowledge is given in *Categories* 4b8–9: 'For it is because the actual thing exists or does not exist that the statement is said to be true or false.' In other words, sentences about real-world objects are true if what they assert corresponds to that reality. Moreover, they are necessarily true if the corresponding reality is unchanging. This clearly suggests that Aristotle adopted a correspondence theory of truth. This account of truth makes the value of linguistic assertions, such as sentences, depend upon the extra-linguistic state of affairs they are representing.

On the death of Alexander in 325 BC Aristotle retired to Chalcis, where he died in 322 BC. The Lyceum was closed by Emperor Justinian I in AD 529, together with other schools of philosophy in Athens, but despite this, Aristotelian scholarship continued in Constantinople until the fall of the Eastern Roman Empire. In the meantime Aristotle's works on logic were known in the West through the works of Boethius until the late fifth and early sixth centuries AD. His other works came to the West by way of the Arabic versions translated into Latin during the ninth to twelfth centuries. Direct translation from Greek texts began only in the twelfth century when manuscripts from Constantinople became known in the West. Within a century Aristotle's influence became overwhelming in the world of learning in Europe. Aristotelian influence reached its peak when it was used by, among others, Thomas Aquinas to present a systematic account of Christian doctrine.

With the Renaissance Aristotle's influence in the intellectual world diminished and was gradually replaced by a greater interest in Platonism. Nevertheless his notion that words have meaning because they correspond to 'mental likenesses' of reality, which has become known as the 'ideational' account of meaning, was fundamental to the work of the British empiricists of the Enlightenment, perhaps most notably John *Locke. It can also be discerned in the structuralist account of meaning developed by Ferdinand de *Saussure. Aristotle's account of all knowledge as derived from experience has been seen as laying the foundations for subsequent empiricist, or 'blank-slate', accounts of language acquisition. It is perhaps for this reason that the influence of Plato's innatism on Aristotle's thought has often been overlooked or forgotten. Aristotle bequeathed to the world of learning a long-lasting vocabulary to describe reality. For example, we owe to Aristotle the idea of a statement being either true or false, that which is false being that which is not true. This has become known as bivalent or classical logic, and is a central idea in Western philosophy. Even when his influence has ceased to be dominating, Aristotle's thought has continued to inspire and intrigue generations of thinkers.

Primary works

(1831–70). *Aristotelis Opera* (5 vols). I. Bekker (ed.). Berlin: G. Reimer.
(1908–52). *Works of Aristotle translated into*

English (12 vols). W. D. Ross and J. A. Smith (eds). Oxford: Clarendon Press.

(1926–91). *Aristotle* (23 vols). Loeb's Classical Library. Cambridge, MA: Harvard University Press.

(1984). *The Complete Works of Aristotle: The Revised Oxford Translation* (2 vols). J. Barnes (ed.). Princeton, NJ: Princeton University Press.

Further reading

Ackrill, J. L. (1981). *Aristotle the Philosopher*. Oxford: Oxford University Press.

Barnes, J. (ed.) (1995). *The Cambridge Companion to Aristotle*. Cambridge: Cambridge University Press.

Bolton, R. (1985). 'Aristotle on the signification of names'. In *Language and Reality in Greek Philosophy*. Athens: Greek Philosophical Society. 153–62.

Charles, D. (2000). *Aristotle on Meaning and Essence*. Oxford: Oxford University Press.

Ghiselin, M. (1974). 'Categories, life and thinking'. *Behavioral and Brain Sciences*. Vol. 4. 269–83.

Lloyd, G. E. R. (1968). *Aristotle: The Growth and Structure of his Thought*. Cambridge: Cambridge University Press.

Modrak, D. (2001). *Aristotle's Theory of Language and Meaning*. Cambridge: Cambridge University Press.

Ross, W. D. (1923). *Aristotle* (5th edition, 1971). London: Methuen.

Agustinus Gianto

ANTOINE ARNAULD

Arnauld, Antoine (b. 1612, d. 1694; French), theologian and philosopher, strongly associated with the controversial Port-Royal school. Recognised for his influential work in linking logic with language and for his extensive correspondence with key philosophers of the day. (*See also* Frege, Gottlob; Leibniz, Gottfried Wilhelm.)

Born in Paris in February of 1612, Antoine Arnauld (also known as the Great Arnauld) was the twentieth child of Antoine Arnauld senior, a renowned lawyer in Paris, and Catherine Marie de Druy. Only half of Arnauld's siblings survived to adulthood, yet all but one of the survivors were involved in some way with Port-Royal, a Cistercian convent and school that would become a centre of theological controversy for many years. In fact Arnauld had planned to follow in his father's footsteps and pursue a career in law until a family friend encouraged him to consider life within the church. He then attended the Collège de Mans, where he received his doctorate in 1641 and was ordained as priest the same year.

Under the leadership of the Abbé St Cyran (the same family friend who had influenced Arnauld to join the church) and later of Arnauld's own sister, Jacqueline, Port-Royal became known for its loyal support of Jansenism, a movement aimed at reform within the Roman Catholic church. Jansenism, so named for its founder Cornelius Jansen, bishop of Ypres, sought a return to the strict moral ideology advocated within the writings of St Augustine. These principles, which included predestination and rigorous piety, sharply contrasted with the teachings of the Jesuits, launching decades of debate of which Arnauld and Port-Royal were at the heart. A particular topic of dispute had to do with the Formulary, a series

7

of five propositions about Jansenism for which Pope Innocent X declared the movement to be heretical. Those, including the Great Arnauld, who would not publicly proclaim their agreement with the Formulary were declared heretics and persecuted, until the Peace of the Church (1669) created a truce across both sides of the disagreement. Arnauld had joined the Sorbonne in 1643 but was expelled from its faculty in 1656 as a direct result of the harsh Jansenist views he had expressed in his writings, including most visibly *De la fréquente communion* (1643), and for his refusal to accept the Formulary. Upon leaving the Sorbonne Arnauld returned to Port-Royal, where he carried on the Jansenist debate through continued correspondence with such prominent thinkers as Nicholas Malebranche, Gottfried Wilhelm *Leibniz and René *Descartes.

The lengthy correspondence between Arnauld and Malebranche focused on the notion of ideas as an extension of the concept of grace. Malebranche's position was that humans see all things and ideas through God, but Arnauld felt that such thinking was unsound and that humans perceive ideas directly and without God's intervention. The dispute began with Arnauld's 1683 publication of *Des vraies et des fausses idées*, continued for several years, and finally ended with a last rebuttal from Malebranche, published five years after Arnauld's death. The communication between Arnauld and Leibniz, who was unknown compared with Arnauld at the time, initially concerned Leibniz's *Discours de métaphysique* and carried on for quite some time

afterwards. Finally, Arnauld's contact with Descartes started when Arnauld was asked to review Descartes' *Meditationes de prima philosophia*, first by a third party and then by Descartes himself.

Through these debates and the many others surrounding his involvement within the Jansenist movement and Port-Royal, Arnauld came to contemplate the nature of argumentation itself. In 1660 and 1662, he published *Grammaire generale et raisonné* and *La Logique, ou l'art de penser*, respectively. Although both were collaborations with other Port-Royalists, Arnauld is typically credited for having contributed the majority of their content. Based on the view that most arguments between men involve a disagreement over language, such as definition of terms, or association between objects, these works outline the grammar of Port-Royal. Arnauld saw language as a manifestation of one's thoughts and so for him clarity in language reflected clarity of mind. Of course to achieve this one must commit to thinking logically to carry out arguments and settle disputes. Arnauld felt that too few of the time's thinkers were properly trained in logic, for they placed too much emphasis on theological beliefs and too little on factual realism. Taking a Cartesian approach to argumentation and logic while focusing on language as a means of expression, Arnauld organised his *Logique* according to four elements of knowledge: conceiving, judging, reasoning and ordering. These elements, of which each depends on the prior, follow the progression of an idea towards a sound scientific claim. That is, an idea is first conceived in its simplest form and then combined with other ideas through judging. Reasoning involves multiple judgements, and ordering occurs when judgements are expressed in the best order to form a valid argument.

The most basic component of any argument is an idea. Here Arnauld makes a distinction between the comprehension of an idea (its representation within the mind, as constituted by a set of attributes the idea represents) and its extension (its existence outside the mind). In Arnauld's view a source of confusion concerning ideas stems from the inevitable ambiguity of language, which he alleges as the main cause for 'defective ideas'. For this he recommends defining up front any ambiguous words used to express ideas, so as to dispel potential misunderstanding. He also stresses that one must be careful not to depend so much on one's words that one loses touch with the ideas that each of those words expresses. Arnauld's definition of ideas helped to lay the framework of modern semantics.

Arnauld's treatment of judging is essentially a study of propositions. He defines judgement as the 'joining' of two ideas, whether affirmatively joining like ideas or negatively joining unlike ideas. In this way a judgement is expressed linguistically as a sentence, and because sentences are built on words, Arnauld dedicates significant attention to types of words, for example nouns, verbs and pronouns, and their function in relation to other words. For the most simple of judgements, two ideas may be joined using the copula *is* and, if the two ideas are dissimilar, the negation word *not*. There also exist complex and compound judgements, expressed as complex and compound sentences.

When linking ideas requires more than a straightforward judgement or assertion, reasoning comes into play. Reasoning is the joining of ideas via an intermediary judgement or series of judgements, resulting in a series of sentences in which the last one derives from those that precede it. Arnauld warns, however, that reasoning itself leads to many errors in argumentation, occurring when the intermediary sentences do not sufficiently support the conclusion expressed in the final sentence. He stresses that one must exercise great caution while reasoning, so as not to discredit one's own argument on the grounds of invalid reasoning alone.

The final element of Arnauld's approach to logical argumentation is the successful ordering of sentences such that each sentence appropriately leads to the next and ultimately substantiates the claim made in the concluding sentence. Early sentences ideally assert inarguable facts, strengthening the basis for the argument as a whole. In the end, skilful ordering demonstrates well-ordered thoughts and minimises any defects of argumentation that may result from ambiguity of language or unsupported, emotional judgements. In his analysis of logical thought Arnauld creates an impressive early study of language and its role within debate and the expression of knowledge.

Although their intellectual contributions to logic, grammar and debate are aptly recognised today, Arnauld and other Port-Royalists were commonly considered, in their day, to be little more than heretical Jansenists.

9

Port-Royal itself witnessed tremendous turbulence throughout the seventeenth century. Founded in 1204 in Chevreuse, a town southwest of Paris, Port-Royal de Champs survived well, schooling both men and women, housing seculars, and eventually opening new schools in Paris. When its name became synonymous with the Jansenist reform movement, however, Port-Royal became a target for religious and political persecution. Its people were forced to disperse and later regroup several times between 1638 and 1669, the year of the Peace of the Church. Port-Royal enjoyed acceptance for only ten years and then, in 1679, fell into controversy once more. In that year, Arnauld left France for a self-imposed exile in the Netherlands, where he died in Brussels in August of 1694. In 1709 Louis XIV ordered Port-Royal to be destroyed.

Primary works

(1660) (with Claude Lancelot). *A General and Rational Grammar*. Menston: Scolar Press, 1968.
(1662) (with Pierre Nicole). *Logic, or the Art of Thinking*. James Dickoff and Patricia James (trans.). New York: Bobbs-Merrill, 1964.

Further reading

Dominicy, Marc (1984). *La Naissance de la grammaire moderne: Langage, logique et philosophie à Port-Royal*. Brussels: Pierre Mardaga.
Donzé, Roland (1967). *La Grammaire générale et raisonnée de Port-Royal*. Bienne: Éditions Francke Berne.
Kremer, Elmar J. (1994). *The Great Arnauld and Some of his Philosophical Correspondents*. Toronto: University of Toronto Press.

Nadler, Steven M. (1989). *Arnauld and the Cartesian Philosophy of Ideas*. Manchester: Manchester University Press.
Weaver, F. Ellen (1978). *The Evolution of the Reform of Port-Royal: From the Rule of Cîteaux to Jansenism*. Paris: Éditions Beauchesne.

Jennifer A. Baldwin

J. L. AUSTIN

Austin, J. L. (John Langshaw) (*b.* 1911, *d.* 1960; British), one of the major English philosophers of the first half of the twentieth century and a leading figure in the British tradition of analytic philosophy. Austin is generally credited with establishing the school of 'ordinary language philosophy' which flourished at Oxford in the years following World War II. He and his supporters held that ordinary language was a suitable focus of philosophical study and indeed was the most reliable guide for philosophical analysis. In linguistics he is best known for introducing the theory of 'speech acts'. (*See also* Ayer, A. J.; Grice, H. P.; Moore, G. E.; Ryle, Gilbert; Searle, John.)

Born in Lancaster on 26 March 1911, Austin was one of five children. His father, G. L. Austin, was an architect when his son John was born, but after military service he moved his family to St Andrews on the east coast of Scotland, where he became secretary to St Leonard's school. In 1924 Austin won a classics scholarship at Shrewsbury school and in 1929 won a scholarship to study classics at

Balliol College, Oxford. After graduation he was a fellow of All Souls (1933–5) and then a fellow and tutor at Magdalen College (1935–52). During World War II Austin served in MI6, a branch of British intelligence. He was an intelligence officer at the Supreme Headquarters of the Allied Expeditionary Force, active in preparations for D-Day, and reached the rank of lieutenant colonel. After the war he was honoured by the United Kindom with an OBE, by the United States when he was made an officer of the Legion of Merit, and by France with the Croix de Guerre. In 1952 he became White's Professor of Moral Philosophy, a position he held for eight years, until his death.

Austin's papers have all (but one) been posthumously collected and published in *Philosophical Papers*, edited by J. O. Urmson and G. J. Warnock, first in 1961 and then in 1970, when two additional papers were added. One of the latter was most probably Austin's first paper, written before 1939, in which he discussed the meaning of the Greek terms *agathon* and *eydaimonia* in the *Ethics* of *Aristotle, his starting point being a paper by Prichard on the meaning of *agathon*. Some of the papers, such as 'A plea for excuses', a 1956 presidential address to the Aristotelian Society, had been published before they appeared in that collection. Other papers, such as the 1940 lecture to the Moral Sciences Club in Cambridge and the Jowett Society in Oxford, 'The meaning of a word', and the transcript of a 1956 BBC talk, 'Performative utterances', had not been published earlier.

Austin's best-known book, *How to Do Things with Words* (1962), is based on his William James lecture series, delivered at Harvard University in 1955. The notes Austin used for those lectures had in turn developed from notes prepared for his 1952–4 lectures at Oxford on 'Words and Deeds'. Most of the notes were full, but some parts were fragmentary and therefore interpreted and supplemented before the volume was published, edited by J. O. Urmson. A second edition of the book was published in 1976, edited by J. O. Urmson and Marina Sbisa, after a thorough re-reading of all the notes and additional materials. Austin's book *Sense and Sensibilia* rests on lecture notes written from 1947 to 1959, mostly under that title. The text of the book is a reconstruction that expanded the length of the text to five or six times the length of the notes. The book was reconstructed by G. J. Warnock and published in 1962.

Austin played a major role in the 'linguistic turn' that took place in philosophy during the first half of the twentieth century, particularly in England and the United States. For Austin, a philosophical project starts from a systematic study of a family of words and phrases that reflect an underlying conceptual framework. Unlike many other philosophers within the mainstreams of analytic philosophy and ordinary language philosophy, who have taken the study of language to be of major importance as a matter of philosophical conviction, Austin took it to be just a matter of common sense and scholarly or scientific responsibility. The results of such a systematic scrutiny of linguistic expressions can be used for two utterly different purposes. First, they can be used as part of an investigation the object of which is language itself. Second, they can be used as a stage in a philosophical analysis of certain problems and attempted solutions that are phrased in terms of expressions that include words and phrases of that family.

The former use is related to the lexical semantics of English, or any other language, as studied by linguists, or to theoretical semantics or pragmatics, as developed by philosophers and linguists in adjacent areas. The latter use, familiar to students of philosophy, both ancient and modern, belongs to a philosophical tradition, stretching from Socrates and *Plato to G. E. *Moore, of carrying out conceptual analysis of some kind before proceeding to a discussion of major claims of philosophical interest and significance made for critical or theoretical purposes.

How to Do Things with Words includes numerous examples of the first kind of use, since it develops a theoretical framework for describing and classifying speech acts in general. *Sense and Sensibilia* is an example of the second kind of use. It is a work in philosophy of perception, which employs an analysis of expressions used in common theories of perception, such as 'appear', 'look' and 'seem', as well as ones used in previous philosophical theories of perception, such as 'sense data'. Some of Austin's earlier papers, written before World War II and not considered here, show another classical style of doing and writing philosophy. Austin's major and characteristic work is commonly held to be that written after the war.

Austin's method of linguistic scrutiny of 'families' of expressions involves two noteworthy steps. First, a family of expressions is collected by a person or by a group of persons, such as Austin's 'Saturday morning group', described by G. J. Warnock in Berlin et al. (1973). This is done on the grounds of their own natural linguistic competence as well as of dictionaries that point out different uses, specify synonyms and show examples of usage. Such a process of collection depends on the linguistic intuitions commonly held by whoever participates in it, *qua* native speaker of a natural language, and on decisions made by writers of dictionaries on grounds of their own linguistic intuitions, *qua* native speakers. A dictionary rests also on some conception of what is a dictionary, but usually this is not an articulate conception of language or of any other object of philosophical discussion, such as perception. Second, participants in the process create 'stories' that involve using an expression that belongs to the delineated family, in a context of utterance that allows it but does not allow replacing it by some other expression or expressions of that family. Again, portrayal of such a 'story' involves just linguistic intuitions with respect to using certain expressions under certain circumstances. Thus the linguistic data collected and created during such a process of linguistic scrutiny is confined to linguistic intuitions held by native speakers of a natural language, independently of any given conception of language or a theory in any branch of philosophy. In this respect Austin's approach is similar to, but independent of, *Chomsky's approach to the issue of data collection. Both are justifiable in terms of a theory of linguistic intuition that takes it to reflect, in different and complex ways, certain underlying conceptions and principles.

Austin took his work on different types of utterance to be among his most significant. His major contributions to this area were his 1946 paper 'Other minds', his 1956 BBC talk 'Performative utterances' (both posthumously published in *Philosophical Papers*, 1961), the similar 1958 paper 'Performatif-constatif' (posthumously published in French in 1962 and then in English translation in 1963), and most importantly his posthumously published *How to Do Things with Words*.

Austin's first step towards his theory of illocutionary forces was to make the distinction between 'constative' and 'performative' utterances. The technical distinction rests on a seemingly simple observation: when I say 'The book is on the desk', under certain circumstances, I describe a certain part of the situation. A natural question that arises is whether what I said is true or false. However, when I say 'I promise to put the book on the desk', under some circumstances I have bound myself to others, and staked my reputation. Similarly when I say 'I know that the book is on the desk', 'I give others my word: I give others my authority for saying' that the book is on the desk (1961: 99). When the latter utterances are made, the question of whether what I have said is true or false does not arise, though elements of the circumstances of utterance can be true and untrue. The 'descriptive

fallacy, so common in philosophy', is to suppose that utterances are descriptive, disregarding the fact that utterance of expressions such as 'I promise etc.', under ordinary appropriate circumstances, 'is not describing the action we are doing, but doing it' (1961: 103).

As much as the idea of drawing a clear distinction between constative and performative utterances seems plausible and applicable, it is easier said than done. Austin himself became aware of the shortcomings of the distinction as suggested. The distinction makes sense when certain utterances are compared with each other, but it became apparent that the theoretical move from clear and seemingly illuminating examples to a general and fruitful, fully fledged theory is rather difficult. Each component of the distinction was found to be a source of problems. First, a constative utterance such as 'The light is red', said by one person to another, when the two approach traffic lights, is descriptive, but at the same time it can function as a warning, which is not descriptive. Second, a performative utterance, such as 'I claim that the light was green', said under ordinary circumstances, gives rise to the question whether it was true or false that the light was green. Moreover it does it to the same extent as the utterance of 'The light was green', said under the same circumstances. Third, the infelicity conditions (the conditions under which 'something goes wrong and the act . . . is therefore at least to some extent a failure' [1962a: 14]) of utterances of both kinds seem quite similar to each other. Preconditions that have to obtain for a constative utterance to be felicitous are on a par with preconditions that have to obtain for a performative utterance to be felicitous.

Thus, for example, under ordinary circumstances of conversation, a constative utterance of the kind of assertion involves as a precondition a justified belief on the part of the person who makes it. Similarly a performative utterance of the kind of promise involves as a precondition a firm intention on the part of the person who makes it. The two preconditions seem to be parallel to each other.

Austin's theory of illocutionary forces solves those problems: the theory of forces is actually a theory of speech acts. Whenever you make an utterance, in an appropriate context, you do something. As a matter of fact, what you do, in a context of utterance, can be described on different, related levels of action. Hence, in a context of utterance you can perform, at one and the same time, a 'phonetic act' of making noises of certain phonetic qualities, as well as a 'phatic act' of uttering words and expressions of certain grammatical qualities.

More interestingly, at the same time you perform three other acts. First, there is a 'locutionary act' of uttering those words and expressions as having certain semantic qualities, in particular sense and reference. Second, there is an 'illocutionary act' of uttering those words and expressions, having their semantic qualities, including sense and reference, as having a certain force, such as that of asserting, warning or promising. Third is a 'perlocutionary act' of uttering those words and expressions, having certain semantic qualities and having a certain force, as achieving of certain effects. One of Austin's examples in *How to Do Things with Words* was:

> Locution: He said to me, 'You can't do that'.
> Illocution: He protested against my doing it.
> Perlocution: He stopped me.

Although Austin specifies five different dimensions of language use it is just one of them, the illocutionary act, that plays the major role in the theory. To put it in terms of speech acts, the first three dimensions (phonetic, phatic and locutionary) involve elements of a speech act, while the fifth one (perlocutionary) has to do with effects of the speech act. The illocutionary dimension is that of the force of the speech act itself. Thus Austin's theory points out the illocutionary act as the unit of language use. Accordingly, '[t]he total speech act in the total speech situation is the only actual phenomenon which, in the last resort, we are engaged in elucidating' (1962a: 148). This deep insight paved the way to a whole research programme of language use that has included *Searle's Speech Acts* (1969) and many illuminating studies of speech acts in general and of particular ones (for a collection of the major ones see Kasher 1998).

An important shortcoming of that research programme, even in its more advanced stages, is that it has hardly brought philosophical theories of action to bear on philosophical theories of language use, which are first and foremost theories of illocutionary and other acts. Austin further proposed a preliminary classification of utterances into five classes, according to their illocutionary force. The first, 'verdictives', are typified by 'essentially giving a finding as to something – fact, or value – which is for different reasons hard to be certain about' (1962a: 151). Examples are those that involve the first person singular present indicative active form of 'acquit', 'diagnose' and 'understand'. The second, 'exercitives', are typified by 'exercising of powers, rights, or influence' (1962a: 151). Examples are 'appoint', 'dismiss' and 'name'. The third, 'commissives', are typified by committing the speaker to doing something, for example 'promise', 'swear' and 'vow'. The fourth, 'behabitives', 'are a very miscellaneous group, and have to do with attitudes and social behavior' (1962a: 152). Austin's examples include 'apologize', 'blame', 'thank' and 'welcome'. The fifth class is 'expositives', which 'are difficult to define. They make plain how our utterances fit into the course of an argument or conversation, how we are using words, or, in general, are expository' (1962a: 152). Examples (which Austin classified into twelve sub-classes) include 'postulate', 'quote', 'revise', 'turn next to' and 'withdraw'.

Austin's proposed classification was followed by a different one put forward by Searle in 1975. Classifications are useful to the extent to which they serve as a starting point for some explanation or theory. But Austin's and Searle's classifications have not been widely used for explanatory exposition or theory construction. A notable exception is Vanderveken (1990, 1991), which is an attempt to construct all speech acts from a core of certain speech acts and a few additional distinctions.

Another fruitful branch of philosophy of language that has emerged from Austin's *How to Do Things with Words* is that of the study of performative utterances. (For the major contributions to this field, by Urmson, Searle, Bach and Harnish and Recanati, see Kasher 1998).

Austin's other major work, *Sense and Sensibilia*, is a discussion of a certain theory of perception, put forward by the contemporary philosophers A. J. *Ayer, H. H. Price and G. J. Warnock. According to that theory 'we never directly perceive or sense material objects (or material things), but only sense-data' (1962b: 2). Austin's analysis of the meaning of 'perceive' and related terms led him to the conclusion that '[t]here is no one kind of thing that we "perceive" but many different kinds' (1962b: 4). The full nature and exact number of those kinds is a matter of scientific research rather than of philosophical investigation.

In a highly illuminating application of his methods of philosophical discussion, Austin rejected the claim 'that we ought to be "realists", to embrace, that is, the doctrine that we do perceive material things' (1962b: 3). Chapter VII of the book is devoted to an elucidation of the meaning of 'real', as contrasted with 'makeshift', 'fake', 'artificial', 'dummy' and other expressions. In understanding Austin's methods and results it is important to notice that he did not consider a theory of perception to be a theory of perception-expressions in a language. As *Sense and Sensibilia* shows, Austin was just as interested in the facts of language as in the facts of perception, and the

15

same holds when he discusses any other topic of philosophical investigation.

Austin married Jean Coutts in 1941 and they had four children. He always preferred secluded family life at his house in the Oxfordshire countryside to the bustle of college society. He was known for his reserve and his austere habits, but also for a dry wit. He died of cancer in February 1960.

Primary works

(1961). *Philosophical Papers*. J. O. Urmson and G. J. Warnock (eds). Oxford: Oxford University Press, 1970.

(1962a). *How to Do Things with Words*. J. O. Urmson (ed.). Oxford: Oxford University Press; Cambridge, MA: Harvard University Press. Second edition, eds J. O. Urmson and Marina Sbisa, 1976.

(1962b). *Sense and Sensibilia*. Reconstructed from the manuscript notes by G. J. Warnock. Oxford: Clarendon Press.

(1962c). 'Performatif-constatif'. In *Cahiers de Royaumont, Philosophie No. IV: La Philosophie Analytique*. Trans. G. J. Warnock as *Philosophy and Ordinary Language*. C. E. Caton (ed.). Urbana, IL: University of Illinois Press, 1963.

(1968). Translation of Gottlob Frege's *The Foundations of Arithmetic: A Logico-Mathematical Enquiry into the Concept of Number*. Evanstone, IL: Northwestern University Press. Second revised edition, 1980.

Further reading

Berlin, Isaiah et al. (1973). *Essays on J. L. Austin*. Oxford: Clarendon Press.

Fann, K. T. (1969). *Symposium on J. L. Austin*. London: Routledge and Kegan Paul.

Furberg, Mats (1971). *Saying and Meaning: A Main Theme in J. L. Austin's Philosophy*. Oxford: Blackwell.

Graham, Keith (1977). *J. L. Austin: A Critique of Ordinary Language Philosophy*. New York: Harvester Press.

Kasher, Asa (1998). *Pragmatics, Critical Concepts. Vol. II: Speech Act Theory and Particular Speech Acts*. London: Routledge.

Searle, John R. (1969). *Speech Acts*. Cambridge: Cambridge University Press.

Vanderveken, Daniel (1990, 1991). *Meaning and Speech Acts. Vols I–II*. Cambridge: Cambridge University Press.

Warnock, G. J. (1991). *J. L. Austin*. London: Routledge.

For a rich list of republications of Austin's works as well as of books and thirty-odd theses and dissertations on those works, see: http//sun3.lib.uci.edu/~scctr/philosophy/Austin/index.html [accessed 27 January 2004].

Asa Kasher

A. J. AYER

Ayer, A. J. (Alfred Jules) (*b.* 1910, *d.* 1989; British), Grote professor of philosophy at University College London (1946–59) and Wykeham professor of logic (1959–78), knighted (1970). Philosopher in the analytic tradition who introduced the ideas of logical positivism to an English-speaking audience in the 1930s. His name is most closely associated with the 'principle of verification', and its implications for the meaning of a variety of different types of sentences. (*See also* Austin, J. L.; Carnap, Rudolf; Kant, Immanuel; Moore, G. E.; Russell, Bertrand; Ryle, Gilbert; Wittgenstein, Ludwig.)

Ayer was born in London to parents of continental European descent. His father, Jules, was from a Swiss Calvinist family, and worked for the Rothschild family before personal bankruptcy forced him to try a fresh start in a new business venture. The maiden name of his mother, Reine, was Citroën; she came from the wealthy Dutch Jewish family that gave its name to the car company. Ayer, known to family and friends throughout his life as 'Freddie', had a classical education at Eton and was introduced to philosophy at Christ Church College, Oxford. Among his tutors there, Gilbert *Ryle discussed with him the ideas of *Russell and *Moore, and introduced him personally to *Wittgenstein. Ayer was impressed by the claim that analytic philosophy enabled the clarification of philosophical concepts by distinguishing the grammatical surface of sentences from their logical form. That is, analytic philosophers argued that the obvious properties of a sentence, such as its words and grammar, are not always an accurate indication of what it says about the world. However, the most important influence on his philosophical development came when he travelled to Austria in 1932 to meet and study with the Vienna Circle. Here he became familiar with the work of *Carnap, and more generally with logical positivism.

On his return to Oxford Ayer set about explaining his own version of logical positivism, incorporating influences from the British analytic tradition, to a wider audience. The resultant book, *Language, Truth and Logic* (1936), was published before Ayer's twenty-sixth birthday. In the generally conservative atmosphere of British philosophy it was unorthodox and controversial, but it quickly became a philosophical classical.

After active war service in the Welsh Guards Ayer moved to London, where he established a thriving philosophy department at University College before returning to Oxford. Despite his long and illustrious career, *Language, Truth and Logic* remains his best-known and most influential publication; it might be said that his life's work was an elaboration and development of the themes established there.

Ayer's greatest impact on the philosophy of language undoubtedly stemmed from his exegesis of the principle of verification. The logical positivists of the Vienna Circle addressed the question of verification by distinguishing between sentences that are meaningful, and therefore amenable to scientific study and discussion, and those that are not. They divided the first category into two basic types. First there are analytic sentences, or sentences which are necessarily true. These include sentences of the type identified by *Kant, which are necessarily true simply by virtue of the meanings of the words they contain. For example, the phrase 'all children are people' is true because the meaning of the predicate is contained within the meaning of the subject, or because 'people' is part of the definition of 'children'. The Vienna Circle also added the statements of mathematics and of logic to the category of analytic sentences, declaring that a sentence such as 'two plus two equals four' is in effect a tautology because of the rules of mathematics. The second category of meaningful sentences is those that are synthetic, or capable of being either true or false, but which can be subject to an identifiable process of verification. That is, there

17

are empirically observable phenomena sufficient to determine the question of truth. Moreover, the process of verification itself, the set of observations, provides the meaning. All sentences which are neither analytic nor verifiable by empirical evidence are meaningless, or without logical form. This includes sentences concerning moral evaluation, aesthetic judgement and religious belief. For the logical positivists, such sentences were not false; they merely had no part in scientific discourse. The doctrine of the Vienna Circle was radically empiricist and strictly anti-metaphysical.

There had been many attempts to formulate the verification principle, but Ayer's own version of it in *Language, Truth and Logic* is characteristically elegant and precise. In the opening chapter, uncompromisingly entitled, 'The elimination of metaphysics', he states that: 'We say that a sentence is factually significant to any given person if, and only if, he knows how to verify the proposition which it purports to express – that is, if he knows what observations would lead him, under certain conditions, to accept the proposition as being true, or reject it as being false' (1936: 48). In other words it need only be possible to identify what state of affairs would, ideally, serve to make a statement true or false. It is not necessary for that state of affairs actually to be available to observation.

This version of the principle of verification claims less than that of the Vienna Circle; for Ayer the means of verification is only an indication of meaningfulness, not a definition of the meaning itself. However, there are problems even with this weaker for-

mulation, and as Ayer became aware of them over the following decades he softened his commitment to verification. For instance, he conceded in *The Central Questions of Philosophy* (1973) that no completely satisfactory formulation of verification has ever been found. In particular, his own earlier version suffered from the flaw that it relied too much on individuals' ability to distinguish appropriate from inappropriate evidence, ignoring the fact that people often act irrationally. Someone who prays for rain and then sees it raining might treat this as sufficient evidence to verify the truth of the metaphysical, and therefore meaningless, sentence 'God exists'.

The significance of Ayer's version of logical positivism to the philosophy of language comes at least in part from the reactions it provoked in his contemporaries. It was initially welcomed by many of his own generation of philosophers because of the challenge it posed to philosophical authority. It dismissed many of the traditional concerns of philosophy on the grounds that they were based on the discussion of meaningless metaphysical statements; it proposed to solve many apparent philosophical problems simply by analysis of the language in which they were expressed; and, of course, it rejected all religious tenets. But over the following decade or so it also brought Ayer increasingly into conflict with another new approach to philosophy. This was the school of 'linguistic philosophy', or 'ordinary language philosophy', which grew out of the work of Ayer's own tutor Ryle, and found a champion in Ayer's near contemporary J. L. *Austin.

The verification principle is based on the premise that the meaning of a synthetic sentence is exhausted by the description of the world that it contains, and ultimately by whether that description is true or false. The verification principle is not concerned with sentences used to ask questions, issue commands, make promises, produce warnings, give invitations, or any of the other uses in which Austin became interested. Ayer and Austin enjoyed lively philosophical arguments during the 1930s, but in later years their differences led to a more embittered and open hostility. Austin's development of 'speech act theory' can be seen, at least in part, as a reaction to Ayer's rigidly truth-theoretical semantics, and the 'descriptive fallacy' that Austin detected at its core. Ayer in turn was openly dismissive of the doctrines and approaches of ordinary language philosophy, particularly its insistence that everyday language was the best, indeed the only legitimate guide to philosophical understanding.

Despite his disdain for philosophy that concerned itself only with the minutiae of language use, Ayer was acutely aware of the linguistic implications of his own work. Drawing on Russell's analytic approach, and with metaphysics removed from the philosophical field, he saw the primary concern of philosophy as being the meticulous analysis and clarification of language. Philosophy should offer 'definitions in use' of problematic expressions, by translating sentences in which such expressions occur into more elementary, logically equivalent sentences in which they do not occur. Ayer frequently cites Russell's

theory of definite descriptions as a model of this type of philosophical analysis.

One controversial area in which Ayer applied his brand of linguistic analysis was his dismissal from philosophical discourse of all sentences expressing ethical judgements. In *Language, Truth and Logic* he acknowledges that his doctrine that the only meaningful synthetic statements are those open to empirical verification is apparently challenged by the existence of 'statements of value'. However, in Ayer's view all such statements must in fact be rejected as meaningless, because there is no identifiable process of verification for them that draws on empirically observable fact. Characteristically Ayer insisted that all philosophy could properly do was to offer an analysis of the language in which moral statements are expressed, not to engage in the discussion of ethical codes. A sentence such as 'you acted wrongly in stealing that money' has just the same logical form as 'you stole the money'. The part of the sentence expressing moral judgement does not, for Ayer, add anything meaningful to the sentence because it does not add anything that could yield to empirical verification. Such meaning as ethical terms do add is not logical but only 'emotivist'; that is, it is only ever an expression of emotional attitude on the part of the speaker. For Ayer, ethical concepts are unanalysable because they are 'pseudo-concepts'. The sentence 'stealing money is wrong' has no factual meaning; it cannot be said to be either true or false.

In later work Ayer modified this uncompromising stance on ethics so far as to concede that sentences expressing moral judgements may have some element of descriptive content and therefore need not be dismissed as completely unanalysable. For instance, in *The Central Questions of Philosophy*, he allows that value judgements, although 'fundamentally' not descriptive, do nevertheless imply that the objects or actions under discussion achieve, or fail to achieve, certain moral standards. However, he notes, uses of such sentences presuppose, without empirical justification, that these standards are generally accepted.

One type of sentence that Ayer saw as more amenable to analysis, and one that continued to exercise him throughout his career, was the type relating to material objects. He notes in *Language, Truth and Logic* that the operation of the principle of verification for an individual is dependent not directly on the physical world, but on that individual's personal sense data. The data we receive through our senses is the only evidence we have available by which to subject sentences which make statements about the world to appropriate processes of verification. This has important implications for the status of statements about material objects, implications that Ayer explored more thoroughly in *The Foundations of Empirical Knowledge*, first published in 1940.

In this book Ayer addresses the question of whether our knowledge is determined by material objects themselves or by our personal sense data. He develops a phenomenalist approach to this question, arguing that beliefs and statements about material objects are only legitimate if they are translated into beliefs and statements about our sense data. However, he maintains that discussion of the status of material objects is primarily a dispute about language. It is a dispute about the best way to analyse statements of experience. Sentences concerned with material objects and those concerned with sense data are simply uses of two different types of language. They refer to the same things in two different ways, rather than describing ontologically different phenomena.

This position, too, he later came to modify, admitting in a later edition of the same book that strict translation from statements about material objects to statements about sense data is not always achievable. Later still he revised his position further, concluding that his attempt at phenomenalism was ultimately unproductive. In *The Central Questions of Philosophy* he suggests instead that, although all we actually have access to is our own sense data, this data is sufficient to warrant belief in material objects and therefore it also warrants independently meaningful statements about them. Such beliefs and statements are hypotheses that we form about the world and are justified by our experience. In this way, the existence of material objects becomes a matter of verifiable objective fact.

Verification also had some striking consequences for statements about past events, and those about the mental states of others. Neither is amenable to a process of verification, but it would be unacceptable to dismiss them as completely meaningless, on a par with metaphysical statements. In *Language, Truth and Logic*, Ayer carried his analysis of these statements through to its logical conclusion by insisting they be translated into statements that can be verified. Statements about past events are in fact statements about the present or even the future: they are about our expectations of the sense data we are encountering or will encounter as a result of those events. Statements about others' mental states are most appropriately translated into statements about their physical states, such as statements about their appearance and behaviour, as perceived through sense data, from which assumptions about mental states are merely inferences.

This radical position, too, was subject to revision throughout Ayer's subsequent work. The argument about mental states in particular may have caused him some anxiety because it came dangerously close to behaviourism, in that it concentrates on observable behaviour and dismisses any discussion of 'underlying' mental states. Behaviourism was an empirical approach to which he was always opposed. In *The Foundations of Empirical Knowledge* he challenged his own claim that it is only statements about one's own mental experiences that can be accepted as they stand, whereas statements about those of others need to be translated into statements about behaviour. Rather, drawing on an argument from analogy, he suggested that it is appropriate to treat the two types of statement in the same way. In other words it is possible to conceive of the thoughts and feelings of others as being like our own, and therefore it is legitimate to ascribe thoughts and feelings to others in the same way as we do to ourselves.

In 1956 Ayer published *The Problem of Knowledge*, in which he reconsidered both his attitude to material objects and his views on past events and other people's mental states by addressing the challenge posed by scepticism. The sceptic would claim that we have no reason to believe in the reality of material objects, of past events, or of the mental experience of others, because our personal sense data does not license such beliefs. Anxious to avoid such a position, Ayer conceded that some empirical statements must go beyond what is strictly licensed by experience of the senses. There are often gaps between our beliefs and the evidence on which they are based. These gaps do not in fact pose the problem that the sceptic would suggest. No definite proof can be offered of past events or the mental experiences of others, so it is not legitimate to demand it.

Later still Ayer worried that this argument did not in fact refute scepticism in the way he had hoped, and he attempted to offer a more robust argument in favour of the belief in events for which we do not have direct sensory evidence. In *Central Questions of Philosophy* he suggested that it may be legitimate to go beyond evidence when this is licensed by probability (when it seems likely that certain events did take place and certain material objects did exist), although his notion of what counts as acceptable probability is never fully defined. Eventually then Ayer was eager to affirm the 'common-sense' view that statements about material objects, the mental experiences of others, and past events are legitimate and meaningful, if not entirely explainable in terms of available evidence. When Bryan Magee put it to him in an interview in 1970 that his philosophy ultimately left things just where they were, Ayer insisted that this was not a problem 'because that's where they are. The point is to clarify, to elucidate, to justify. If such fundamental beliefs as these seem to be are capable of justification, the thing is to find it' (Magee 1986: 86).

In general Ayer's career was built on exploring the implications of the position he set out in his first book and, very often, softening his original stance on a number of philosophical issues. However, he never abandoned his insistence on an empirical approach to the explanation of knowledge and the language in which it is expressed, or his belief in the essentially analytic nature of philosophy.

Although he remained in academic appointments throughout his adult life, Ayer's engagement with and appetite for the outside world were legendary. He enjoyed parties and loved to dance, was passionate about football in general and Tottenham Hotspur in particular, and engaged in a long succession of love affairs, as well as three marriages. His rhetorical skills and natural flamboyancy made him an inspiring and popular teacher and, in later life, a successful and regular broadcaster on both radio and television. Although seen by some as arrogant and aloof, he inspired lasting friendship in some colleagues and admiration in many students. Ayer died on 27 June 1989, his position as one of the best-known British philosophers of the twentieth century firmly established. Some commentators have suggested that Ayer's greatest contribution was not in the originality of his ideas, but in the elegance and clarity with which he interpreted and presented the ideas of others. These are valuable skills, and *Language, Truth and Logic* has never gone out of print. Ayer's presentation of logical positivism, together with the reaction it provoked, were one of the most significant catalysts in the development of twentieth-century philosophy of language.

Primary works

(1936; second edition 1946). *Language, Truth and Logic*. Harmondsworth: Penguin, 1971.
(1940). *The Foundations of Empirical Knowledge*. London: Macmillan, 1964.
(1956). *The Problem of Knowledge*. Harmondsworth: Penguin, 1990.
(1969). *Metaphysics and Common Sense*. London: Macmillan, 1973.
(1973). *The Central Questions of Philosophy*. Harmondsworth: Penguin, 1991.
(1981). *Philosophy in the Twentieth Century*. London: Phoenix, 1992.

Further reading

Foster, John (1985). *A. J. Ayer*. London: Routledge.
Hahn, L. E. (ed.) (1972). *The Philosophy of A. J. Ayer*. La Salle, IL: Open Court.
Macdonald, Graham and Wright, Crispin (eds) (1986). *Fact, Science and Morality: Essays on A. J. Ayer's 'Language, Truth and Logic'*. Oxford: Oxford University Press.
Magee, Bryan (1971). *Modern British Philosophy*. Oxford: Oxford University Press, 1986.
Phillips Griffiths, A. (ed.) (1991). *A. J. Ayer: Memorial Essays*. Cambridge: Cambridge University Press.
Rogers, Ben (2000). *A. J. Ayer: A Life*. London: Vintage.

Siobhan Chapman

MIKHAIL BAKHTIN

Bakhtin, Mikhail M. (Mikhailovich) (*b.* 1895, *d.* 1975; Russian), intellectual and literary scholar who was concerned with intertextuality and the linguistic construction of the self. His name is most closely associated with the ideas of dialogism, polyphony and heteroglossia. (*See also* Barthes, Roland; Kant, Immanuel; Kristeva, Julia; Saussure, Ferdinand de.)

Bakhtin was born into a well-to-do family of the minor nobility in imperial Russia. His father's position as a bank executive meant that the family had to move frequently and Bakhtin was first educated at home and later went to school in Vilnius and Odessa. During his early years he had a German governess and so he grew up bilingual in Russian and German. At the time, Vilnius and Odessa were two of the great cosmopolitan and multilingual cities of the Russian empire. In Vilnius, the young Bakhtin would have heard Lithuanian, Polish, Yiddish and Hebrew on a regular basis. Odessa was another important centre of East European Jewry and also a busy port on the Black Sea where people from many different cultural and linguistic backgrounds were in contact. Given this background it is not surprising that Bakhtin developed an intense interest in heteroglossia, or 'many-languagedness'.

At university, first in Odessa and then in St Petersburg, Bakhtin enrolled in classical languages. In 1918, in the chaotic aftermath of the Soviet revolution and World War I, he left St Petersburg for a small rural town, Vitebsk, where he became a member of an intense group of intellectuals who were later to be known as the 'Bakhtin circle'. These included the musicologist Valentin N. Voloshinov and the literary scholar Pavel Medvedev. At the beginning of the twenty-first century there is an ongoing debate as to whether it was really Bakhtin who was the author of several texts published under the names of Voloshinov and Medvdev. Most notable among these are *The Formal Method in Literary Scholarship: A Critical Introduction to Sociological Poetics*, published in 1928 under Medvedev's name, and *Marxism and the Philosophy of Language*, published in 1929 under Voloshinov's name.

The Bakhtin circle's philosophical interest was in Neo-Kantianism, which dominated Russian and German intellectual life at the time. Like *Kant these intellectuals insisted on the dialectical relationship between the mind and the material world. Neo-Kantians also tried to integrate the major developments that the exact sciences went through at the time – the general theory of relativity in physics, for example, or the study of the central nervous system in physiology – with problems in philosophy. Bakhtin's life-long concern with questions of perception stems from there.

In the mid-1920s Bakhtin returned to St Petersburg, by then renamed Leningrad after the first Soviet leader. Because he had contracted a debilitating bone disease in Vitebsk and because he was politically suspect, Bakhtin could not get a job and had to rely on his wife's earnings for his living. However, not having a job meant that he had enough time to write, and he wrote feverishly. Some of his main works were produced during those years: in addition to the above-mentioned titles whose authorship is disputed, there were *Problems in the Work of Dostoevsky* (1929; only a later version of 1963 has been translated into English) and a host of essays. The importance of Bakhtin's work of this period lies in the fact that the emphasis on variation, plurality and point of view increases at a time when, with the advent of Stalinism, life in the Soviet Union became increasingly homogenised.

Bakhtin felt the direct impact of Stalinism when he was arrested in 1929 and sentenced to exile in Kazakhstan. The reasons for his arrest and sentence are ultimately unclear except for the obvious fact that he was an intellectual. In Kazakhstan he taught book-keeping during the day and, with the help of influential friends who supplied him with books, he continued his studies at night. Despite the hardship of his situation Bakhtin completed a number of essays and monographs, including *Discourse in the Novel* (1934–5; published in English as part of the reader *The Dialogic Imagination* in 1981). When his sentence in exile in Kazakhstan ended, he moved around the Soviet Union for a number of years, probably to escape re-arrest, and worked as a high-school and university teacher in various places. During this period he completed another two important manuscripts. One was the original version of *Rabelais and his World*

(published in 1965), which he submitted as a PhD thesis to the Gorky Institute of World Literature. It was accepted in 1947 but, for political reasons, for a lower degree only. The other was called *The Novel of Education and its Significance in the History of Realism*, but this manuscript did not survive World War II. There were only two copies. One was lost when the publishing house where it was to appear was raided and burnt by the Germans. The other copy was with Bakhtin himself, and when cigarette paper became inaccessible during the war he used its pages, one after the other, to roll cigarettes.

After the war Bakhtin became the chair of Russian and world literature in a newly established provincial university in Saransk, a city about 500 kilometres southeast of Moscow. The post allowed him to lie low during the anti-intellectual purges of the 1950s and he managed to escape re-arrest. His obscurity was such that a group of young intellectuals who read his dissertation about *Rabelais and his World* at the Gorky Institute in the early 1960s did not expect him to be alive; they thought he would have perished like many intellectuals of his generation. When they discovered him living in Saransk, Bakhtin's fortunes changed and his books *Problems of Dostoevsky's Poetics* (1963) and *Rabelais and his World* (1965) were published to high acclaim in the Soviet Union. As a result he could finally move away from the provinces, and he spent the last years of his life in Moscow where he continued to live an intellectual life of writing, philosophical discussions and producing new editions of his early works.

Bakhtin was 'discovered' by Western scholars in the 1960s and 1970s but became well known only in the 1980s, during a time when poststructuralism and postmodernism became dominant frameworks for scholars in the humanities and social sciences. This is perhaps unsurprising since Bakhtin attacked structuralism at a time when it was at the height of its influence. He criticized Ferdinand de *Saussure, for example, for his unitary view of language, which Bakhtin said failed to take into account everyday speech as well as the historicity of language. For Bakhtin, language cannot be understood as a unitary phenomenon. He argues that language is always heteroglossic because it consists of different styles, genres and registers. Therefore linguistic meaning does not exist independently of the level of words, sentences or even individual discourses. Rather, an individual speech act derives its meaning from other speech acts to which it is historically or socially related. In other words meaning is always 'intertextual' (it depends on the relationships and points of overlap between texts or speech acts), since speakers always have to draw on other utterances that have been made by other speakers. Bakhtin says: 'Any utterance is a link in a very complexly organized chain of other utterances' with which it 'enters into one kind of relation or another' (1986: 69). It was Julia *Kristeva who coined the term 'intertextuality' for these relations between utterances, and she is sometimes even credited with 'discovering' Bakhtin for a Western audience.

Bakhtin accuses Saussure of 'abstract objectivism' because he is said to treat language as a system of phonetic, grammatical and lexical laws over which an individual speaker has no control. At the same time Bakhtin also finds Saussure's account of language overly mentalistic, in that it tends to treat language as residing solely in the mind of the individual speaker. While these two criticisms may seem contradictory, they are not. Saussure described language as a tripartite system of 'langage' (objective norms), 'langue' (the system on which the individual speaker draws) and 'parole' (the concrete utterance). Like many idealists he gave short shrift to 'parole' because he saw it as essentially chaotic; that is, too flawed by vernacular speech, processing errors and individual idiosyncracies to be a worthy object of scientific enquiry. By contrast Bakhtin argues that it is precisely the individual utterance that should be made the central object of enquiry because it is there that the voices of self and other engage in an ongoing power struggle over meaning.

Through a number of 'voices' various speakers are present in a conversation or a text. Many speakers – identified or unidentified – achieve voice in a particular text, which thus becomes 'dialogic', 'heteroglossic', 'polyphonic' or even 'carnivalesque'. In this view language use is never completely original but is always an activation of voices that have been heard before. Or, as a frequently quoted passage from *Discourse in the Novel* puts it: 'Language is not a

25

neutral medium that passes freely and easily into the private property of the speaker's intentions; it is populated, overpopulated – with the intentions of others' (1929a: 273–4). Thus, whenever speakers or writers use language they do so in three ways:

> One can say that any word exists for the speaker in three aspects: as a neutral word of a language, belonging to nobody; as an *other's* word, which belongs to another person and is filled with echoes of the other's utterance; and, finally, as *my* word, for, since I am dealing with it in a particular situation, with a particular speech plan, it is already imbued with my expression. (1986: 88)

Not surprisingly for a literary scholar, Bakhtin considered novels to be the prototypical examples of heteroglossic texts, which he regarded as the democratic ideal of language use. This should be seen in contrast to monologic texts, in which there is only one voice, or one dominant, hegemonic voice and a number of submerged voices. The latter aspect of Bakhtin's work – the democratic acknowledgement of difference in a text vs. texts in which consensus is manufactured by the use of a hegemonic voice – has been of particular interest to critical discourse analysts. In a narrative text these distinct voices are shaped as conscious reactions to the ideological positions of other voices. At the same time Bakhtin sees intertextuality as a broader principle of discourse that goes beyond narrative texts and operates in all language use. Novels and dramas, which Bakhtin calls 'secondary' or 'complex' speech genres, draw upon ordinary speech: 'they absorb and digest various primary (simple) genres that have taken form in unmediated speech communion' (1986: 62). Linguists have taken this notion of 'appropriation' of utterances beyond literature and now employ it to describe the ways in which people learn to use language – be it children in first language acquisition or adult learners in second and foreign language learning.

The discovery of Bakhtin in linguistics is a much more recent phenomenon than in literary theory and cultural studies, and his influence continues to grow in the early twenty-first century, mostly among linguists who are dissatisfied with formal linguistics. Consequently, his influence has been greatest in (critical) discourse analysis, stylistics and sociolinguistics, and has only recently expanded into areas of applied linguistics, particularly work in language acquisition. Bakhtin died in 1975, four years after his beloved wife Elena Alexandrowna, whose faithful support had been crucial for his work. Michael Holquist, one of the foremost authorities on Bakhtin, provides a summary evaluation of Bakhtin's long life and his work: '[Bakhtin] argued early and late that what a person said was meaningful to the degree his or her utterance answered a question, and the particular set of questions he himself addressed may be understood as growing out of problems that confront anyone seeking to heed Socrates' injunction to "Know thyself!"' (Holquist 2002: 11–12).

Primary works

(1928) (credited to P. N. Medvedev). *The Formal Method in Literary Scholarship: A Critical Introduction to Sociological Poetics*. A. J.

Wehrle (trans.). Baltimore and London: Johns Hopkins University Press, 1978.

(1929a). *The Dialogic Imagination: Four Essays*. C. Emerson and M. Holquist (trans.). Austin, TX: University of Texas Press, 1981.

(1929b) (credited to V. N. Voloshinov). *Marxism and the Philosophy of Language*. L. Matejka and I. R. Titunik (trans.). Cambridge, MA: Harvard University Press, 1986.

(1963). *Problems of Dostoevsky's Poetics*. C. Emerson (trans.). Manchester: Manchester University Press, 1984.

(1965). *Rabelais and his World*. H. Iswolsky (trans.). Bloomington: Indiana University Press, 1984.

(1986). *Speech Genres and Other Late Essays*. C. Emerson, M. Holquist and V. W. McGee (trans.). Austin, TX: University of Texas Press.

(1994). *The Bakhtin Reader: Selected Writings by Bakhtin, Medvedev, Voloshinov*. P. Morris (ed.). London: Edward Arnold.

(1995). *Bakhtinian Thought: An Introductory Reader*. S. Dentith (ed.). London: Routledge.

Further reading

Holquist, M. (2002). *Dialogism: Bakhtin and his World*. London: Routledge.

Vice, S. (1997). *Introducing Bakhtin*. Manchester: Manchester University Press.

Ingrid Piller

ROLAND BARTHES

Barthes, Roland (*b*. 1915, *d*. 1980; French), teacher, lexicographer, writer and professor of literary semiology at the Collège de France. Barthes is a key figure in the development of semiotics and a major influence on structuralism and poststructuralism, particularly as they relate to literary theory and textual analysis. His work addresses the disjuncture between language (what we say) and utterances (the way we say it), and is the foundation for many of the theories popular in the 1960s and 1970s that apply linguistic theory to culture and myth. (*See also* Bakhtin, Mikhail; Greimas, Algirdas; Saussure, Ferdinand de; Todorov, Tzvetan.)

Barthes was born in the naval town of Cherbourg on the coast of northwest France. His father was killed in action at sea when Barthes was just a year old, and he moved with his mother to Bayonne where he spent his early childhood. He was educated at schools in Paris and at the Sorbonne, where he studied for a degree in French and classics. But from the age of 19 until his early thirties Barthes suffered with tuberculosis and spent a great deal of time resting in sanatoriums in the Pyrenees and Switzerland. He took advantage of this enforced leisure to read, but never managed to achieve the sustained effort required to pass the *agrégation* exams mandatory for French university lecturers. In the 1930s Barthes worked as a teacher in Hungary, in Biarritz and in Paris. In the years immediately after World War II he contributed to *Combat*, a journal published by the existentialist philosopher Albert Camus. Barthes also worked as a librarian and teacher in Bucharest, Hungary, and as a lecturer at the University of Alexandria, Egypt. It was here that his interest in linguistics was sparked by *Greimas, a fellow lecturer, in 1949. While working as a lexicographer in 1953 Barthes published *Writing Degree Zero*, the book that came to represent his early position on the problem of the relationship between writing, reading and the dominant cultural discourse.

Perhaps the most important philosophical influence on Barthes was the structuralist thinker and early linguist *Saussure. Famously, Saussure's contribution to linguistics is in outlining the composition of the sign (a sound image interpreted as meaningful) as comprising a signifier (a word, for example) and a signified (the concept represented by the signifier). Using this linguistic model Saussure set about trying to identify the structure of sign systems beyond language itself, a discipline he called the 'general science' of semiology – known since the late twentieth century as semiotics. Semiology was adopted by many other thinkers, from linguists and psychoanalysts to anthropologists and political scientists. But while Saussure viewed linguistics as a discipline within semiology, Barthes viewed semiology as a sub-discipline of linguistics. While he is better known as a literary and cultural critic, it is important to recognise that Barthes viewed language as the key to his diverse writings on subjects from fashion to photography, and from literature to his own life.

Barthes's political activism, fighting against fascism in the 1930s and 1940s, and writing in radical and left-wing journals, also informs his early attempts to critique and interpret bourgeois culture. For example, the structuralist idea that meaning is agreed rather than determinate challenged the idea that certain works of art were inherently superior to others. So, for example, the idea that the architecture of a cathedral is in some way more meaningful than the design of a car is quite illogical. Rather it is simply that a powerful group of people – the French bourgeoisie – agreed at the time that the cathedral had more artistic value. In fact by 1957, when his essay 'The new Citroën' appeared in the book *Mythologies*, he was able to argue that, like the great Gothic cathedrals, cars had become 'the supreme creation of an era'. In other words the Gothic cathedrals and Citroën cars have meaning only within the myth structures of their own time.

This application and extension of a linguistic theory of meaning to wider cultural expressions took shape in books such as *Mythologies* and *The Fashion System* (1967). But Barthes's linguistic approach to art, culture and myth often left him out of step with other thinkers of his time. For example, where Jean-Paul Sartre assumed that realist writing could be an accurate representation of the world, Barthes remained sceptical. For him the layers of myth, bad faith and outright misinformation are impossible to disassemble naively. Barthes's belief that signs are arbitrary allowed him to recognise the political and ideological foundation of all writing; to claim that language has meaning independent of its use is mistaken.

In books such as *Writing Degree Zero* and *Michelet* (1953) Barthes developed an approach to reading texts that, in various incarnations, came to dominate the study of narrative and culture in the late twentieth century. His emphasis on formal linguistic structures in texts became known – often pejoratively – as *nouvelle critique* (new criticism), arguably the single most influential critical approach of the 1960s. The anti-establishment and radical possibilities of new criticism were perhaps one reason why Barthes's structuralism acquired such resonance in the period. *Writing Degree Zero*, for example, attacks canonical realist writers who claim to have created an objective representation of reality independent of their history, beliefs and personal mythologies. On the contrary, Barthes argues that writing in denial of its historicity is the writing on which history has made its strongest imprint. To gain freedom writers must isolate themselves in a form of language where history is a linguistic 'zero'.

In *Criticism and Truth* (1966) Barthes provides an answer to those who attacked the new criticism and argues for a more scientific and theoretical critical approach. This can be summarised as privileging the reader and the text over the author, an idea expressed most famously in the essay 'The death of the author' (1968). In making this case Barthes can be credited with originating the development of linguistics-based critical theory as a central feature of humanities scholarship.

As more of his work appeared in English, Barthes's influence outside France grew quickly; he was especially influential in the United States. He became more explicit in his attempts to decode the apparently natural characteristics of narratives of all kinds. In *The Fashion System*, for example, Barthes attempts to identify the language of fashion and in doing so finds that it is a system in which writing about fashion, rather than fashionable clothing itself, constitutes the sign of fashion. Similarly, in *S/Z* (1970), he separates the 'textuality' of Balzac's short story 'Sarrasine' from judgements based on its canonical status. As with the fashion system, it is the textuality of the story – all aspects of the writing – not the story itself that constitutes the sign. In other words, for structuralist critics it is not simply that the way of reading is as important as what is being read, but rather that how we read *is* what we read.

In a line-by-line analysis of 'Sarrasine', *S/Z* outlines five 'codes' that Barthes identifies in all realist narrative and establishes a framework for structuralist criticism in general. But in many ways *S/Z* also marks the beginning of a change in Barthes's approach. Whereas he had begun by exploring the limitations of realist writing by revealing its hidden rootedness in arbitrary narrative codes, by the 1970s he became more playful and less overtly concerned with theory as such. Later writings, such as *The Pleasure of the Text* (1973) and *Roland Barthes* (1974), intermingle fictionality, autobiography, and criticism. *A Lover's Discourse* (1977) in particular moved towards a form of critical writing Barthes described as 'novelistic'. Such playfulness emerges directly from earlier ideas in that it implies a loss of self; in terms of his autobiographical writings in *Roland Barthes*, the subject Roland Barthes is interpreted and 'read' rather than described. Such later work moves away from his structuralist beginnings in that it recognises that writing can never free itself from the influence of dominant ideologies and history; in poststructuralist thinking, to which

Barthes made an important contribution, writing can never achieve degree zero.

Barthes's application of linguistic theory to art, literature and culture made possible such academic areas as critical theory and cultural studies, while his later work laid the foundations for poststructuralism and deconstruction, among the most influential philosophical concepts of the late twentieth century. By the 1990s semiotics, the discipline of which he was an outstanding practitioner, had become embedded in critical practice across the humanities. Barthes was knocked down while crossing the road in Paris on 23 March 1980 and died a month later from his injuries.

Primary works

(1953). *Writing Degree Zero*. Annette Lavers and Colin Smith (trans.). Boston, MA: Beacon Press, 1970.
(1957). *Mythologies*. Annette Lavers (trans.). London: Jonathan Cape, 1972.
(1964). *Elements of Semiology*. Annette Lavers and Colin Smith (trans.). New York: Hill and Wang, 1977.
(1967). *The Fashion System*. Matthew Ward and Richard Howard (trans.). London: Jonathan Cape, 1985.
(1970). *S/Z*. Richard Miller (trans.). New York: Hill and Wang, 1974.
(1982). *Selected Writings*. Susan Sontag (ed.). London: Fontana Press, 1989.

Further reading

Culler, Jonathan (1983). *Barthes*. London: Fontana Press.
Lavers, Annette (1982). *Roland Barthes: Structuralism and After*. London: Methuen.
Rylance, Rick (1994). *Roland Barthes*. London: Harvester Wheatsheaf.

Thody, Philip, and Course, Ann (1999). *Introducing Barthes*. Cambridge: Icon Books.
Todorov, Tzvetan (1988). *Literature and its Theorists: A Personal View of Twentieth Century Criticism*. Catherine Porter (trans.). London: Routledge.
Ungar, Steven (1983). *Roland Barthes: The Professor of Desire*. London: University of Nebraska Press.

Christopher Routledge

ÉMILE BENVENISTE

Benveniste, Émile (*b*. 1902, *d*. 1976; French), director of studies in comparative grammar and Iranian at the École Pratique des Hautes Études (1927–37), professor of comparative grammar at the Collège de France (1937–76). Made valuable contributions to the study of Indo-European and general linguistics. Working within a broadly functionalist perspective, developed key concepts such as subjectivity and enunciation as well as a notion of speech acts, independently of similar work done at Oxford. (*See also* Austin, J. L.; Saussure, Ferdinand de.)

Benveniste was born into a Sephardic Jewish family in Aleppo in what was then part of the Ottoman Empire. As a small child he was taken to Paris and enrolled at a rabbinical school. But very early on Benveniste developed a flair for languages, and at the age of 16 he was admitted to the Sorbonne to study classical languages. Later he became a disciple of Antoine Meillet. He was also profoundly influenced by the teachings of early structuralist Ferdinand de *Saussure.

However, Benveniste challenged one of Saussure's foundational principles: the arbitrariness of the sign relation. While conceding that the relation between the sign and its referent may indeed be arbitrary, Benveniste argued that the connection between the signifier and signified is necessary in the sense that the two invariably invoke each other under all circumstances. The idea of semiotic necessity highlights how the two components that together constitute the linguistic sign are actually associated in the speaker's mind. As a functionalist (a linguist who insists that any account of language must pay attention to the purposes for which it is used, not just its formal properties), Benveniste loathed theorising in the abstract and treating the sign as a concept closed unto itself. Instead he sought to validate theoretical constructs from the language users' perspective – a trait that he shared with the ordinary language philosophers at Oxford, notably J. L. *Austin. This explains why Benveniste developed a notion of speech acts quite independently of work in progress across the English Channel.

The functionalist thrust of Benveniste's thinking is also clearly discernible in his theory of enunciation (according to which the speaking subject makes his or her presence felt in – not through – language), particularly his emphasis on the notion of subjectivity, which in turn is closely tied to his important distinction between history (*histoire*) and discourse (*discourse*). Unlike historical language, where there is no scope for speaker participation, discourse is the domain where the speaker actively intervenes. This intervention is signalled by the use of deictics such as 'I', 'here' and 'now'. The idea is further explored in his influential work on pronouns.

Benveniste's work has had a great impact on literary theory, especially in the area of 'narratology', and is clearly perceptible in the writings of Gérard Genette, Roland *Barthes and Tzvetan *Todorov. A prolific writer who produced eighteen volumes and some 300 papers, Benveniste spent his last years in poor health. He suffered a heart attack in 1956 and a stroke in 1969 that crippled him and robbed him of the ability to speak for the rest of his life.

Primary works

(1966). *Problèmes de linguistique générale (Problems in General Linguistics). Vols 1 and 2.* Paris: Gallimard.

Further reading

Lotringer, S. and Gora, T. (eds) (1981). *Polyphonic Linguistics: The Many Voices of Émile Benveniste. Semiotica: Special Supplement.* The Hague: Mouton.

Kanavillil Rajagopalan

GEORGE BERKELEY

Berkeley, George (*b.* 1685, *d.* 1753; Irish), empiricist philosopher and Anglican bishop best known for his argument that the material world exists only in our perception of it.

Despite critics who suggested his ideas were not serious, his major works, especially *An Essay Towards a New Theory of Vision* (1709) and *A Treatise Concerning the Principles of Human Knowledge* (1710), established him as one of the most important figures in philosophy at the time and a major influence on the direction of British empiricism. (*See also* Bloomfield, Leonard; Hume, David; Locke, John; Quine, W. V. O.; Saussure, Ferdinand de.)

Born near Kilkenny, Ireland, Berkeley attended Kilkenny College and Trinity College, Dublin, which he entered at the age of 15. In 1707 he became a fellow at Trinity and in 1709, aged just 24, he published *An Essay Towards a New Theory of Vision*, one of his most important works. In it Berkeley explored the question of whether someone blind from birth whose sight was restored would recognise a cube by sight having previously recognised it only by feel. Berkeley argued that since ideas were entirely dependent on sense perception, and since a person who had never seen a cube before would have no relevant perception, it would not be possible for him or her to recognise the cube.

This argument marked the beginnings of Berkeley's best-known position, that to exist is to be perceived or to perceive and nothing more. In other words, things that are not perceived or do not themselves perceive do not exist; the material world exists only as ideas. But while some of Berkeley's critics read this as denying the existence of anything that is out of sight, in fact Berkeley gives a neat – some would argue rather too neat – solution: everything in the material world is perceived at all times by the eye of God.

For Berkeley, then, we have no way of knowing if our perceptions measure up to an independent reality or if perceptions have any causal link with such an independent reality. Rather, God causes perceptions of the material world, and subsequent thoughts we have about such perceptions are our own doing. Language is the inadequate system we have devised to communicate our knowledge of the world, but since language itself is 'immaterial' it tends to obscure the very knowledge it is designed to convey. Where *Locke blamed our inability to understand the world on our physical failings, Berkeley took a more moralistic approach; our ignorance is down to our failure to use our perceptive faculties wisely. Language is the most powerful barrier to knowledge since it forces us to substitute words for ideas. The repercussions of this idea were felt as late as the twentieth century in the theories of poststructuralism and deconstruction.

In 1728 Berkeley moved to Newport, Rhode Island, to help set up a college for ministers, in the hope of increasing the number of churches in the American colonies, but returned to London four years later when promised funding failed to materialise. In 1732 he became bishop of Cloyne and spent his time attending to the rural Irish poor and promoting the medicinal qualities of tar water, about which he wrote *A Chain of Philosophical Reflexions and Inquiries Concerning the Virtues of Tar-Water* (1744), a book later known as *Siris*. In 1752 Berkeley and his wife retired to Oxford, where he died quite unexpectedly at home a year later.

Primary works

(1709). *An Essay Towards a New Theory of Vision*. In Colin Murray Turbayne (ed.), *Works on Vision*. Westport, CT: Greenwood Press, 1981.

(1710). *A Treatise Concerning the Principles of Human Knowledge*. Jonathan Dancey (ed.). Oxford: Oxford University Press, 1998.

(1980). *Berkeley: Philosophical Works*. M. R. Ayers (ed.) London: Everyman's University Library.

Further reading

Armstrong, D. M. and Malet, David (1988). *Berkeley's Theory of Vision: A Critical Examination of Bishop Berkeley's Essay 'Towards a New Theory of Vision'*. London: Garland.

Warnock, G. J. (1982). *Berkeley*. Oxford: Blackwell.

Christopher Routledge

BASIL BERNSTEIN

Bernstein, Basil (*b.* 1924, *d.* 2000; British), reader in the sociology of education at the University of London (1965–9), professor of sociology of education at the University of London (1967–90), distinguished research fellow at the University of Wales, Cardiff. His major contribution, a perceptive and rigorous analysis of language codes, helped to explain why working-class children underachieved at school. Whereas middle-class children had access to both elaborate language, including academic discourse, and more intimate personal speech forms, working-class children were often limited to the latter – their restricted code. (*See also* Jakobson, Roman; Labov, William; Sapir, Edward.)

Born in London, Basil Bernstein graduated from the London School of Economics (LSE), then trained as a teacher at Westminster College. He worked at the Bernhard Baron Settlement in Stepney and as a teacher of General Post Office workers studying at the City Day College, experiences that provided him with raw working-class material for early studies on language. It was while holding a Social Science Research Council fellowship at University College, London, that he encountered Frieda Goldman-Eisler, whose work on pause data in conversations was related to planning speech forms. He also read in the field of linguistics, including *Sapir and *Jakobson. In 1962 he published 'Linguistic codes: hesitation phenomena and intelligence', where the concept of language codes first appeared. He was appointed as a senior lecturer at the Institute of Education in 1963 and as the first Karl Mannheim professor of sociology of education at the University of London in 1967.

Bernstein defined language codes in terms of the ease or difficulty of predicting the syntactic choices of speakers. In an elaborated code, for example, the speakers explore more fully the resources of the grammar and therefore have more possibilities of combination. The 'restricted' code allows more intimate personal speech forms. However, the term 'restricted' code does not refer to restricted vocabulary and the 'elaborated' code does not entail so-called flowery use of language. Rather the restricted code works better than the elaborated code where there is shared knowledge between speakers. In contrast, the elaborated code necessarily includes more information in order to aid understanding.

Bernstein has been criticised for his view that restricted codes cannot deal with new knowledge and ideas (see *Labov), and his justifications became extremely abstract. However, his original research on language codes has been developed into models for understanding authority relationships and for classifying cultures. As such his work has influenced a wide range of researchers and policy makers around the world.

Primary works

(1971). *Class, Codes and Control. Vol. 1*. London: Routledge and Kegan Paul.
(1973). *Class, Codes and Control. Vol. 2*. London: Routledge and Kegan Paul.
(1977). *Class, Codes and Control. Vol. 3*. London: Routledge and Kegan Paul.
(1990). *Class, Codes and Control. Vol. 4*. London: Routledge.
(1996). *Pedagogy, Symbolic Control and Identity: Theory, Research and Critique*. London: Taylor and Francis.

Further reading

Labov, W. (1969). 'The logic of nonstandard English'. Reprinted in P. Giglioli (ed.), *Language and Social Context*. Harmondsworth: Penguin, 1990.

Sapir, Edward (1929). 'The status of linguistics as a science'. In D. G. Mandelbaum (ed.), *Selected Writings of Edward Sapir*. Berkeley, CA: University of California Press.

John Williams

LEONARD BLOOMFIELD

Bloomfield, Leonard (*b.* 1887, *d.* 1949; American), instructor in German at the University of Cincinnati (1909–10) and the University of Illinois (1910–13), assistant professor of comparative philology and German at the University of Illinois (1914–21), professor of German and linguistics at Ohio State University (1921–7), professor of Germanic philology at the University of Chicago (1927–40) and Sterling professor of linguistics at Yale University (1940–9). Linguist frequently associated with American structuralism, who advocated an analysis of language conducted according to scientific, descriptive principles. He helped found the Linguistic Society of America in 1924 and is known for his accounts of indigenous languages and for innovative views concerning phonetics, semantics, foreign language study and reading instruction. (*See also* Boas, Franz; Brugmann, Karl; Chomsky, Noam; Hockett, Charles; Pike, Kenneth; Sapir, Edward; Saussure, Ferdinand de; Skinner, B. F.)

Bloomfield, the son of Sigmund and Carola Buber Bloomfield, was born in Chicago, Illinois, but he moved at an early age to Elkhart Lake, Wisconsin, where his parents managed a hotel. Earning his AB at Harvard College in 1906, he started graduate studies at the University of Wisconsin, but later transferred to the University of Chicago, where he studied linguistics and earned a PhD in 1909, completing a dissertation entitled 'A semasiologic differentiation in Germanic secondary ablaut'. During his graduate education, his postgraduate work in Leipzig (1913–14) and his early professional career at the University of Illinois and Ohio State University, Bloomfield was exposed to various influences, including the methodology of comparative and structural linguistics, the increased popularity of empiricism in the natural sciences, and the shift from mentalism (the idea that mental processes are independent of physical interaction) to behaviourism (the idea that mental activity is not distinct from behaviour) in psychology. Bloomfield married Alice Sayers in 1909 and the couple eventually adopted two boys.

Bloomfield's exposure to comparative linguistics came as a result of his work with Eduard Prokosch at the University of Wisconsin in the United States, with *Brugmann, August Leskien and Hermann Oldenberg at the Universities of Leipzig and Göttingen in Germany, and with Jacob Wackernagel at the University of Basel in Switzerland. Studying the work of these scholars, Bloomfield gained experience with four groups within the Indo-European language family: Germanic, Indic, Slavic and Hellenic. While learning the principles of diachronic linguistics (the study of language through time), he became familiar with the limitations of comparative and historical linguistics, acquiring a healthy scepticism towards relying solely on written documents when formulating generalisations about language and language change. Bloomfield was also familiar with the works of *Saussure and admired the accomplishments of the American anthropologists *Boas and *Sapir, who published descriptive analyses of Native American Indian languages. His acquaintance with the grammar of Sanskrit by the ancient Hindu grammarian Panini provided him with a further example of a systematic descriptive organisation of morphology, syntax and vocabulary. Characteristic of each man's efforts was the reference to internal linguistic structure to explain language phenomena.

Bloomfield also lived at a time when profound changes were occurring in scientific methodology and in scholars' understanding of the goals and objectives of language study. Since the last half of the nineteenth century, great thinkers in the natural sciences had become increasingly attracted to empiricism, and they sought to establish strictly prescribed fields of investigation and accurate methodologies. While the philology of the nineteenth century had tended towards the study of world cultures and their histories, using language and literature as a means to chart a people's intellectual achievements, linguists in the late nineteenth and early twentieth centuries began to work towards creating a more scientific study of language. For example, August Schleicher urged his fellow linguists to follow the model of the natural sciences by substituting dispassionate investigation for biased commentary, while Saussure worked to define more precisely the different fields of enquiry within linguistics, and supported the idea of studying language as it exists at a specific moment in time without considering its historical development.

A further source of influence on Bloomfield was the change occurring in psychology as the field shifted its emphasis from mentalism to behaviourism. It has been suggested that Bloomfield was introduced to the basic tenets of behaviourism and to John B. Watson, one of its strongest proponents, through his close association with Albert P. Weiss, a psychologist, while Bloomfield and Weiss were on the faculty of Ohio State University. A central idea of behaviourism was the claim that human behaviour could be interpreted as a series of learned habits that had been acquired as a result of a prolonged process of responding in specific ways to specific stimuli; behaviourists also maintained that human behaviour could be predicted once scientists had thoroughly studied the various stimuli and responses present in a society. Behaviourists limited their enquiries to observable and measurable phenomena, rejecting concepts such as intuition, soul and consciousness. In the 1930s and 1940s, linguists were increasingly of the opinion that the structures, forms and uses of language could be explained by theories founded on the principles of behaviourism.

These influences contributed to Bloomfield's distinct view of the field of linguistics. He believed that linguists should be trained in the methods of scientific enquiry and that they should conduct their research in an unbiased manner. He claimed that serious language study did not include the analysis of writing or literature, since those areas involved cultural and social issues that were the subject matter of other disciplines. And he rejected categorically speculation about unobservable phenomena. He developed a preference for basing linguistic enquiry on samples of spoken language and exhibited a reluctance to rely on written language, since he felt most languages lacked a one-to-one correspondence between sounds and letters. Bloomfield favoured the image of language as a building constructed of small blocks of sound and meaning, each block having a specific place and function and exhibiting specific characteristics. Believing that it was a linguist's duty to describe rather than prescribe language usage, Bloomfield advocated a hands-on approach for scholars, one requiring fieldwork and interaction with native speakers. Bloomfield also was convinced that scientific enquiry for its own sake was of questionable value. He saw the importance of knowledge gained through linguistic science in its relevance to everyday life and sought to find practical applications for his theoretical insights. Indeed, he thought that the goal of all intellectual enquiry was ultimately to improve the welfare of human beings worldwide, by leading them to an awareness of their potential and an understanding of their environment.

Bloomfield wrote extensively on a wide variety of topics during the course of his career, and he also published reviews of works by other linguists. He was an energetic contributor to *Language*, a periodical published by the Linguistic Society of America, and to other well-known publications, such as the *Modern Language Journal*, the *American Anthropologist* and the *Journal of English and Germanic Philology*. In addition he published a number of dictionaries and grammars of North American Indian languages, foreign language textbooks and the monograph for which he is most remembered: *Language* (1933), a thoroughly reworked version of his earlier *An Introduction to the Study of Language* (1914). Readers can gain an idea of the intellectual depth and breadth of his writings by considering his comments concerning the nature of language, foreign language study and reading education.

Revealing his philosophy of language most elaborately in his book *Language*, Bloomfield saw the substance of language as consisting of two types of material. The first is sound. Bloomfield is credited with popularising the concept of the phoneme, a theoretical construct introduced by the Russian-Polish Baudouin de Courtenay in 1812 and developed further by various groups of scholars, including the Prague Linguistic Circle founded in 1927. Bloomfield was the first to state in such uncompromising terms that linguistic study involved isolating and categorising the finite number of phonemes in a given language (its smallest significant units of sound) and describing how these units join together to form larger units of language. Bloomfield insisted that studying sounds meant examining an utterance without considering meaning.

The second type of material is meaning. According to Bloomfield, phonemes join together to form morphemes, the smallest units of meaning in a language; morphemes, in turn, join together to form words and words form phrases, leading to sentences. It must be noted that Bloomfield felt uncomfortable including meaning in his scientific study of language because he believed that it was impossible to investigate fully all factors that might contribute to the meaning of an utterance. In other words, the meaning of an utterance is determined not only by the string of phonemes and morphemes, but also by cultural, psychological, physiological and idiosyncratic matters relating to the speaker and hearer.

Bloomfield's view of language and his description of the scientific study of language met with a mixed reaction. On the one hand his efforts were greeted with derision by those who chose to cling to traditional interpretations of the essence of language and conventional approaches to the study of language. In particular, his views were regarded as controversial by philosophers who held language to be a manifestation of certain universal truths or logic and by teachers at all levels who sought to prescribe rather than describe language usage. His attempt to demystify language brought him into conflict with the Roman Catholic church in the United States, and his text *Language* was banned in certain schools. On the other hand, his relentless demand for limiting the subject matter of scholarly linguistic investigation to observable phenomena was greeted with jubilation by those who had complained about the fanciful treatises of the past. Bloomfield's portrayal of linguistics as a science served as a model for American structural linguistics practiced by American academics, such as *Pike, *Hockett, Bernard Bloch and Zellig Harris.

Bloomfield's interests were not limited to esoteric topics. For example, he was critical of foreign language teaching in the United States and sought to remedy its shortcomings. He felt that schools failed to provide any practical competence in foreign languages, and he claimed that teachers were using outdated methods, that they had little knowledge of how language worked and that they spent too much time teaching students to read printed texts. Bloomfield thought that priority in foreign language education should initially be given to developing speaking and listening proficiencies. He asserted that students should progress to reading literature and writing compositions only after they had become familiar with pronunciation, vocabulary and grammar. Most importantly, he defined a high level of language proficiency as thorough acquisition of a native speaker's linguistic behaviour patterns.

During World War II Bloomfield had the chance to introduce innovations into the field of foreign language teaching. At that time, he and other linguists worked with the Army Specialized Training Program to help prepare members of the armed forces to interact with the military and civilians in allied or enemy countries. In *Outline Guide for the Practical Study of Foreign Languages* (1942a) and 'About foreign language teaching' (1945), Bloomfield describes his methodology and relates how he and other linguists developed intensive courses in numerous languages. Only hand-picked, highly motivated students took part in the courses, and participants were divided into groups of ten, studying together fifteen hours a week for nine months. The methods used each week in a given course included at least ten hours of oral drill with native speakers, and at least three hours of grammar explanation and practice with instructors who were proficient in the particular foreign language and in new trends in linguistics. According to Bloomfield the courses accomplished their goal, producing speakers who could function independently in environments where only the foreign language occurred.

The success of the American Army Method, as the experiment came to be known, was based in part on the special methods employed, but the enthusiasm of the learners, who could devote almost all their time to language study, also played an important role. Bloomfield himself cautioned against regarding the procedure as any type of quick-fix method to be implemented in schools. But his warning fell on deaf ears. In the late 1940s educators began considering ways to modify foreign language teaching in the United States, and after the launching of the first Sputnik satellites by the Soviet Union in 1957 there arose a fear that schools offered insufficient work in the sciences, mathematics and modern foreign languages. In 1958 the United States Congress passed the National Defense Education Act, providing financial support for foreign language programmes and teacher training through the Language Development Program, and as a result, schools instituted or expanded foreign language offerings. Finding inspiration in the theoretical writings of Bloomfield and the behavioural psychologist B. F. *Skinner, as well as in descriptions of the American Army Method, methodologists and textbook authors created programmes that emphasised speaking and listening, dialogues and pattern drills, and contrastive analyses. Most programmes made extensive use of language laboratories. The audiolingual method, as this approach was called, was popular during the 1960s.

Bloomfield also found fault with the way reading was taught to young children in the United States. He maintained that teachers lacked a thorough understanding of alphabetic writing and the relationship of letters to phonemes. He felt that successful reading took place when children became aware of the connection between the spoken word and the printed word and when they were able to recognise written representations of their sound system. According to Bloomfield, accomplished readers developed an accelerated, effortless ability to connect sounds with written characters. To help children begin to achieve this level of proficiency, Bloomfield suggested a four-step plan. The first step involved teaching children to recognise letters and preparing them for left-to-right scanning. It also included practice with reading material containing letters with only one phonetic value, for example *b* in *bat*, *bun* and *bin*. Later steps introduced irreg-

ular spelling patterns, multi-syllabic words and connected texts. Bloomfield made no effort to avoid nonsense syllables, since he believed that they appealed to children's natural playful attitude towards language while allowing them to demonstrate mastery of a particular sound–symbol correspondence. Eventually Bloomfield prepared a manuscript version of a textbook for teaching schoolchildren to read and write English. When the book was substituted for the regular textbook in a private school in Chicago in the early 1940s, it delighted the children and earned the praise of teachers and parents. A published version of his efforts, *Let's Read: A Linguistic Approach*, written together with Clarence L. Barnhart, eventually appeared in 1961.

The post-war period should have been a time of contentment and continued creativity for Bloomfield. Enjoying international respect, the Linguistic Society of America had grown significantly, and Bloomfield's particular brand of linguistics was attracting more and more attention and admiration. In addition, the valuable work he had performed for the military, contributing to a revitalisation of the field of foreign language teaching, was recognised, and he was enjoying the fame that accompanied his appointment as a Sterling professor at Yale. Unfortunately personal problems overshadowed his professional success and Bloomfield faced days filled with sorrow and hardship. His wife was a victim of recurring bouts of depression, and Bloomfield himself suffered a stroke in 1946. Although his family, friends and colleagues never gave up hope that he would recover enough to return to teaching, he remained too weak for most activity, and during the last three years of his life, he was able to complete very little academic work. A number of projects remained unfinished, including a Menomini grammar that was to be the most extensive account of a North American Indian language ever prepared.

In the end Bloomfield was confined to his bed and died on 18 April 1949 in New Haven, Connecticut. In the 1950s his ideas and techniques grew in popularity among scholars, especially in the United States. Structural linguistics remained prominent until the early 1960s, and the so-called Army Method was transformed into the audiolingual method of foreign language teaching, remaining in favour throughout the 1960s. However, with the advent of the generative-transformational school of linguistics (in which the sentences of a language are described as 'generated' by a basic set of rules internal to individual speakers) and the communicative competence approach to language teaching in the 1970s, Bloomfield's reputation as a progressive thinker in linguistics was challenged, and his teachings were often neglected. Critics such as *Chomsky claimed that structural linguistics did not take into account the workings of the human mind or the creativity of language. Some educationalists asserted that the lessons prepared according to the audiolingual method tended to be boring, repetitive and ineffective. In the 1980s Bloomfield's contributions to the field of linguistics were re-examined and a more balanced view

of his efforts appeared. In general he is hailed for his introduction of scientific rigour into the study of language and for inspiring a re-evaluation of foreign language teaching methods. With his major work *Language* and his many articles readily accessible, Bloomfield manages to interest and inspire each new generation of scholars seeking to understand and appreciate the uniqueness of language.

Primary works

(1914). *An Introduction to the Study of Language*. New York: Henry Holt.
(1925). 'Why a linguistic society?' *Language*. Vol. 1: 1–5.
(1933). *Language*. New York: Henry Holt.
(1939). 'Menomini morphophonemics'. *Travaux du Cercle Linguistique de Prague*. Vol. 8: 105–15.
(1942a). *Outline Guide for the Practical Study of Foreign Languages*. Baltimore, MD: Linguistic Society of America.
(1942b). 'Linguistics and reading'. *Elementary English Review*. Vol. 19: 125–30, 183–6.
(1945). 'About foreign language teaching'. *Yale Review*. Vol. 34: 625–41.
(1961) (with Clarence L. Barnhart). *Let's Read: A Linguistic Approach*. Detroit, MI: Wayne State University Press.

Further reading

Hall, Robert A., Jr (1990). *A Life for Language: A Biographical Memoir of Leonard Bloomfield*. Philadelphia: John Benjamins.
Harris, Zellig S. (1951). *Methods in Structural Linguistics*. Chicago: University of Chicago Press.
Hockett, Charles F. (ed.) (1970). *A Leonard Bloomfield Anthology*. Bloomington: Indiana University Press.
Lado, Robert (1964). *Foreign Language Teaching: A Scientific Approach*. New York: McGraw-Hill.

Matthews, Peter H. (1993). *Grammatical Theory in the United States from Bloomfield to Chomsky*. Cambridge: Cambridge University Press.

Rivers, Wilga M. (1964). *The Psychologist and the Foreign-Language Teacher*. Chicago: University of Chicago Press.

David V. Witkosky

FRANZ BOAS

Boas, Franz (*b.* 1858, *d.* 1942; German, naturalised American 1887), geographer, physicist, ethnologist, linguist, professor of anthropology at Columbia University (1899–1942), founder and editor of the *International Journal of American Linguistics*. Acclaimed anthropologist best known for his descriptive accounts of numerous Native American languages at the verge of extinction. (*See also* Bloomfield, Leonard; Sapir, Edward.)

Branded the father of American anthropology, Franz Boas brought to the fields of anthropology and linguistics an objectivity virtually unparalleled in his time. The child of a successful merchant and a kindergarten teacher, Boas enjoyed a settled childhood in Minden, Germany. His liberal Jewish parents, active in the German revolution of 1848, instilled into Boas a distaste for racism and anti-semitism, which ultimately contributed to his emigration to the United States in the 1880s.

Boas's formal education at Heidelberg, Bonn and Kiel was in physics and geography, disciplines whose rigour and technique influenced his approach towards his future anthropological and linguistic work. In the early 1880s Boas embarked on a one-man geographical expedition to Baffin Island (then known as Baffin Land), an experience that turned the young scientist's interests further towards anthropology: his ethnological articles on the native people, then known as Eskimos, surpassed in number the geographical articles for which his trip had been funded.

Over the remainder of his lifetime, Boas held academic positions, briefly at Clark University (during which the first American PhD in anthropology was conferred) and later at Columbia University, as well as positions at the American Museum, the Bureau of American Ethnology, and the International School of American Archaeology and Ethnology. Simultaneously, he studied Native American cultures on the north Pacific coast of North America, visiting tribes in Washington and British Columbia frequently over many years to observe and record their culture, language and folklore. He systematically gathered valuable information on countless languages, including Chinook, Kathlamet, Tsimshian, Tlingit, Kutenai, Keresan, Bella Bella, Dakota, Haida, Bella Coola, Nootka and – most extensively – Kwakiutl.

What sets his work apart from others of the time is its freedom from preconception; Boas approached each new language as a unique representation of its speakers' culture and in doing so developed more thorough and organised ways of collecting language data than had previously existed. It is his work with Native Americans that constitutes Boas's greatest contribution to anthropology and linguistics, since the population of native speakers of these languages was steadily dwindling to the point of extinction. Without his dedication and that of his associate Leonard *Bloomfield and his former student Edward *Sapir, many Native American cultures and languages would have disappeared without ever having been recorded. An active anthropologist and outspoken advocate of racial and religious equality through to his old age, Boas died in New York in December 1942.

Primary works

(1911). *The Mind of Primitive Man*. New York: Macmillan.
(1940). *Race, Language, and Culture*. New York: Macmillan.

Further reading

Benedict, Ruth, Emeneau, Murray B., Herskovits, Melville J., Kroeber, A. L., Alden Mason, J. and Reichard, Gladys A. (1943). 'Franz Boas: 1858–1942'. *Titles in the Memoir Series of the American Anthropological Association* No. 61.
Goldschmidt, Walter (ed.) (1959). 'The anthropology of Franz Boas: essays on the centennial of his birth'. *American Anthropologist*. Vol. 61.
Stocking, George W. (ed.) (1974). *The Shaping of American Anthropology, 1883–1911: A Franz Boas Reader*. New York: Basic Books.

Jennifer A. Baldwin

FRANZ BOPP

Bopp, Franz (*b.* 1791, *d.* 1867; German), extraordinary professor (full professor 1825–67) of Oriental languages and general philology, Berlin, member of the Royal Prussian Academy (1825–67). Comparative-historical linguist whose (1816) monograph, the first major Indo-European comparative grammar, exerted considerable influence on several generations of researchers on Indo-European comparative linguistics. (*See also* Brugmann, Karl; Greenberg, Joseph; Grimm, Jacob; Humboldt, Wilhelm von; Rask, Rasmus.)

Born in Mainz, Bopp attended the Gymnasium (college) in Aschaffenburg, Bavaria, where he studied classical and Oriental languages and literatures under Karl Joseph Windischmann. Inspired by Friedrich von Schlegel's *Über die Sprache und Weisheit der Indier* (1808), he moved to Paris on a grant from the Bavarian king to study Sanskrit, largely on his own. There he met such giants as fellow Orientalist Alexander Hamilton. Bopp also studied Arabic and Persian with Antoine Isaac Silvestre de Sacy, one of the greatest Orientalists of the time. After four years of intensive research, Bopp's *Über das Conjugationssystem der Sanskritsprache in Vergleichung mit jenem den griechischen, lateinischen, persischen und germanischen Sprache* appeared in 1816 with an introduction by his teacher, Windischmann. Bopp is often credited as the founder of Indo-European comparative linguistics; his grammars of Sanskrit were the first to use Western terminology rather than the Indian grammatical tradition.

On a visit to London Bopp met the Prussian ambassador to the court of St James, Wilhelm von *Humboldt, whom he taught Sanskrit. In 1820 Bopp published his 'Analytical comparison of the Sanskrit, Greek, Latin and Teutonic languages', a revised version of the linguistic parts of his 1816 monograph. He is probably best known for his *Vergleichende Grammatik des Sanskrit, Send, Griechischen, Lateinischen, Lithauischen, Gothischen und Deutschen*, which appeared in six parts in Berlin in the Proceedings of the Prussian Academy from 1833 to 1852. This work made him by far the most important Indo-Europeanist and Sanskritologist of the first half of the nineteenth century. In it he systematically investigated the *Lautgesetze* (sound laws) as well as morphemic and allomorphic origins in many of the Indo-European languages, at the same time as he continued to deepen his knowledge of Avestan, Albanian, Lithuanian, Gothic, Slavic and Celtic. One of his central ideas was that the endings of the verb 'be' and the personal pronouns were the origin of the inflectional affixes.

Bopp was a very prolific scholar, producing monographs on Teutonic (1836), Celtic (1839), Old Prussian (1853), Albanian (1854) and the accent in Greek and Sanskrit (1854). He also had a number of distinguished students, including August Friedrich Pott, William Dwight Whitney and Michel Bréal. However, like a few twentieth-century comparative-historical linguists such as *Greenberg, Bopp became one of the 'long rangers' (linguists who believe that language families across great distances are 'genetically' related, such as the Nostraticists) by hypothesizing that the Malayo-Polynesian and Caucasian languages were related to Indo-European.

Primary works

(1816). *Über das Conjugationssystem der Sanskritsprache in Vergleichung mit jenem den griechischen, lateinischen, persischen und germanischen Sprache*. Frankfurt Andreäischen Buchhandlung.
(1820). 'Analytical comparison of the Sanskrit, Greek, Latin and Teutonic languages, shewing the original identity of their grammatical structure'. *Annals of Oriental Literature*. Vol. 1(1):1–64.
(1833–52). *Vergleichende Grammatik des Sanskrit, Send, Griechischen, Lateinischen, Lithauischen, Gothischen und Deutschen*. Third edition, 1868–71. Berlin: Dümmler.

Further reading

Lefman, Salomon (1891–5). *Franz Bopp, sein Leben und seine Wissenschaft* (2 vols). Berlin: Reimer.
Verburg, P. A. (1950). 'The background to the linguistic conceptions of Franz Bopp'. *Lingua*. Vol. 2: 438–68.

Alan S. Kaye

PIERRE BOURDIEU

Bourdieu, Pierre (*b.* 1930, *d.* 2002; French), director of studies at the École Pratique des Hautes Études (1964–81), chair of sociology at the Collège de France (1981–2002). Sociologist who extended the market model to many forms of social and cultural expression, including language.

(*See also* Austin, J. L.; Bernstein, Basil; Labov, William; Saussure, Ferdinand de.)

When Pierre Bourdieu died in 2002 at the age of 71 the widespread public and media response was an indication of his standing not only in the field of sociology, but also among the French cultural industries that were so often his targets. He was also known to the public as a politically engaged intellectual who supported railway strikes and anti-globalisation protests. Born and raised in Denguin, southern France, the son of a civil servant, Bourdieu studied philosophy at the École Normale Supérieure before his two-year conscription to the French army in Algeria in 1956. He stayed in Algeria until 1960, undertaking ethnographic work that informed much of his later thinking.

Bourdieu's analysis of the symbolism of a Berber house is a classic example of structuralist criticism, but his 'theory of practice' stems from his reaction against structuralism. He argued that while the sociologist should be distanced from the 'subjective' experience of the individual, an 'objective' position produced a description of the norms rather than the practices of social actors. He wanted to capture how the individual is not engaged in rule following, but not acting out of rational self-interest either. The notion of 'habitus' explains how individuals are disposed towards certain actions and classifications through interactions with each other and their environment, which then serve to reproduce society and culture.

Further material for Bourdieu's prolific analytic output included the farmers of his native Bèarn, the education system, museums, photography, television, the media and language. These 'fields' or markets are structured by power struggles over unequally distributed capital that can be economic, social, cultural or symbolic. The arbitrary cultural preferences of the dominant classes are imposed through legitimated 'symbolic violence'. Taste is not innate, but rather it is used to maintain cultural – that is, class – boundaries. Certainly Bourdieu owed debts to *Marx, Weber and Durkheim among others, but he consistently claimed an original reworking of his predecessors.

Language or linguistic capital, in this view, cannot be separated from 'the linguistic market' and the conditions of its production. Bourdieu's critique of formalist linguistics is not unique, but in his attempts to integrate linguistic exchanges with social theory he is considered more radical than sociolinguists and sociologists of language. He was rather more sympathetic to *Austin's speech act theory, but insisted that felicity conditions are primarily social. Bourdieu's most significant treatment of language may be on the way academics use elaborated linguistic codes to accumulate and retain cultural and other kinds of capital.

Primary works

(1979). *Algeria 1960*. Cambridge: Cambridge University Press.
(1990). *The Logic of Practice*. Cambridge: Polity.
(1991). *Language and Symbolic Power*. John B. Thompson (ed.). Cambridge: Polity.

Further reading

Robbins, Derek (ed.) (2000). *Pierre Bourdieu*. London: Sage.
Wacquant, Loic (1989). 'Towards a reflexive sociology: a workshop with Pierre Bourdieu'. *Sociological Theory*. Vol. 7: 26–63.

Claire Cowie

KARL BRUGMANN

Brugmann, Karl (Friedrich Christian) (*b*. 1849, *d*. 1919; German), lecturer at Leipzig University (1877–84), professor at Freiburg (1884–7), then professor of Indo-European linguistics at Leipzig (1887–1919). A vastly influential historical linguist, both in his youth as a leading member of the 'neogrammarians', who revolutionised the study of diachrony (the study of language in time), and later as the author of the key compendium for Indo-European historical and comparative linguistics. (*See also* Bloomfield, Leonard; Bopp, Franz; Grimm, Jacob; Rask, Rasmus; Saussure, Ferdinand de.)

Brugmann was born 'Brugman' in Wiesbaden, into a well-to-do family. His family changed the spelling to 'Brugmann' when he was 33. In 1867, he left to study linguistics, already well established at German universities, first for one year at Halle, and then at Leipzig. One interruption came directly after he submitted his doctoral thesis (1871), when he took a teacher training qualification in Bonn. After a year's teaching in Wiesbaden,

he moved back to Leipzig, first to teach in a school, and then after four years returned to the university.

His university teaching career was all spent at Leipzig, apart from an early move to Freiburg when he was 35. He began publication of some of his key works there, but stayed for only three years, until his *alma mater* offered him a chair. Returning to Leipzig, he helped build the university into the then world-centre of linguistics, with Brugmann himself its leading light. Germany was then the capital of linguistics, and the discipline essentially a historical and comparative one (although other trends were also pursued, for example by *Humboldt). Brugmann belonged to the third generation of serious nineteenth-century linguists. The first comprised pioneers such as *Rask, *Bopp and *Grimm. The second, including such figures as August Schleicher, established linguistics as an academic discipline, both in universities and as a developing paradigm of knowledge, with scholars aware of and consciously building on colleagues' work.

Brugmann thus found linguistics a relatively mature discipline (he reckoned it sixty years old in 1878). Its primary goal was the reconstruction of Proto-Indo-European, and Brugmann's first influential articles were both contributions to this goal. Published in 1876, while he was still a school teacher, they were distinctly controversial, also a defining characteristic of some of Brugmann's later writings. These first major contributions substantially but simply reshaped Indo-European phonology by reinterpreting its inventory of vowels and recognising that it had underlying syllabic nasals. The latter illustrates his openness to developments in general phonetics and phonology, unlike many historical linguists who had gone before.

Brugmann is best known as a leader among the 'neogrammarians'. This handful of scholars and their contemporary co-thinkers were academically young; they set out to revitalise linguistics and save it from what they saw as non-scientific, romantic faults. The translation 'neogrammarian' does not well convey the humorously meant 'young upstart' flavour of the original *Junggrammatiker*, and the confidence with which they set about revising old results was as infuriating for some contemporaries as it was inspiring for others.

Brugmann co-founded the quasi-journal *Morphologische Untersuchungen*, to publicise neogrammarian ideas, and its first volume's preface (1878) is now known as the 'neogrammarian manifesto'. Written by Brugmann (also signed by Hermann Osthoff), this sets out the theoretical assumptions of the neogrammarian movement. These were not stunningly new in 1878 – as the 'manifesto' explains, they had been assumed in some previous work – but their formulation by Brugmann in a concise and coherent manner had a considerable impact due to their explicitness and clear contradiction of the assumptions of predecessors and contemporaries.

Using modern terminology, these principles can be summed up as follows. First, phonological change proceeds through the innovation of regular, subconscious 'sound laws' that do not allow exceptions. That is, for any change all occurrences of a segment in the environment concerned will be changed (this is referred to as the 'regularity' or 'exceptionlessness' hypothesis; it aided the shift in linguistics from plain comparative reconstruction to attempts to link reconstructed to attested forms through the formulation of historical phonological processes). Second, the other key mechanism that can lead to changes in a morpheme's form is an analogy with a member of a parallel morphological paradigm. This is sometimes referred to as 'form association'. Third, the languages that linguists reconstruct had exactly the same kind of linguistic properties as languages have today, a feature often referred to as 'uniformitarianism'. Finally, language exists in the human mind and is not an autonomous organism that might 'be young', 'grow old', 'improve' or 'decay'.

The first and second points are the key methodological principles, and all four are now fundamental assumptions in much linguistics, apart perhaps from the first, which may have been complicated in the light of 'lexically diffusing' changes that seem to spread gradually through the lexicon so that not all words are affected at the same time even though they feature the same phonological environment. Even so, many twenty-first-century linguists would still claim some version of the regularity hypothesis as a crucial guiding methodological assumption. The principles fitted well with the general assumption of universal laws and uniformity in nature in nineteenth-century science.

Brugmann applied these principles in many contributions to the history of Indo-European languages, especially Latin and Greek. For the latter, he produced a detailed grammar (1885), recognised as one of the clearest and most comprehensive for any individual language: although historically focused, it also described the synchronic phonology, morphology and syntax of ancient Greek. Indeed, synchronic description (description of a language at a given time) was taken for granted by the neogrammarians, although not seen as a goal in its own right.

Brugmann's greatest work was his vast compendium of knowledge about Indo-European and the Indo-European languages, the *Grundriß*. This was published in several parts (some written by Berthold Delbrück), beginning in 1886, with a second edition following soon after. A mammoth undertaking, the *Grundriß* summed up the state of the art in comparative and historical Indo-European studies, the linguistic pilot science. It contained the results of many scholars' work, including Brugmann's own, and encouragement for subsequent researchers to address unexplained problems. Naturally, subsequent scholarship has revised the results that Brugmann records. Thus his four series of Indo-European obstruents are now normally reduced to three, while the discovery of Tocharian and Hittite has widened the Indo-European data set. But Brugmann's *Grundriß* has stood the test of time as a remarkable source of data and hypotheses concerning older Indo-European languages.

The second edition of the *Grundriß* was nearing completion when Brugmann died. In the meantime he had published a shortened, still-read, one-volume version, co-founded the journal *Indogermanische Forschungen*, and published a remarkable number of other pieces, mostly on phonology and morphology, but also on syntax and meaning.

While the controversy regarding some of his opinions and analyses did not and still will not die down, even in the twenty-first century, Brugmann achieved immense respect during his lifetime, undiminished among those who read his work today. He was an absolute master of the live topics in linguistics, and also a great teacher, organiser and networker. Many students and colleagues came to Leipzig, including *Saussure, *Bloomfield and *Trubetzkoy, all of whom played major roles in the later development of 'modern' synchronic linguistics; Brugmann's influence is by no means limited to those who work on historical problems. The neogrammarian systematic, scientific approach has been passed on to contemporary formal linguistics. The 'regularity' hypothesis was the first explanatory principle in linguistics: sound laws could be shown to be right or wrong because they made predictions about which segments in which environments would change. If a word could be found where a segment targeted by a law had not changed, either a principled (phonological, dialectological or analogical) explanation had to be found, or the sound law had to be reformulated or rejected. This type of argumentation has been passed on to feature crucially in generative linguistics. A further neogrammarian contribution was in fully legitimising the investigation of speaker-internal, endogenously changing language in its own right; that is, as an autonomous system that can undergo changes caused and constrained by purely linguistic (phonological and morphological, for example) factors. Brugmann never shied from academic debate where he felt his science demanded it, but most of his work was painstaking and creative explanation of data. He had a happy family life, was well liked by his colleagues, and died in post at Leipzig in 1919.

Primary works

(1876a). 'Nasalis sonans in der indogermanischen Grundsprache'. *Sudien zur griechischen und lateinischen Grammatik (Curtis' Studien)*. Vol. 9.

(1876b). "Zur Geschichte der stammabstufenden Declinationen. Erste Abhandlung: Die Nomina auf -ar- und -tar-'. *Sudien zur griechischen und lateinischen Grammatik (Curtis' Studien)*. Vol. 9.

(1878). Preface to *Morphologische Untersuchungen auf dem Gebiet der indogermanischen Sprachen*. Vol. 1. Winfred Lehmann (trans.). In Winfred Lehmann (ed.), *A Reader in Nineteenth-Century Historical Indo-European Linguistics*. Bloomington: Indiana University Press, 1963.

(1885). 'Griechische Grammatik'. In Iwan Müller (ed.), *Handbuch der klassischen Altertumswissenschaft*. Vol. 2. Munich: Beck. Later published, in a much expanded form, as a separate volume (the third edition, 1900, with 632 pages).

(1886–93). *Grundriß der vergleichenden Grammatik der indogermanischen Sprachen*. First two volumes, on phonology and morphology (vols 3–5, on syntax, were written by Berthold Delbrück). Strasburg: Trübner.

(1888–95). *Elements of the Comparative Grammar of the Indo-Germanic Languages*. Joseph Wright, R. Seymour Conway and W. H. D. Rouse (trans.). Second edition 1897–1916. London: David Nutt, Kegan Paul, Trench, Trübner.

Further reading

Collinge, N. E. (1995). 'History of historical linguistics'. In E. F. K. Koerner and R. E. Asher (eds), *Concise History of the Language Sciences*. Oxford: Elsevier.

Lehmann, Winfred (1993). *Theoretical Bases of Indo-European Linguistics*. London: Routledge.

Morpurgo Davies, Anna (1997). *History of Linguistic. Vol. 4: Nineteenth-Century Linguistics*. London: Longman.

Robins, R. H. (1997). *A Short History of Linguistics* (fourth edition). London: Longman.

Streitberg, Wilhelm (1919). 'Karl Brugmann'. *Indogermanisches Jahrbuch*. Vol. 7.

Patrick Honeybone

DEBORAH CAMERON

Cameron, Deborah (*b.* 1958; British), Rupert Murdoch professor of linguistics at Oxford University (2003–), professor of languages in education at the Institute of Education, London University (1999–2003), senior lecturer and professor of English language at Strathclyde University (1991–9), assistant professor of English, College of William and Mary, VA (1988–90), lecturer in English language, Roehampton Institute (1983–8). Discourse analyst and sociolinguist, whose greatest influence has been in feminist linguistics. (*See also* Tannen, Deborah.)

Cameron received her BA in English language and literature from the University of Newcastle upon Tyne, and her MLitt in general linguistics from the University of Oxford. She has held academic positions in the UK and the USA and is a major figure in the study of language and gender. Her monograph *Feminism and Linguistic Theory* (1985) is one of the central texts in the field, as is an edited reader, *The Feminist Critique of Language* (1990). She has also made important contributions to discourse analysis and the study of language ideologies. Her book on purist ideologies, *Verbal Hygiene* (1995), was awarded the 1996 British Association for Applied Linguistics book prize.

Cameron's 1985 monograph *Feminism and Linguistic Theory* is a foundational text for poststructuralist approaches to language and gender. Earlier work in the field tended to treat gender as a given and was concerned with the ways in which men and women speak differently, either as a result of socialisation (see Deborah *Tannen) or patriarchy. By contrast, poststructuralists such as Cameron argue that it is language that calls the (gendered) identity of speakers into existence. In other words, gender is no longer treated as a given, but the linguistic concern is now with the way in which gendered subjectivities are constituted in language. Furthermore, Cameron is an archetypal 'engaged' scholar who has consistently argued for the importance of not only describing linguistic practices, but also challenging linguistic practices that disadvantage groups of speakers. In her work on language and gender this has meant challenging what is typically considered as the norm of feminine talk as well as the negative judgements that women's speech, whether it is 'feminine' or 'unfeminine', attracts. Similarly, in her book *Good To Talk?*

Living and Working in a Communication Culture (2000) she takes issue with the exploitation of communication workers in late twentieth-century neo-capitalist economies.

The appeal of Cameron's work lies in the innovative and novel ways in which she has been able to combine outspoken feminism with linguistic theory. Outside linguistics, she has also published a book about sexual murder.

Primary works

(1985). *Feminism and Linguistic Theory*. Second edition 1992. London: Macmillan.
(1987), (with E. Frazer). *The Lust To Kill: A Feminist Investigation of Sexual Murder*. Cambridge: Polity.
(1990) (ed.). *The Feminist Critique of Language: A Reader*. Second edition 1998. London: Routledge.
(1995). *Verbal Hygiene*. London: Routledge.
(2000). *Good To Talk? Living and Working in a Communication Culture*. London: Sage.

Ingrid Piller

RUDOLF CARNAP

Carnap, Rudolf (b. 1891, d. 1970; German, naturalised American 1941), professor of philosophy at the German University of Prague, the University of Chicago and University of California, Los Angeles (UCLA). One of the leading figures of logical positivism, who made important contributions to the philosophy of science, the philosophy of mathematics, the philosophy of language, the foundations of probability theory and epistemology.

RUDOLF CARNAP

(*See also* Ayer, A. J.; Frege, Gottlob; Goodman, Nelson; Quine, W. V. O.; Russell, Bertrand; Tarski, Alfred; Wittgenstein, Ludwig.)

Carnap was born in Ronsdorf, Germany. His parents, Johannes Carnap, a factory owner, and Anna Carnap (neé Dörpfeld), a teacher, were deeply religious. After completing his studies of mathematics, philosophy and physics, Carnap took up a position as a *privatdozent* (untenured professor) in Vienna, where he became one of the most active members of the Vienna Circle, a group of philosophers, mathematicians, physicists and social scientists who met regularly to discuss problems in the foundations of the empirical and formal sciences. After the Nazis came to power in Germany in 1933 the political and cultural atmosphere became unbearable for Carnap. In 1935 he moved to the United States, where he held positions at the University of Chicago, Harvard, the Institute for Advanced Study in Princeton and UCLA.

Two early influences left their mark on Carnap's thinking. As a student in Jena, he took courses with Gottlob *Frege, the founder of modern logic, which started Carnap's life-long interest in the subject. In 1919 Carnap became acquainted with the work of Bertrand *Russell, in particular his *Our Knowledge of the External World*, as well as Russell and Whitehead's monumental *Principia Mathematica*, which pursued the logicist programme of grounding all of mathematics on a logical basis. Russell's philosophical outlook and methodological orientation were a deep influence on Carnap's approach to philosophy, which was that philosophy ought to be pursued in a scientific spirit and is capable of the same rigour as the sciences. In other words, the tools of formal logic can be fruitfully applied to philosophical problems. Throughout Carnap's career, his aim was to reconstruct rationally familiar everyday, philosophical or scientific concepts; that is, to work out precise, scientifically viable counterparts for these (often vague) concepts. In his first major philosophical work, *Der logische Aufbau der Welt* (*The Logical Structure of the World*) (1928), Carnap presented an account of our knowledge of the empirical world on a phenomenological basis. Much discussed at the time in the Vienna Circle, the project was pursued further in the late 1940s by Nelson *Goodman.

Through the Vienna Circle Carnap made contact with Ludwig *Wittgenstein, Kurt Gödel and Alfred *Tarski. Gödel had proved that no consistent mathematical system that meets certain constraints can prove its own consistency. For this, he had invented the method of arithmetisation, which allows one to encode and reason about syntactic notions in arithmetic. Tarski had given a formally precise account of the concept of truth, thereby laying the foundation for formal semantics. Carnap was one of the first to realise the importance of the work of Gödel and Tarski, and made use of their insights in his own work.

One major theme in the Vienna Circle was the idea that philosophy, unlike the empirical sciences, was stagnant because most traditional problems of philosophy are pseudoproblems and many philosophical claims are, as they stand, meaningless. As a criterion of meaningfulness the circle considered the criterion of verifiability; a sentence is meaningful only if either it or its negation can be verified by observation. But this criterion had two major drawbacks. First, it ruled out as meaningless a great many statements of the empirical sciences, and second, it ruled out as meaningless all of the statements of mathematics.

A substantial portion of Carnap's work addressed these two problems. In a series of articles he investigated weaker criteria of meaning which were still in the empiricist spirit and would allow one to classify most ordinary scientific statements as meaningful. Carnap tackled the second problem in one of his most important books, *Die Logische Syntax der Sprache* (*The Logical Syntax of Language*) (1937). There he pursued two aims. First he proposed that genuine philosophical problems are metatheoretical; that is, they are problems concerning the language(s) employed in the empirical (natural, social, and formal) sciences. Genuine philosophical questions, he maintained, can be reconstrued as questions about language, and those that cannot are meaningless. The second aim was to show that mathematics is analytic, that the truths of mathematics are determined solely by the syntactical properties of the language of mathematics. Carnap set up the apparatus to determine for any language (meeting certain requirements) which truths are truths in virtue of the formal properties of the language. This treatment made mathematics compatible with empiricist criteria of meaning in that it established that mathematics did not

aspire to the kind of meaning these criteria were set out to measure.

Under the influence of Tarski, Carnap started working on the semantics of languages containing modal operators (such as 'is necessary', 'is possible'). In 1947 he published *Meaning and Necessity*, in which he gave the first precise formal reconstruction of Frege's important notions of *Sinn* ('meaning', or 'intension' in Carnap's reconstruction) and *Bedeutung* ('reference', or 'extension' for Carnap) within what amounts to a possible-world semantics. In Carnap's account the intension (meaning) of an expression is a function from a possible state of affairs to an extension appropriate to the expression. The intension of a name is referred to as an 'individual concept', that of a predicate as a 'property' and that of a sentence as a 'proposition'.

Two major challenges were presented to Carnap's work on semantics. First, *Quine and others complained that Carnap's use of abstract entities (such as properties and propositions) was incompatible with an empiricist-scientific outlook concerned with physical properties. Second, Quine objected that while semantic notions such as meaning and synonymy could be introduced for formal languages, they are empty terms when applied to natural languages. Carnap attempted to meet both challenges. In order to defend his appeal to abstract entities he introduced, in 'Empiricism, semantics, and ontology' (1950), his well-known distinction between internal and external questions. Questions internal to a linguistic framework are asked and answered relative to the linguistic resources and evidential standards of that framework. On the other hand, questions external to a linguistic framework demand answers independent of the evidential standards of the framework. For example, in Carnap's view the question whether there are propositions is either meant as internal to the framework of semantics, in which case it has a trivially affirmative answer, or is meant to be external to that framework, in which case it reduces to the pragmatic question of whether we should adopt the framework of semantics.

We choose frameworks on pragmatic grounds, not because we believe that the entities appealed to in the framework really exist but rather because if theorising in terms of properties or propositions proves fruitful, we should not deprive ourselves of these modes of theorising on the grounds of misguided metaphysical scruples. As far as this second challenge is concerned, Carnap argued that when confronted with an unfamiliar language a field linguist may break into the language and, using empirical observational methods, develop a translation manual that allows one to determine what the expressions of the language mean. These arguments led Quine to put forward, in *Word and Object*, his famous argument for the indeterminacy of translation, according to which observational data is not sufficient to pin down a unique translation manual. Quine concluded that there is no place for meaning in the scientifically acceptable study of language.

Through both his writing and his teaching Carnap had an enormous impact on the development of analytical philosophy. He did pioneering work in the semantics of modal languages, and several important works in the philosophy of language were developed in direct response to his views on semantics. The scientific outlook and formal rigour introduced into philosophy by Carnap and other logical positivists left its mark on the subject. From the 1950s onwards, analytic philosophy proceeded from criticism of the perceived shortcomings of logical positivism and in particular the work of Carnap. But the 1990s saw a substantial reassessment of Carnap's work, one which revealed it to be more subtle than earlier critics had realised.

Primary works

(1937). *The Logical Syntax of Language*. Amethe Smeaton (trans.). London: Routledge and Kegan Paul.

(1942). *Introduction to Semantics*. Cambridge, MA: Harvard University Press.

(1947). *Meaning and Necessity: A Study in Semantics and Modal Logic*. Chicago: Chicago University Press.

(1950). 'Empiricism, semantics and ontology'. *Revue Internationale de Philosophie*. Vol. 4.

(1967). *The Logical Structure of the World*. Rolf George (trans.). Berkeley, CA: University of California Press.

Further reading

Carnap, Rudolf (1963). 'My intellectual development'. In Paul Schilpp (ed.), *The Philosophy of Rudolf Carnap*. Library of Living Philosophers, Vol. 11. La Salle: Open Court, 1963.

Coffa, Alberto (1991). *The Semantic Tradition: From Kant to Carnap*. Cambridge: Cambridge University Press.

Iris Einheuser

NOAM CHOMSKY

Chomsky, (Avram) Noam (*b.* 1928; American), professor, Massachusetts Institute of Technology (1961–6), Ferrari P. Ward professor of modern languages and linguistics (1966–76), Institute professor (1976–). Linguist and philosopher; founder of transformational generative grammar, linked with the claim that human language is a psychological, ultimately biological object which should be studied using the methods of the natural sciences and that human beings possess a species-specific language acquisition device. (*See also* Bloomfield, Leonard; Descartes, René; Humboldt, Wilhelm von; Plato; Putnam, Hilary; Quine, W. V. O.; Skinner, B. F.)

One of the central figures of twentieth-century linguistics, Noam Chomsky was born on 7 December 1928 in Philadelphia, Pennsylvania. The two areas in which he would become best known, linguistics and politics, were a part of his life almost from birth. His parents were both teachers of Hebrew, and his father William published scholarly articles on medieval Hebrew grammarians. At the same time his family was very active politically, particularly in various left-wing and cultural Zionist organisations.

Chomsky's early school years were spent at a Deweyite experimental school in Philadelphia. He attended the Oak Lane Country Day School until the age of 12, a school where, in line with the educational system devised by John Dewey, children were encour- aged to learn whatever they wanted, either individually or in groups, at whatever pace they wanted. It was there that Chomsky's first political writings appeared, in the form of an editorial in the school newspaper about the fall of Barcelona during the Spanish Civil War. Although he would go on to become one of the most influential linguists of the twentieth century, his political writings on American foreign policy, state power, the security services and the military-industrial complex have made Chomsky famous as a commentator and voice of the radical liberal left. So well known is Chomsky's political commentary, in fact, that many of his admirers in that area are hardly even aware of his huge stature in linguistics and the philosophy of language.

After transferring to Philadelphia's Central High School, Chomsky went on to the University of Pennsylvania. But he was soon unhappy with the replication of the imposed hierarchies and manipulated competition that had characterised his high school experience and was on the verge of dropping out of university. However, in 1947 he met Zelig Harris, a charismatic professor with whom he shared a broad range of intellectual and political interests, and stayed on to study linguistics, philosophy and logic.

The roots of what came to be known as 'generative' grammar go back as far as Chomsky's undergraduate thesis, which he revised for his master's thesis and which was subsequently published in 1979 under the title *Morphophonemics of Modern Hebrew*. Chomsky's ambitious goal in that work, only partially realised, was to provide a complete grammar of the language, providing every sentence with an explicit, formal description at the syntactic, morphological, morphophonemic and phonemic levels. Unlike some earlier works that could be taken to be generative in spirit (for example, Leonard, *Bloomfield's treatment of Menomini morphophonemics or Roman *Jakobson's Russian conjugations), Chomsky's explicitly incorporates devices from mathematical logic in aid of an economical description of linguistic phenomena.

In 1955 Chomsky was awarded his PhD by the University of Pennsylvania on the strength of one chapter of a book that he had written. It eventually saw publication by Plenum Press in 1975 under the title *The Logical Structure of Linguistic Theory*, though it was rejected twenty years earlier by the precursor to MIT Press. Later in 1995 he began work in the Research Laboratory for Electronics at the Massachusetts Institute of Technology (MIT), and was eventually made a full-time member of staff. As part of his teaching obligations, he took over an undergraduate course on language that had been in the catalogue. It was the lectures for this course which eventually became the basis for his seminal 1957 book *Syntactic Structures*.

In this volume, Chomsky attempts to put the study of language on a modern scientific footing by providing an explicit theory of the internal structure of languages. In a way that would be familiar to researchers in the more 'natural' sciences, Chomsky provides an axiom system (a finite number of postulated rules that can generate an infinite number of results, in this case in the form of a phrase-structure grammar and generalised transformations) and then proceeds to explore the various consequences of that system and the predictions that are derivable from it.

However, it was in the area of methodology that *Syntactic Structures* constituted a radical break from the past, providing a new conception of what linguistics was about. The emphasis in structuralist linguistics, the prevailing approach at the time, had been on 'discovery procedures': mechanical procedures for arriving at the correct description of a language starting from the lowest (phonetic) level and working upward. Chomsky argued that since the actual practice of theory construction involved all manner of factors such as intuition, past experience and the like, the formulation of procedures for this seemed an overambitious goal. Instead, *Syntactic Structures* shifted the focus from discovery to evaluation; in other words he began to look at methods for determining which grammar of several possible ones is the correct one.

Syntactic Structures also marked the appearance of the famous example sentence 'Colorless green ideas sleep furiously.' With this example Chomsky is attempting to illustrate that intuitive judgements about well-formedness are in principle independent of meaning. Whatever bizarre non-meaning this sentence has, the sentence clearly has a different status from the one obtained by putting the words in the reverse order 'Furiously sleep ideas green colorless.' The difference is that the first sentence is syntactically well-formed, and the second is not.

Syntactic Structures was generally received very favourably, marking Chomsky as a linguist to watch. His status was further enhanced by his enormously influential 1959 review of B. F. *Skinner's Verbal Behavior*, in which Chomsky argued against a behaviouristic account of language acquisition. In 1961 he received tenure at MIT, where he has remained for his entire career. A year later, he was one of only five invited plenary speakers at the Ninth International Congress of Linguists, and a revised version of his address to that congress was published in 1964 as *Current Issues in Linguistic Theory*.

In *Current Issues*, Chomsky for the first time articulated a number of distinctions that have become central to his approach. It is here, for example, that Chomsky introduces his distinction between competence and performance. Although similar kinds of distinctions had been proposed in the past (and Chomsky explicitly claims to be reinterpreting Ferdinand de *Saussure's langue–parole* distinction), Chomsky's formulation has become particularly well known. 'Competence' refers to a speaker's knowledge about his or her grammar, whereas 'performance' refers to the way in which the speaker puts that knowledge to use in actually speaking and understanding a language. Chomsky sees his enterprise as the study of competence.

It is also in *Current Issues* that Chomsky first elaborates his famous distinction between 'observational', 'descriptive' and 'explanatory' adequacy. Observational adequacy is attained by a grammar that just states the correct facts, merely producing,

for example, the correct form in the correct environment. A descriptively adequate grammar, by contrast, treats the surface data in terms of generalisations and underlying regularities, expressing a given distribution by postulating a single underlying form which is then affected by processes that have more general application within the language. The highest level of adequacy, explanatory adequacy, is attained when there is a general theory of grammars that provides the basis for selecting the most descriptively adequate grammar from a selection of possible grammars.

In *Aspects of the Theory of Syntax* (1965a) Chomsky attempted his most detailed exposition of syntactic theory since *Syntactic Structures*, and *Aspects* became the standard reference work for a generation of syntacticians. Looking at the 'base component', one of the most important theoretical changes seen in *Aspects* was the introduction of the level of 'Deep Structure' (later often D-Structure) which determined the semantic interpretation of a sentence, as opposed to the 'Surface Structure' (or S-Structure) which determined its phonetic form. It is also in *Aspects* that Chomsky introduces the lexicon as the locus of idiosyncratic information.

Aspects also sees Chomsky for the first time examining the question of language acquisition, phrasing certain theoretical problems as the problem of constructing a hypothetical language acquisition device. Concern for language acquisition issues would come to play a crucial background role in Chomsky's thinking, and many of the changes to the theory throughout his career are directly related to his position on this issue.

In elaborating his views on language acquisition in *Aspects* Chomsky identifies two historical approaches to the acquisition of knowledge, of which he takes knowledge of language to be a sub-case. Chomsky allies himself with the rationalist tradition, exemplified by René *Descartes and Wilhelm von *Humboldt, who take there to be innate ideas and principles of various kinds over and above elementary processing mechanisms. In the rationalist tradition these innate principles then shape the acquired knowledge, sometimes in very specific ways. This is in contrast to the empiricist tradition, as exemplified in this context by W. V. O. *Quine or Skinner, which takes the view that the knowledge acquisition device consists only of weak principles of association or generalisation. Chomsky would reiterate his connection to the rationalist epistemological and linguistic tradition in *Cartesian Linguistics* (1965b), his first extended foray into the history of linguistic ideas. Although Chomsky in *Aspects* argues that it was not possible at that time to formulate assumptions about this initial, innate language acquisition device that were sufficiently rich and structured to account for the fact of language acquisition, it would be an issue that he would return to again and again during his career.

In addition to his work on syntactic theory, Chomsky also published some articles on phonology. His major contribution in this field came in 1968 with the publication of *The Sound Pattern of English*, co-authored with his MIT colleague Morris Halle. In this work, Chomsky and Halle extended the *Aspects* programme into phonology, capturing regularities in English by postulating underlying representations and ordered phonological rules to generate surface forms. A major innovation in *The Sound Pattern of English* was that these phonological rules were stated in terms of distinctive features, rather than undivided phonemes (see Jakobson).

During the 1970s one of Chomsky's central concerns was to constrain the transformational operation. He had noted as far back as *The Logical Structure of Linguistic Theory* that the transformation as a theoretical device was undesirably powerful and unconstrained. As a result only a very weak claim was made about what constituted a possible language, and this made it more difficult to explain language acquisition, since it wasn't then possible to postulate a single innate device from which all languages originate. In 'Conditions on transformations' (1973), Chomsky proposes a number of general constraints on the transformational operation. These included the requirement that all transformations leave a trace marking the original position of the moved element. 'Conditions' thus represents the first step on the programme inaugurated in *Aspects* but put aside as premature: the outline of the content of Universal Grammar (UG), a species-specific language acquisition device that might provide a principled account for the fact of language acquisition.

In 1981's *Lectures on Government and Binding* Chomsky continued this process, providing his most explicit and detailed unification of his conceptual work and his technical work. Chomsky suggests that Universal Grammar consists of a number of sub-systems relating to phenomena such as case assignment and anaphora. He also argues for various principles of UG which play a role across the grammar, such as 'government'. In arguing for these various sub-systems of UG, Chomsky shows how they interact to provide a wide range of empirical coverage. In addition to containing principles, he suggests that UG also contains parameters – options from a limited set provided by UG that can be instantiated differently in individual languages. The principles express the language-universal aspects and the parameters account for the variation (Saussurian arbitrariness aside).

Although Chomsky had been discussing some of these ideas since the mid-1970s, his 1986 volume *Knowledge of Language* brought together much of his thinking on some of the more philosophical aspects of his approach to language. It was here that he most extensively discussed what he referred to as '*Plato's Problem' (also sometimes '*Russell's problem'). This is the problem of how human beings come to know so much, given that their contacts with the world are so limited. With respect to language acquisition, Plato's problem manifests itself in the 'poverty of the stimulus', the claim that one's knowledge of one's language is vastly underdetermined by the data available during the course of language acquisition.

By the late 1980s and early 1990s, Chomsky had once again become concerned about the complexity of his theory and the attendant problems for explanatory adequacy and language acquisition. At the same time a striking property of the Principles and Parameters research programme began to become clear: a lack of redundancy with respect to linguistic principles. Very often when the ungrammaticality of a given sentence could be explained by two different principles, it had been shown that one or the other was disposable or incorrectly formulated. As Chomsky noted, this is unexpected, in that this kind of 'perfection' is more a feature of the inorganic world than the organic world, which is often characterised by 'mess' and redundancy. These two issues led Chomsky to a radical theoretical restructuring that came to be known as the 'Minimalist Program'. The 1995 volume of the same name collects three of Chomsky's articles from the early 1990s together with a new chapter in which he develops some of the ideas further.

The central research intuition pursued by the Minimalist Program is that the computational system is a 'perfect' solution to the constraints imposed by virtual conceptual necessity. With respect to the organisation of the grammar, for example, it implies that the only levels of representation with any linguistic significance are Phonetic Form (the interface with pronunciation) and Logical Form (the interface with meaning). These two interfaces seem inescapable if the computational system is to relate sound and meaning. However, Deep Structure and Surface Structure are not levels which have any significance for the grammar.

Principles that were previously stated in terms of these levels thus required revision. Since its inception questions of economy, both with respect to derivations and representations, have gained new importance within the context of the Minimalist Program.

The Minimalist Program also re-opened questions about adequacy. In 1964's *Current Issues in Linguistic Theory*, Chomsky laid out the distinctions between observational, descriptive and explanatory adequacy. But as the twenty-first century begins, Chomsky suggests that the Minimalist Program allows one even to go beyond explanatory adequacy. Not only can our general theory of grammars select the most descriptively adequate grammar, but we are also in a position to explain why/how it does so. If language truly is a 'perfect' solution given the constraints imposed, then we can explain why a grammar with a Minimalist character ends up being the most descriptively adequate.

In addition to his work on formal linguistic theory, Chomsky has also made significant contributions in the area of more traditional philosophy of language and mind. His book *New Horizons in the Study of Language and Mind* (2000) provides a comprehensive overview of his philosophical views, especially as they developed during the 1990s. One of the recurring themes of the volume is that various traditional and influential philosophical discussions on language and mind are fundamentally misconceived.

One such misconception concerns reference, Chomsky suggests. There is a long-standing debate, going back in its modern form to Gottlob *Frege, regarding the way in which words pick out or refer to things in the world. Chomsky is in fact doubtful that any such relation exists. He argues that even simple examples such as 'book' or 'city' can be used in a way that requires whatever object is being referred to to have contradictory properties. For example: 'That book about linguistics which John wrote in his head weighs two kilos in hard cover' or 'The city of London is so unpleasant and frenetic that it should be destroyed utterly and rebuilt ten miles further up the Thames'. Crucially though, whatever the reference relation between words and things is that is being discussed in the philosophy literature, Chomsky claims that it is a technical notion internal to some (often implicit) theory about human cognition. Yet if this is the case then information gleaned from thought experiments such as Hilary *Putnam's 'Twin Earth' may not be relevant: thought experiments about what 'angular momentum' means are irrelevant for the study of physics, for example.

Perhaps even more strikingly, Chomsky also claims that the so-called 'mind–body' problem does not exist and that debates about it are predicated on a crucial misunderstanding. The 'mind–body' problem is not only a centuries-old question in its own right, but also lies behind a number of major trends in twentieth-century philosophy, particularly the 'naturalisation' of philosophy. However, Chomsky observes that to even formulate the problem requires having a coherent notion of 'body', and he believes that no such notion exists. For the Cartesians, 'body' was formulated in terms of contact mechanics. Things in the physical world can only interact if they are in physical contact. Newton's theory of gravitational attraction, however, showed that the contact mechanics view of the universe could not be sustained. Since that time 'body', the physical universe, has simply expanded and changed as necessary to account for whatever phenomena are observed in the world. It then becomes unclear why certain phenomena of the physical world (the mental ones) are in principle beyond its scope.

Chomsky is among a select group of scientists and intellectuals who have continued to provide revolutionary new ideas throughout the entire length of their career. Perhaps because of his prolific output as both a linguist and a political commentator, he inspires both strong devotion and strong antagonism. Interestingly, for most of his professional life these two strands have remained almost completely separate, and though audiences for his books and talks in both areas are always huge, he is better known by far as a dissident than as a linguist. Chomsky is known for his relentless pace of work and for robust defence of his current thinking. This conviction is often viewed as intellectual arrogance, but there is no doubt that he is one of the most important thinkers of the twentieth century in any sphere. Throughout much of the mid- to late twentieth century, linguistic researchers of whatever theoretical persuasion felt the at least

to need take account of the issues that Chomsky and his work have raised. It is a trend that shows no sign of abating in the twenty-first century.

Primary works

(1957). *Syntactic Structures*. The Hague: Mouton.

(1964). *Current Issues in Linguistic Theory*. The Hague: Mouton.

(1965a). *Aspects of the Theory of Syntax*. Cambridge, MA: MIT Press.

(1965b). *Cartesian Linguistics*. New York: Harper and Row.

(1968) (with Morris Halle). *The Sound Pattern of English*. New York: Harper and Row.

(1973). 'Conditions on transformations'. In S. R. Anderson and P. Kiparsky (eds), *A Festschrift for Morris Halle*. New York: Holt, Reinhart and Winston.

(1975). *The Logical Structure of Linguistic Theory*. New York: Plenum Press.

(1981). *Lectures on Government and Binding*. Dordrecht: Foris.

(1986). *Knowledge of Language*. New York: Praeger Press.

(1995). *The Minimalist Program*. Cambridge, MA: MIT Press.

(2000). *New Horizons in the Study of Language and Mind*. Cambridge: Cambridge University Press.

Further reading

Barsky, Robert F. (1997). *Noam Chomsky: A Life of Dissent*. Cambridge, MA: MIT Press.

Lyons, John (1991). *Chomsky*. Fontana Modern Masters series, third edition. London: Fontana.

Newmeyer, Frederick J. (1996). *Generative Linguistics*. London: Routledge.

Smith, Neil (1999). *Chomsky: Ideas and Ideals*. Cambridge: Cambridge University Press.

Geoffrey Poole

DONALD DAVIDSON

Davidson, Donald (Herbert) (*b*. 1917, *d*. 2003; American), Willis S. and Marion Slusser professor, University of California at Berkeley (1986–2003). Instructor then professor of philosophy at: Queen's College New York (1947–50), Stanford University, California (1950–67), Princeton University (1967–9), Rockefeller University, New York City (1970–6), University of Chicago (1976–81), University of California at Berkeley (1981–2003). John Locke lecturer, University of Oxford (1970). An analytical philosopher whose work covers a wide range of topics in the philosophies of action, mind and language, Davidson's most obvious influence was his teacher W. V. O. *Quine, but his work has influenced and been influenced by a wide range of philosophers and linguists. Two of his most important contributions are his proposed solution to the mind–body problem, and his groundbreaking work on the nature of a semantic theory for natural languages, based on a notion of truth developed by Alfred *Tarski. (*See also* Descartes, René; Dummett, Michael; Frege, Gottlob; Hume, David; Lewis, David; Montague, Richard; Plato; Putnam, Hilary; Quine, W. V. O.; Tarski, Alfred; Wittgenstein, Ludwig.)

Davidson was born in 1917 in Springfield, Massachusetts. His father, Clarence Herbert Davidson, was a civil engineer and his mother, Grace Cordelia Anthony, was the daughter of a fairly prosperous industrialist. His father's work caused the family to travel frequently and this meant that Davidson received little formal education until he was around 9 or 10 years old, when he enrolled at a public (that is, 'state') school on Staten Island, New York. He gained a BA at Harvard in 1939 and a PhD, also at Harvard, in 1949. Before completing his PhD, he interrupted his studies to serve with the United States Navy in the Mediterranean from 1942 until 1945. While carrying out his undergraduate work in English, comparative literature and classics, he attended classes taught by Alfred North Whitehead, and this influence inspired him to study philosophy as a graduate student. His graduate thesis, under the supervision of Quine, explored *Plato's *Philebus* and demonstrated an interest in classical philosophy. But he was already interested in analytical philosophy and went on to become one of the most important analytical philosophers of the twentieth century. Since the early 1960s his vast output of essays has had a major influence in a wide range of philosophical areas.

At the time when Davidson began his graduate studies, American philosophy was heavily influenced by empiricism and in particular by logical positivism. Davidson studied both of these carefully before rejecting them in his mature work. He saw the attempt to refute empiricism as one of his most important endeavours. He made a significant contribution to work on decision-making in the 1950s, before moving on to the areas for which his work is best known. His most important work covers a wide range of topics in analytical philosophy, but it can be thought of as dividing into two broad areas: work on reasons, causes, events and actions, and work on the philosophy of language, including work on the semantics of natural languages. Davidson saw rationality and language as closely linked, and it is possible to see his work as part of one overall project to understand what it is to be a rational, language-using being.

In 1963 Davidson published the essay 'Actions, reasons and causes' (see Davidson 2001a), which had a huge impact on the philosophy of mind and action. Davidson argued against the then standard view, inspired partly by the work of *Wittgenstein and *Hume, that a reason for acting could not be a cause of the relevant action. Hume had suggested that it is not possible for one thing to cause another if there is a logical connection between them. Davidson argued instead that the existence of a logical connection does not rule out a causal relationship. For example, an individual's beliefs both that a particular action is harmful and that he or she doesn't want to do anything harmful may be both logically and causally connected to a decision not to do the harmful thing.

A crucial idea that both underpins and is supported by several strands of Davidson's work is his suggestion that an event is a concrete, dated particular entity. This notion is exploited in his account of causation, in his account of the mind–body problem and in his work on the study of meaning. He saw causation as a relation between events, and he saw the mind–body problem in terms of the relation between mental and physical events, while his work on meaning exploited his view that events have concrete existence.

He developed an account of the semantics of adverbial modifiers that both exploits and provides support for his view of events as concrete particulars. He argued that the fact that an infinite number of adverbial modifiers can be attached to a sentence such as 'John hit Bill' requires the assumption that the event of John hitting Bill is a concrete entity. If we assume this, then the meaning of a sentence with multiple adverbial modifiers, such as 'John hit Bill at six in the bedroom', can be explained as a series of conjunctions as follows: 'There is an event e and e is a hitting of Bill by John and e occurs at six and e occurs in the bedroom.' This is an alternative to postulating a separate event for each of: 'John hitting Bill', 'John hitting Bill at six', 'John hitting Bill at six in the bedroom' and so on. Similarly Davidson argued that a sentence such as 'the short circuit caused the fire' can be understood as saying that a relationship of causation exists between an event of short circuit and an event of fire.

Davidson's approach to the mind–body problem was in terms of the relation between mental and physical events; he developed a new perspective on the problem in his theory of 'anomalous monism'. This theory holds that everything in the world is physical, in particular that mental events are physical events (monism), but also that (anomalously) one cannot be reduced to the other. The failure of mental events to reduce to physical events is based on the assumption that there are properties that can be predicated of one but not of the other. For example, the transitivity of length is constitutive of physical entities while principles of rationality are constitutive of mental entities.

One way of summarising the traditional mind–body problem is in terms of the following assumptions:

1. No mental event is a physical event.
2. Some mental events cause physical events.
3. The only causes of physical events are physical events.

Davidson's solution involves abandoning assumption (1) while retaining assumptions (2) and (3); that is, he argues that mental events are just physical events. The difference between mental events and physical events is in fact only a difference in how they are described. Davidson's view is therefore a materialist one in that he claims that it is possible for one thing to have both mental and physical properties. This kind of materialism is often referred to as an 'identity theory', since the mental is seen as identical to the physical. For Davidson, unlike *Descartes and other 'dualists', mind and matter are not distinct substances. Mind and matter, like mental and physical events, are distinct in terms of how they are described.

One of the first important ideas Davidson proposed in his work on the philosophy of language was an adequacy criterion for theories of linguistic meaning. He insisted that an adequate theory must be 'compositional'; that is, the meaning of each sentence in a language must be generated from the meanings of its parts (of which there is a finite set). This criterion follows from the fact that human beings with finite brains can potentially understand the meanings of an infinite number of utterances in languages they speak. This notion of compositionality was present in the work of earlier philosophers, notably Gottlob *Frege, but Davidson's work helped to make it a standard assumption in subsequent theories of linguistic meaning.

He claimed that a semantic theory should not make explicit reference to notions of meaning but instead needed only to refer to notions of truth. This claim partly reflects the influence of Quine, but the most significant problem Davidson saw with the notion of meaning was the problem of 'semantic opacity': the fact that the expression 'means that' is semantically opaque while the expression 'is true if' is not. If, for example, we claim that a particular linguistic expression 'means that' a cat climbed the big tree in my garden, it is not clear whether this means that a cat climbed the chestnut tree in my garden, even if we know that 'the big tree' and 'the chestnut tree' are the same thing. Applying Tarski's formal theory of truth, which also originated in the work of Frege, to the semantics of natural languages, Davidson suggested that to give the meaning of a sentence such as the German expression 'Schnee ist weiss', we should state a theorem such as: 'Schnee ist weiss' is true in German if, and only if, snow is white'. To understand this theorem it is important to distinguish the 'object language' being studied (in this case German) and the 'metalanguage' being used to analyse it (in this case English). If the distinction between object language and metalanguage is fully grasped, then there is no oddity in using a particular language, say English, as both object language and metalanguage, and claiming that 'snow is white' is true in

English if, and only if, snow is white'. This is a form of 'correspondence theory'; that is, a view of meaning in terms of a correspondence between the meaning-bearing expression and another kind of expression or entity: correspondence theories originate in the work of *Aristotle. Davidson goes against traditional approaches by suggesting that we do not need to analyse the notion of 'truth' in order to develop an adequate analysis, but he also suggests that truth is central to an account of linguistic meaning.

A Davidsonian semantic theory for a particular language would involve a finite set of axioms giving the meanings of basic terms in the language, rules for the meanings of connectives (such as 'and' and 'or') and quantifiers (such as 'some' and 'all'), and rules for assessing whether expressions in the language are well-formed. From this it should be possible to state the truth conditions of an infinite set of utterances in the language. This truth-conditional approach has not been universally adopted, but it has been extremely influential and is a useful starting point in defining any approach to the study of meaning. So far a detailed account along these lines has been developed only for a small number of linguistic expressions. The main areas of difficulty in developing such an account relate to expressions that do not seem to be analysable in terms of truth conditions, such as indexicals, attributive adjectives, indirect speech contexts and non-declarative sentences. Davidson made significant contributions to the analysis of a number of these areas, which are still the subject of considerable interest and debate.

Another criterion Davidson suggested was that an adequate theory must hold under the practice of 'radical interpretation'. A radical interpreter is someone who knows nothing about the language he or she is attempting to interpret and has no access to bilingual speakers, dictionaries or other sources. A radical interpreter can usually determine whether an informant 'holds true' a sentence even if the interpreter does not understand the sentence. So a radical interpreter can gather data by checking what is true at the time when a speaker agrees that a particular assertion is true. For example, it might be clear to the radical interpreter that a particular speaker holds 'es regnet' true whenever it is raining. This criterion will prevent the radical interpreter from assuming that, for example, 'es regnet' is true whenever grass is green, even though it is true that grass is green every time a speaker says 'es regnet'. There is a sense in which everyone who acquires a language does so from the point of view of a radical interpreter. Davidson saw the truth theory to be applied to natural languages as an empirical one to be confirmed for a speaker or linguistic community. In Davidson's view nothing that cannot be worked out on the basis of evidence can be part of meaning.

Further to this, Davidson invoked a 'principle of charity' that rules out the possibility that a community of speakers might all happen to be wrong about the meaning of an expression in their language. The principle of charity assumes that speakers are in general rational, well intentioned and well informed about their language. Quine made reference to this principle in his discussion of 'radical translation'; that is, cases where translators are unfamiliar with the culture of the speakers of the language to be translated. In the context of radical interpretation, the principle of charity says that where a speaker's utterances can be interpreted in more than one way, the interpretation to prefer is the one that makes the most statements come out as true or inviting assent. In later work Davidson replaced the principle of charity with a 'principle of humanity', stating that the interpretations to prefer are those that make most utterances come out as 'reasonable' rather than true. This line of reasoning also led Davidson to reject global scepticism, the view that it is possible for an individual to hold beliefs most of which are false. Davidson suggests that the way beliefs are arrived at will mean that they are mostly true.

Davidson has argued against the notion that language is representational, since this is based on the assumption that language represents facts and he claims that there are no facts for language to represent. His account of meanings proposes a correspondence between sentences in the object language and statements in a meta-language, not between sentences and facts. He argues that there can be at most one fact so that if true sentences correspond to anything they all correspond to the same 'Great Fact'. If any sentence is made true by a particular fact, then all sentences that agree in truth value with that sentence are made true by the same fact. This conclusion depends, of course, on Davidson's approach to meaning in terms of truth.

Davidson also developed a strong position on the relationship between language and thought, arguing that the ability to think requires an ability with language. This view depends partly on the notion of 'semantic opacity' mentioned above. He claims that semantic opacity occurs only when language is linked to thought, and that the only evidence strong enough to support the view that particular creatures can think would be evidence that they possess a language.

Davidson also links the question of whether people in different cultures have different conceptual schemes to questions about language. If we assume both that thought requires language and that any concept is expressible in a language, then this entails that a difference in conceptual schemes between two people will mean that some of the language of one of them will not be translatable into the language of the other. Davidson argues that no sense can be made of the notion of non-translatable languages and therefore that we cannot judge whether anyone has a conceptual scheme radically different from our own.

He rejects the traditional idea, originally inspired by the work of Descartes, that beliefs about our own mental states are central to our structure of justified beliefs. He argues that 'first person authority', the idea that an individual's assumptions about his or her own mental states are more reliable than another individual's assumptions about them, follows from the more accurate knowledge an individual has about his or her own words. He suggests that knowledge of the world is autonomous from knowledge of our own minds and that it cannot be explained in terms of inferences from knowledge in our own minds. He also rejects empiricism, arguing that our knowledge of the world is based not on sensory experience but on the fact that we are rational, communicating animals.

For Davidson language, mind and action are inseparable. He claims that a semantic theory can only be adequate if it combines a finite basic vocabulary with a set of rules of composition. He treats the theory of truth for a language as an empirical theory and sees the stance of the radical interpreter as a means of confirming it. He sees the theory of meaning in a context of rational agency. He rejects Cartesianism, empiricism, conceptual relativism, global scepticism and representationalism.

Davidson has influenced a wide range of other scholars working in the philosophy of language and linguistics. Arguably his greatest influence in these areas has been in that of semantics, where he both developed and argued against ideas proposed by previous thinkers, including Aristotle, Descartes, Frege, Hume and Tarski. He has both influenced and been influenced by other scholars working on a truth-conditional approach to meaning, or with a more general interest in the relationship between truth and language, including *Dummet, *Lewis, *Montague and *Putnam. An account of any approach to the semantics of natural languages is now likely to begin by stating whether it is based on adopting or rejecting a truth-conditional approach inspired by Davidson's work.

Besides his enormous influence on the philosophy of language Davidson also lived an adventurous non-academic life. He took part in a wide range of activities including surfing, mountain climbing, skiing, piloting two-engine planes, script writing, piano playing and drama. He died in 2003 at the age of 86.

Primary works

(1972) (ed. with Gilbert Harman). *Semantics of Natural Language*. Dordrecht: Reidel.

(2001a). *Essays on Actions and Events*. Second edition. Oxford: Clarendon Press.

(2001b). *Inquiries into Truth and Interpretation*. Second edition. Oxford: Clarendon Press.

(2001c). *Subjective, Intersubjective, Objective*. Oxford: Clarendon Press.

(forthcoming a). *Problems of Rationality*. Oxford: Clarendon Press.

(forthcoming b). *Truth, Language and History*. Oxford: Clarendon Press.

Further reading

Evnine, Simon (1991). *Donald Davidson*. Cambridge: Polity.

Hahn, Lewis Edwin (ed.) (1999). *The Philosophy of Donald Davidson*. Library of Living Philosophers XXVII. Chicago: Open Court.

Lepore, Ernest (ed.) (1986). *Truth and Interpretation: Perspectives on the Philosophy of Donald Davidson*. Oxford: Blackwell.

Lepore, Ernest and McLaughlin, Brian (eds) (1985). *Actions and Events: Perspectives on the Philosophy of Donald Davidson*. Oxford: Blackwell.

Malpas, Jeff E. (1992). *Donald Davidson and the Mirror of Meaning*. Cambridge: Cambridge University Press.

Ramberg, Bjorn (1989). *Donald Davidson's Philosophy of Language: An Introduction*. Oxford: Blackwell.

Vermazen, Bruce and Hintikka, Merrill (eds) (1985). *Essays on Davidson: Actions and Events*. Oxford: Clarendon Press.

Zeglen, Ursula M. (ed.) (1991). *Donald Davidson: Truth, Meaning and Knowledge.* London: Routledge.

Billy Clark

JACQUES DERRIDA

Derrida, Jacques (*b*. 1930, *d*. 2004; Algerian, naturalised French), taught at the Sorbonne (1960–4) and the École Normale Supérieure (1965–84). Became directeur d'études at the École des Hautes Études en Sciences Sociales in Paris. A leading figure in the movement called deconstruction, closely associated with poststructuralism and, perhaps in less obvious ways, with postmodernism, postcolonialism, feminist theory and struggles by various minorities. Derrida is one of the most celebrated, quoted, cited and derided figures of late twentieth-century philosophy. From the early 1970s on he was a frequent visitor to the United States, on teaching assignments at Johns Hopkins, Yale, and the University of California at Irvine. (*See also* Austin, J. L.; Husserl, Edmund; Searle, John.)

Jacques Derrida was born in El-Biar on the suburbs of Algiers in an assimilated petit bourgeois Jewish family, the third son of Aimé and Georgette (née Safar) Derrida. As a child, he had a taste of growing anti-semitism when in 1942, barely a year after he had been admitted to the *lycée* of Ben Aknun near his home town, he was expelled under a recently introduced law that placed an upper limit on the number of Jews in state schools. Despite the traumatising experience and the interruption to his formal education, Derrida kept himself busy reading widely among the works of Rousseau, Gide, Nietzsche, Valery and Camus. He also had a brief stint writing poems, which he later came to detest, for local North African journals and even toyed with the idea of becoming a professional footballer. Derrida finally passed his *baccalauréat* in 1948 after a failed attempt the year before. At the age of 19 he moved to France and spent a year as a boarding student at the Lycée Louis-le-Grand, during which time he read the works of Simone Weil amidst precarious living conditions and frail health. After two unsuccessful earlier attempts, he was admitted to the École Normal Supérieure in Paris in 1952. There he became a friend of fellow student Pierre *Bourdieu.

During 1953–4 Derrida worked hard on his degree and attended lectures by Michel Foucault, but 1955 brought another setback: he failed the oral part of the philosophy *aggregation*, which would have guaranteed him a life-long tenure as a teacher at a state school. A year later he did pass the examination and at about the same time was awarded a grant as a special auditor at Harvard University, where he undertook a translation of Edmund *Husserl's *Origin of Geometry* into French. In 1957 he married Marguerite Aucouturier, a psychologist of Polish descent, whom he had met in Paris five years before. They had two children, Pierre and Jean. Between 1957 and 1959 Derrida served in the French army during the Algerian war, where he taught French and English in a school in Kolea, near Algiers, to children of soldiers.

Derrida is undoubtedly one of the most important names in philosophy in the late twentieth and early twenty-first century. Yet even as he is revered by many, so too there are many others who hasten to dismiss him as a passing fad at best or a charlatan at worst. Perhaps the most striking testimony to the controversial nature of his work is an unsuccessful but much-publicised attempt by the president of the American Philosophical Association to convince the French government to veto the unanimous election of Derrida as director of the International College of Philosophy on the charge of *obscurantisme terroriste*. In 1992 he was again in the media spotlight when his name was suggested for the award of an honorary degree by Cambridge University in the UK. He did receive the honour, but only after a lengthy debate that brought to the fore some of the profound differences between analytic and continental approaches to philosophy. Both these reactions from Anglophone philosophers resulted from an earlier debate between Derrida and John *Searle, which began as a difference of opinion over the work of the Oxford philosopher J. L. *Austin and soon became an extended disagreement in the pages of the *New York Review of Books*.

The main reason why Derrida is such a controversial figure is that his thinking is uncompromisingly radical, to the point of even defying description in terms of conventional concepts and categories. These concepts and categories are after all the product of the very mainstream philosophy

Derrida rejoices in challenging. As a philosopher he has called into question practically every one of philosophy's foundational claims. So there is a sense in which, like Nietzsche before him, Derrida is a philosopher only by default; he does not seem to have chosen philosophy in any active sense. As Bertrand *Russell once remarked, philosophers, unlike clerics, do not have the option of quitting their chosen vocation even in the face of radical differences. Even to voice their fundamental differences with established opinions, true philosophers have no alternative but to continue doing philosophy.

Derrida's challenge to prevailing ideas in the 1960s was aimed at the belief that all ideas must somehow be 'tethered' to facts or things in the concrete world or, in terms of phenomenology, mental phenomena must have the property of intentionality. On the contrary, structuralism, which was the predominant intellectual current when Derrida began in academia, posited the total autonomy or separation of ideas from empirical facts. For structuralism, ideas or conceptual units formed a system of their own, autonomous and fully closed unto itself. In a structure, as Ferdinand de *Saussure explains, there is no room for origin or history; in fact Saussure argued that diachronic (language studied through time) and synchronic (language studied at a given time) linguistics must be treated separately. Derrida found both these positions equally problematic. On the one hand he saw the phenomenologist's quest for the innermost self as futile. But on the other he was suspicious of the decentring of the phenomenological subject as promoted by structuralism, saying the individual units in a structure display a temporal as well as a spatial difference from one another, a feature he referred to by the French neologism *différance* (an amalgam of difference and deferment). In this sense, Derrida may be said to have influenced poststructuralism, whose key feature is the reinscription of the historical subject right inside the structure. For Derrida, the apparent totality of a structure is based on an illusion of meaning at its centre. It is through this forever absent centre that history, and with it, the subject, makes itself present.

Derrida's name is closely associated with the movement called deconstruction. As far as philosophical movements go, deconstruction is so radical in its thrust that any attempt to encapsulate it within the confines of a definition will deprive it of whatever gives it its distinctive quality. Indeed, deconstruction underscores the very impossibility of definitions as the rationalist tradition in philosophy might know them. For Socrates, as portrayed in *Plato's early *Dialogues*, one could only claim to have adequately explained something once one had come up with an accurate definition for it. It has been one of Derrida's favourite themes to show that philosophy in this sense is doomed to default on its own promise. Deconstruction is Derrida's answer to the ambition of traditional philosophy to get to grips with the ultimate essence of things. Against philosophy's incessant and self-reassuring search for foundational concepts, Derrida argues that all a philosopher in fact ever succeeds in doing is re-reading his or her predecessors and proposing fresh interpretations of their work. He thus follows on from Nietzsche, who decreed that there are no ultimate facts of the matter or stable meanings, only interpretations.

The first use of the word 'deconstruction' dates back to the early 1960s, and an early example is to be found in the introduction to Derrida's 1962 translation of Husserl's *Origin of Geometry*. Through a close reading of Husserl's rhetorical strategies, Derrida shows how the Husserlian text may be seen as ultimately thwarting its own sustained logical rigour, as soon as attention is directed at small details that are normally ignored or swept aside as marginal to the central argument. Incidentally, *Margins of Philosophy* is the title chosen for one of Derrida's volumes of collected papers (1972); deconstruction itself could be described as the revenge of the margins on the centre. The things marginalised by philosophical discourse might be a trope, an incidental or casual remark, or even a Freudian slip: Derrida himself has acknowledged deconstruction's close connection to Freudian psychoanalysis, although he has also insisted on the importance of not losing sight of the textuality of Freud's own writings, a mistake often made in psycholanalysis itself.

According to Derrida, it has been philosophy's primary concern to cover up its own textuality or relegate it to its own margins. But to quote one of Derrida's most quoted and perhaps most misunderstood remarks: 'Il n'y a pas de hors-texte' ('There is nothing outside of the text'). A reading of a given text therefore is not an accretion to it; rather it is part and parcel of the text itself. This means no text can aspire to a stable meaning unaffected by the successive readings to which it is submitted. Rather the text's meaning, if there is anything that answers to such a description, is what is 'iterable' about it ('iterable' being a neologism that highlights its reproducibility in the absence of a unitary or stable identity).

These ideas were further developed in *Of Grammatology* (1976b), one of Derrida's early published works and probably his most famous in the English-speaking world. There Derrida begins with the claim that the entire edifice of Western thought is erected on the premise that speech or *logos* is anterior to writing, not only in the temporal sense of order of acquisition but in a deeper, ontological sense. It is a 'metaphysics of presence' in that speech is believed to provide the closest possible public access to the otherwise inaccessible psychic interior where meanings are believed to exist in their pristine purity. Western philosophy is unrepentantly 'logocentric', to use yet another term made popular by Derrida. Modern linguistics from Saussure on has remained faithful to this logocentrism by electing speech as the true manifestation of language, relegating writing to a secondary, marginal status. Unlike writing, whose texuality is readily conceded, speech is believed to be uncontaminated by the effects of textuality. Yet in denying its own textuality, philosophy is thus emphatically reaffirming its trademark logocentrism. In fact, the logocentrism of Western philosophy manifests itself in modern linguistics in the form of 'phonocentrism' (concentrating on sounds).

As Derrida warns, writing continually returns to haunt linguistics and play havoc with the discipline's foundational certainties. Where Saussure assumed that signs remained independent of contexts, for Derrida the birth of the linguistic sign depends on establishing a sense of stable identity out of irreducible differences. In other words, for Derrida, Saussure's insistence on the autonomy of the sign is a sleight of hand. For if the planes of both signifieds and signifiers are made up equally in the endless interplay of differences, Saussure's description of the linguistic sign as a self-contained identity, far from identifying a secure foundation stone upon which to erect the science of language, instead rather wills its existence. Saussure's inaugural gesture is thus not an ontological discovery, but an exercise in the will to power. Similarly, if the putative superiority of speech over writing is premised on the belief that it is only in the case of the former that meaning supposedly lends itself to unmediated scrutiny, such a move is conditional upon the prior relegation writing to its secondary status (the representation of a representation, in *Aristotle's famous formulation). And once it is admitted that speech is a representation of a psychic interiority, there is no principled reason for affording it superiority, because what makes speech what it is is precisely what it has in common with writing: its irreducible mediatedness or non-immediacy, or what Derrida calls 'arch-writing'.

Yet in this mistaken insistence on stable meaning and identity linguistics is only being faithful to its origin in the

Western philosophical tradition. Deconstruction of the fundamental postulates of linguistics can be carried out in other domains too, in fact wherever the project of system building is carried out by postulating a series of binary opposites. Closer inspection reveals all dichotomous pairs to be cleverly camouflaged hierarchies. To deconstruct a pair of such opposites is to begin by showing how tenuous and arbitrary the underlying hierarchy is. This may be done through a strategic reversal of the terms that constitute the hierarchy, by teasing out the crucial criterion utilised in justifying the hierarchy and showing how it in fact underlies both the terms. The deconstruction of the opposition 'speech vs. writing' is done by exposing the 'writerliness' of speech itself (or by pointing to the unacknowledged notion of arch-writing that makes the very distinction between speech and writing possible to begin with). Derrida has tirelessly carried out deconstructive readings of the works of great names in Western thought, subjecting writers as diverse as Plato, *Descartes, *Kant, *Hegel, *Marx, Nietzsche, Freud, Heidegger, Sartre and Foucault to close readings.

But where does deconstruction take us? Anyone expecting to be told that it opens a window on a completely new paradigm of philosophy or, more ambitiously, shows us a way out of philosophy is headed for frustration. As for the first option, Derrida has insisted that that precisely has been philosophy's stock in trade; showing how wrong past attempts at philosophising were and how the new approach holds out the only promise. For Derrida, this strategy is nothing but the quest for new centres and it is doomed from the very start. For it is the very logic unleashed by affirming a centre at the expense of a margin that is responsible for destabilising existing paradigms. The task of deconstruction is therefore endless.

As for the second alternative, namely leaving philosophy behind once and for all, Derrida is categorical about the impossibility of doing so. For philosophy is inextricably tied to its textuality, so if texts have no exterior it follows that there is no way one can stay out of philosophy to critique it from a privileged, transcendental perspective. In fact, deconstruction of philosophy underscores the very limit and unserviceability of the opposition between transcendental and immanent. We are always already caught up in philosophy. This in turn takes us to the rather staggering conclusion that there is, strictly speaking, no plain or ordinary language as such, uncontaminated by philosophy. The very fact of speaking the language we do commits us to the basic tenets of a whole metaphysics that underwrites all our thinking. This is quite contrary to what the logical positivists had hoped.

In the early twentieth century, Bertand Russell came near to reaching apparently the same conclusion as Derrida on the problem of ordinary language and philosophy. But in fact Russell could not have reached Derrida's philosophical position without a radical re-evaluation of his ideas. Analytic philosophers on both sides of the ordinary language divide are at one in their presupposition that there is such a thing as ordinary language, different from the language of, say, philosophy. Many, perhaps most, philosophers of language advocate the idea that their own metalanguage is qualitatively different from the object language they investigate. All through his career Russell never doubted this principle, although he famously reviewed many of his other positions along the way.

Yet one corollary of Derridean deconstruction is the questioning of this last cornerstone of the Western philosophical tradition. Philosophy is like any other mode of enquiry and is not entitled to any privileged discourse. From the 1990s on, Derrida was actively engaged in exploring the ethical and political aspects of the deconstructive enterprise. He also campaigned to make philosophy an activity for everyone in a practical sense: he advocated teaching it to children in schools as part of their regular school curriculum.

Primary works

(1962). *Origin of Geometry: An Introduction.* John P. Leavey, Jr (trans.). Lincoln, NE: University of Nebraska Press, 1989.

(1967a). *Speech and Phenomena and Other Essays on Husserl's Theory of Signs.* David B. Allison (trans.). Evanston, IL: Northwestern University Press, 1973.

(1967b). *Of Grammatology.* Gayatri Chakravorty Spivak (trans.). Baltimore, MD: Johns Hopkins University Press, 1976.

(1967c). *Writing and Difference.* Alan Bass (trans.). Chicago: Chicago University Press, 1978.

(1972). *Margins of Philosophy.* Alan Bass (trans.). Chicago: Chicago University Press, 1982.

(1977). *Limited Inc, abc...* Samuel Weber (trans.). Supplement to *Glyph.* vol. 2. 1977. Derrida's debate with Searle, reprinted.

Further reading

Hartman, Geoffrey (1981). *Saving the Text: Literature/Derrida/Philosophy.* Baltimore, MD: Johns Hopkins University Press.

Norris, Christopher (1987). *Derrida.* London: Fontana.

Kanavillil Rajagopalan

RENÉ DESCARTES

Descartes, René (*b.* 1596, *d.* 1650; French), philosopher. Often described as the 'father of modern philosophy', Descartes is one of the most influential philosophers of all time, having made significant contributions not only to philosophy but also to mathematics, metaphysics, physics, psychology and science in general. His main philosophical project was to replace the dominant approach of his time, Scholasticism, with a system of knowledge that did not depend on the authority of the church or previous thinkers, but instead could be achieved by one thinker working alone. Starting from a position of extreme scepticism, where the one indubitable assumption was 'I am thinking, therefore I exist' ('Cogito ergo sum'), he attempted to establish the existence of God and of the physical world, the general reliability of human reason, the possibility of error, the distinction between mind and body ('Cartesian dualism'), and the existence of innate ideas. (*See also* Aristotle; Chomsky, Noam; Davidson, Donald; Hume, David; Leibniz, Gottfried Wilhelm; Locke, John; Mill, J. S.; Wittgenstein, Ludwig.)

Descartes was born into a fairly affluent family in 1596 in the Touraine region of France, in the town of La Haye, which was later renamed La Haye-Descartes in his honour and is now known simply as Descartes. His father, Joachim, was a councillor at the parliament of Brittany, his paternal grandfather was a doctor, and most of the family of his mother, Jeanne Brochard, were legal officials. His mother died when he was 1 year old, and Descartes and his siblings were raised by his maternal grandmother, Jeanne Sain. He was never close to his father and did not attend his funeral when he died. Descartes's poor health as a child meant that he was allowed to stay in bed every morning until 11 o'clock. He stuck to this regime as an adult and used his mornings for thinking. He never had to work for a living and he eventually dedicated his life to reflection and the development of his new philosophical system. From the age of 8 he attended the Jesuit school of La Flèche in Anjou. He then took a law degree at the University of Poitiers, but did not go on to practise law.

Instead he began to travel and enlisted in more than one army, first in Holland with the forces of Prince Maurice of Nassau and later in Germany with the forces of Maximilian of Bavaria. It is not known exactly what he did for these armies, but it seems likely that he was a kind of military engineer, applying mathematical techniques to the solution of military problems. After leaving the military he began working on his ambitious project to develop a secure philosophical foundation for all human knowledge.

Perhaps the prime motivation for all of Descartes's work was his dissatisfaction with the then traditional approach to philosophy, known as Scholasticism. Scholasticism was based on, and aimed to reconcile, the various authorities of God, the church and previous thinkers, most notably *Aristotle. At La Flèche, Descartes received what he considered a good education, and this would have given him a good grounding in the assumptions and methods of Scholasticism, which he nevertheless came to regard as unreliable, vacuous and not explanatory. He was equally unimpressed with the approaches of those of his contemporaries who also rejected Scholasticism. In Descartes's eyes, these approaches were either unduly pessimistic about the possibility of reliable human knowledge or they were based on assumptions which were as unreliable as those of Scholasticism. Descartes set out to develop a system of knowledge whose conclusions were not open to doubt and could be achieved by one thinker working alone. His aim was to reach conclusions which were believed not because they were professed by himself or any other thinker, but because they were clear and convincing to a rational mind.

It was Isaac Beeckman, a doctor from Caen, who encouraged Descartes to be a philosopher rather than a military man. Descartes was fully persuaded to dedicate himself to the pursuit of knowledge after wintry weather forced him to take shelter in a stove-heated room near Ulm on the Danube. After a day spent deep in thought, he fell asleep in an agitated state and had three vivid dreams. In the first dream, he was attacked by phantoms and caught in a whirlwind that would not allow him to stand up properly. Trying to take shelter in a college, he was approached by a friend who offered him what he understood to be a melon from a foreign country. He woke up afraid and in pain, and could not sleep for two hours. When he did fall asleep again, he heard a loud thunderclap and found himself in a room full of fire and sparks. His third dream was more peaceful and more pleasant. He found himself looking through a pile of books by his bed and in particular consulting a dictionary and an anthology of poems. Descartes decided that the dictionary stood for the sciences and the anthology of poems for 'philosophy and wisdom'. His conclusion was that the dreams were telling him to remove himself from the troubles of the world and devote his time to philosophy and the pursuit of wisdom. After continuing to travel for some years, he spent two years in Paris, where he made a life-long friend of the Franciscan friar Marin Mersenne, and then settled in Holland in 1629. By this time, he had already published a number of works, including *Rules for the Direction of the Mind*, but his most significant works were written during his time in Holland.

The first work he began in Holland was called *The World* and aimed to develop a new kind of physics, based on mathematics rather than on philosophy or the evidence provided by the senses. The approach he presented in *The World* rejected the assumptions of Scholasticism and, like Galileo's work, was consistent with the Copernican view of the universe. When Descartes heard that Galileo had been condemned by the Inquisition in Rome, he decided not to publish *The World*. But he did not abandon his larger project and instead worked towards presenting his ideas in a way that was less likely to cause offence.

In 1635 Descartes fathered a child, Francine, whose mother, Hélène, was a servant in his place of lodging. Francine's early death, at 5 years of age, had a powerful effect on him and he had no more children. In the next ten years, he produced his most famous works, *Philosophical Essays* (which included the *Discourse on the Method of Rightly Conducting One's Reason and Seeking the Truth in the Sciences*) in 1637, *Meditations on First Philosophy* in 1641 and *Principles of Philosophy* in 1644.

Philosophical Essays was published anonymously at first, since Descartes wanted to make sure they did not cause offence before admitting responsibility for the ideas he expressed there. The three essays in this volume, on 'Optics', 'Geometry' and 'Meteorology', are intended to illustrate the application of the methodology presented in the introductory *Discourse on the Method*. But *Discourse on the Method* turned out to be far more influential than the essays that followed it. It is both an explanation of the method and a biographical account of how Descartes came to develop it. There is considerable overlap between the *Discourse* and the *Meditations*, which are Descartes's most important texts from a purely philosophical point of view. In these works, he sets out the method he will use for his project and presents some of the conclusions he has reached using the method.

Probably the most famous of Descartes's ideas is what is now known as the 'cogito argument'. Starting from a position of extreme doubt, Descartes finds that there is one thing that an individual can never doubt as long as that individual is thinking (Descartes uses the term 'I' throughout, but it seems that the 'I' refers not to Descartes but to any individual thinker). The fact that 'I' am thinking is conclusive evidence for the assumption that I exist. In Latin this assumption is expressed as 'Cogito ergo sum', and the most appropriate English translation is 'I am thinking, therefore I exist' (rather than the better known 'I think therefore I am'). Having decided that it is possible to trust neither the senses, which are not fully reliable, nor reason, since human reason sometimes makes mistakes, Descartes suggested that nevertheless the very fact that 'I' am doubting means that I must exist. Even if an evil demon were tricking me into thinking something false, it would still be the case that I am thinking and therefore that I must exist. From this first principle, Descartes then set out to build a firm foundation for all human knowledge.

First he set out to prove the existence of God. The two most important arguments he presented for this have become known as the 'trademark argument' and the 'ontological argument'. The trademark argument is based on the recognition that human beings, who are not perfect, nevertheless have an idea of perfection within them. Descartes argued that this idea could not have been put there except by a perfect being, namely God. The ontological argument starts from the assumption that God is perfect. From this it follows that God exists, since existence is one aspect of perfection. Having established God's existence, Descartes then attempted to establish the existence of physical entities in the world. The evidence for this depends on the existence of God. God exists and has allowed the idea of physical entities to exist within humans. If physical entities did not exist, then God would be deceiving us and hence not perfect. Therefore, the physical entities must exist.

Another important idea presented in the *Meditations* is the distinction between mind and body. This idea is now known as 'Cartesian dualism'. Descartes proposed that the universe was made out of two kinds of entity: minds and bodies. He believed that animals were essentially machines, possessing only bodies, while humans also possessed souls. So human beings are composed of two kinds of entity: the mental (mind) and the corporeal (body). He proposed an explanation of how minds and bodies interact, suggesting that the pineal gland was the location of their interaction. This idea was not generally accepted and the notion of non-corporeal mind is puzzling, particularly to later thinkers. One major problem that Descartes fails to explain is how a non-physical mind can ever cause movement in a physical entity. How, for example, can my mind ever cause my arm to move? If the pineal gland is the one organ that my mind can control, why can my mind not move the pineal gland itself? Despite these difficulties, Descartes's work in this area has been hugely influential. He was not the first thinker to propose a distinction between mind and body, but he was the first to propose a systematic account.

One of the most influential aspects of Descartes's work was the doubt he cast on the evidence supplied by the senses. His famous illustration of this refers to a piece of wax. He considers a hard, cold piece of wax which has recently been removed from a honeycomb, then considers the changes the wax undergoes if placed near a fire. But although it becomes liquid and soft, and smells, tastes and feels different, we continue to perceive it as wax. Since two different sets of sense data can lead to the perception of wax, Descartes argues, then it is not our senses that allow us to perceive the wax, or any other physical entity. Rather he suggests they are perceived by 'the mind alone'. The notion that the senses do not provide direct evidence, with the emphasis on 'the mind alone', have been very influential in subsequent philosophy, psychology and linguistics. This influence is particularly clear in approaches that explore the nature of innate ideas and the creativity of the human mind, two important ideas in the linguistics of Noam *Chomsky.

While he made little explicit reference to language, Descartes did refer to it in exploring the distinction between humans, whom he saw as possessing a mind or soul, and animals, which he saw as mindless machines

or automata. He claimed that all animal behaviour could be explained on the assumption that animals were machines, or automata, but that certain human behaviours could not be explained on the basis of that assumption alone. One type of behaviour that Descartes referred to here was the use of language. He suggested that no animal or machine could produce behaviour comparable to what humans do when they produce appropriate utterances in a particular context. In *Cartesian Linguistics*, Chomsky (1966) suggested that what Descartes is referring to here is the creativity of human language. While animals or machines could be designed so as to produce a particular utterance in response to a particular stimulus, they could not, as humans regularly do, produce an appropriate response to any stimulus that can be envisaged. This is one of the key reasons for Chomsky's suggestion that his approach to linguistics is 'Cartesian'.

Principles of Philosophy contains the most comprehensive account of Descartes's system. It covers physics and metaphysics and attempts to explain the nature of the universe in terms of the physics and metaphysics proposed. There is also an account of the history of the earth and Descartes's famous metaphor for knowledge seen in terms of a tree, where the roots are metaphysics, the trunk is physics and the other sciences are branches.

In 1643 he began to correspond with Princess Elizabeth of Bohemia. She was then 24 years old and in exile in Holland. Her perceptive comments initiated a discussion of the relationship between mind and body and the relationship between reason and the passions. These topics were discussed in *The Passions of the Soul*, which was published in 1649.

In that year Descartes was invited to Stockholm by Queen Christina of Sweden. After being initially wary, he accepted the invitation. In Sweden, he became depressed. He was asked to rise and visit the queen to give her tuition at 5 o'clock in the morning. Perhaps as much because of the early rising as the cold climate, he soon became ill, and died from pneumonia on 11 February 1650. When Descartes died he was a Catholic in a Protestant country. Because of this he was buried in a cemetery for unbaptised children. His remains were later taken to France and then, during the French Revolution, they were disinterred for burial in the Pantheon. His tomb is now in the church of St Germain des Prés.

Descartes's intellectual legacy can hardly be overstated. Despite various kinds of resistance during his lifetime, by the end of the seventeenth century 'Cartesianism' was seen as the dominant approach to physics, and Descartes's rationalist approach to philosophy was seen as the 'new philosophy', to be contrasted with the 'ancient' philosophy of Scholasticism. His influence in physics diminished as the influence of Newton grew, although Newton carefully studied the work of Descartes, and twenty-first-century physics is very much based on mathematics, as Descartes had proposed. Within philosophy, his ideas were either developed or challenged in most of the significant work of the century following his death. Notable challengers include Hobbes, *Leibniz, *Locke and Pascal. One recent opponent of the Cartesian tradition in philosophy is Donald *Davidson, who explicitly rejected the view that knowledge of our own mental states plays an important role in acquiring knowledge of the world. Davidson argued that these two types of knowledge are wholly distinct. Nevertheless, Descartes's emphasis on the role of the self rather than the authority of other thinkers or doctrines has been an important idea for most subsequent philosophy, whether it accepts or rejects this notion. His influence is felt in discussions of the nature of human knowledge, of the relationship between reason and the senses, of the role of innateness, and in considerations of rationalism and empiricism in general. In linguistics the most celebrated explicit link has been made by Noam Chomsky, whose book *Cartesian Linguistics* explicitly explores the links between his approach to linguistics and Cartesian concepts. But Cartesian ideas are important for any approach which explores the role of innateness in language or treats language as a cognitive phenomenon.

Primary works

(1911). *The Philosophical Works of Descartes* (2 vols). Elisabeth S. Haldane and G. R. T. Ross (eds). Cambridge: Cambridge University Press.

(1952). *Descartes's Philosophical Writings*. Norman Kemp Smith (ed. and trans.). London: Macmillan.

(1954). *Descartes: Philosophical Writings*. Elisabeth Anscombe and Peter Thomas Geach (eds). Edinburgh: Nelson.

(1964–76). *Oeuvres de Descartes*. Charles Adam and Paul Tannery (eds) (revised edition, 12 vols). Paris: J. Vrin in association with the Centre National de la Recherche Scientifique.

(1980). *Descartes: Philosophical Letters.* Kenny, Anthony (ed. and trans.). Oxford: Oxford University Press.

(1985). *The Philosophical Writings of Descartes* (2 vols). John Cottingham, Robert Stoothoff and Murdoch Dugald (eds and trans.). Cambridge: Cambridge University Press.

Further reading

Baillet, Adrian (1691). *La Vie de Monsieur Descartes* (2 vols). New York: Garland, 1987.

Chomsky, Noam (1966). *Cartesian Linguistics: A Chapter in the History of Rationalist Thought.* Lanham, MD: University Press of America.

Cottingham, John (1986). *Descartes.* Oxford: Blackwell.

Doney, Willis (ed.) (1967). *Descartes: A Collection of Critical Essays.* New York: Doubleday.

Gaukrogger, Stephen (1995). *Descartes: An Intellectual Biography.* Oxford: Clarendon Press.

Kenny, Anthony (1993). *Descartes: A Study of his Philosophy.* Bristol: Thoemmes Press.

Moyal, Georges (ed.) (1991). *René Descartes: Critical Assessments* (4 vols). London: Routledge.

Rée, Jonathan (1974). *Descartes.* London: Allen Lane.

Robinson, Dave and Garratt, Chris (1998). *Introducing Descartes.* Cambridge: Icon Books.

Sorell, Tom (1994). *Descartes: A Very Short Introduction.* Oxford: Oxford University Press.

Williams, Bernard (1978). *Descartes: The Project of Pure Enquiry.* Second edition. Harmondsworth: Penguin.

Billy Clark

MICHAEL DUMMETT

Dummett, Michael (Anthony Eardley) (*b.* 1925; British), Wykeham professor emeritus of logic (Wykeham professor 1979–92). Dummett began his academic career as a fellow at All Souls College, Oxford (1950). He was assistant lecturer in philosophy at Birmingham University (1950–1), and reader in philosophy of mathematics in Oxford (1962–74). He has held a number of positions at American colleges and universities including Berkeley, Stanford, Princeton and Harvard, and received a knighthood for services to philosophy and to racial justice in 1999. His major contributions to the philosophy of language include his interpretations of *Frege and his works on the notions of truth and meaning. (*See also* Davidson, Donald; Frege, Gottlob; Russell, Bertrand; Wittgenstein, Ludwig.)

Educated in the tradition of the Anglican church, Dummett converted to Catholicism in 1944 after declaring himself an atheist for most of his teens. He studied at Winchester College and at Christ Church College, Oxford, graduating with first class honours in philosophy (1950). He received his MA from Oxford in 1954. Dummett belongs to the Anglo-American tradition of modern analytical philosophy and the main themes of his thought deal with the problems of logic and truth, mathematical philosophy and the philosophy of language. According to his line of reasoning these themes, and the theoretical problems connected with them, are closely linked to each other. His point of departure in trying to contribute to solving the problems was an historical study, *Frege: Philosophy of Language* (1973). This book examines the thoughts of Frege on the logical foundations of mathematics, and led Dummett to consider in what way the notion of truth functions as the basis of linguistic meaning and how truth conditions are (or should be) assumed to be the basis of the meanings and understandings of sentences. Therefore after the initial interpretation of Frege, Dummett's main work has been on matters concerning general problems in logic and language. Dummett's work is widely acknowledged as a major contribution to the philosophies of logic, mathematics and language. He is considered one of the most influential British philosophers of the second half of the twentieth century, but he has also published on other subjects and themes, among them Catholicism, the game of Tarot, voting and election procedures, and proper grammar and style, as well as immigration and refugee issues. He was, especially in the 1960s, very much engaged in the fight against racism.

Dummett published a number of reviews and articles between 1953 and the beginning of the 1970s, but his first book wasn't published until 1973. His reflections on Frege have often been informed by the later works of *Wittgenstein, and in particular his claim that the meaning of a word is a matter of somebody having the knowledge of understanding that word and that to understand a word is to be able to use it correctly. Dummett relates this train of thought to Frege's assumption (and attempt to prove) that all true propositions in arithmetic can be deduced from logical premises. Known as 'logicism', this basic position was also held by *Russell. Frege himself called his formal language applied to arithmetic 'logic', but

Dummett conceives of Frege's contributions as 'philosophy of language'. He sees Frege's work as the foundation of the 'linguistic turn' in philosophy and as the outset of real analytical philosophy.

However, Dummett dissociates himself from Frege's idea that the distinction in natural language semantics between *Sinn* ('sense') and *Bedeutung* ('reference') can be applied to the meaning of numbers, for the obvious reason that it is hard to point to the entities to which the meaning of numbers is supposed to be the reference. A great deal of Dummett's work is dedicated to solving this problem of Frege's. On the other hand Dummett clearly acknowledges Frege's contribution to semantics, saying that Frege had offered a semantic theory by making the distinction mentioned above. By doing so Frege had also clarified one of the ways the notion of truth can be used; that is, as the relation of reference between the words that refer to some objects and the objects that are the referents of these words. In other words, if the words of a sentence refer to some existing objects then that sentence is true.

But as is well known, it is not always easy to decide whether some objects should be taken as existing objects or not. Take, for instance, the referents of numbers, of other minds, or of entities beyond the perceivable surroundings. Suppose, for example, that somebody claims that things do not exist if you do not perceive them. In such a case it is very difficult to give good reasons for the opposite point of view. The position that claims that there are objects in the world (as referents of linguistic expressions) whether we perceive them or not is called (semantic) 'realism', and the view of which Dummett is considered one of the most prominent proponents is called (semantic) 'anti-realism'. Anti-realism about arithmetical (mathematical) objects is in general called 'intuitionism'.

By relating Wittgenstein's view that meaning is use to Frege's semantics, Dummett points to the problem mentioned above; that is, sometimes, in certain 'domains', it is hard to find the referents of words and sentences. But it should be noted that Dummett does not accept the Wittgensteinian view that metaphysics is meaningless and a result of linguistic misunderstandings. Rather he tries to solve the metaphysical problems by considering them as matters of truth, meaning and understanding (see Dummett 1991b). Intuitionism and anti-realism offer ways of handling the problem of metaphysics as well as many of the issues raised by Frege.

For example, intuitionism argues that mathematical objects are constructed; that is, they are artificial. This view is also called 'constructivism'. Therefore propositions about these objects are only reports about constructs. Intuitionism is consequently opposed to the views of Fregean 'logicism', in which it is argued that all arithmetical propositions have a logical, or natural, basis. According to the Dummettian version of anti-realism you have to reject the assumptions of realism, such as the idea that any sentence has a truth value but that you may not be able to decide its truth value – the principle called the 'principle of bivalence' – and that con-sequently any sentence has a number of 'truth conditions' (the state of affairs of the referents of that sentence). Dummett's ideas encounter problems with, among other things, the past and the future, and to solve such problems he appeals to 'assertability conditions'. Since truth cannot be used to explain what these conditions are, he proposes that the answer is a 'meaning theory'. For Dummett, such a theory deals with the meaning of sentences and it is important to acknowledge that this is fundamental in his philosophy: he favours 'molecularism'; that is, the idea that sentences, not words or sets of sentences, have truth value or may be asserted. He also defends the view that the meanings of sentences are made up by the meanings of their parts. If sentences are being asserted, but their truth value cannot be determined, Dummett assumes, following Wittgenstein, that they have meaning because someone is able to have an understanding of the assertability conditions of that sentence, and that the speaker does so because she or he has knowledge of language and has access to the 'best possible evidence'.

How these thoughts have been put together, how debates over the issues are settled, and which arguments are defended and which rejected are all themes of the books published by Dummett. Of these the most important are *Truth and Other Enigmas* (1978), *The Logical Basis of Metaphysics* (1991b) and *The Seas of Language* (1993). The book last mentioned is primarily a compilation of papers published or lectures given in the 1970s and 1980s, and it summarises the key notions of Dummett's philosophy. In one of his later books, *Frege: Philosophy of Mathematics* (1991a), Dummett takes up once more the question of how to interpret Frege's contributions to the philosophy of mathematics. The book is mostly a detailed comment on Frege's basic works, and Frege is praised by Dummett as one of the greatest philosophers of mathematics. Dummett's work is unquestionably difficult to read, and it may be appropriate to quote one of Bernhard Weiss's conclusive remarks, made in 2002: 'I am not in a position to offer such a summary [of Dummett's work], not having an encompassing view of his work. But neither is anyone else in such a position'.

Primary works

(1973). *Frege: Philosophy of Language.* London: Duckworth, 1981.
(1978). *Truth and Other Enigmas.* London: Duckworth.
(1991a). *Frege: Philosophy of Mathematics.* London: Duckworth.
(1991b). *The Logical Basis of Metaphysics.* London: Duckworth.
(1993). *The Seas of Language.* Oxford: Oxford University Press.

Further reading

McGuiness, Brian and Olivieri, Gianluigi (eds) (1994). *The Philosophy of Michael Dummett.* Dordrecht: Kluwer.
Weiss, Bernhard (2002). *Michael Dummett.* Chesham: Acumen.
Wright, Chris (1992). *Realism, Meaning and Truth.* First edition 1986. Oxford: Blackwell.

Hans Götzsche

J. R. FIRTH

Firth, J. R. (John Rupert) (*b.* 1890, *d.* 1960; British), professor of English at the University of the Punjab, Lahore (1920–8), senior lecturer at University College London (1928–38), then senior lecturer, reader and professor of general linguistics at the School of Oriental and African Studies, University of London (1938–56). An important figure in the foundation of linguistics as an autonomous discipline in Britain; known for his original ideas on phonology and the study of meaning. (*See also* Halliday, M. A. K.; Malinowski, Bronislaw.)

J. R. Firth was a man of his time. He was born in Keighley, Yorkshire, in late nineteenth-century Britain, which still held much of the world in imperial subjugation, and his career was marked by the existence of the British Empire. He attended the local grammar school, studied for a BA and MA in history at Leeds University, and briefly taught the subject at a Leeds teacher training college. Just after the start of World War I he went to India, still part of Britain's empire, to work for the Indian Education Service. He also undertook military service in India during the war (and in Afghanistan and Africa), returning to the imperial education service after the armistice as a professor of English at the University of the Punjab. There Firth began his study of the area's languages, which were to provide linguistic data for later publications; his time in India had a lasting effect on his career.

He returned to Britain first for a year in 1926, then long-term in 1928, to a position in Daniel *Jones's Department of Phonetics at University College London (UCL), interspersing his UCL teaching with part-time work at the London School of Economics (LSE), what was to become the School of Oriental and African Studies (SOAS), and Oxford. While at the LSE he met Bronislaw *Malinowski, who was then working on language from an anthropological point of view. Some of Malinowski's ideas were to influence Firth considerably – much more than those of Jones, whom Firth regarded as theoretically barren and intellectually insular (he did, however, rate highly the work of the experimental phoneticians at UCL).

Firth published his only books while at UCL. Meant for non-academic audiences, these none the less contain the basics of much of what was later recognised as 'Firthian' linguistics. The populist approach of these texts, *Speech* (1930) and *The Tongues of Men* (1937), is the first sign of Firth's constant striving to promote linguistics in Britain. Both books end, after a tour through many linguistic issues, with a call for the establishment of linguistic institutes. Firth writes on the last page of *Speech* that Britain needs to promote the investigation of English (as the only possible world language) and of other languages, together with its 'partners in a world empire with hundreds of millions of Asiatics and Africans speaking hundreds of languages'. The books cover similar points and such repetition is frequent in Firth's writing. A positive way of viewing this is to recognise that Firth's ideas, which were not of the linguistic mainstream, were, with the exception of his phonological work,

remarkably consistent throughout his working life.

Firth's main writing interests can be split into four: (1) the idea that the study of 'meaning' and 'context' should be central in linguistics; (2) discussion of the history of linguistics, especially of linguists from Britain; (3) work on phonology, particularly the development of a model called 'prosodic analysis'; and (4) linguistic descriptions and encyclopedia articles on Indian and southern Asian languages, particularly their orthography and phonology. Aspects of (1), (2) and (4) are present in his writing from the start; (3) only developed later. He is best known for (1) and (3), where he laid out his views as to how language works and how linguists should approach its analysis. While they are by no means incompatible, there is, however, no necessary connection between his ideas in these two areas.

Firth's ideas on meaning and context are fundamental to his conception of language, as he considered the analysis of the meaning of utterances to be the main goal of linguistics; this was unusual at a time when contemporaries such as *Bloomfield were positively excluding meaning from linguistic study. Firth rejects any kind of distinction between 'langue' and 'parole' (such as *Saussure made before him) or 'competence' and 'performance' (such as *Chomsky made after him), because, for Firth, language was not an autonomous entity and was not to be studied as a mental system. Rather, in keeping with the behaviourist and positivist ideas of the contemporary intellectual environment (see the work of *Skinner, for example), Firth saw language as a set of events which speakers uttered, a mode of action, a way of 'doing things', and held that therefore linguists should focus on speech events themselves. This rejected the common view that speech acts are only interesting for linguists to gain access to the 'true' object of study – their underlying grammatical systems.

As utterances occur in real-life contexts, Firth argued that their meaning derived just as much from the particular situation in which they occurred as from the string of sounds uttered. This integrationist idea, which mixes language with the objects physically present during a conversation to ascertain the meaning involved, is known as Firth's 'contextual theory of meaning' or his theory of 'context of situation', a phrase which he borrowed from Malinowski.

Some of Firth's ideas on meaning were developed in his misleadingly titled article 'The technique of semantics' (1935). Much of the article deals with the history of usages of the term 'semantics' and of the study of meaning, although it does make a start at recognising a taxonomy of possible situation types (never developed further). Firth proposes to use the term 'semantics' to describe his whole approach to language, which is to link all levels of linguistic analysis (from phonetics to lexicography) with their contexts and situations. He does not maintain this usage elsewhere in his writings, but he does extend the meaning of 'meaning' in remarkable ways, writing about the 'phonological meaning' of phones and the 'grammatical meaning' of constituents. This was due to his overarching definition of meaning as the function or effect of an item in a particular context; thus phonological entities have meaning because they can contrast and have relations with other entities in particular phonological environments. At a lexical level, this embraces the notion of the 'collocation'; that is, which other words a particular word consistently co-occurs with (part of the 'meaning' of words in collocations, such as 'an egregious ass', is that they co-occur). These usages of 'meaning' allowed Firth to perceive a fundamental unity among linguistic levels, linked through the search for statements of 'meaning' at each level. It has frequently been pointed out, not least by Lyons (1966), that this stretches the meaning of 'meaning' until it snaps, and that while situations must be understood for the interpretation of utterances, considerably more is required to give a full description of meaning.

Given Firth's anti-mentalist views, he expected the analytical levels that linguists employ to have different properties and to be described in their own terms; no universals or structural analogies were to be expected or sought. The number and nature of entities which could be postulated were unlimited because Firth's instrumentalism meant that a linguist was not thought to be describing the uniquely 'true' (or 'psychologically real') form of a language; linguists were free to use whatever theoretical constructs were necessary, and to mix information from different linguistic levels. Furthermore, Firth considered it perfectly proper to focus on only one very small sub-system of a language, ignoring other sub-systems if it made descriptive sense to do so, a principle referred to as 'polysystemacity'.

Firth also published several pieces on the phonology of languages such as Burmese and Tamil while at UCL. Following a 15-month research fellowship, spent in India working on languages such as Gujarati and Telugu, Firth moved in 1938 to the Department of Phonetics and Linguistics at London University's SOAS (then still called the School of Oriental Studies), where he was to stay for the rest of his career, being made a reader two years later and head of department in 1941. The development of SOAS was in part due to the existence of the British Empire, as SOAS was the UK centre for teaching and research on the cultures and languages of vast areas of the world in Britain's imperialistic thrall. Firth's expertise in southern Asian languages, gathered from his time in India, fitted SOAS's remit well, enabling him to prosper there, and the School was to prove an excellent base for Firth's ambitions to establish linguistics on a firm academic footing.

The year after Firth moved to SOAS, World War II began, oddly strengthening Firth's position. When Japan entered the war in 1941, Firth ran intensive training courses in Japanese for members of the armed services. This led to a substantial increase in the staff employed in his department, and Firth was awarded the Order of the British Empire in 1946 for this work. He had been given a full professorship in 1944, which meant that he was the first professor of general linguistics in Britain (long after such appointments had been made in other countries). Firth's department flourished after the war, with contin-

ued government support following the recognition of SOAS's strategic importance, given Britain's imperial interests. Firth's charisma and inspirational abilities also lured several people to work at SOAS who before the war had worked at UCL.

Just after the war, Firth published 'The English school of phonetics' (1946), his main contribution to the history of linguistics. This article illustrates Firth's conviction that he was working in a long linguistic tradition, stretching back centuries (including Henry Sweet, Alexander Melville Bell, John Hart, and even Orm and Ælfric). The article is coloured by the impression that Firth finds it important to praise the work of those who wrote in England, but his interests in this area were important in stimulating other work in the field (for example, in co-workers such as R. H. Robins).

While at SOAS Firth developed his ideas on phonology, which many see as his greatest contribution to linguistics. Many of the ideas in 'prosodic analysis' (or 'London School Phonology') were, however, best written about by others, and the most impressive analyses in this framework were published by Firth's co-workers (mostly colleagues at SOAS), who formed the 'London School', a group inspired and encouraged by Firth. The first publication where Firth set out his phonological ideas is 'Sounds and prosodies' (1948), although it is not easy to extract them from the article. One fundamental idea is a rejection of purely phonemic analysis, as practised by others working in phonology at the time (such as *Trubetzkoy and Bloomfield). This approach still uses segmentation (into what are called 'phonematic units'), but crucially, it allows the phonologist also to assign features of phonetic form to 'prosodies', which are non-segmental entities that can be tied to any piece of phonological structure – spread over a whole word, or syntactic unit, or part of a syllable, for example. The metaphor 'spread' should not be taken dynamically, however, as no notion of 'phonological process' is countenanced; rather the static domain of a prosody is described. Thus assimilations and vowel harmony are simply described in terms of the span the feature (the 'prosody') has in the observable form of an utterance. Phonematic units can be nearly empty of distinctive phonological specification if this is analysed as prosodic. Furthermore, anything that is described with reference to syntagmatic, rather than paradigmatic, structure can be a prosody, including 'juncture' phenomena, which mark out linguistic boundaries, and features restricted to particular positions in a syllable.

Prosodic analysis further assumes a clear separation between 'phonetics' and 'phonology'. Phonematic units and prosodies are not assumed to have 'intrinsic' or obvious phonetic content. They must be accompanied by 'exponency' statements which state formally how a particular piece of phonological structure maps onto the phonetics. This allowed Firthians to combine an abstract phonology with detailed phonetic description.

Firth's general assumption of instrumentalism and polysystematicity meant that phonologists became free to recognise a phonological system in any piece of linguistic structure, rather than needing to provide a coherent account of the whole phonological system of a language. There is no necessary expectation that the same phonological entities and systems should be relevant in, for example, both syllable onsets and syllable rhymes, function words and lexical words, noun phrases and adverb phrases; this also illustrates the countenanced mixing of linguistic levels.

Some of Firth's phonological ideas are re-expressed in his last major publication, 'A synopsis of linguistic theory, 1930–1955'. This also repeats many of his other main ideas, quoting directly from *Speech* and *The Tongues of Men*, and served as the introduction to a volume of articles by his colleagues. It appeared in 1957, the same year as a collection of Firth's articles, *Papers in Linguistics 1934–1951*. These volumes served as a summary of, and practically the end-point to, his career: he had retired from SOAS in 1956. Firth lived only a further four years leaving, many have argued, much unwritten, in part because he was already quite ill (although by no means infirm – he lectured part-time at Edinburgh).

At the time of his death Firth was recognised in Britain as a central, distinguished figure in linguistics. He had been president of the Philological Society and awarded honorary degrees. He had published around forty items but, notably, had never set out all his ideas in a clear and coherent manner. Firth was well aware of developments in linguistics in continental Europe and America, but his work was not influential outside Britain. He lectured abroad, attended conferences and was an invited teacher at an LSA Linguistic Institute, a prestigious summer school organised by the Linguistic Society of America. None the less, some claim that Firth shared some of Britain's insularity, lacking ambition to persuade those elsewhere of his ideas. He was certainly not understood in the United States, except by such figures as Kenneth *Pike. Within Britain, however, Firth's personal influence is indisputable. He was widely acclaimed as an inspiring teacher with organisational skill and the means to get his own way. While his writing is bad, his performance in lectures and personal conversation could be enthralling. A generation of linguists arose around him; they helped spread linguistics to newly founded departments in Britain, with an identifiably 'Firthian' approach.

Some recognise both malign and positive aspects of Firth's influence, describing him as autocratic and impolite. He controlled what most members of the London School could publish and suppressed linguistic ideas of which he disapproved, such as the phonology done at UCL. This aggressive attitude, coupled with the need for personal contact to perceive his inspirational quality, may have contributed to the waning of interest in Firthian ideas. Work in prosodic analysis continued in Britain in some quantity into the 1960s and 1970s, but was then overtaken by the progress of generative phonology, developed by Morris Halle and Noam Chomsky, just as other Firthian ideas were challenged by general generative linguistics.

The true extent of Firth's posthumous intellectual influence is difficult to assess. Some linguists (mostly tending towards the 'applied' end of the spectrum) overtly claim Firth as an inspiration; others work with ideas which are reminiscent of his, although a direct line of influence is not easily recognisable. His ideas on meaning and context now find echoes, sometimes with citation, in discourse analysis, corpus linguistics, pragmatics and sociolinguistics. Several fundamental ideas were taken up by M. A. K. *Halliday, who founded systemic functional linguistics, now widely pursued. Halliday's ideas, originally labelled 'neo-Firthian', picked up Firth's general approach of considering the function of language in context, working in the realm of grammar (which Firth himself had not), expanding on the notion of linguistic systems as paradigmatic sets of choices, and developing new ideas, arguably compatible with Firth's (although essentially monosystemic).

Firth is still inspiring work in phonology, especially around a group at the University of York (see Ogden and Local 1994). Furthermore, many twenty-first-century phonological ideas were foreshadowed by Firth's, although mostly in a different form. It is now widely accepted that the autonomous phoneme is an untenable object, and there are echoes of London School positions in (1) the common, non-linear, 'autosegmental' understanding of segments; (2) the widespread use of information from other linguistic levels in phonological analyses; (3) many phonologists' rejection of dynamic phonological 'processes', in favour of static description of (and constraints on) the domain-span of a feature; and (4) the assumption among some phonologists (but no longer the majority) that an 'unnatural' phonology should be divorced from phonetics.

Firth died suddenly on 14 December 1960 in Lindfield, Sussex. He had seized the opportunities that came his way and left British linguistics stronger than when he entered it. His connections with the British empire enabled his career, but he repaid this by working on many under-investigated languages of the empire. His theories were the product of novel, inspirational thinking: a posthumous festschrift was published in 1966, full of ideas.

Primary works

(1930). *Speech*. London: Benn's Sixpenny Library. Reprinted in Peter Strevens (ed.), *The Tongues of Men and Speech*. London: Oxford University Press, 1964.

(1935). 'The technique of semantics'. *Transactions of the Philological Society*. 1935: 36–72.

(1937). *The Tongues of Men*. London: Watts. Reprinted in Peter Strevens (ed.), *The Tongues of Men and Speech*. London: Oxford University Press, 1964.

(1946). 'The English school of phonetics'. *Transactions of the Philological Society*. 1946: 92–132.

(1948). 'Sounds and prosodies'. *Transactions of the Philological Society*. 1948: 127–52.

(1957a). *Papers in Linguistics 1934–1951*. London: Oxford University Press.

(1957b). 'A synopsis of linguistic theory, 1930–1955'. In J. R. Firth et al., *Studies in Linguistic Analysis*. Special volume of the Philological Society. Oxford: Blackwell.

Further reading

Brown, Keith and Law, Vivien (eds) (2002). 'R. E. Asher', 'M. A. K. Halliday', 'Frank Palmer', 'R. H. Robins' and 'J. L. M. Trim'. In *Linguistics in Britain: Personal Histories*.
Publications of the Philological Society 36. Oxford: Blackwell.

Joseph, John, Love, Nigel and Taylor, Talbot (2001). *Landmarks in Linguistic Thought II: the Western Tradition in the Twentieth Century*. London: Routledge.

Lyons, John (1966). 'Firth's theory of "meaning" '. In C. E. Bazell, J. C. Catford, M. A. K. Halliday and R. H. Robins (eds), *In Memory of J. R. Firth*. London: Longman.

Mitchell, T. F. (1975). 'Introductory'. In *Principles of Firthian Linguistics*. London: Longman.

Ogden, Richard and Local, John (1994). 'Disentangling autosegments from prosodies: a note on the misrepresentation of a research tradition in phonology'. *Journal of Linguistics*. Vol. 30: 477–98.

Robins, R. H. (1961). 'John Rupert Firth: obituary'. *Language*. Vol. 37: 191–200.

Patrick Honeybone

JERRY FODOR

Fodor, Jerry (*b*. 1935; American), professor of philosophy at Rutgers University (1988–); previously professor at the Massachusetts Institute of Technology (MIT) in the departments of humanities, philosophy and psychology (1959–86); distinguished professor at the City University of New York (CUNY) graduate centre (1986–8). A prolific, empirically minded and often humorous philosopher of mind, language and cognitive science, Fodor is famous for his 'language of thought' hypothesis, his defence of a causal theory of meaning, and an interdisciplinary integration of traditional philosophical enquiry with empirical research in cognitive psychology, neuroscience and computer science. (*See also* Chomsky, Noam; Skinner, B. F.)

Born in New York City, Fodor received his PhD in philosophy from Princeton in 1960, then took a teaching job at MIT that would greatly influence the shape of his philosophical career. There he worked alongside Noam *Chomsky, renowned for his ideas about how native speakers of a language can learn its grammatical rules. The central tenet of Chomsky's theory, and the part that most resonated with Fodor, was the idea that grammatical rules are encoded in innate neural structures. In *The Language of Thought* (1975), Fodor absorbed this idea into a general thesis about the nature of thought that has since remained central to his theory of mind.

Fodor's 'language of thought' (LOT) thesis held that thinking should be understood as a relation thinkers bear to neurally realised, internal representations – sentences in a private language, known as 'mentalese'. When you believe that Aristotle was wise, for instance, you stand in a certain sort of relation (the belief relation) to a complex neural state of your brain that says, in its own version of syntax and vocabulary, that Aristotle was wise. As Fodor made perfectly clear, the LOT thesis was directly opposed to the then-popular theory of mind known as 'logical behaviourism' (see B. F. *Skinner). For behaviourists, thinking amounts simply to being disposed to behave in certain sorts of ways in the presence of certain sorts of stimuli: as long as something behaves like a thinker, it thinks. Fodor in contrast was placing highly non-trivial restrictions on what the internal constitution of a thinking organism must be like. For

example, if a thing does not possess an internal system of representation that shares certain essential features with natural language, then it cannot be a thinker. Fodor's thesis also opposed the tradition of seeing thoughts as unmediated relations to abstract 'propositions' (for example, the proposition that Aristotle was wise), for the reason that abstract entities are not spatially located anywhere, much less inside the head.

In what has become a trademark interdisciplinary and empirical style, Fodor supported his LOT thesis with discoveries in Gestalt psychology (the study of perception and behaviour as a whole rather than discrete 'events') and results from laboratory experiments on everything from human brains to rats. The core of Fodor's argument was that (1) processes of thought consist of computational processes, and (2) computation requires a language over which the computations are performed. The process of concept acquisition, for instance, consists of computing and comparing the degree of confirmation of various hypotheses about the extension of the concept. Does the concept you are supposed to attach to the word 'tomato', for instance, apply to all red edible things or just those red edible things you are supposed to put in spaghetti sauce? The various hypothesised extensions, furthermore, must be represented by and to the learner in a 'medium of computation' that shares the distinctive properties of natural language. As Fodor elaborated in later writings, those distinctively linguistic properties are 'productivity' and 'systematicity'. Your representational system is productive because it is always possible to think of something that is not yet in our representational vocabulary: if, for instance, you can think of something being a tomato and also think of something being in spaghetti sauce, then you can think of something *either* being a tomato *or* being in spaghetti sauce; you can also think of something being *both* a tomato *and* in spaghetti sauce; and so on. Your representational system is systematic, furthermore, because bits of different thoughts can be detached and recombined in ways reminiscent of cutting and pasting words in a sentence: if you can think of a tomato being in spaghetti sauce and also think of spaghetti sauce being red, then you can think of a tomato being red.

One idea in *The Language of Thought* that received substantial defence in Fodor's subsequent writings was that the mental categories used in 'folk psychology' – our ordinary, everyday practice of ascribing mental states to our fellow thinkers – are real, important and causally potent. In 'Three cheers for propositional attitudes' (1978, reprinted in Fodor 1981), Fodor summarised his case against a behaviourist reduction or elimination of folk psychology: folk psychological categories are indispensable to an adequate understanding of the mind in general, and in particular to adequate psychological explanations of intentional behaviour.

A more controversial idea present in the LOT theory, which Fodor defended at length in 'Propositional attitudes' (1978) and 'Methodological solipsism considered as a research strategy in cognitive psychology' (1980), was that thoughts are relations to something inside the head. In 1975, the year that Fodor published *The Language of Thought*, Hilary *Putnam and Tyler Burge had both published seminal papers marking the beginnings of 'externalism' or 'anti-individualism' – the prevailing idea in philosophical circles at the start of the twenty-first century that the contents of thoughts, the denotations of 'that'-clauses in ordinary, folk psychological ascriptions of mental states, are 'wide'; that is, not fully determined by what is in the head. To think that water is wet, for instance, one must have had appropriate causal interactions with the substance in the past; it is not sufficient simply to be in a certain kind of internal state. Accordingly, one consequence of Putnam's and Burge's arguments was that two people can be internally indistinguishable – that is, microphysically indiscernible from the skin inward – and yet think thoughts with different contents. And if that is possible then the things our thoughts are relations to cannot be fully determined by what lies inside our heads. Such an idea is at odds with Fodor's idea that thoughts are relations to neural sentences in an internal language of thought.

Fodor's defence of internalism rested on evidence for a 'computational theory of mind' (CTM), which he argued provided the best explanation of a variety of mental phenomena. According to CTM, our thoughts are relations to 'formal' representations. This means that their semantic properties, such as what they mean and what they refer to, are irrelevant. When doing behavioural psychology, then, we should be 'solipsistic' in our methodology: explanations of a person's thought processes and resulting actions, in terms of their previous thoughts, need make no mention of anything outside of that person herself or himself.

With Fodor's development of CTM, and an increased emphasis on the formal or non-semantic nature of our internal representations, came new challenges: most immediately, how do our thoughts get their semantic properties? In 'A theory of content (I and II)' (reprinted in Fodor 1990), Fodor took up this challenge by developing a semantics for the language of thought that was, importantly, externalistic, in the sense that the meanings of our internal representations, and hence the contents of our thoughts, depend on our relations to our external and past environment. In particular, Fodor endorsed a straightforward causal semantics for proper names, in the language of thought, along the lines defended by Saul *Kripke for proper names in natural language; and for predicates, Fodor endorsed an informational semantics of the sort developed by Fred Dretske. So in Fodor's example from the Greek tragic play *Oedipus Rex*, the internal sentences that realise Oedipus' thought that Jocasta was his mother succeed in referring to Jocasta because they contain a constituent whose causal ancestry included, in an appropriately central way, Jocasta herself. And they were about motherhood because they contained a constituent that covaries in an appropriate way with mothers: roughly, it is a law that someone has representations containing that constituent when and only when in the presence of a mother.

Fodor expended considerable energy defending an externalist semantics, including developing a novel response to the traditional objection he called the 'disjunction' problem: why does your mother-concept denote mothers instead of a disjunction of mothers with all of the other things that have ever caused you to have mother-thoughts, such as paintings of your mother or other people who resemble her? But unlike other semantic externalists, Fodor was also committed to methodological solipsism, and so had to confront the question of how mental content can be causally relevant to behaviour. For mental content depends on what the world outside of the mental subject and/or in the subject's past is like (that is, Fodor's semantic externalism), while all that is relevant in causal explanations of behaviour is 'in the head' (that is, Fodor's methodological solipsism).

One tactic Fodor explored, for example in 'Making mind matter more' (1989, reprinted in Fodor 1990), following some ideas presented in earlier work (see Fodor 1968), was explaining how so-called 'special sciences' can provide true causal laws even though the events they describe are at a higher level of abstraction than the more fundamental sciences. One might wonder, for instance, how geological laws can tell a true causal story (one example of Fodor's was 'rivers erode their outer banks'), since, you might think, all that is relevant to the causal behavior of a riverbank is the motion of sub-atomic particles. Fodor derided this 'epiphobia' (the fear of becoming an epiphenomenalist) as misguided, since special sciences can provide true causal laws as long as those laws are implemented by the phenomena mentioned by the more fundamental sciences. Fodor urged resolving the tension between semantic externalism and methodological solipsism in a similar way: content-based psychology can provide true causal laws even though what is immediately causally relevant to a person's behaviour is the formal, non-semantic properties of the person's internal representations. This is because psychological laws are implemented by computational laws defined over those representations. So although the explanation of Oedipus' behaviour offered by CTM will mention only the formal properties of Oedipus' internal representations, it can still be true that he poked his eyes out because he learned that Jocasta was his mother. This is because the law relating his learning to his behaviour was implemented by the computational processes mentioned by CTM.

Fodor explored a more radical, and correspondingly controversial, strategy of resolving the tension between semantic externalism and methodological solipsism in *Psychosemantics* (1987) and 'A modal argument for narrow content' (1991). There he hypothesised the existence of something he called 'narrow content'. While ordinary folk psychological content, as we have seen, is 'wide' – in the sense that, for instance, you can have a belief with the content that water is wet only if you have had appropriate causal interaction with water – Fodor suggested that mental states have 'narrow' content in addition to the ordinary wide kind. So although wide contents, and hence ordinary folk psychological contents, cannot

figure in good psychological explanations of the causes of behaviour (because of the truth of methodological solipsism), that does not mean that mental content as a whole is epiphenomenal, or that we have to give up viewing psychology as a respectable science. Instead it is narrow content, not folk psychological content, that figures in good psychological explanations of behaviour.

The final decade of the twentieth century saw some unexpected pronouncements from Fodor. First, in *The Elm and the Expert* (1994), he argued that we do not, after all, need 'narrow' content in order to give adequate psychological explanations of intentional behaviour. The reason he previously thought that folk psychological content would not suffice, Fodor reminded us, was that because of semantic externalism it is possible for one and the same sentence of the language of thought to express different contents in different contexts (those are what Fodor called 'Twin-cases') as well as for one and the same content to be implemented by two different sentences in the language of thought (what Fodor called 'Frege-cases'). The possibility of Twin- and Frege-cases seemed incompatible with the existence of scientific laws relating folk psychological content to behaviour, because all that is relevant to a person's behaviour is what is inside the person's head. Fodor's new proposal was to accept that semantic externalism reveals the possibility of folk psychology pulling apart from computational psychology, but to conclude that this proves the existence of laws that prevent Twin- and Frege- cases from arising too often. It can still be the case, for instance, that you jump in the lake because you believe it to be filled with water, even though the combination of an externalist semantics with CTM makes it possible for you to believe that very same thing without jumping into the lake and also makes it possible for you to jump into the lake without believing anything similar. All that follows, says Fodor, is that there is a law keeping your belief and your behaviour from coming too far apart from each other in the actual world. Folk psychology is fine as it is, even granting CTM and externalism: there is, as Fodor put it, 'life without narrow content'.

In *The Mind Doesn't Work that Way* (2000), Fodor took aim at some of the more extreme versions of CTM. In particular, as the title suggests, his target was the so-called 'New Synthesis' view expressed by Stephen Pinker in *How the Mind Works* (1997). As Fodor saw it, the New Synthesis urged an extreme sort of optimism about CTM as a way of explaining how all aspects of the mind work, a degree of optimism that Fodor alleged he had never have endorsed. On the contrary, Fodor now argued, some of the most central, important and distinctively human aspects of thought simply cannot be captured by CTM – in particular, the making of what he called 'abductive' inferences (or equivalently, 'global', 'holistic' 'inferences to the best explanation').

An abductive inference is one that is reasonable and compelling, yet not formally valid: an example Fodor uses is the inference from the belief that it is cloudy to the conclusion that one should bring an umbrella. This sort of inference gives way to the so-called 'frame problem', in that whether the inference is justified depends on an unknown number of the believing subject's other beliefs, including whether the clouds are nimbus or cirrus; whether there are cloud-producing factories around; whether one's clothes could use a good washing, and so on. Hence all of a person's beliefs are potentially relevant to such an inference. But it cannot be reasonable for any finite mind to check all of its beliefs in making every such inference, so abductive inference has to be context-sensitive: whether the above inference, for instance, is reasonable depends on whether one is near any factories, for instance. If CTM is right, then thought should consist in computations defined over the formal properties of internal representations, and hence should be context-insensitive. Again, Fodor does not conclude that CTM is entirely misguided; rather, it is the right story to tell about certain mental processes, such as 'rational" processes that involve deductive reasoning. But CTM does not capture much of what is uniquely human, namely, 'practical" mental processes that involve abduction.

Fodor has also written extensively on matters based more in empirical psychology than in analytic philosophy; for example, in 1983, defending the so-called 'modularity thesis" (the idea that the mind is made up of more-or-less subject-specific information-processing 'modules'), and in 1998, defending 'atomism' about concepts (the idea that concepts are gained and can be defined individually, rather than together as a whole). Because he continues to write on a variety of subjects that cross academic boundaries and also employs a rare combination of traditional *a priori* philosophical reasoning with a respect for empirical scientific research, Fodor's impact has been felt not only in linguistics and philosophy of language but also in cognitive science, cognitive psychology, neuroscience and computer science. His views about mind and language have changed over the course of his career, but the basic shape remains constant: mental states are real, causally potent relations to innate, atomic, formal representations in an internal language of thought, and rational mental processes consist in computations defined over those representations.

Primary works

(1968). *Psychological Explanation*. New York: Random House.
(1975). *The Language of Thought*. New York: Thomas Y. Crowell.
(1978). 'Propositional attitudes'. *Monist*. Vol. 61: 501–23.
(1980). 'Methodological solipsism considered as a research strategy in cognitive psychology'. *Behavioural and Brain Sciences*. Vol. 3: 63–109.
(1981). *RePresentations*. Cambridge, MA: MIT Press.
(1983). *The Modularity of Mind*. Cambridge, MA: MIT Press.
(1987). *Psychosemantics*. Cambridge, MA: MIT Press.
(1990). *A Theory of Content and Other Essays*. Cambridge, MA: MIT Press.
(1991). 'A modal argument for narrow content'. *Journal of Philosophy*. Vol. 88: 5–26.
(1994). *The Elm and the Expert*. Cambridge, MA: MIT Press.

(1998). *Concepts: Where Cognitive Science Went Wrong*. Oxford: Oxford University Press.
(2000). *The Mind Doesn't Work that Way*. Cambridge, MA: MIT Press.

Further reading

Baumgartner, Peter and Payr, Sabine (eds) (1995). *Speaking Minds: Interviews with Twenty Eminent Cognitive Scientists*. Princeton, NJ: Princeton University Press.
Chomsky, Noam (1968). *Language and Thought*. New York: Harcourt, Brace and World.
Dretske, Fred (1981). *Knowledge and the Flow of Information*. Cambridge, MA: MIT Press.
Loewer, Barry and Rey, Georges (1991). *Meaning in Mind: Jerry Fodor and his Critics*. Cambridge, MA: Blackwell.
Pinker, Stephen (1997). *How the Mind Works*. New York: W. W. Norton.

Anthony Newman

GOTTLOB FREGE

Frege, (Friedrich Ludwig) Gottlob (*b.* 1848, *d.* 1925; German), mathematician and logician, the father of modern mathematical logic and one of the founders of analytic philosophy. Frege was professor of mathematics at the university of Jena, being appointed *Professor Extraordinarius* in 1879 and *ordentlicher Honorarprofessor* in 1896. He made signal contributions to the philosophy of mathematics, philosophical logic and the philosophy of language. (*See also* Carnap, Rudolf; Leibniz, Gottfried Wilhelm; Montague, Richard; Russell, Bertrand; Wittgenstein, Ludwig.)

Gottlob Frege was born in Wismar (Mecklenburg-Vorpommern) on 8 November 1848. His father was Karl Alexander Frege, the founder and principal of a private girls' high school in Wismar, a position he held until his death in 1866. His mother, Auguste (Bialloblotzky) Frege, was a teacher and later herself principal of the school. Frege attended the Gymnasium in Wismar (1864–9) and then entered the University of Jena, where he studied chemistry, mathematics and philosophy. After four semesters at Jena, he transferred to the University of Göttingen. In December 1873, he received a PhD in mathematics for a dissertation entitled 'Über eine geometrische Darstellung der imaginären Gebilde in der Ebene' ('On a geometrical representation of imaginary figures in a plane'), written under the supervision of Ernst Schering. In May 1874 Frege was admitted to the position of *Privatdozent* in mathematics (an unsalaried lecturing position) at the University of Jena, where he would remain until his retirement in 1918. He lectured on all branches of mathematics, although his publications in mathematics outside the field of logic are scarce. At Jena, he did not have much contact with either his students or colleagues. Rudolf *Carnap, a student of Frege in the autumn of 1910, recalls in his autobiography: 'Frege looked old beyond his years. He was of small stature, rather shy, extremely introverted' (1963: 5). Little is known about Frege's family. He was married to Margaret Lieseburg and had at least two children, who died at an early age. They later adopted a son, Alfred, whom Frege had to raise alone when

Margaret died in 1905. Although Alfred took care of Frege's unpublished papers after his death, much of this material was destroyed during World War II.

Frege was radically opposed to the 'psychological' stance on logic and the philosophy of mathematics that was dominant among his contemporaries. For him, mathematics could not be reduced to something empirical or psychological, and he looked down on foundational approaches to the field that went in this direction. In his 'Begriffsschrift' ('Concept Script', 1879), which is perhaps the single most important paper on mathematical logic of the nineteenth century, Frege set out to find a solid scientific foundation for mathematics and demonstrate that the truths of arithmetic can follow from logical axioms and principles. He achieved this latter goal in 'Die Grundlagen der Arithmetik' ('The foundations of arithmetic', 1884), where he presented an axiomatic theory of arithmetic.

In the five years of work that led to the 'Begriffsschrift', Frege realised that natural language was inadequate for his enterprise (that is, unfit to express mathematical reasoning precisely) and so he developed 'a formula language of pure thought' as a substitute. His determined efforts resulted in the first rigorous and self-contained axiomatic theory of propositional logic. However, the real logical breakthrough in 'Concept Script' came with the introduction of quantification theory and the notion of variable binding. Building on the idea of function-argument analysis in mathematics, Frege hypothesised that semantic composition is the result of saturating an unsaturated meaning component. For instance, he took sentences like 'Felix is a cat' to be the value that the unsaturated functional expression '____ is a cat' yields when it takes the expression 'Felix' as an argument. Frege then made the crucial observation that a quantified expression such as 'Every cat' in a sentence like 'Every cat meows' is qualitatively very different from the proper name 'Felix', because the noun 'cat' can itself be construed as an unsaturated expression. This led him to the realisation that quantified statements of the form 'Every A is a B' involved not one but two unsaturated functional expressions, in this case '____ is an A' and '____ is a B', such that if an argument is true of the former it must also be true of the latter. Frege is often credited with being the first to consider that the meaning of statement such as 'Every cat meows' is 'for all values of x, if x is a cat, then x meows', a move that constituted a complete departure from the 'subject–predicate' analysis of Aristotelian syllogistic theory which had dominated logic over two millennia. Frege was promoted at Jena upon publication of the 'Begriffsschrift', but very few people at the time appreciated the great significance of this piece of work.

Frege did substantial work in the philosophy of language, an interest which was motivated in part by his desire to find a secure grounding for his research in logic and mathematics. The essay 'Über Sinn und Bedeutung' ('On sense and reference', 1892a) stands out among his other works in the philosophy of language.

In this paper he presented two perplexing puzzles about language, which led him to the conclusion that considering the denotations of the singular terms (that is, names and definite descriptions) that occur in certain types of sentences was not enough to explain the meaning and logical behaviour of those sentences. The first of these intricate problems concerns the informativeness of identity statements with co-referential singular terms; the second is about identity statements that occur as sentential complements of propositional attitude verbs like 'believe', 'know' or 'think'. Let's look at them in turn.

'Phosphorus' is an ancient name for the Morning Star, and 'Hesperus' was the name used to refer to the Evening Star. One of the earliest astronomical discoveries was that Phosphorus and Hesperus were, in fact, the same; that is, the planet Venus. Frege observed that the meaning, or cognitive significance, of redundant identity statements such as 'Hesperus is Hesperus' is different from that of true non-redundant identity statements such as 'Phosphorus is Hesperus', even if 'Phosphorus' and 'Hesperus' are co-referential terms. In particular, while the statement 'Hesperus is Phosphorus' expresses an empirically significant discovery (made by astronomers in Roman times), the statement 'Hesperus is Hesperus' is a trivial truth of logic. This difficult problem of substitution of co-referring terms in identity statements is often nicknamed 'Frege's puzzle'. Frege also identified a related problem concerning the substitution of co-referential terms in contexts reporting propositional attitudes, like belief ascriptions. If 'Hesperus' and 'Phosphorus' are co-referential terms, why is the sentence 'Mary believes that Hesperus is Hesperus' trivially true while the sentence 'Mary believes that Hesperus is Phosphorus' may be false?

Frege explained these apparent paradoxes by drawing a fundamental distinction between an expression's *Sinn* ('sense') and its *Bedeutung* ('reference'), a distinction which was already present in his earlier lecture 'Funktion und Begriff' ('Function and concept', 1891). According to him, proper names like 'Hesperus' (and also descriptions like 'the Morning Star') are associated with both a reference and a sense. The reference of a proper name (or description) is typically the individual it designates, which in the case of 'Hesperus" is the planet Venus. On the other hand, a Fregean sense is, so to speak, the way the reference is given to us, its particular mode of presentation. For example, although 'Hesperus' and 'Phosphorus' have identical reference (that is, the second planet in order of distance from the sun), they clearly have different modes of presentation, 'Hesperus' being the first star to appear in the evening sky and 'Phosphorus' being the last star to disappear in the morning sky.

Frege believed that the 'true meaning" of an expression is given to us by its sense and not simply by its reference, which gave him a way of explaining the perceived difference between identity statements such as 'Hesperus is Hesperus' and 'Hesperus is Phosphorus'. Since 'Hesperus' and 'Phosphorus' express different senses, the sense of the identity statements in which they occur will be different in each case too. Frege also proposed that proper names and descriptions that occur in propositional attitude contexts, such as following verbs like 'believe' or 'think', denote their senses. This explains why in such contexts a singular term cannot be simply substituted for another having the same reference in a truth-preserving way.

The discussion above is related to what has been called 'Frege's principle' (of the compositionality of meaning). A view commonly attributed to Frege is that the reference of a complex expression is a function of (is determined uniquely by) the reference of its component parts. Just as a mathematical function always returns the same value when applied to the same argument, a complex expression retains the same reference when we replace any of its parts by another which has the same reference. For example, if we replace 'Hesperus' in 'Hesperus is Phosphorus' by the co-referential expressions 'Venus' or 'the Morning Star', we obtain a sentence which must have the same reference. This observation may also be extended straightforwardly to the senses of composite expressions. A version of Frege's principle was adopted by Richard *Montague in his groundbreaking work on the formal semantics of natural language, and this principle (broadly construed) still informs much current theorising in this area.

The paper 'Über Begriff und Gegenstand' ('On concept and object', 1892b) was also influential. In it Frege introduced an intuitive but nevertheless important distinction between concepts and objects. Take the sentence 'Felix is a cat.' According to Frege, a sentence such as this naturally breaks down in two parts: an object denoting expression, 'Felix', which picks out the particular individual referred to in the sentence, and a concept denoting predicate, 'is a cat', which, as we would expect, denotes the concept of being a cat. This simple distinction paved the way for subsequent work in mathematics, as it was particularly useful in the conceptualisation of notions such as being the element of a set.

The next step in Frege's logicist project, that is, the derivability of arithmetical propositions from logical laws by definition, appeared as the first volume of *Grundgesetze der Arithmetik* (*The Basic Laws of Arithmetic*, 1893). But Frege's work continued to be unfavourably received, and he published the second volume of this series (1903) entirely at his own expense. In June 1902, while it was still in press, he received a letter from Bertrand *Russell in which Russell expressed concerns about one of Frege's axioms (Frege's 'Basic Law (V)'). In this letter, Russell showed that a contradiction could be derived in Frege's logical system. This came to be known as Russell's paradox, and is perhaps the most famous of the classical paradoxes of set theory.

The paradox arises if we assume that for every property P, there is a set that consists of all and only those entities which have P. It goes like this: consider the set S of all entities that are not members of themselves. Is the set S a member of itself? Let us assume first that S is a member of itself. Then in order to satisfy its own requirement for membership, S must not be a member of itself. So, clearly, our assumption is wrong and S cannot be a member of itself. On the other hand, if we assume that S is not a member of itself, then we must conclude that S is a member of itself, for it satisfies its own condition for membership. But this is impossible. So, contrary to our assumption, S must be a member of itself. Notice that we have concluded both that S is and that it is not a member of itself, which is paradoxical.

Frege, who immediately realised the difficulty which Russell's observations posed for the logical foundations of his theory, was dismayed. Although he added an appendix to his 'Grundgesetze' in which he identified what he perceived to be the faulty axiom and tried to address Russell's comments to him, Frege could not resolve the problem which they raised. However, his response to Russell was not bitter, and Russell himself considered the intellectual pleasure with which Frege embraced the news 'almost superhuman, and a telling indication of that of which men are capable if their dedication is to creative work and knowledge instead of cruder efforts to dominate and be known' (Heijenoort 1967: 127) Frege eventually felt compelled to abandon many of his long-standing views on logic and mathematics.

After Frege's death, the brilliant logician Kurt Gödel published his incompleteness theorems, showing that Frege's logicist enterprise was impossible.

Frege published a series of important papers after his retirement in 1918. Among them were 'Der Gedanke' ('Thoughts', 1918a), 'Die Verneinung' ('Negation', 1918b) and 'Gedankengefüge' ('Compound thoughts', 1923). He intended these last three papers, which have the originality of his earlier work, to be published in a book to be called *Logical Investigations*. An English translation was published posthumously under this title (edited by Peter Geach in 1977). In these papers, Frege provided the most comprehensive and detailed account of the nature of thoughts. He endorsed the view that thoughts are abstract, structured objects. Since we are able to identify parts in a thought which correspond to the parts of a sentence, he hypothesised that the structure of the sentence can be a fitting model of the structure of the thought.

Frege is a central figure of our intellectual heritage. He practically founded the modern discipline of mathematical logic, and his philosophy of language is still considered to be full of interesting insights. Besides his perceptive distinction between an expression's sense and its reference, he argued extensively against subjective theories of meaning (for example, the dictum that meaning is internal to the individual), and in favour of giving meanings the status of mind-independent abstract entities. His 'context principle', the view that words have meaning only in the context of the sentences in which they occur, has been subsequently defended by renowned philosophers such as W. V. O. *Quine. Although Frege's work was largely ignored by his contemporaries (with the notable exceptions of Rudolf Carnap, Bertrand Russell, Ludwig *Wittgenstein and some others), his ideas have become a profound influence on the development of philosophical logic, philosophy of language and natural language semantics. In fact, they are so ingrained in our current thinking in these areas that it can be difficult sometimes to realise fully their originality and significance. His achievements are even more impressive if we consider that we have got so comparatively short a way from the point he reached. Gottlob Frege died on 26 July 1925 in Bad Kleinen (some 15 miles south of Wismar) at the age of 77.

Primary works

(1879). 'Begriffsschrift, eine der arithmetischen nachgebildete Formelsprache des reinen Denkens'. Halle: Louis Nebert. Trans. J. van Heijenoort as 'Concept Script, a formal language of pure thought modelled upon that of arithmetic'. In J. van Heijenoort (ed.), *From Frege to Gödel: A Source Book in Mathematical Logic, 1879–1931*. Cambridge, MA: Harvard University Press, 1967.

(1884). 'Die Grundlagen der Arithmetik, ein logisch-mathematische Untersuchung über den Begriff der Zahl'. Breslau: W. Koebner.

Trans. J. L. Austin as *The Foundations of Arithmetic: A Logico-Mathematical Enquiry into the Concept of Number*. Second edition. Oxford: Blackwell, 1953.

(1891). 'Funktion und Begriff'. Vortrag, gehalten in der Sitzung vom 9. Januar 1891 der Jenaischen Gesellschaft für Medizin und Naturwissenschaft. Jena: Hermann Pohle. Trans. P. Geach and M. Black as 'Function and concept'. In Geach and Black (eds), *Translations from the Philosophical Writings of Gottlob Frege*. Third edition. Oxford: Blackwell, 1980.

(1892a). 'Über Sinn und Bedeutung'. *Zeitschrift für Philosophie und philosophische Kritik*. vol. 100: 25–50. Trans. P. Geach and M. Black as 'On sense and reference'. In Geach and Black (eds), *Translations from the Philosophical Writings of Gottlob Frege*. Third edition. Oxford: Blackwell, 1980.

(1892b). 'Über Begriff und Gegenstand'. *Vierteljahresschrift für wissenschaftliche Philosophie*. vol. 16: 192–205. Trans. P. Geach and M. Black as 'On concept and object". In Geach and Black (eds), *Translations from the Philosophical Writings of Gottlob Frege*. third edition. Oxford: Blackwell, 1980.

(1893). *Grundgesetze der Arithmetik. Band I.* Jena: Hermann Pohle. Trans. (of preface, introduction and part I) M. Furth as *The Basic Laws of Arithmetic: Exposition of the System*. Berkeley, CA University of California Press, 1964.

(1903). *Grundgesetze der Arithmetik. Band II.* Jena: Hermann Pohle. Trans. of extracts P. Geach and M. Black as *The Basic Laws of Arithmetic*. In P. Geach and M. Black (eds), *Translations from the Philosophical Writings of Gottlob Frege*. Third edition. Oxford: Blackwell, 1980.

(1918a). 'Der Gedanke, eine logische Untersuchung'. *Beiträge zur Philosophie des Deutschen Idealismus*. vol. 1: 58–77. Trans. P. Geach as 'Thoughts'. In P. Geach (ed.), *Logical Investigations*. Oxford: Blackwell, 1977.

(1918b). 'Die Verneinung, eine logische Untersuchung'. *Beiträge zur Philosophie des Deutschen Idealismus*. vol. 1: 143–57. Trans. P. Geach as 'Negation". In P. Geach (ed.),

Logical Investigations. Oxford: Blackwell, 1977.

(1923). 'Logische Untersuchungen, Dritter Teil: Gedankengefüge'. *Beiträge zur Philosophie des Deutschen Idealismus*. vol. 3: 36–51. Trans. P. Geach as 'Compound thoughts". In P. Geach (ed.), *Logical Investigations*. Oxford: Blackwell, 1977.

(1979). *Posthumous Writings*. H. Hermes, F. Kambartel and E. Kaulbach (eds). Oxford: Blackwell.

Further reading

Beaney, Michael (1996). *Frege: Making Sense*. London: Duckworth.

Beaney, Michael (ed.) (1997). *The Frege Reader*. Oxford: Blackwell.

Carl, Wolfgang (1994). *Frege's Theory of Sense and Reference*. Cambridge: Cambridge University Press.

Carnap, Rudolf (1963). 'Intellectual autobiography'. In P. A. Schilpp (ed.), *The Philosophy of Rudolf Carnap*. La Salle: Open Court.

Currie, Gregory (1982). *Frege: An Introduction to his Philosophy*. Sussex: Harvester.

Dummett, Michael (1973). *Frege: Philosophy of Language*. London: Duckworth.

Heijenoort, Jean van (ed.) (1967). *From Frege to Gödel*. Cambridge, MA: Harvard University Press.

Kenny, Anthony (2000). *Frege: An Introduction to the Founder of Modern Analytic Philosophy*. Oxford: Blackwell.

Noonan, Harold W. (2001). *Frege: A Critical Introduction*. Cambridge: Polity.

Reck, Erich H. (ed.) (2002). *From Frege to Wittgenstein: Perspectives in Early Analytic Philosophy*. Oxford: Oxford University Press.

Salmon, Nathan (1986). *Frege's Puzzle*. Cambridge, MA: MIT Press.

Sluga, Hans D. (1980). *Gottlob Frege*. London: Routledge and Kegan Paul.

Sluga, Hans D. (ed.) (1993). *The Philosophy of Frege* (4 vols). New York: Garland.

Iván García-Álvarez

PETER GEACH

Geach, Peter (Thomas) (*b.* 1916; British), emeritus professor at the University of Leeds, fellow of Balliol College, Oxford (1979), and fellow of the British Academy since 1965. He taught philosophy at the Universities of Birmingham (1951–66) and Leeds (1966–81), where he was appointed professor of logic. Geach is an analytical philosopher and logician, whose greatest influence on linguistics has been in the application of logical techniques to problems of language and metaphysics. (*See also* Frege, Gottlob; Montague, Richard; Wittgenstein, Ludwig.)

Geach was born in London, the son of George Hender and Eleonora Frederyka Adolfina Geach. His father worked in the Indian Educational Service as professor of philosophy at Lahore and later as principal of a teacher training college at Peshawar. Eleonora Geach, the daughter of Polish emigrants, returned to Britain for her son's birth after a short period of time in India, and Geach spent his earliest years in his maternal grandparents' house in Cardiff. When he was 8 years old Geach was sent by his father to the Llandaff Cathedral boarding school, and later he attended Clifton College. Geach was educated at Balliol College, Oxford (BA, 1938; MA, 1951), and at Cambridge University (MA, 1971). In 1941 he married the Cambridge philosopher Elizabeth Anscombe, whom he had met in Oxford while a student.

Peter Geach has written on many philosophical topics of linguistic interest. For instance, in his first book, *Mental Acts: Their Content and their Objects* (1956), he provided a logical analysis of the notion of mental act and criticised the view that concepts are acquired by abstracting them from recurrent features of experience. He claimed that the limitations of this empiricist doctrine are most clearly perceived when one considers logical concepts such as negation, for clearly a concept like 'not red' cannot simply be derived from abstracted particulars, but rather from the previously acquired concept of 'red' together with an appreciation of the concept of 'negation'.

In linguistic circles Geach is perhaps best known for bringing attention to a number of puzzles regarding the use of referring expressions and expressions of generality in natural language and thought. The most striking of these puzzles, addressed in his book *Reference and Generality: An Examination of some Medieval and Modern Theories* (1962), concerns the interpretation of 'donkey sentences', so called because the examples that he used in his discussion involved donkeys. Donkey sentences are sentences in which a pronoun is anaphoric to an indefinite noun phrase, as in the example: 'Every man who owns a donkey beats it.' Geach noticed that the interpretation of indefinites in donkey sentences is problematic, because they characteristically act as universal quantifiers in that context. How can the sentence 'Every man who owns a donkey beats it' mean that every man beats every donkey he owns if, as has been standard practice, indefinites usually operate like existentially quantified terms? Geach's observations that the simple binding mechanisms of predicate logic do not give us the interpretation of donkey sentences afforded by our intuitions paved the way for a fruitful line of research in linguistic semantics in the early 1980s (Kamp 1981; Heim 1983).

In *Reference and Generality*, Geach paid a great deal of attention to the intricacies of pronominal reference. For example, he claimed that since pronouns vary in the way in which they get their reference, they should be represented in different ways. On the one hand, there are what he called 'pronouns of laziness'; that is, pronouns that simply duplicate the content of their antecedents and can be replaced by them without affecting the meaning of the sentence. To use one of Geach's examples, the pronoun 'he' in 'Smith broke the bank at Monte Carlo, and he has recently died a pauper' is one of laziness, merely going proxy for its antecedent. On the other hand, there are pronouns that have quantifier expressions as antecedents, as does 'her' in the sentence 'Every girl dated a boy who liked her', and appear to be functionally analogous to the bound variables in predicate logic. Geach's contention that every anaphoric term can be treated in one of these two ways was challenged by the Oxford philosopher Gareth Evans (1977). Evans argued that there are pronouns whose antecedents are quantifiers, but which do not appear to behave as if they were bound by those quantifiers. The debate surrounding the adequacy of the two-way distinction in the treatment of pronominal reference postulated by Geach has given rise to countless articles in the linguistics literature.

In 1972 Geach published *Logic Matters*, an edited collection of papers mainly concerned with issues in philosophical logic. Logical themes are interwoven with almost all the topics he has covered, and he has been a staunch defender of the value of logic in philosophy and education. His love for the discipline stemmed from early on in his life, when his father first exposed him to Neville Keynes's 1887 textbook *Studies and Exercises in Formal Logic*. In 'Identity', one of the papers in the collection cited above, we find a clear statement of Geach's influential albeit quite contentious view on identity statements. He puts forward the thesis that there is no single, all-embracing relation of identity, but rather that identity statements are expressed relative to some general term. Thus, according to Geach, identity statements of the form '*a* is the same as *b*' are meaningless unless we identify the particular identity relation we have in mind by appealing, for example, to a countable noun like 'planet': '*a* is the same planet as *b*.' Geach also believed that the transitivity of identity – that is, the claim that if '*a* is the same as *b*' and '*b* is the same as *c*', then it follows that '*a* is the same as *c*' – holds only when there is a single identity relation concept at work. Is it possible for two things, '*a*' and '*b*', to be identical relative to one kind-term, but to fail to enter into the identity relation relative to some other kind-term even if the latter term applies to both '*a*' and '*b*'? Geach argued that this question should receive a positive answer. Although his ideas on this topic continue to be discussed, the theory of relative identity he put forward has now been mostly rejected.

Geach's writings on the philosophy of religion constitute a significant corpus that stands out from his other work. His interest in the subject was sparked by John McTaggart's *Some Dogmas of Religion* (1930), which Geach had read by the time he was 13. Interestingly, Geach remains a respected authority on this British philosopher. As an adult, Geach converted to Roman Catholicism and subsequently became a leading figure of (analytic) Thomism, a body of philosophical and theological ideas that seeks to articulate the intellectual content of Catholic Christianity. He combined elements of philosophical analysis and analytic-linguistic techniques with the content of Thomism, and showed that an appreciation of Aquinas was not categorically incompatible with sympathy for the work of philosophers such as Gottlob *Frege and Ludwig *Wittgenstein.

Peter Geach's work in philosophical logic has been very relevant to linguistic semantics and the philosophy of language. In his many writings, he has not only called attention to novel example sentences of great linguistic interest, but also formulated creative and seminal analyses of such data. He must also be credited with the coinage of certain phrases that have become terms of art in the linguistics literature (for example, 'pronouns of laziness'). Curiously enough, in his philosophical autobiography (Lewis 1991), he appears to be somewhat sceptical about the efforts of some professional linguists to get the facts about language right.

Primary works

(1956). *Mental Acts: Their Content and their Objects*. London: Routledge and Kegan Paul.

(1962). *Reference and Generality: An Examination of some Medieval and Modern Theories*. Ithaca, NY: Cornell University Press.

(1967). 'Identity'. *Review of Metaphysics*. Vol. 21: 3–12. Reprinted in Geach (1972).

(1969). *God and the Soul*. London: Routledge and Kegan Paul.

(1972). *Logic Matters*. Oxford: Blackwell.

(1977). *The Virtues: The Stanton Lectures 1973–4*. Cambridge: Cambridge University Press.

(1979). *Truth, Love, and Immortality: An Introduction to McTaggart's Philosophy*. Berkeley, CA: University of California Press.

Further reading

Evans, Gareth (1977). 'Pronouns, quantifiers, and relative clauses'. *Canadian Journal of Philosophy*. Vol. 7: 467–36.

Heim, Irene (1983). 'File change semantics and the familiarity theory of definiteness'. In R. Bäuerle, C. Schwarze and A. von Stechow (eds), *Meaning, Use and Interpretation of Language*. Berlin: De Gruyter.

Kamp, Hans (1981). 'A theory of truth and semantic representation'. In J. Groenondijk, T. Janssen and M. Stokhof (eds), *Formal Methods in the Study of Language*. Amsterdam: Mathematisch Centrum.

Lewis, Harry A. (ed.) (1991). *Peter Geach: Philosophical Encounters*. Dordrecht: Kluwer.

McTaggart, John M. E. (1930). *Some Dogmas of Religion*. London: Arnold.

Neville Keynes, John (1887). *Studies and Exercises in Formal Logic: Including a Generalisation of Logical Processes in their Application to Complex Inferences*. Second edition. London and New York: Macmillan.

Iván García-Álvarez

NELSON GOODMAN

Goodman, Nelson (*b.* 1906, *d.* 1998; American), considered – alongside *Quine – the most important representative of the branch of analytical philosophy that wanted to describe and solve philosophical problems with the aid of modern logic. (*See also* Carnap, Rudolf; Quine, W. V. O.; Russell, Bertrand.)

Goodman was born in Somerville, Massachusetts. He attended Harvard University, where he received a BS in 1928 and PhD in 1941. As he was Jewish and thus not eligible for a fellowship, he financed his studies by working as director of the Goodman-Walker Art Gallery in Boston (1929–40). He was always a collector of ancient and modern art and showed a broad interest in, and active support of, various fields of art. His wife was the artist Katharine Sturgis. During World War II he served in the United States Army, then taught briefly at Tufts College (1945–6). He was then professor at the University of Pennsylvania (1946–64), and taught philosophy at Brandeis University (1964–7). In 1968 he returned to Harvard University, where he had studied, and retired in 1977. He received numerous honours and rewards, and was president of the Eastern Division of the American Philosophical Association (1967) and vice-president of the Association for Symbolic Logic (1950–2).

Goodman contributed to diverse fields of philosophy, including logic (the branch of philosophy and mathematics that deals with the formal principles, methods and criteria of validity of inference, reasoning and knowledge), epistemology (the philosophy of knowledge) and aesthetics (the philosophy of art), as well as language in general. His first published book, *The Structure of Appearance* (1951), elaborates the ideas of a mereology (a branch of logic that investigates part–whole formal relationships), called the 'calculus of individuals', that he developed as graduate student. He took up a nominalist view, which can be summarised as a rejection of classes and argues that worlds are made or constructed by symbol systems that supply structure.

Goodman made his best-known and most discussed contribution to the study of language in *Fact, Fiction and Forecast* (1954). There he investigates the problem of counterfactual conditionals and the problem of induction (just because all the swans we have ever seen are white doesn't make it legitimate to assume that all swans are white). First noted by *Hume, this problem concerns the logical basis of inferences from the observed to the unobserved. Goodman has recommended replacing Hume's 'old riddle' with a 'new riddle of induction', known as the 'grue paradox'. This paradox may be explained with a possible account of the colour of emeralds. If all the emeralds ever discovered up to a certain point are green, inductive reasoning would suggest that all emeralds are green. Yet this does not discount the possibility that emeralds are in fact grue, that is, green if observed before future time '*t*', when a blue emerald is discovered. Emeralds in fact have always have been grue, but we use the word green simply to make things easier for ourselves.

Goodman's broad interest in art is reflected in *Languages of Art* (1968), where he develops a symbol theory and argues that art makes and reveals worlds, just as do the sciences. He died in Needham, Massachusetts on 25 November 1998, at the age of 92. His highly original work covers great range and depth and he is among the most important philosophers of the twentieth century.

Primary works

(1951). *The Structure of Appearance*. Third edition 1977. Boston: Reidel.
(1954). *Fact, Fiction, and Forecast*. Fourth edition 1983. Cambridge, MA: Harvard University Press.

Further reading

Elgin, Catherine (ed.) (1997). *The Philosophy of Nelson Goodman*. New York: Garland.

Eva Herrmann-Kaliner

JOSEPH GREENBERG

Greenberg, Joseph (*b.* 1915, *d.* 2001; American), professor of anthropology at Columbia University (1948–62) and professor of social sciences at Stanford University (1962–2001); anthropologist, historical linguist and classifier of world languages, who carried out extensive research of languages spanning vast geographical and temporal spaces. He is best known for his work in language universals and linguistic typology. (*See also* Chomsky, Noam; Jakobson, Roman; Sapir, Edward; Whorf, Benjamin Lee.)

Greenberg was born in Brooklyn, New York, to parents of German-Polish descent. He was exposed to German and Yiddish at an early age. The former was spoken by his mother's family and the latter by his father's. In addition to these languages, he also learned Hebrew, Arabic, Greek and Latin. From his early childhood he showed a gift for music; he was a talented pianist, who performed in public in his early teens. His family expected him to pursue a career in music, but he decided to enrol at Columbia to study social anthropology. After his graduation he enrolled at Northwestern University, where he obtained a PhD in anthropology in 1940. During World War II he served in the army, and was stationed in North Africa and Italy from 1940 to 1945. Thereafter he taught at the University of Minnesota for a year before joining the faculty at Columbia.

Greenberg is best known for his research in typology, one of the two major approaches that intend to define the basic properties of 'human language' by investigating their common characteristics. The other approach is the universal paradigm, proposed by *Chomsky. Although these two approaches share the same goal, their methodological frameworks are completely different. The typological method compares languages and classifies them into types by their structural similarities. The universal approach, on the other hand, asserts that human language is biologically determined; hence, all human languages have the same core, or basic, properties. Proponents of this perspective rely on their intuition as native speakers to formulate a set of rules governing the grammaticality of linguistic units.

Greenberg is often referred to as an Africanist because of his influential work in the reclassification of African languages. However, the first piece of African research he conducted was anthropological. In 1938–9 he spent a year in North Nigeria studying the influence of Islam on the native Nigerians' beliefs and practices, research that was the subject of his doctoral dissertation at Northwestern. His African field trip ignited his interest in African languages, and marked the beginning of a series of research endeavours that culminated in the publication of his important classification of Africa's 1,500 languages into four families. These are the Afro-Asiatic, the Nilo-Saharan, the Khoisan and the Niger-Kordofanian families.

Greenberg's classification of African languages was significant for a number of reasons. One of them is that Africa is the most linguistically diverse continent. The majority of these languages do not have a written form, which makes the classification task even harder. When Greenberg's classification of African languages was published in 1955, the findings of his research were heavily criticised. Most of the criticism questioned his methodological approach, which used word similarity as a determinant of typologising languages in the same

family. Despite the criticism, Greenberg's classification is now accepted as the norm by the majority of Africanists. In fact, genetic research findings have confirmed that modern humans originated in Africa, a conclusion Greenberg reached on purely linguistic evidence.

There are different criteria by which languages are classified. The major approaches are phonological, morphological, syntactic, lexicosemantic, holistic and sociolinguistic (see Lyovin 1997). One of Greenberg's significant contributions to the field of typology was his morphological approach to the classification of languages, published in 'A quantitative approach to the morphological typology of language' (1960). Traditionally languages were classified into four morphologically distinct types. These are: (1) analytic languages, (2) agglutinative languages, (3) fusional languages and (4) polysynthetic languages. The main difference between these is that in types (1) and (2) the morphological composition of words can easily be determined with respect to boundaries and significance. In types (3) and (4), such determination is not always possible. According to Lyovin, this classificatory system is problematic because a single language may exhibit morphological characteristics pertaining to more than one of the four types. To remedy the situation, Greenberg (1960) proposed what he considered a superior paradigm for typologizing languages. The main merit of this paradigm, which consists of ten typological indexes, is that it is relative, not absolute. In other words, a language does not have to exhibit the characteristics of a certain type all the time in order for it to be considered a member of that type.

The Conference on Language Universals held in Dobbs Ferry, New York, in 1961 was a landmark in the history of typology. The conference was significant because it was held at a time when linguistic research was dominated by the structuralist approach, which warned against comparative methods. The linguists at the meeting in Dobbs Ferry felt that the structuralist approach to language study, despite its detailed analysis of individual languages, failed to address the broader question of what is common to all languages. To overcome this shortcoming, an archived corpus of data from a large number of diverse languages was needed to facilitate the task of using the comparative method to carry out typological studies. Despite the success of the conference, Charles Ferguson, an associate editor on *Universals of Human Language* (1978), stated in an article in that book that Greenberg was the only participant who continued his research endeavours in that direction, notably in Greenberg (1978).

Not only did Greenberg continue his classification of the languages of the world using a comparative method that had fallen out of favour for over a century, but he also stressed the need for taking both synchronic (language at a given moment) and diachronic (language through history) factors into consideration to determine language types and linguistic universals. This approach was foreign to typology, which, until then, had embraced the structuralist synchronic perspective. Although both synchronic and diachronic linguistic analyses were first

employed by *Jakobson to explain the phonology of a Proto-Indo-European language, Greenberg was a pioneer in applying them as a methodological framework to comparing all aspects of language.

Some of the important recommendations of Dobbs Ferry were realised through the Project on Language Universals, which started at Stanford in 1967. This project was co-directed by Greenberg and Ferguson. The project's goal, as stated by Greenberg in the first issue of *Working Papers in Language Universals*, was two-fold: the formulation of generalisations about languages through comparison, and the establishment of a large data bank that would make the verification of these generalisations possible. This important project culminated in the publication of *Universals of Human Languages*, a four-volume set published in 1978. It includes forty-six papers covering 750 languages.

In 1971 Greenberg proposed a classification of the languages of New Guinea into a single family. This was considered a radical project because New Guinea is the most linguistically diverse region in the world, where several hundred languages are spoken in a small geographical area. At the time of writing (2003) no analysis of all the languages of New Guinea has yet been accomplished, although linguists have studied the area for decades. After his New Guinea research Greenberg turned his attention to the classification of the languages of the so-called New World. His book *Languages in America* was published in 1987. There he proposed the classification of the 650 native languages of

North and South America into three families, which he called Na-Dene, Eskimo-Aleut and Amerind.

Greenberg's last research project attempted to prove the relationship between the languages of Europe, Asia and North America. He called this family of languages Euroasiatic, and published a first volume, containing the grammatical support of his classification, in 2000. He finished the second volume, including the lexical evidence of the relationship between Euroasiatic languages, the day before he was diagnosed with his terminal illness.

Although Greenberg has been criticised by many linguists who questioned his methodology, genetic and archaeological research in the late twentieth and early twenty-first centuries has provided support for many of his classifications. What is more impressive than his classifications of the languages of the world, however, is his quest to discover a proto-universal human language. The first issue of volume 6 of *Linguistic Typology* has a section titled 'Remembering Joseph H. Greenberg' (2000). There nine of his friends and colleagues in linguistics discuss not only his seminal legacy in a variety of disciplines, but also his modest and unassuming personality.

Primary works

(1955). *Studies in African Linguistic Classification*. New Haven, CT: Compass Press.
(1960). 'A quantitative approach to the morphological typology of language'. *International Journal of American Linguistics*. Vol. 26: 178–94.
(1963a) (ed.). *Universals of Language*. Cambridge, MA: MIT Press.
(1963b). 'Some universals of grammar with reference to the order of meaningful elements'. In Greenberg (1963a).
(1978) (with Charles Ferguson and Edith Moravcsik) (eds). *Universals of Human Language* (4 vols). Stanford, CA: Stanford University Press.
(1987). *Languages in America*. Stanford, CA: Stanford University Press.
(2000). 'The concept of proof in genetic linguistics'. In Spike Gildea (ed.), *Reconstructing Grammar: Comparative Linguistics and Grammaticalization* Amsterdam: John Benjamins.
(2000–2). *Indo-European and its Closest Relatives: The Eurasiatic Language Family* (2 vols). Stanford, CA: Stanford University Press.

Further reading

Lyovin, Anatole (1997). *An Introduction to the Languages of the World*. New York: Oxford University Press.
(2002). 'Remembering Joseph H. Greenberg (1915–2001)'. *Linguistic Typology*. Vol. 6(1): 3–47.

Yousif Elhindi

ALGIRDAS GREIMAS

Greimas, Algirdas (Julius or Julien) (*b.* 1917, *d.* 1992; Lithuanian, naturalised French 1949), leading semiotic theorist and director of studies in Social Sciences at the École Pratique des Hautes Études. His project on text semiotics led to the establishment of the Paris school in the 1960s. He is especially remembered for his application of the universal model of the 'semiotic square' to narrative structures. (*See also* Barthes, Roland; Hjelmslev, Louis; Jakobson, Roman.)

Greimas was born in Tula, Russia, of Lithuanian parents on 19 March 1917. He attended Rygiskiu Jono gymnasium in Marijampole, Lithuania, in 1934, and later studied law at Kaunas University, commencing postgraduate studies on the history of the French language at the University of Grenoble. He returned to Lithuania in 1940, where he taught and wrote critical essays on contemporary culture. After returning to France in 1944 and studying at the Sorbonne, he completed a doctoral thesis on the vocabulary of fashion. In 1950 he accepted a lectureship in French at the University of Alexandria, Egypt, where he met Roland *Barthes and was influenced by the ideas of Roman *Jakobson and Louis *Hjelmslev. Greimas became professor of French language at Ankara, moving to the University of Istanbul, then to the University of Poitiers. In 1965 he succeeded Barthes as director of studies in social sciences at l'École Pratique des Hautes Études.

The three major aspects of Greimasian semiotics correspond to three distinct phases of his career. From the 1950s to the late 1960s, he was establishing basic semantic principles. From the late 1960s to the mid-1970s, his works became the core of the Paris school of structuralism with a syntactic analysis of discourse. The school places less emphasis than other versions of structuralism on cultural codes and conventions that enable readers to recognise that a text requires a certain kind of interpretative reading. Consequently Greimas is perceived as reducing meaning to method and language to forms and relationships. The third phase, beginning in the 1970s, is characterised by his focus on a transformational process linking more abstract and deep structures with surface structures.

The significance of any element in a text for Greimas lies in its difference from other elements. These differences, conceived as a bundle of features, establish meaningfulness. The minimum meaningful unit would have a structure, the 'semiotic square', a crossing of logic and language which identifies logical conjunctions and disjunctions relating semantic features in a text, as Figure 1 demonstrates.

Axis S1–S2 could be called the temperature assertion; s1–s2 would be the negation of this, and called the non-temperature assertion. The square offers a number of logical relations or 'transformations'; opposition, contradiction and implication, the elementary structures of signification.

Applying the semiotic square to narrative syntax, the four-element model provides the only complete system ever devised for investigating narrative structure. Although Greimas died in Paris in 1992, the school he founded continues to broaden its structural analysis to cultural phenomena such as gesture, painting, legal discourse and social science.

Primary works

(1966). *Structural Semantics*. Lincoln, NB: University of Nebraska Press.
(1970). *Du sens*. Paris: Seuil.

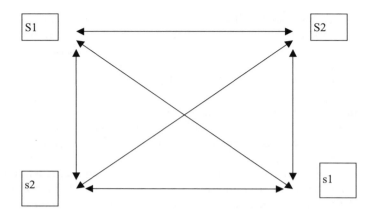

The semiotic square

S1 This solid is hot

S2 This solid is cold

s1 This solid is cool

s2 This solid is lukewarm

Figure 1   The semiotic square.

(1976). *Maupassant: The Semiotics of Text.* Amsterdam: John Benjamins.
(1986). *Semiotique: Dictionnaire raisonné de la théorie du langage.* Vol. 2. Paris: Hachette.
(1987). *Du sens II.* Paris: Seuil.

Further reading

Noth, W. (1995). *Handbook of Semiotics.* Indianapolis: Indiana University Press.
Ubersfeld, A. (1977). *Lire et theatre.* Paris: Editions Sociales.

John Williams

H. P. GRICE

Grice, H. P. (Herbert Paul) (*b.* 1913, *d.* 1988; British), fellow of St John's College, Oxford (1939–67), and professor of philosophy at the University of California, Berkeley (1967–80). A central figure in ordinary language philosophy and a major influence on the development of pragmatics in the late twentieth century; in later life he also worked on theories of rationality, ethics and metaphysics. (*See also* Austin, J. L.; Strawson, P. F.)

Grice grew up in Harborne, Birmingham. His father, Herbert, owned a manufacturing business, and his mother, Mabel (née Felton), ran a small school for local children, including her two sons, in the family home. However, from the age of 13 Grice received a conventional elite education, first at Clifton College, Bristol, and then at Corpus Christi College,

Oxford. His degree was in classics, then the only part of the Oxford curriculum to include philosophy, and he discovered an interest in subtleties of meaning, together with an enthusiasm for philosophical argument. After graduating with first class honours, Grice worked for a year as assistant master at Rossall public (fee-paying) school in Lancashire. He returned to Oxford in 1936, spending two years in graduate study at Merton College and one year as lecturer in philosophy at St John's College, before being elected to a fellowship. World War II almost immediately interrupted his career; he joined the Royal Navy, seeing active service in the North Atlantic, and then working in intelligence at the admiralty. He did not return full-time to St John's until 1945, by which time he was married to Kathleen (née Watson). Grice always preferred his middle name, and was known as Paul to family, friends and colleagues. His early publications are credited to 'H. P. Grice', but in later and less formal days he was generally referred to, and published as, 'Paul Grice'.

Soon after the war Grice became associated with 'ordinary language philosophy', which was to be predominant at Oxford for about twenty years. He always denied that this constituted a single school of thought, but he did acknowledge some general characteristics. There was a respect for 'common-sense' responses to the questions of philosophy, and for the language in which these responses were expressed. Above all there was a belief that ordinary language was not just a legitimate focus for philosophical study, but a valuable resource that could play an active part in address-

ing philosophical questions. Ordinary language had been used to make sense of the world by succeeding generations, something the fashionable jargons of philosophy generally failed to do. In fact, such jargon helped to perpetuate error.

The generally acknowledged leader of ordinary language philosophy was J. L. *Austin; its focus was a regular discussion group on Saturday mornings, which Grice jokingly but irreverently christened 'The Play Group'. Grice was a central member of this, but his own work increasingly differed from Austin's, and he began to doubt some of the basic assumptions of ordinary language philosophy itself. Nevertheless he retained throughout his life a belief in the importance of paying attention to common sense, and to the subtleties of everyday language. He also remained committed to the shared, discursive nature of ordinary language philosophy; he preferred working, and sometimes writing, in collaboration with other philosophers. Writing, however, was a different matter from publishing. Grice wrote prolifically, but was notoriously reluctant to submit his work for publication, perhaps because his perfectionism refused to allow that a piece of work could ever be truly finished. As a result, much of his work remained inaccessible for years, even after it had become successful by reputation.

During the 1950s Grice worked and wrote with fellow philosophers of ordinary language. He collaborated with Geoffrey Warnock on the philosophy of perception and also worked with his colleague and former pupil P. F. *Strawson. The only publication resulting from these collaborations was a joint paper with Strawson, 'In defence of a dogma' (1956), published at Strawson's instigation. Grice and Strawson argue against W. V. O. *Quine's dismissal of the analytic–synthetic distinction. Not only has the distinction proved valuable to philosophers for centuries, they argue, it also has resonances in ordinary language, in the use of such phrases as 'meaning the same as'. Grice later declared himself dissatisfied with the rather simplistic argument of this article, but maintained that the analytic–synthetic distinction should be defended, being of fundamental importance to the philosophy of language. Grice's only solo article during this period was 'Meaning' (1957), also published at Strawson's insistence.

'Meaning' begins with a canonically 'ordinary language' procedure: Grice proposes to approach the philosophical study of meaning by considering the different ways in which the verb 'mean' is ordinarily used. He notes that there are at least two distinct uses, exemplified by 'Those spots mean measles' and 'Those three rings on the bell mean that the bus is full.' In the first case, no agent is involved; it is not possible to say that someone 'meant something by' the spots. This is an example of 'natural meaning'; the spots are a natural sign, or symptom, of the disease. The second case does suggest an agent. The bus conductor meant something by the rings; he intended to communicate that the bus was full, a fact independent of whether the bus was actually full or not. Grice describes this as 'nonnatural meaning', abbreviated to 'meaning$_{NN}$', of

which linguistic meaning is one type. Using the term 'utterance' for any example of meaning$_{NN}$, he argues that the intention of the utterer is central. For meaning$_{NN}$ to succeed it is necessary for an utterer to intend an audience to adopt some belief, and also for the audience to recognise that intention. Using 'A' to stand for the utterer and 'x' for the utterance, ' "A meant$_{NN}$ something by x" is roughly equivalent to "A uttered x with the intention of inducing a belief by means of the recognition of this intention" ' (1989: 219). Grice notes that this definition needs to be expanded to include instances of promoting action (imperatives) as well as inducing belief (declaratives).

The article 'Meaning' has attracted much attention in the philosophy of language, although commentators have often had as much to say about the problems it raises as the elegance of its solutions. Grice was not just offering a philosophical theory based on the common-sense idea that the effect of our utterances depends on what we intend to communicate. His project was much more ambitious. He argued that an account of what A meant$_{NN}$ by x was necessarily prior to an account of the meaning$_{NN}$ of x. In other words, linguistic meaning depends on speaker meaning, itself explained by the cognitive phenomenon of intention; semantics is explained by psychology. This brought criticism from a number of philosophers, including John *Searle, and Stephen Schiffer, whose contribution to the debate was eventually published in Meaning (1972). In response to such critics, and the increasingly elaborate counterexamples they suggested, Grice modified his account during the 1960s, and presented a revised version in 1967 when he delivered the annual William James lecture series at Harvard. In these lectures, entitled 'Logic and Conversation' (published in Grice 1989), he allowed that what an utterer can legitimately intend is constrained by the 'conventional' meaning of an utterance. Although he still maintained that this conventional meaning must ultimately be explained in psychological terms, some saw this concession as fatally weakening Grice's original idea. Generally, however, the revised account of meaning was overshadowed by the earlier lectures in the William James series, in which Grice introduced his concept of 'conversational implicature'.

Grice had been working for some years on a theoretical mechanism to explain a number of philosophical problems, drawing on another common-sense belief about language: that what we say is often different from what we mean. He argues that it is often necessary to distinguish between 'what is said' and 'what is implicated by what is said', introducing the verb 'implicate' and the noun 'implicature' as technical terms. 'What is said' is something close to the troublesome notion of conventional meaning, with the addition of any necessary reference assignment and disambiguation. 'What is implicated' is often central to the significance of an utterance, but is never a factor in determining its literal truth or falsity. In a few cases it depends simply on conventional meaning. So in 'He is an Englishman; he is, therefore, brave', what is said is simply that the referent in question possesses the two qualities of Englishness and bravery. What is convention-

ally implicated is that the bravery is a consequence of the Englishness. Most cases of implicature, however, depend on other factors, outside the language. Grice's central claim is that these factors can be explained in terms of one general principle of human behaviour.

Grice describes conversation as essentially end-driven; it succeeds because people behave in a way most likely to bring about a desired result, either of imparting information or of influencing behaviour. Grice sums this up in his 'co-operative principle': 'Make your conversational contribution such as is required, at the stage at which it occurs, by the accepted purpose or direction of the talk exchange in which you are engaged' (1989: 26). This is characterised in four 'categories', Quantity, Quality, Relation and Manner, each containing a number of 'maxims'. The first three categories are concerned with the information in an utterance. The maxims of Quantity state that there must be neither too little nor too much for the present purposes. Quality stipulates that the speaker must believe the information to be true, and have adequate evidence for it. Relation specifies simply that it must be relevant. Manner is rather different, in that it concerns how the utterance is delivered rather than its content. Grice offers the following maxims as examples: 'Avoid obscurity of expression', 'Avoid ambiguity', 'Be brief', 'Be orderly.'

The categories and maxims may appear to be a disparate collection but, for Grice, to observe them is simply to observe the single co-operative principle in different specific ways. Seen as such, they demonstrate impressive explanatory power. For instance, the use of the indefinite pronoun often suggests that the item specified lacks a particular relation to a relevant person. In Grice's example, 'X is meeting a woman this evening' suggests that the woman is not X's wife, mother or sister. Yet this specific suggestion can hardly be part of the linguistic meaning of 'a', and if it were discovered that the woman was X's relative, the speaker could be accused of being misleading, but not of saying something false. This problem can be explained with reference to Quantity. If the speaker were in a position to give more information, to specify some relationship between X and the woman, it would be most co-operative to do so. Therefore, the hearer is entitled to infer that no more specific information can truthfully be offered; the fact that the woman is not related to X is a conversational implicature of the utterance.

This is an example of a 'generalised conversational implicature'. Many implicatures, however, are 'particularised'; they depend on a wider context. If A says 'Smith doesn't seem to have a girlfriend these days' and B replies 'He has been paying a lot of visits to New York lately', B implicates that he knows or guesses that Smith has a girlfriend in New York; otherwise he would be ignoring the demands of Relation. The successful interpretation of implicature, then, depends on the assumption that the speaker is adhering to the co-operative principle. In some cases, this assumption requires more work. 'Miss X produced a series of sounds that corresponded closely with the score of

"Home Sweet Home"' is a great deal less brief and more obscure than its apparent paraphrase 'Miss X sang "Home Sweet Home"'. On the assumption that the speaker is being co-operative and is not simply disregarding Manner, the hearer recovers the implicature that there was some severe defect in Miss X's performance. In such cases, the speaker is said to be 'flouting' a maxim: deliberately and ostentatiously disregarding it in order to convey an implicature.

Grice's achievement in 'Logic and Conversation' was to offer a systematic model of linguistic interaction, taking account of the fact that context is often crucial to the difference between literal and intended meaning. In so doing he was distancing himself from ordinary language philosophy, in which the concentration of ordinary use as the best – indeed the only – guide to meaning did not allow for the 'levels' of interpretation Grice was suggesting. Moreover, ordinary language philosophy was given to descriptive attention to subtleties of use, rather than to general theories. But Grice's move away from Oxford philosophy was not just intellectual; in 1967 he took up a post at the University of California, Berkeley, where he spent the rest of his career, becoming full professor in 1975. At Berkeley he continued to enjoy discussion and collaboration with students and colleagues, and found an appreciative audience for his ideas.

'Logic and Conversation' was an almost immediate success in philosophy and more particularly in linguistics. Some linguists, particularly 'generative semanticists', were beginning to think beyond the exclusively grammatical approach offered by the theories of Noam *Chomsky, looking for ways to incorporate context into linguistic theory, and Grice's ideas seemed to provide just that. Although generative semantics ultimately failed in its ambitious project, it introduced into linguistics a serious interest in aspects of meaning beyond the logical and truth-conditional, and Grice's work played a central part in the emergence of the discipline of pragmatics. This was despite the rather chequered publication history of the William James lectures, which appeared piecemeal over the years following their original presentation. Such was the demand for the lectures that they were circulated widely in mimeograph for a number of years. The lecture introducing the theory of conversation was first published in 1975, also under the title 'Logic and conversation'. Some critics have concentrated on the vagueness of the theory: the underspecified nature of 'what is said', and the lack of clarity over the justifications for, and divisions between, the maxims. Others have accused Grice of an idealistic view of human nature, even of attempting to lay down rules of etiquette for conversational practice. In fact, his interest was not in legislating how conversation should be conducted, but in identifying certain end-driven tendencies in interactive behaviour, and explaining how they contribute to communication. Chiefly he was suggesting a sensitivity to how language is used as a solution to certain philosophical problems. Nevertheless the theory of conversation has proved an immensely suggestive tool for linguistic analysis, being applied to data as diverse as jokes, gendered language, literature, classroom interaction, legal proceedings and advertising. There have been various proposed revisions or more complete reworkings. For instance, in the 1980s Dan Sperber and Deirdre Wilson's 'Relevance Theory' (1995) suggested that the Gricean maxims could be reduced to a single 'principle of relevance', not a generalisation that could be followed or flouted, but a necessary and inescapable aspect of human cognition.

Grice's later work is less well known in linguistics, partly because he moved away from a direct engagement with language to concentrate on other aspects of human nature, particularly rationality and ethics. However, he maintained a respect for language as a guide to philosophical thought, and as a form of behaviour in need of sophisticated explanation. In his 1979 lecture series on rationality (published as Grice 2001) he draws on the various uses of the word 'reason', and related vocabulary, to propose a single cognitive faculty of reasoning concerned with both practical and nonpractical reasoning: with wanting and believing. In his 1981 article 'Meaning revisited' he offers a place for language in rational psychology; it is highly desirable for rational creatures to be able to communicate their beliefs and wants so as to induce beliefs and promote behaviour, or at least the intention to behaviour, in others. In his 1983 lecture series on ethics (published as Grice 1991), he approaches ethical value by considering the sentences in which ethical judgements are generally expressed. He argues that objective ethical value exists, but only because rational creatures exist whose defining property is the ability to attribute value; value exists because people exist. Grice was always wary of divisions of philosophy into branches and fields, and at the end of his life he was working on an account of metaphysics as a unified philosophical approach to the full range of human experience.

Grice believed that philosophy could and should be fun. This belief is apparent in the wit of his writing, the bizarre humour of many of his examples, and his enjoyment of discussion. Philosophy was much more than a job for him; it was an all-consuming interest that he continued to pursue after his retirement in 1980. He found time for more conventional pastimes too, such as bridge and chess. He was also a passionate fan of cricket. During his active days he played for a number of clubs, and even at county level for Oxfordshire. Grice was a heavy smoker and during the 1970s was increasingly affected by a chronic cough. He gave up smoking in 1980, but a few years later was diagnosed with emphysema and suffered deteriorating health. Nevertheless, he oversaw work on *Studies in the Way of Words* (1989), bringing together the complete William James lectures and many of his other essays on the philosophy of language. The manuscript was completed just before he died in Berkeley on 28 August 1988. The lecture series on rationality and on value were later edited by former colleagues and published as *Aspects of Reason* (2001) and *The Conception of Value* (1991). However, it is for his psychological treatment of meaning and most of all for his account of communication as an essentially co-operative, end-driven form of behaviour that Grice's work continues to be most celebrated.

Primary works

(1989). *Studies in the Way of Words*. Cambridge, MA: Harvard University Press.
(1991). *The Conception of Value*. Oxford: Clarendon Press.
(2001). *Aspects of Reason*. Oxford: Clarendon Press.

Further reading

Chapman, Siobhan (2005). *Paul Grice: Philosopher and Linguist*. Basingstoke: Palgrave.
Grandy, Richard and Warner, Richard (eds) (1986). *Philosophical Grounds of Rationality: Intentions, Categories, Ends*. Oxford: Clarendon Press.
Levinson, Stephen (1983). *Pragmatics*. Cambridge: Cambridge University Press.
Schiffer, Stephen (1972). *Meaning*. Oxford: Clarendon Press.
Sperber, Dan and Wilson, Deirdre (1995). *Relevance*. Second edition. Oxford: Blackwell. First edition 1986.

Siobhan Chapman

JACOB GRIMM

Grimm, Jacob (Ludwig Carl) (*b*.1785, *d*. 1863; German), librarian in Kassel, professor and librarian at Göttingen University (1829–37), finally professor at Berlin University (1840–63). Historical linguist, philologist, folklorist, anthropologist, lexicographer and Germanist, whose pioneering and enduring work is foundational in all these areas. (*See also* Bopp, Franz; Brugmann, Karl; Humboldt, Wilhelm von; Rask, Rasmus.)

Grimm was born in Hanau, one of six children (including his younger brother Wilhelm, a life-long collaborator). After studying law at Marburg, Grimm began a prolific working life, sometimes interrupted by political engagement (he and Wilhelm were dismissed from Göttingen for political protests). He spent over a third of his working life as a librarian with light duties, giving him time to write.

One of the best known of all linguists, Grimm's greatest fame came as one of the 'Brothers Grimm' (with Wilhelm) publishing folkloric collections of fairy tales that were seen as serious contributions to the study of folklore. This was linked with Grimm's linguistics by the then widespread Romantic worldview and by his politics: both the fairy tales and his work on the history and origins of the German and Germanic languages were a link to a mythical medieval past. They were also a link to Germanic culture among Germans who had suffered from foreign occupation and from the proliferation of small German statelets. Among general linguists his fame derives from his description of the phonological changes (now known as 'Grimm's Law') which describe how Germanic consonantal systems differ spectacularly from other Indo-European languages (for example, English *FaTHer* corresponds with Latin *PaTer*).

This was set out in the second edition of his monumental *Deutsche Grammatik* (which translates as 'Germanic Grammar', 1819–37), quite an early work at its commencement, but not his first. It forms only one part of the *Grammatik*, however, which for the first time described the historical development of the phonology, morphology and simple sentence syntax of all Germanic languages. The *Grammatik* established historical work (particularly historical phonology) as the centrepoint of linguistics, following *Bopp's pioneering comparative work, and providing the foundations for the neogrammarians' sound laws (see *Brugmann). While his results have often since been revised, the concepts Grimm discovered, shaped or named (such as *auslaut, umlaut* and *ablaut*) often still underlie linguistic work, diachronic (language change) and synchronic (language at a particular time), Germanic and general.

He published much other work, typically descriptive rather than theoretical, but paradigm-creating, none the less. The last years of his life were largely spent working on another key work, the vast *Deutsches Wörterbuch* (*German Dictionary*, 1854–1960) which he founded jointly with Wilhelm. This was the first such compendious (and non-prescriptive) dictionary on historical principles.

With *Rask and Bopp, whose work he valued, Grimm is seen as a pioneer of nineteenth-century, scientific, uniformitarian historical linguistics, which eventually led to the development of modern formal linguistics. He was certainly the founder of German(ic) historical linguistics and his work was immediately recognised as crucial by his contemporaries. He survived his brother by four years and was still working on their dictionary when he died at the age of 78.

Primary works

(1819–37; second edition of vol. 1, 1822). *Deutsche Grammatik* (4 vols). Göttingen: Dieterich'sche Buchhandlung. Reprinted in facsimile, 1999. London: Routledge.
(1854–1960) (with Wilhelm Grimm and later collaborators). *Deutsches Wörterbuch* (16 vols). Leipzig: Hirzel.

Further reading

Collinge, N. E. (1985). 'Grimm's Law' and 'Appendix II'. In N. E. Collinge, *The Laws of Indo-European*. Amsterdam: John Benjamins.
Koerner, E. F. K. (1989). 'Jacob Grimm's place in the foundation of linguistics as a science'. In E. F. K. Koerner, *Practising Linguistic Historiography*. Amsterdam: John Benjamins.
Morpurgo Davies, Anna (1997). *History of Linguistics*. Vol. 4: *Nineteenth-Century Linguistics*. London: Longman.

Patrick Honeybone

M. A. K. HALLIDAY

Halliday, M. A. K. (Michael Alexander Kirkwood) (*b.* 1925; British), professor of general linguistics at University College London (1965–70), professor of linguistics at University of Illinois, Chicago (1973–5), and then at University of Sydney (1976–87); since 1987, emeritus professor at the Universities of Sydney and Macquarie. Linguist in the functional tradition who has developed an all-embracing model of language in its sociocultural context known as Systemic Functional Linguistics (SFL). Perhaps the most salient features of his theory are the emphasis on language as a system network of choices, and the division of language into three metafunctions, each corresponding to different sets of choices in the grammar. (*See also* Bernstein, Basil; Firth, J. R.; Hjelmslev, Louis; Malinowski, Bronislaw; Sinclair, John; Whorf, Benjamin Lee.)

Michael Halliday was born in Leeds, England. Both his parents were teachers and after studying Chinese language and literature as an undergraduate, he himself taught Chinese for several years. One of his university tutors, who was to have an important influence on his thinking, was *Firth; and it was through Firth that Halliday came across the ideas of *Malinowski. Halliday worked on his doctoral thesis, 'The Language of the Chinese *Secret History of the Mongols*', at the Universities of Peking and Lingnan in China, and the PhD was awarded by the University of Cambridge in 1955. During his time in London in the 1960s Halliday was in contact with *Bernstein, whom he regards as one of the few sociologists who took full account of language in his theories of cultural transmissions. In the same period, Halliday engaged with the approaches that had emerged as dominant in America, particularly that of Noam *Chomsky and his followers.

But Halliday rapidly became disenchanted both with what he saw as the restrictive narrowness of these approaches and with the dismissive response given to his attempts to explore their wider implications. He claims a closer affinity with the alternative American tradition, represented in different ways by linguists such as *Whorf, *Sapir and *Pike; and his work also falls very much into the European tradition from *Saussure to *Hjelmslev and Firth. This tradition has typically been more interested in function and meaning than has the American mainstream.

Halliday's early thinking on linguistic theory is best represented by his 1961 paper 'Categories of the theory of grammar', in which he sets out a general approach to grammatical description known as scale and category grammar. He proposes four types of linguistic categories, related by three scales, as the basis for the description. Only a brief illustration of this model is necessary, since although it underlies much of the later theory, the emphases have shifted radically. One of the categories proposed is the unit. The four units Halliday argues are needed are clause, group, word and morpheme (sentence was originally included but was later dropped, since it is seen as an orthographic rather than a grammatical unit). Units are related to each other by the scale of rank: clauses are made up of one or more groups, which are made up of one or more words, which in turn are made up of one or more morphemes. So in the utterance 'our cats won't eat fish', the clause is made up of three groups 'our cats', 'won't eat' and 'fish'; the group 'our cats' is made up of two

words; and the word 'cats' is made up of two morphemes 'cat' and 's'. The rank scale was hypothesized to be exhaustive – that is, every part of an utterance could be accounted for at all ranks – although this requirement was later relaxed in certain respects. Nevertheless the concept continues to be used in exploring the different kinds of choices available at different ranks, especially clause and group. The paper more generally reflects Halliday's ongoing interest in 'grammatics', the study of possible ways of thinking about grammar.

During the 1960s Halliday's ways of thinking developed along two main lines, which became increasingly interdependent and formed the basis of SFL as it stands at the beginning of the twenty-first century. First, in the papers collected in the 1976b volume, the idea of system, one of the original categories in scale and category grammar, took over a central role, to the point where it appears in the name of the theory ('systemic' means roughly 'based on systems'). This change of emphasis follows naturally from a focus on function rather than structure as the generative heart of language. For Halliday the most illuminating way of looking at language functions is to see them in terms of choices in context. To take a very simple example: speakers have a range of greetings available in English, which include 'how do you do' and 'hiya'. The choice between these is influenced by contextual factors such as the relationship between the speaker and addressee. But Halliday stresses that the influence is not one-way: while speakers show their understanding of what the context is by their choices, those language choices simultaneously create the context. By choosing 'hiya', they project (the technical term is 'construe') a more informal atmosphere: for both speaker and addressee, part of the meaning of 'hiya' is that it has been chosen rather than other possible greetings.

The same principle, of there being sets of choices in context that are meaningful in relation to other possible choices, can be applied to cases that are more clearly grammatical and more complex. For example, there is a choice between modalised expressions such as the following: 'The problem *seems* to arise because...', '*It appears that* the problem arises because...' and '*I think that* the problem arises because...'. These are close in meaning, but one will feel more appropriate in certain contexts than the others. In order to show these more complex choices, Halliday uses systems. A system is a set of choices that become available once an entry condition is satisfied; once one choice has been made in the system, more delicate choices are opened up. Figure 2 illustrates this with part of the system network of mood in the clause in English.

The set of choices in Figure 2 has the entry condition 'independent clause'. Reading across the figure from left to right, the choices become increasingly more delicate; delicacy was one of the original scales in scale and category grammar. An independent clause may be either indicative or imperative; if indicative, it may be interrogative or declarative; if interrogative, it may be WH- or yes/no; and so on. In this model structures are the means by which functions are realised or expressed and the boxes in the figure give the realisation statements. If yes/no interrogative is chosen, for example, this is realised by the presence of Subject and Finite (inherited from the realisation of indicative), in the order Finite followed by Subject; for example, '*did you* lock up?'.

Working in this way, we can establish an immensely complex network of interlocking systems. Halliday argues that three large-scale groupings of systems then emerge, with interactions between systems within each grouping but with relatively little interaction

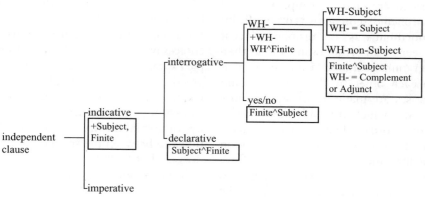

Figure 2 The mood system.

between the groupings. This is the basis of the hypothesis that there are three 'metafunctions', that is, three overarching functions realized through language, each expressed through different aspects of the grammar. For example, language is used to represent the speaker's view of the world, and this is known as the ideational metafunction, corresponding to the traditional view of 'content'. Language is simultaneously used to enact social relations with the addressee through the interpersonal metafunction, and it is used in a way such that these two functions are carried out in text that is recognisably fitted to its context, known as the textual metafunction. Every utterance performs these three functions; the three strands of grammatical realization are interwoven in the wording of the clause. If we take a sample clause, 'You can shoot images for email', the writer represents a physical process of 'shooting' involving an Actor 'you', a Goal 'images' and a Circumstance 'for email'. These equate roughly to 'doer', 'doing', 'done-to', 'purpose' (the ideational perspective). The clause is a positive, modalised declarative, functioning to offer information to the addressee (the interpersonal perspective), and the starting point for the clause, the Theme in Hallidayan terms, is the Subject 'you', which in English is the unmarked choice (the textual perspective). Each of these sets of choices can be manipulated separately to give a different configuration: 'You can see images on email' (Senser, mental process, Phenomenon, Circumstance of location); 'Can you shoot images for email?' (interrogative, demanding in-

formation from the addressee); 'For email you can shoot images' (Circumstance as marked Theme). Halliday gives a detailed description of English in terms of the three metafunctions in *An Introduction to Functional Grammar* (1985).

Halliday argues that one key advantage in working with metafunctionally organised system networks is that it 'free[s] the grammar from the restrictions imposed by structure' (2002: 12). Since there is only one sequential unfolding of wording when we speak or write, it is extremely difficult to force descriptions of the different kinds of meaning into a single set of labels, particularly since different strands of meaning are realised through different parts of the clause, which are not necessarily coextensive. Even more importantly, the way in which different kinds of meaning are realised varies: Halliday adopts Pike's comparison of the clause to matter in physics, which can be viewed as particle, field or wave. Breaking the clause into constituents – concrete-seeming 'particles' of language – privileges the ideational perspective; this has been the dominant, often exclusive, methodology in structural linguistics. But in order to capture the full meaning we also need the interpersonal perspective, viewing it in terms of prosodic meanings which, field-like, encompass whole units such as the clause in their scope. From the textual perspective it can best be seen as 'wave', pulses of informational prominence running through the text.

The second major emphasis that emerged in Halliday's thinking is the importance of modelling language as social phenomenon, or as the title of his 1978 book puts it, 'social semiotic'. One stimulus for this shift was his work with teachers. During the 1960s, for example, he directed two projects which resulted in language awareness textbooks for schools. This interest continued after he moved to Australia in 1976. There a group of linguists and teachers formed around him and subsequently did groundbreaking work on the language of education, introducing genre-based approaches to literacy across the schools' curriculum. As mentioned above, Halliday sees the relationship between language and social context as reflexive. Language reflects sociocultural norms, but it simultaneously constructs, maintains and changes them. Our experience of the world is mediated primarily through language, and as Whorf argued, the linguistic resources available to us shape the way that we see the world. Furthermore, the way we see the world shapes the way we use language and the way language has evolved.

Halliday's approach to modelling context in relation to language is based on the three metafunctions projected 'upwards'. Any of the contexts in which language is situated can be described in terms of three dimensions of variation: field, tenor and mode. Note that 'field' is here used in a different sense than in the physics terminology above. Here field relates to the nature of the social action involving language, including what is being talked about; tenor relates to the people involved in the interaction and the relationship between them; and mode relates to how the language is functioning in the interaction, for example whether it is written or spoken. Recurrent configurations of field, tenor and mode – that is, types of situation that we recognise as distinctive, such as school lessons, or giving instructions for cooking dishes – are construed by different registers, indicated by recurrent configurations of linguistic choices; for example, the higher than average occurrence of imperatives with certain types of processes in recipes. The interdependence with language is shown in the fact that, Halliday argues, field primarily influences and is construed by ideational choices in the grammar; tenor stands in the same relation to interpersonal choices, and mode to textual choices.

In 1976 Halliday published the book for which he is probably best known by scholars outside the SFL community, *Cohesion in English*. This was co-authored with his wife, Ruqaiya Hasan, who is an important linguist in her own right. While figures such as Roland *Barthes, working in the field of semiology, were also interested in taking linguistic analysis beyond the sentence, Halliday and Hasan's book played a major role in establishing text as a viable focus of linguistic study, in contrast to the insistence in mainstream linguistics on the sentence as the upper limit. For Halliday, text is central, since it represents the instantiation of the language system. Rather than positing grammar as an abstract competence that each speaker in some sense possesses, he sees the language system as the sum of all its instantiations in text. As such it is therefore essentially a social phenomenon that can only be properly explored through instances of use. He shares with *Sinclair a firm belief in the importance of the corpus, explaining this by using the simile of the relation between weather and climate. Weather is what we experience on a daily basis; climate is the picture we get if we stand back and examine the patterns from a long-term perspective. These include the same phenomena, but seen on different time-scales. Another way of putting this is that the weather 'instantiates' the climate in the same way as text, our daily experience of language, instantiates the language system. Since the climate is the sum of patterns of weather, the weather on any individual day represents (part of) the climate and simultaneously affects it, however slightly. Similarly, each time someone uses language, they are both activating (part of) the system and, to an infinitesimal degree, changing it. The system is therefore meta-stable but constantly in a state of gradual change.

Halliday's contribution to linguistic thinking can be highlighted by a comparison of his approach with the dominant theoretical approaches of the second part of the twentieth century, especially those associated with Chomsky. The latter set out to explain linguistic form in terms of the genetically determined characteristics of a hypothesised language faculty that each human inherits. In contrast, Halliday has consistently argued that language must be explained in terms of social factors: language is as it is because of the functions that it is designed to serve in social communication. For the 'biological' approaches, modularity is a key methodological and theoretical tenet. Different aspects of language can best be studied separately and are hypothesised to call on different parts of cognitive resources. Thus lexis and syntax are kept apart; lexical items are seen essentially as fillers that, with some constraints, can be inserted into syntactic structures that are generated independently. More generally, meaning is kept distinct from syntax, and is studied in semantics, with some aspects further segregated in another division, pragmatics. For Halliday, on the other hand, meaning is central. Language is above all a resource for making meaning. Therefore his model of language begins from an analysis of the kinds of meanings that can be made. Lexis is seen as intimately involved in meaning-making, as 'the most delicate grammar' ('grammar' in his usage is in fact short-hand for 'lexico-grammar'). The lexico-grammar is 'natural' – that is, motivated by the semantics – rather than arbitrary, and can only be understood in relation to the semantics. Since meaning is reflexive of context, pragmatic use is also part of the core. Nor does Halliday find it necessary to distinguish what is generally called sociolinguistics, as proposed by *Labov and others. Halliday holds that linguistics should be inherently oriented towards the social. One major aspect of his importance is that, in the face of an aggressively promoted view of linguistics as mentalist, formal and compartmentalised, he has maintained the viability of an alternative tradition, that is social, semantic and holistic.

As the *Collected Works* show, Halliday's linguistic interests are remarkably wide-ranging. He has written not only on grammar and grammatics, but on language acquisition, discourse analysis, language in education, social semiotics, the language of science, and computational and quantitative approaches to linguistics. His work is used in these and other areas such as critical discourse analysis and natural language generation, and has been applied to a variety of languages including Chinese, Japanese, Tagalog and indigenous Australian languages. Although formally retired, he has continued to extend the SFL model of language. One recent extension is summarised in the subtitle of the 1999 co-authored book, *A Language-Based Approach to Cognition*. This explores in depth his belief that 'the development of the brain is the development of the ability to mean' (2002: 3) in both phylogenetic (language evolution) and ontogenetic (child language acquisition) terms. Intriguingly, at a conference in 2002 he raised the possibility that systems, one of the pillars of the theory, may have outlived their usefulness and that other forms of representation may be more appropriate. At the time of writing (2003), it remains to be seen what these might be.

Primary works

(1961, reprinted in vol. 1 of the *Collected Works*, 2002). 'Categories of the theory of grammar'. *Word*. Vol. 17(3): 241–92.

(1973). *Explorations in the Functions of Language*. London: Arnold.

(1975). *Learning How to Mean: Explorations in the Development of Language*. London: Arnold.

(1976a). (with Ruqaiya Hasan). *Cohesion in English* (English Language Series 9). London: Longman.

(1976b). *System and Function in Language* (Selected Papers). G. Kress (ed.). Oxford: Oxford University Press.

(1978). *Language as Social Semiotic: The Social Interpretation of Language and Meaning*. London: Arnold.

(1985, second edition 1994, third edition with Christian Matthiessen 2003). *An Introduction to Functional Grammar*. London: Arnold.

(1993) (with James R. Martin). *Writing Science: Literacy and Discursive Power*. London and Washington, DC: Farmer Press.

(1999) (with Christian Matthiessen). *Construing Experience through Meaning: A Language-Based Approach to Cognition*. London and New York: Cassell.

(2002–). *Collected Works of M. A. K. Halliday* (10 vols). J. Webster (ed.). London and New York: Continuum.

Further reading

de Beaugrande, Robert (1991). *Linguistic Theory: The Discourse of Fundamental Works*. London: Longman.

Butler, Christopher, S. (2003). *Structure and Function: A Guide to Three Major Structural-Functional Theories* (2 vols). Amsterdam: John Benjamins.

Eggins, Suzanne (1994). *An Introduction to Systemic Functional Linguistics*. London: Pinter.

Thompson, Geoff (2003). *Introducing Functional Grammar*. Second edition. London: Arnold.

Geoff Thompson

G. W. F. HEGEL

Hegel, G. W. F. (Georg Wilhelm Friedrich) (*b.* 1770, *d.* 1831; German), tutor, newspaper editor, secondary school principal, professor, chair of philosophy and finally rector at the University of Berlin (1818–31). Philosopher who shaped nineteenth-century discussions concerning semiology, the value of speech and writing, and the debate over alphabetic and hieroglyphic scripts. (*See also* Derrida, Jacques; Leibniz, Gottfried Wilhelm; Marx, Karl; Mill, J. S.; Russell, Bertrand; Saussure, Ferdinand de.)

Born in Stuttgart, Hegel was the son of Georg Ludwig Hegel and Maria Magdalena Louisa Fromm Hegel. Raised in a religiously conservative environment, Hegel first studied to be a minister. Soon realising that his interests lay elsewhere, he devoted his energy to studying culture and philosophy, earning degrees at Tübingen and Jena. His professional career as an educator and writer took him to Bern, Frankfurt, Jena, Nürnberg, Heidelberg and Berlin. He married Maria Helena Susanna von Tucher in 1811, and they had three children. Hegel is well known for his treatment of history, language, psychology and religion in his philosophical system.

Although Hegel makes frequent reference to language, *Philosophy of the Mind*, part three of his *Encyclopaedia of the Philosophical Sciences* (1830 edition), contains the most extensive references to his understanding of language. He portrays the emergence and development of the entire system of language as an evolutionary process in the expression of thoughts and ideas; he sees a progression from images to symbols, from symbols to signs, and finally from signs to arbitrary sequences of sounds, each stage representing less of a visual connection to the object or concept in question and a greater reliance on conventionality to convey meaning.

Assigning a great deal of importance to language, Hegel believed that human thought is impossible without words. He states that language consists of two elements: (1) speech sounds that have lost any independent meaning they might have once had, and (2) grammar that represents a system of rules and relationships introduced into language by the human intellect. Unlike *Leibniz, Hegel argues that an alphabetic script is preferable to a hieroglyphic script. Alphabetic scripts simplify communication, reveal properties of the spoken word and focus attention on words as separate, distinct entities. Finally Hegel gives spoken language priority over written language.

Hegel influenced many subsequent philosophies. *Marx based his theory of the dialectic and his linguistic speculations, in part, on Hegel's writings, while *Saussure supported Hegel's analysis of signs and symbols. *Mill and *Russell expanded on Hegel's belief that words are understood as distinct entities, not as conglomerations of small individual parts, and *Derrida found intellectual stimulation in Hegel's work on semiology. Hegel died of cholera in Berlin in 1831.

Primary works

(1830). *Hegel's Philosophy of Mind: Part Three of the Encyclopaedia of the Philosophical Sciences*. William Wallace (trans.). Oxford: Clarendon Press, 1971.

Further reading

Derrida, Jean Jacques (1972). 'The pit and the pyramid: an introduction to Hegel's semiology'. In *Margins of Philosophy*. Alan Bass (trans.). Chicago: University of Chicago Press, 1982.

Pinkard, Terry (2000). *Hegel: A Biography*. Cambridge: Cambridge University Press.

David V. Witkosky

LOUIS HJELMSLEV

Hjelmslev, Louis (Trolle) (*b.* 1899, *d.* 1965; Danish), reader at Aarhus University in Denmark (1934–7) then appointed professor in 'comparative linguistics' at the University of Copenhagen (1937), a position he held till his death in 1965. Hjelmslev founded the so-called Copenhagen School of Linguistics and set up the special programme in 'structural linguistics' called 'glossematics'. Besides his inflence on structuralism, he inspired a generation of Danish linguists and was celebrated for the rigour of his theoretical reasoning. (*See also* Chomsky, Noam; Greimas, Algirdas; Jakobson, Roman; Rask, Rasmus; Saussure, Ferdinand de.)

Hjelmslev was born in Copenhagen. His father was a professor of mathematics with a special interest in geometry, a field in which he was well known. Hjelmslev's father was totally absorbed by his professional life, while his mother's health was fragile, so Hjelmslev had ample opportunity to spend his time as he liked, and lan-

guage soon became his main interest. He later explained that at 10 years old he paid the family's housemaid a penny an hour for allowing him to teach her Italian and that, aged 13, he read Otto Jespersen's *The Logic of Language*. One other inspiration was his study of the translation of one of Hans Christian Andersen's fairy tales, 'The Story of a Mother', into fifteen languages. He would later go on to edit the publication of another fairy tale translated into twenty-five languages. It was a natural choice for him to study linguistics. He made his first academic journey abroad in 1921 to study Lithuanian, an experience of which traces can be found throughout his works. He earned his MA in 1923.

He studied abroad for some years, in Prague (1923–4) and Paris (1926–7). Given that *Jakobson was a major figure in structuralist linguistics in Prague at the time, it is surprising that he and Hjelmslev apparently did not actually meet during Hjelmslev's stay in the city. In 1925 he both got married and read *Saussure's *Cours de linguistique générale* (1916), and he spent his time in Paris writing a book: *Principes de grammaire générale* (1928), in which he tried to identify the principles governing the grammars of all languages. The book offers some of the basic theoretical thoughts of 'glossematics', an attempt to provide a formal, scientific explanation for language as a whole. It was quite an achievement, almost 350 pages of mostly theoretical reasoning, and it prepared the ground for his later theoretical ambitions.

Back in Copenhagen in 1931, and inspired by the Prague Linguistic

Circle, Hjelmslev founded the Copenhagen Linguistic Circle. He received his doctorate in 1932 for a thesis on sound changes in the Baltic languages: *Etudes baltiques*. The 1930s were in many ways the most creative period in Hjelmslev's life: he developed his theory of 'glossematics'; he was the editor of *Rask's *Udvalgte Afhandlinger* (*Selected Writings*) (1932–5), and in 1939 he founded, and became with Viggo Brøndal (1939–42) the editor of, the journal *Acta Linguistica* (from 1965 *Acta Linguistica Hafniensia*), including *Jakobson in the journal's International Council (1939–78). The detailed theory of glossematics was developed in Aarhus between 1934 and 1937, while Hjelmslev was working with Hans Jørgen Uldall (1907–57). In fact Uldall coined the new theory's name. Although by 1937 an almost completed piece of work, the glossematic programme was, apart from minor papers and presentations at conferences, not published until 1943, with Hjelmslev as the sole author. At the outset Hjelmslev and Uldall had intended to publish a book on 'glossematics' with the working title *An Outline of Glossematics*. They produced the preliminaries of a major work in the 1930s. A manuscript 'Sprogteori' (language theory) is recorded in the year 1943, but it was not published, and in 1943 Hjelmslev published *Omkring sprogteoriens grundlæggelse* (*Prolegomena to a Theory of Language)* (1953). The major theoretical account (*Sprogteori*) was not published until 1975 in an English translation: *Résumé of a Theory of Language*. This is the only publicly accessible account of the technical details of the theory.

These two later ones are the central ones on 'glossematics', the ultimate goal of which was to establish linguistics as a science, and which is an attempt to create a thoroughly formal system to grasp the whole of language as an immanent structure. One should observe that the *Prolegomena* is, according to Hjelmslev, not an account of a theory of linguistics but an exposition of the prerequisites of any such theory. Another observation is that, in order to make linguistics a science, in principle all previous linguistics has to be abandoned. This is also the point of departure of 'glossematics'; it claims to start from scratch. This is likewise what is signalled by giving this new science a special name, derived from Greek *glossa* 'language'.

Hjelmslev's project was much inspired by 'logical positivism' (see *Ayer) in that he abandons 'metaphysical claims' and 'psychology', and sees 'an algebra of language' as the only adequate instrument in linguistics revealing the 'structure of language'. When inaugurating his scientific programme Hjelmslev makes some implicit assumptions. First, language is a system of linguistic 'signs', much in the spirit of Saussure but in a revised mode: not as a sign for something else but as an internal structure, the relation of which to something else is not relevant to linguistic theory. Second, a 'linguistic sign' is a connection between 'expression' and 'content', a relation for which Hjelmslev chooses the term 'function', so that 'expression' and 'content' become the 'functives' ('the terminals of a function') of that relation. At this point Hjelmslev may be the most extreme structuralist of all, since he claims that only the 'functions have scientific existence'. In other words, the only thing that exists is structures, and structures are nothing but (dependence) relations. Accordingly he develops a complicated nomenclature of 'functions' and 'functives', the most important of which are the terms 'constant', a 'functive whose presence is a necessary condition for the presence' of another functive, and 'variable', which is a 'not necessary' condition.

The wealth of special names makes it sometimes hard to follow the line of reasoning, and the abstractness of the notions makes it hard to evaluate what they refer to. This also applies to two specific features of the theory: first, the idea that both sides of the linguistic sign, 'expression' and 'content', should be analysed by the same principles; and second, the theoretical concepts of 'form' and 'substance'. The first assumption implies that minimal units of the same nature can be found on both sides of the linguistic sign; that is, just as the phoneme is the minimal expressional unit so there is a minimal unit in the 'content', though Hjelmslev never develops the claim. The other problem concerns 'form' vs. 'substance', notions the history of which goes far back, but Hjelmslev has a special interpretation of their meaning. 'Form' is not in fact expression but 'structure'. Thus there is 'expression form' as well as 'content form', while 'substance' can best be understood as a kind of formed matter. The term for formed matter used by Hjelmslev is, in Danish, *mening*, the English cognate of which is *meaning*, while the Hjelmslev tradition of translations into English has chosen the word 'purport'. The organisational structure this terminology supports has consequences for the methodological principles, in that Hjelmslev claims that 'glossematics' is able to find the structures of language and languages without reference to 'substance'. Whether the claim is justified is still a matter of debate among scholars.

In connection with his professional life Hjelmslev travelled a lot and, especially after World War II, he held a number of honorary and other offices, both domestic and abroad. Among them he became an honorary member of the Linguistic Society of America. Hjelmslev was an outstanding scholar and a special character with a thorough-going knowledge of a very large number of languages, and he carried out and inspired much reflection on linguistic matters. Glossematics itself has not had an obvious, long-lasting effect on linguistics, but nevertheless Hjelmslev is a key figure in the 'algebraic turn' of the discipline and its attempts to become more rigorous and scientific. One reason for the relative obscurity of Hjelmslev's legacy may be that his opinions in linguistics were radical and his thoughts were extremely abstract, or, as phrased by one scholar, he was 'digging for the roots while trying not to get dirty' (de Beaugrande 1991: 122).

Primary works

(1928). *Principes de grammaire générale.* Copenhagen: Høst and Søn. Reprinted Copenhagen: Munksgaard, 1968.

(1932). *Etudes baltiques.* Copenhagen: Levin and Munksgaard.

(1943). *Omkring sprogteoriens grund-lashggelse.* Copenhagen: University of Copenhagen. Reprinted Akademisk Forlag, 1966. *Prolegomena to a Theory of Language.* Francis J. Whitfield (trans.). Baltimore: Waverly Press, 1953.

(1957) (with Hans Jørgen Uldall). *Outline of Glossematics.* Copenhagen: Nordisk Sprog-og Kulturforlag.

(1959). *Essais linguistiques.* Copenhagen: Nordisk Sprog- og Kulturforlag.

(1973). *Essais linguistiques* II. Copenhagen: Nordisk Sprog- og Kulturforlag.

(1975). *Résumé of a Theory of Language.* Copenhagen: Nordisk Sprog-og Kulturforlag.

Further reading

de Beaugrande, Robert (1991). *Linguistic Theory: The Discourse of Fundamental Works.* New York: Longman.

Fischer-Jørgensen, Eli (1967). 'Form and substance in glossematics'. *Acta Linguistica Hafniensia.* Vol. X, 1–33.

Fischer-Jørgensen, Eli (1975). *Trends in Phonological Theory: A Historical Introduction.* Copenhagen: Akademisk Forlag.

Togeby, Knud (1957). *Structure immante de la langue française.* Paris: Larousse.

Hans Götzsche

CHARLES HOCKETT

Hockett, Charles (Francis) (*b.* 1916, *d.* 2000; American), taught at Cornell (1945–82), theoretical linguist, musician, composer. His classic 1958 textbook is an elegant statement of the last generation of American structural linguists. (*See also* Bloomfield, Leonard; Chomsky, Noam; Pike, Kenneth L; Sapir, Edward.)

Charles Francis Hockett was born on 17 January 1916 in Columbus, Ohio. After completing his MA in ancient history at Ohio State University in 1936, he started to study linguistics and anthropology with Edward *Sapir at Yale, and obtained his PhD in 1939 with a dissertation based on his fieldwork on the Potawatomi Indians of Northern Wisconsin. He did two years of post-doctoral studies at the University of Chicago, where he met *Bloomfield. In 1946, after serving in the armed forces as a language instructor, Hockett began his long career at Cornell as assistant professor, associate professor, then professor, and finally Goldwin Smith professor until his retirement in 1982. He was elected to the American Academy of Arts and Sciences in 1972, and a year later to the National Academy of Science.

Hockett's impact on linguistics was first felt in a 1954 paper where he advocated the 'item and process' approach over the dominant 'item and arrangement' analysis (for example, *farm+er+s*) in order to give a more satisfactory account for derivational processes (for example, *sink–sank*). According to Hockett, a model to explain the system of a language must be general, but at the same time also specific in that it can be applied to a given language; it has also to be inclusive of all the observable data, and productive in the sense that it can generate constructions in that language while keeping to the efficiency of the description.

Hockett's 1958 classic textbook, *A Course in Modern Linguistics*, presents language as a complex system of habits consisting of five principal sub-systems: grammatical, phonological, morphophonemic, semantic and phonetic. The first three are called 'central' and consist of purely linguistic patterns, in contrast to the two 'peripheral' sub-systems, which include real-world situations and speech organs. These peripheral sub-systems, however, provide clues to the understanding of the more abstract patterns, in the central ones. Hockett also allows more room for semantics than do other structuralists of his time. He is known to give special importance to the notion of topic and comment in the study of syntax.

Hockett consistently maintained a critical view of transformational grammar from its beginning. In his 1968 monograph *The State of the Art* he summarised *Chomsky's position in nineteen statements and reviewed them critically. His main objection is directed against the claims that the grammar of a language consists of a finite system characterising an infinite set of well-formed sentences, and that this system mirrors the innate grammar in the mind. Hockett died on 3 November 2000. His obituary in the *Cornell Chronicle* (16 November 2000) also mentions his musical talents, highlighting some of his compositions.

Primary works

(1954). 'Two models of grammatical description'. *Word*. Vol. 10: 210–31.

(1958). *A Course in Modern Linguistics*. New York: Macmillan.
(1968). *The State of the Art* (Janua Linguarum, Series Minor 73). The Hague: Mouton.

Further reading

Gair, James W. (2003). 'Charles Hockett'. *Language*. Vol. 79: 600–13.
Hymes, D. and Fought, J. (1975). *American Structuralism* (Janua Linguarum, Series Maior 102). The Hague: Mouton.
Matthews, P. (2001). *A Short History of Structural Linguistics*. Cambridge: Cambridge University Press.

Agustinus Gianto

WILHELM VON HUMBOLDT

Humboldt, (Karl) Wilhelm (Freiherr) von (*b.* 1767, *d.* 1835; German), linguist, humanist, Prussian diplomat, and educational reformer; founder of general linguistics as a science and linguistic anthropology. Humboldt's rationalist approach to language has its roots in *Kantian rationalism and this is perhaps the reason why it was so enthusiastically adopted by the new discipline of linguistics. (*See also* Bloomfield, Leonard; Descartes, René; Kant, Immanuel; Katz, J. J.)

Humboldt was born into a noble family during the planning stages of Frederick the Great's unification of Prussia in the era of Enlightenment. Scholarly endeavours came easily to him and his younger brother, scientist and explorer Alexander von

Humboldt. Wilhelm studied with a private tutor, Johann Jakob Engel, and was well grounded in classical (especially Greek) philology, studying it formally in 1788–9 at the University of Göttingen. But he read copiously in many other fields, especially political science, philosophy and literature. His first publication was a translation of selections of Xenophon's rendering of Socrates and Plato for a Prussian school reader. He maintained a lifelong interest in classical Greek.

The Humboldt brothers were among the intellectual giants of their day, accomplished in a wide range of disciplines and skills. Wilhelm, according to a comment attributed to his brother, was able apparently 'to penetrate deeper into the structure of a larger number of languages than have probably yet been encompassed by any single mind'. In addition to being a linguist and philologist (there was little separating philology from linguistics in those days), Wilhelm was also a lawyer and statesman. Having studied law at the University of Frankfurt an der Oder in 1787–8, he worked in 1790 as a law clerk in the Prussian Supreme Court, representing Prussia at the Vatican (1801–8) and serving as the Prussian ambassador in Vienna and London (1810–19). He was Prussia's chief negotiator at the surrender talks with Napoleon's army. But perhaps his most visible legacy in the twenty-first century is the university named after him, Humboldt Universität in Berlin, founded in 1809 as Friedrich Wilhelm Universität, the first university in which research and teaching went together. In the year the university was founded

Humboldt himself joined the Royal Prussian Academy of Science. He served sixteen months as minister of public instruction, and the pillar of his educational philosophy was the humanistic Gymnasium. Because of political differences with Metternich and Hardenberg, he was dismissed from the Prussian government in 1819.

Through his wife Karoline von Dacheröden, Humboldt met such luminaries as Friedrich Schiller and Johann Wolfgang Goethe, with whom he became good friends. He is well known as an early generativist or, at least, a Cartesian (thinker after the philosopher René *Descartes) anticipator of transformational generative grammar, although some would dispute this point. Noam *Chomsky asserts that Humboldt was in fact one of the founders of 'the first cognitive revolution'. In the twenty-first century it is likely that most linguists know of Humboldt through the writings of Chomsky, especially his book *Cartesian Linguistics* (1966). Humboldt's maxim 'Language makes infinite use of finite means' has been propagated by many scholars across a wide range of humanistic and social scientific disciplines. His generative credentials stem from his idea that language is not a fixed object (as in the Greek *ergon*), but a fully generative system (as in the Greek *energeia*).

It seems that writing did not come easily to Humboldt, who tended towards perfectionism and so procrastinated, often not completing a work begun. However, another probable factor for his delaying publication on language and linguistic matters is the amount of time he spent trying to master numerous exotic languages, including the language isolate Basque, which he studied in Spain. From 1824 to 1826 he concentrated on Native American languages, under the influence of his brother. From 1827 to 1829 he focused on Sanskrit, under the tutelage of Franz *Bopp, and on the languages of the South Pacific, and from 1829 until his death he concentrated on Malayo-Polynesian languages. The enormous diversity of languages with which he came into contact must have influenced his conception of 'linguistic relativity', and indeed most scholars of the *Sapir-*Whorf hypothesis trace this legacy back to his writing. As Humboldt himself noted: 'Just as without language no concept is possible, so also [without language] there can be no object for the mind' (Losonsky 1999: xvii), and 'since language is involved in structuring human cognition, and languages are diverse in their structure, there resides in every language a characteristic world-view (*Weltansicht*)'. In the Humboldtian view, no thinking can occur without words. Of course, one of the presuppositions of the Sapir-Whorf hypothesis (the idea that the language one learns determine's one's view of the world) is that thinking means linguistic thinking. Although this has not been proven right, neither has anyone proved it wrong, at least in its milder version (linguistic relativity rather than the stronger version, linguistic determinism).

At the beginning of the twenty-first century Humboldt's work continues to resonate in modern linguistics, for example in the debate about transformational generative grammar. Chomsky and Humboldt differ about what is infinite in language structure. While Chomsky sees language as consisting of an infinite number of possible grammatical sentences, for Humboldt the claim is often made that rather than infinite sentences, infinite thoughts are key. But these two positions are not necessarily incompatible: if every language consists of an infinite number of possible sentences, then those sentences are capable of expressing an infinite number of thoughts.

The Humboldtian view of linguistic typology is also important. Here, following in the footsteps of Friedrich and August Wilhelm von Schlegel, he affirmed that Chinese is a root-isolating language, that Greek, Latin and Sanskrit are highly inflectional, that Turkish and Japanese are agglutinating languages which can be viewed as between isolating and inflectional, and that Nahuatl is an example of an incorporating language. Humboldt unquestionably considered the inflectional type as the most developed, and therefore the best kind of language. For him, this is the reason why they helped yield the superb Greek and Indian literatures. In this he differs from Sapir-Whorf, who argued that all types of language are equally expressive vehicles for thoughts and concepts, but are shaped in practice by the needs of the culture in which they develop.

A century and a half after his death, Humboldt's life and career continue to generate new works, including a two-volume biography (Sweet 1978–80), the exhaustive publication of seventeen volumes of his collected writings (Humboldt 1903–36), a five-volume collected writings (Humboldt 1960–81), a treatise on the philosophical foundations of the linguistic theory underlying his work (Manchester 1985), and Losonsky's edition of Humboldt's *On Language* (1999). Humboldt died in Tegel, now part of modern Berlin, on 8 April 1835.

Primary works

(1836a). *Über die Verschiedenheit des Menschlichen Sprachbaues und ihren Einfluss auf die geistige Entwicklung des Menschengeschlecht.* Berlin: F. Dümmler.
(1836b, 1838, 1840). *Über die Kawi Sprache auf der Insel von Java.* Berlin: Königlich Akademie der Wissenschaften.
(1903–36). *Gesammelte Schriften* (17 vols). Berlin: Königlich Akademie der Wissenschaften. Reprinted, Berlin: Mouton de Gruyter, 1967–8.
(1960–81). *Werke* (5 vols). Darmstadt: Wissenschaftliche Buchgesellschaft.

Further reading

Aarslef, Hans (1982). *From Locke to Saussure.* Minneapolis: University of Minnesota Press.
Chomsky, Noam (1966). *Cartesian Linguistics: A Chapter in the History of Rationalist Thought.* New York: Harper and Row.
Chomsky, Noam (2000). *New Horizons in the Study of Language and Mind.* Cambridge: Cambridge University Press.
Cowan, Marianne (ed.) (1963). *Humanist without Portfolio: An Anthology of the Writings of Wilhelm von Humboldt.* Detroit: Wayne State University Press.
Losonsky, Michael (ed.) (1999). *Wilhelm von Humboldt: On Language – On the Diversity of Human Language Construction and its Influence on the Mental Development of the Human Species.* New York: Cambridge University Press.

Manchester, Martin L. (1985). *The Philosophical Foundations of Humboldt's Linguisic Doctrines.* Amsterdam: John Benjamins.
Sweet, Paul R. (1978–80). *Wilhelm von Humboldt: A Biography* (2 vols). Columbus: Ohio State University Press.

Alan S. Kaye

DAVID HUME

Hume, David (*b.* 1711, *d.* 1777; British), arguably the most important philosopher of the Scottish Enlightenment, known as a leading British empiricist, but more broadly as a key figure in the development of rationalism and scepticism in the eighteenth century. Hume's theories of human nature place human beings alongside the 'higher' mammals in terms of cognitive ability, the ability to reason being a function of language, rather than a God-given innate superiority. But while language in Hume's view gave human beings the advantage of rationality, it was also responsible for many misconceptions and falsehoods. In particular, Hume saw language as potentially misleading in that it helps perpetuate the 'illusion' of causality. (*See also* Berkeley, George; Kant, Immanuel; Leibniz, Gottfried Wilhelm; Locke, John; Mill, J. S.)

Hume was born in Edinburgh, the son of a landowner near Berwick on the border with England. His father died when Hume was just 2 years old, and he was raised and partly educated by his mother, who pushed him towards studying law. He attended Edinburgh University from the age of 12 but did not take his degree, preferring instead to study philosophy under his own direction. He published the first two parts of his *Treatise of Human Nature* in 1739 and the third part in 1740. But although this has since become his best-regarded work, its publication went almost unnoticed, even after Hume himself published an abstract as a form of anonymous publicity. Many of the ideas from the *Treatise* reappeared in revised, reduced and sometimes contradictory form in *An Enquiry Concerning Human Understanding* (1748) and *An Enquiry Concerning the Principles of Morals* (1751).

Hume's influence on the philosophy of language is largely in the areas of psychology, perception and causality. In particular, he divides perceptions into 'impressions' and 'ideas'. Impressions are the stronger of the two, since they consist in sensations and emotions deriving from direct engagement with the world. Ideas, on the other hand, are caused by impressions; they are distilled from them through reasoning and language. In other words, Hume did not privilege reason over sensation but saw them operating together in a complex system of interrelations. Having established that ideas are always caused by impressions, Hume goes further, dividing propositions into two: those that relate to things that are 'certain', such as statements of mathematics or geometry, and what he calls 'matters of fact'. The first of these types of proposition, which he calls 'relations of ideas', cannot be contradicted: the proposition $A + B = C$, for example, must necessarily be either true or false according to its terms. In the case of matters of fact, however, propositions themselves are not necessarily true or false. For example, the proposition that 'the sun will rise tomorrow' is no more necessarily true than its contradiction, that 'the sun will not rise tomorrow'. Rather, the truth status of such propositions depends on external evidence and inductive reasoning.

Yet even apparent evidence must be treated with caution. Hume's view of causation, for example, is that cycles of cause and effect are established as fact out of a kind of habit, rather than reasoning. Thus the proposition 'fire is hot' is considered true not because we have empirical evidence that it is true, but because our psychology and our language lead us to believe that since placing one's hand in the fire is usually followed by the sensation of burning, there must be a causal link. In fact, there is no guarantee that the presence of fire will be accompanied by heat on each and every future occasion. Hume uses causality to explain the persistence of beliefs in the absence of proof derived from inductive reasoning. But while causality is problematic for Hume's philosophy, he is more categorical on the subject of religion. Because he rejects all ideas that do not originate in sensation, he had no place for God in his system of thought.

Such sceptical views made Hume a controversial figure in Britain during his lifetime, and despite his best efforts he failed to gain recognition in the form of an academic post. Instead he worked as a private tutor, as a law librarian, and as secretary to various military commanders and diplomats overseas. Even so he managed to become well known as a writer, especially in France, where he was a popular figure. Hume died at home in the house he had built in Edinburgh after an illness lasting two years.

Primary works

(1739, books I and II; 1740, book III). *A Treatise on Human Nature*. L. A. Selby-Bigge (ed.), rev. P. H. Nidditch. Oxford: Oxford University Press, 1978.
(1748). *An Enquiry Concerning Human Understanding*. L. A. Selby-Bigge (ed.), rev. P. H. Nidditch. Oxford: Oxford University Press, 1996.
(1751). *An Enquiry Concerning the Principles of Morals*. L. A. Selby-Bigge (ed.), rev. P. H. Nidditch. Oxford: Oxford University Press, 1996.

Further reading

Passmore, J. (1980). *Hume's Intentions*. London: Duckworth.
Penelhum, T. H. (1975). *Hume*. London: Macmillan.
Smith, N. Kemp (1941). *The Philosophy of David Hume: A Critical Study of its Origins and Central Doctrines*. London: Macmillan.

Christopher Routledge

EDMUND HUSSERL

Husserl, Edmund (b. 1859, d. 1938; German), philosopher and epistemologist, *privatdozent* at the University of Halle (1887–1901), associate professor (1901–6) and professor of philosophy (1906–16) at the University of Göttingen, eventually professor of philosophy at the University of Freiburg im Breisgau (1916–28). Husserl laid the foundations of modern phenomenology, which profoundly influenced important strands in modern philosophy, especially existentialism, hermeneutics, poststructuralism, the philosophy of mind in general and more recently analytic philosophy. (*See also* Arnauld, Antoine; Derrida, Jacques; Frege, Gottlob; Saussure, Ferdinand de.)

Husserl was born in Moravia, in a town called Prossnitz (Prostějov, then in the Austrian Empire, in the twenty-first century in the Czech Republic), into a family of German-speaking Jews. He moved to Leipzig in 1876 to study mathematics, physics, astronomy and philosophy. He continued his studies in Berlin (1878–81) and in Vienna, where he received a doctorate for his dissertation *Beiträge zur Theorie der Variationsrechnung* in 1883. After attending lectures in philosophy given by Franz Brentano (an early influence on phenomenology) in Vienna, Husserl went to Halle, where he converted to Protestantism in 1886. In Halle he wrote his 'Habilitation' thesis *Über den Begriff der Zahl* (1887) under Carl Stumpf, a student of Brentano. His first published book, *Philosophie der Arithmetik* (1891), was based on that thesis and deals with the foundations of mathematics. The book was reviewed very critically by Gottlob *Frege, who regarded it as an example of the then common view that mathematics, like formal logic, could be founded on psychology. Frege was a well-known opponent of this idea. A decade later, however, Husserl was himself to deal the death-blow to psychologism in logic and philosophy with the publication of *Logische Untersuchungen* in 1900–1 (1975, 1984), the two volumes of which are often regarded as Husserl's *magnum opus*, even though they were published early in his career as a philosopher. He moved to Göttingen in 1906. His son Wolfgang was killed on the Western Front at Verdun, and after a period of mourning during which Husserl wrote nothing, he moved to Freiburg im Breisgau in 1916.

Over the first four decades of the twentieth century Husserl produced a huge amount of shorthand manuscript (approximately 40,000 pages), all of which was rescued and transferred to Leuven in Belgium shortly after his death, before the Nazis could confiscate and destroy it. In the twenty-first century the Husserl Archive in Leuven is still one of the most important centres for phenomenology in the world. In these manuscripts, which have been carefully transcribed for publication (since 1950) in the *Husserliana* edition, Husserl tirelessly revised and refined his countless analyses of human mental activities ('acts') and how the 'objects' of knowledge are constituted through them. His considerable influence on his contemporaries was largely a result of his novel, refreshing and truly undogmatic way of philosophising. Many of his talented disciples and colleagues adopted his approach as a starting point for their own research. Husserl fascinated many younger philosophers at the time because his philosophical credo promised to be not only a challenge to psychologism but also a viable alternative to all kinds of speculative trends in philosophy at the turn of the century, in particular those of a neo-*Kantian and neo-*Hegelian origin. Unlike phenomenology, these trends were highly aprioristic (advocating the idea of prior knowledge), and peculiarly remote from the compelling questions of knowledge that philosophy was facing at a time when sciences like physics, biology and chemistry were chalking up one success after another. In such a context Husserl's famous appeal 'To the things themselves!' (*Zu den Sachen selbst!*) must have come as a relief to many academics who saw philosophy losing its status to the natural sciences.

Husserl's thought developed through different stages, although it is now generally acknowledged that this development took place gradually and should not be represented as a succession of ruptures. He proceeded from a philosophical account of the foundations of mathematics in the 1880s to a detailed elucidation of 'natural logic' and of cognitive processes including expressing thoughts, intentionality, abstraction and so on in the *Logische Untersuchungen*. In the first decades of the twentieth century he further widened his scope to encompass many important methodological issues, including the difference between realism and idealism, the problem of time consciousness, the genesis of logical categories out of everyday life experience, transcendental philosophy and the relation between the individual and the community; many texts of this period were published only posthumously. Husserl's writings bear witness to his enduring ambition to present phenomenology as a well-founded general perspective from which all important philosophical problems could in principle be tackled. Even during the last stage in the development of his thought, when he set out to write a comprehensive critique of the pervasive objectivism and scientism he detected in the history of the sciences since Galileo, Husserl's own alternative view – an analysis of the foundations of all scientific reasoning in the human 'life world' (*Lebenswelt*) – continued to build on the principles of philosophical research he had been conducting in previous decades.

Phenomenological philosophy was initially, and rather infelicitously, labelled a kind of 'descriptive psychology' by Husserl himself. But its general objectives are relatively clear from the outset, in particular from the *Logische Untersuchungen* onwards. Husserl's phenomenology is a multi-faceted enterprise in which philosophical (including ontological), epistemological and logico-linguistic analyses go hand in hand to such an extent that the whole cannot be adequately understood if its parts are regarded in isolation. But phenomenology is less a fully fledged theory or method that could be said to be fixed once and for all than an intellectual attitude, a way of 'doing philosophy'. Phenomenology is a specific way of 'looking' at the world and the ways human beings experience that world: the 'phenomena' themselves. Its ultimate aim is to describe and explain the conditions of knowledge, and it does this by unravelling the complex relation between what is constituted through mental activity and the ways the objects of knowledge present themselves through experience. In this way, phenomenology accounts for what is rendered evident through the phenomena themselves. In such a framework, signs and processes of signification play an important role. Husserl must be credited for developing a thought-provoking theory of meaning that does justice not only to intentionality in general but also to some of the essential features of natural language and linguistic meaning. This is not to say, however, that he could be termed a philosopher of language as such. While linguistic signs did play an important part in his work, they were never a central concern. Furthermore, as a philosopher and epistemologist he was always restrained in his claims about language.

Husserl's contribution to the philosophy of language and linguistic theory can best be highlighted from two different angles, a theoretical and a metatheoretical one. First, the phenomenological focus he propounded in *Logische Untersuchungen* and more clearly in *Ideen zu einer reinen Phänomenologie und phänomenologischen Philosophie* (1952b, 1952a, 1977) has major consequences for the methodology of linguistic research; phenomenology serves as an epistemological guideline for all kinds of research within the field of the humanities. Second, Husserl's phenomenology of meaning, expounded most fully in his logicolinguistic analyses in the *Logische Untersuchungen*, can be regarded as his major achievement towards the theory of language. Some of his findings remain valuable in the context of the late twentieth-century debates in linguistics concerning the theory of meaning.

After the publication of the *Logische Untersuchungen*, Husserl spent much time clarifying the philosophical method he deemed necessary to carry out phenomenological analyses. This method is based on what he called 'reductions', which consist in abstractions of all kinds. For example, it is crucial for phenomenologists not to appeal to their belief in the factual existence of the objects in the world, since these are merely experienced as phenomena. This attitude of retreat and non-involvement is a prerequisite for directing attention to one's intentionality towards the phenomena. Intentionality is the central phenomenological concept; for Husserl, consciousness is not a mental state but a dynamic attitude that always implies a 'directedness' towards some object. In focusing on one's intentionality, a phenomenologist also has to abstract away from the accidental features of the phenomena under consideration and seize what is essential to them. This can be achieved, according to Husserl, by intuiting the objects *as* objects; that is, as immanent parts of the intentional focus itself.

If applied to linguistics as an academic discipline, phenomenological reductions have a number of remarkable consequences. First of all, linguists have to recognise that everyday language use is only a component part of very complex cognitive and communicative processes. In actual life, language is not given as a bare phenomenon but interwoven with acts of reference, knowledge of the world, a multitude of psychological attitudes and associations, and so on. Therefore the study of language necessarily presupposes a reductive abstraction through which language proper can be distinguished from the innumerable concomitant aspects present in language use. Together, these aspects form the highly complex preliminary knowledge upon which linguistics is based. Such a distinction is in keeping with a central concern of structuralist linguistics. For example, in his famous *Cours de linguistique générale* (1916) Ferdinand de *Saussure urged linguists not to mix up *langue* (the language system) with *parole* (language use).

Another convergence between structural linguistics and the Husserlian theory of phenomenological reductions is that structuralists also seek to define 'essences'. Not only do structuralists, like Husserl, consider the definition of the essence of language to be the theoretical basis of all empirical linguistic research, but meaning-bearing elements like words, linguistic categories and rules of grammar are said to correspond to 'essential meanings' on the level of *langue*. These meanings are to be distinguished from their (potentially infinite) instantiations in referential contexts. From a structuralist point of view, a linguistic meaning is an 'essence', both as part of a system of structurally related meanings and as an abstract, homogeneous mental entity that lies at the basis of all its 'uses' in context. Considered from a phenomenological stance, this view is entirely adequate, yet Husserl's theory of intentionality would require something important to be added. Whenever a meaning is instantiated in a particular act of language use, the meaning itself is not present to the mind, because consciousness is then focused on the object or state of affairs referred to. The meaning, which is the necessary condition of the act of reference, remains implicit in language use; hence meanings can only become 'objects' when a reduction is performed, and when one's belief in the applicability of meanings to the extra-linguistic world is suspended for the sake of analysis.

Even so, the parallels between phenomenology and structuralist linguistics should not be exaggerated. Linguistic differences among languages can hardly be said to be the object of a phenomenology of language. Unlike Saussure and his followers, Husserl was never seriously interested in what makes one particular language different from other languages. Whenever he talks about 'grammar', 'expressions', 'meaning' and so on, Husserl is dealing with abstractions. He consistently refers to aspects of language in general, not to any actual language or languages. It should be borne in mind that the German examples he gives throughout the *Logische Untersuchungen* (as well as in some other, lesser manuscripts on language and meaning) are merely illustrations of general statements about linguistic signs, not claims about German. It comes as no surprise then that Husserl was particularly sensitive to René *Descartes's and Gottfried Wilhelm *Leibniz's doctrine of a *characteristica universalis* (universal code or grammar). In fact, he partly tried to revive this doctrine in his outline of a theory of 'pure grammar'. In this outline, Husserl is concerned not so much with what twenty-first-century grammarians mean by 'grammar' (including 'syntax' and 'semantics') as with the structures of logical reasoning and their genesis in experience and consciousness, including the structure

of judgements of the form S *is* p, the difference between simple and complex meanings (*man* vs. *a man of iron*) and so on. Crucially, however, such laws of logic can only be assessed adequately if one understands what terms such as 'meaning', 'expression', 'sentence' might mean with regard to linguistic signs. Husserl's outline of pure grammar might also be seen as an antecedent of the late twentieth-century idea of Universal Grammar (see *Chomsky).

The most detailed and influential exposition of this theory can be found in the *Logische Untersuchungen*. Although Husserl revised his findings on a number of points in later work, he did not deal again with meaning in such an extensive and linguistically convincing way. But his theory of meaning should not be thought of as an end in itself; rather it is a central part of his theory of logic and reasoning. According to Husserl, meanings are abstract, ideal entities that have to be distinguished both from the mental acts in which the meanings are put to use and from the objects to which the speaker refers on a particular occasion. Granting that meanings are ideal entities not only implies that they belong to a unique mental sphere and that communication – the uttering of actual words and sentences – is not essential to meaning; it also implies that meanings are fixed, while acts of reference are variable. The meaning of a word or of some rule of grammar does not change just because it is used to refer to different objects or states of affairs. For example, the lexical item 'woman' has a general, clearly delineated meaning that remains the same whenever reference is made to a woman. For Husserl, it is even irrelevant whether the intended object really exists or is a mere object of thought or imagination. What is crucial is that, as he puts it in the first investigation of his *Logische Untersuchungen*, entitled 'Expression and Meaning' ('Ausdruck und Bedeutung'), 'the object never coincides with the meaning'.

Conversely, entirely different meanings can be used to refer to one and the same object or state of affairs. Husserl cites examples like 'the victor of Jena' and 'the vanquished at Waterloo' – both of which refer to Napoleon – and 'a is larger than b' and 'b is smaller than a'. One could add as a telling example the semantic difference between active and passive; for example, 'Husserl calls meanings ideal objects' vs. 'Meanings are called ideal objects by Husserl.' Husserl's list of examples could also be extended from a cross-linguistic perspective. Saussure, for example, pointed out that a linguistic category like 'plural' has a different meaning in languages like German and French from that it has in Sanskrit and classical Greek. In the second pair, the 'singular' is in opposition not only to a 'plural' but also to a 'dual'. As a consequence, while the referent of an English 'plural' and a Greek 'plural' may be identical, their invariant meanings are clearly different.

Husserl further emphasises that not all that a native speaker of a given language interprets as absurd or nonsensical is meaningless. There is indeed a clear distinction between ill-formed expressions that are said to be meaningless, such as 'a round or' or 'a human being and is', and expressions to which no object or state of affairs is known to correspond but which nevertheless have a perfectly homogeneous meaning, such as 'a round square' or 'all rectangles have five angles'. Such examples not only evince that meaning combinations in the Husserlian sense can be homogeneous only if the meaning parts of an expression are compatible with one another. They also show that the objectivity of some intended meaning, and thus ultimately the truth of a given expression, is dependent on the phenomena in the world and cannot possibly be rendered by linguistic signs and significations alone.

By distinguishing meanings from objects or states of affairs referred to, Husserl was able to pinpoint a number of issues that will always be at the heart of a theory of semantics. This assessment of his meaning for the philosophy of language remains valid even though several of his claims have since been stated more precisely and empirically better substantiated in more recent theories of language. Husserl retired from teaching in 1928, but his final decade was overshadowed by the rise of the Nazis in Germany, and he was troubled by the way Jews were treated by the regime. He died, apparently of pleurisy, in 1938.

Primary works

Works in the *Husserliana* edition (HUA, founded in 1950), first published by Martinus Nijhoff (The Hague), since 1989 by Kluwer (Dordrecht, Boston and London); 2002 saw the publication of vol. XXXV:
(1939, 1985). *Erfahrung und Urteil*. L. Landgrebe.

(1950, reprinted 1973). *Cartesianische Meditationen und Pariser Vorträge.* S. Strasser (ed.). (HUA I).

(1952a, reprinted 1971). *Ideen zu einer reinen Phänomenologie und phänomenologischen Philosophie.* Vol. III: *Die Phänomenologie und die Fundamente der Wissenschaften.* M. Biemel (ed.). (HUA V).

(1952b, reprinted 1984). *Ideen zu einer reinen Phänomenologie und phänomenologischen Philosophie.* Vol. II: *Phänomenologische Untersuchungen zur Konstitution.* M. Biemel (ed.). (HUA IV).

(1954). *Die Krisis der europäischen Wissenschaften und die transzendetale Phänomenologie. Eine Einleitung in die phänomenologische Philosophie.* W. Biemel (ed.). (HUA VI). Hamburg: Felix Meiner.

(1974). *Formale und transzendentale Logik. Versuch einer Kritik der logischen Vernunft.* P. Janssen (ed.). (HUA XVII).

(1975). *Logische Untersuchungen.* Vol. I: *Prolegomena zur reinen Logik.* E. Holenstein (ed.). (HUA XVIII).

(1977). *Ideen zu einer reinen Phänomenologie und phänomenologischen Philosophie.* Vol. I: *Allgemeine Einführung in die reine Phänomenologie.* K. Schuhmann (ed.). (HUA III).

(1984). *Logische Untersuchungen.* Vol. II: *Untersuchungen zur Phänomenologie und Theorie der Erkenntnis.* U. Panzer (ed.). (HUA XIX).

(1987). *Vorlesungen über Bedeutungslehre. Sommersemester 1908.* U. Panzer (ed.) (HUA XXVI).

(1999). *The Essential Husserl: Basic Writings in Transcendental Phenomenology.* Donn Welton (ed.). Bloomington and Indianapolis: Indiana University Press.

Further reading

Bernet, Rudolf, Kern, Iso and Marbach, Eduard (1993). *An Introduction to Husserlian Phenomenology.* Evanston, IL: Northwestern University Press.

Cobb-Stevens, Richard (1990). *Husserl and Analytic Philosophy.* Dordrecht, Boston and Lancaster: Kluwer.

Holenstein, Elmar (1976). *Linguistik, Semiotik, Hermeneutik: Plädoyers für eine strukturale Phänomenologie.* Frankfurt: Suhrkamp.

Mohanty, Jitendra Nath (ed.) (1977). *Readings on Edmund Husserl's 'Logical Investigations'.* The Hague: Martinus Nijhoff.

Smith, Barry and Woodruff Smith, David (eds) (1995). *The Cambridge Companion to Husserl.* Cambridge: Cambridge University Press.

Spiegelberg, Herbert (1982). *The Phenomenological Movement. A Historical Introduction.* Third edition. The Hague, Boston and Lancaster: Martinus Nijhoff.

Klaas Willems

ROMAN JAKOBSON

Jakobson, Roman (Osipovich) (*b.* 1896, *d.* 1982; Russian, naturalised American 1941). Though he spent the second half of his life in the United States, Jakobson is generally acknowledged as a principal founder of the European movement in structural linguistics. His views in some respects differ substantially from those of other representatives of structuralism. (*See also* Bloomfield, Leonard; Boas, Franz; Hjelmslev, Louis; Peirce, C. S.; Saussure, Ferdinand de; Trubetzkoy, N. S.; Whorf, Benjamin Lee.)

Jakobson was born in Moscow, the son of a chemical engineer and successful industrialist. In 1914 he embarked on his academic studies at the University of Moscow, and at the age of 19 he wrote his first scholarly article, on the phonetics of a North Great Russian dialect. With six other students he founded the Moscow Linguistic Circle. Jakobson moved to Prague in 1920, where he and *Trubetzkoy co-founded the Prague School of Linguistics in 1926. In 1939 Jakobson left Czechoslovakia because of the Nazi occupation, and during 1939–41 he was in Copenhagen (Denmark) and Oslo and Uppsala (Sweden) as a visiting professor. In 1941 he emigrated to the United States, where he stayed till his death. There he held a number of positions, among them at Columbia University (1943–9), Harvard (1949–66), and Massachusetts Institute of Technology (MIT, 1957–82).

According to Bradford (1994), Jakobson's first significant contribution to language studies was a paper on Russian poetry, published in 1921 (published in Russian in *Selected Writings*, vol. V: 299–354), specifically the poetry of his friend Velimir Xlebnikov. Jakobson's interest in poetry is reflected in his later work, where he argues that language is essential in human understanding and the way we encounter the world, but poetry is special because it reflects on the nature of language itself. Accordingly Jakobson sees the poet both as a person who analyses language and as an artist. The eight volumes of Jakobson's *Selected Writings* (2002) demonstrate that these initial interests became the guidelines of Jakobson's professional life, since he contributed to the various fields of linguistics proper, literary theory, the nature of poetry, philological investigations of literary texts, Slavic folklore and mythology as well as the cultural history of the Slavs, and literary criticism of modern Russian

poetry. His linguistic competence is overwhelmingly manifested in the authorship of works in a number of different languages, including Russian, German, French and English. Even so, he never tried to adapt his pronunciation to match the accents of native speakers. His Russian accent in English did not fade even after many years in the United States, and in fact he became well known for it: it has been said that he spoke Russian in fifty languages.

The primary intellectual background for Jakobson's kind of linguistics was the ideas of *Saussure. Jakobson kept the Saussurian notion of the 'linguistic sign' as a basic conceptual framework in his work on linguistics and poetics. Saussure's 'linguistic sign' is composed of the relation between expression and content, in the English version 'the signifier' and 'the signified' respectively, but Jakobson preferred the Latin terminology: 'signum' (the linguistic sign), 'signans' (sound form) and 'signatum' (meaning). Most of Jakobson's subsequent work is concerned either with sound forms, in the development of a theory of phonology, or with the interference between sound forms (rhythm and rhyme) and grammatical structures, in the development of a theory of poetics. In the period of his early intellectual maturation, Jakobson was also influenced by, among others, *Husserl concerning the phenomenology of language. Jakobson was inspired by the development of modern physics, especially by Einstein's theory of relativity, and later on he used these insights in his reflections on 'diachrony' and 'synchrony' in linguistic investigation and on analyses of the structures of poems.

When Jakobson moved to Prague in 1920, the Moscow Linguistic Circle dissolved. The Prague years were in many respects the most creative period in his life. He received his doctorate in 1930 from Prague University, and in 1933 he started a job as a teacher at T. G. Masaryk University in Brno, where, in 1937, he was appointed chair in Russian philology and Old Czech literature. In Prague he found a perfect intellectual environment and in 1926 he was a co-founder of the Prague Linguistic Circle. It is widely acknowledged that this group of people became some of the most influential figures in European linguistics under the label 'structuralism', a term that Jakobson was possibly the first to use.

Jakobson's life-long work on phonology had its outset here, and together with Trubetzkoy he elaborated (mainly during the 1920s and 1930s) the basic notion of the 'phoneme' as an entity the existence of which is a matter of its relations to other phonemic entities. The set of all the relations of all phonemes of a language make up the phonological system of that language, and thus the phonemes become functional elements in the language, establishing its sound structure. Phonemes therefore are not seen as groups of similar (acoustic and auditive) sounds lumped together but as elements of linguistic sounds that are able to make differences between words. Take, for instance, the English words *pin* and *bin* (Waugh and Monville-Burston 1990), in which the *p* in *pin* is unvoiced while the *b* in *bin* is voiced. *p* and *b* are said to be two phonemes (normally written /p/ vs. /b/) because they make the words in question different. Pairs of words such as *pin* and *bin* are known as 'minimal pairs' because they are distinguished phonetically by only one feature and that feature brings about a semantic difference. This is opposed to the situation relating to the pair *pin* and *spin*, where in the first the *p* is aspirated and in the second the *p* is unaspirated, but this difference is not the only one that distinguishes between the words (the occurrence or absence of the *s* also makes this distinction).

Such contextually different manifestations of the 'same' sound are sometimes called allophones. Since the functional differences seem to coincide across sets of phonemes, they are often related in pairs, and Jakobson proposed another key notion in linguistics, that of 'markedness'. If we reconsider the *pin* vs. *bin* opposition, then the property of the phoneme /b/ in *bin* being voiced is seen as justifying the label 'marked' for that phoneme, while /p/ in *pin* is unvoiced and therefore, because of the absence of the property mentioned, is regarded as 'unmarked'. The theoretical notion of 'markedness' became essential in phonology, but it also diffused into morphology, syntax and even semantics. In phonology proper, this train of thought led Jakobson to propose so-called 'implicational laws' (or 'rules'), saying that there exist certain co-occurrence relations between phonemic properties in the same system.

These principles correspond to the ideas and principles in *Hjelmslevian glossematics (an attempt to establish the structural characteristics of all languages), in which they are applied to the description of any kind of linguistic structure, but Jakobson approved neither of this nor of the extreme of formalisation presupposed by glossematics. Jakobson's principles were applied to Slovak in an article in 1931, and most of his theoretical contributions were published in minor papers or longer monographs on specific subjects, but his work also embraced some general problems, one of them concerned with utilising the new structuralist paradigm to question the eighteenth-century understanding of historical linguistics and language change. He became convinced that 'linguistic changes are systematic and goal directed', and this teleological approach was presented in the programmatic paper 'The concept of the sound law and the teleological criterion' (a brief extract from this paper is found in 2002, vol. I: 1–2), delivered in the Prague Circle in 1927. Another general problem was the question of to what extent he wanted to accept the basic assumptions normally attributed to Saussure: the primacy of 'synchrony' (language at a given moment) over 'diachrony' (language over time), the primacy of *langue* (the language system) over *parole* (language use), and the primacy of paradigmatic structures over syntagmatic structures. In Jakobson's view, Saussure's formulation of these dichotomies was a necessary starting point, but he considered the Saussurian one-sidedness too simplistic. Jakobson conceived of the linguistic dimensions as being complementary to the structural dimensions rather than existing as part of a hierarchy.

During the 1930s Jakobson clarified his theory of phonemes and especially the notion of 'distinctive features'. This became the technical term for the properties of phonemes that make each phoneme distinct from any other, and thereby make syllables and words distinct from each other. As is well known, some words are phonetically (almost) identical, and this is one of the reasons why the theoretical concept of 'distinctive features', such as the notion of 'markedness', diffused into other areas of linguistics, among them syntax and semantics, in which it plays a key role in some theoretical models. A basic assumption in Jakobson's theory of phonemes is that the relations of features are all binary, like the voiced /b/ vs. unvoiced /p/ opposition mentioned above. According to this kind of analysis, phonemes in a language-specific system are all regarded as clusters of binary relations of 'features'. What is important then is not the absolute occurrence of a property, such as consonantal voice, but the system of phonemic relations in a language or dialect: in other words, the phonological structure. This line of reasoning, known as 'structuralism', became the model for other areas in linguistics, but it should be noted that the structuralist movement was not a uniform intellectual community. In fact, Jakobson dissociated himself, more or less, from several different kinds of 'structuralism': Saussurian, contemporary European (represented by Hjelmslev) and American (represented by, for example, *Bloomfield).

This general theorising on methodology and structures led Jakobson and Trubetzkoy to assume the existence of universal principles governing the structure and change of phonemic systems. The first detailed account of their thoughts was given by Trubetzkoy in his paper *Grundzüge der Phonologie* (1939; English translation, *Principles of Phonology*, 1969), and Jakobson's best-known theoretical account is *Kindersprache, Aphasie und allgemeine Lautgesetze* (1941; English translation, *Child Language, Aphasia, and Phonological Universals*, 1968). This monograph was written in Oslo and Stockholm during 1939–41 and was published both in a volume of proceedings (1940–42) from the association of Swedish linguists and also as a separate publication in Uppsala (1941). As is indicated by the title of the book, Jakobson had become interested in language acquisition and language loss as a way of underpinning his theories on phoneme structures, but he did not personally do much work with children or aphasics. Rather he consulted the results of others and ingeniously extracted the facts in order to adopt them in support of his theories.

When Jakobson arrived in the United States in 1941, his thoughts on linguistics were received with scepticism by some American structuralists, but he established friendly relations with among others, *Boas, *Whorf and Bloomfield, and by 1943 he was engaged in the founding of the Linguistic Circle of New York. He moved to Harvard in 1949, and in 1957 he became professor at nearby MIT while keeping his professorship at Harvard. His years in the United States partly meant a refinement of the previously developed theories of phonology and linguistics in general, and partly broadened his interests in fields outside linguistics proper. Besides poetics, literary theory, metrics and philology, he took up issues in semiotics, mythology and Slavic studies.

Jakobson's reflections on linguistics carried further his basic view that on the one hand language is structure and on the other hand language is function – that is, the use of language in human communication. In his opposition to the Saussurian line of reasoning, Jakobson shifted his focus even further from structures and systems to the theory of language use. One kind of impulse was the development, during World War II, of the field of communication technology. Jakobson even substituted some of his theoretical linguistic terms with words used in this field; for example, *langue* became 'code' and *parole* became 'message'.

One outcome of this communicational turn was the well-known model of 'factors . . . involved in verbal communication' (2002, vol. III: 22). This model, shown in figure 3, allows for six factors, including addresser and addressee, that make up verbal communication; if the addresser or addressee (not necessarily limited to two parties, or, in the case of text generated by an institution, to individuals) are not explicitly mentioned in an exchange, then they will at least leave evidence or 'tracks'

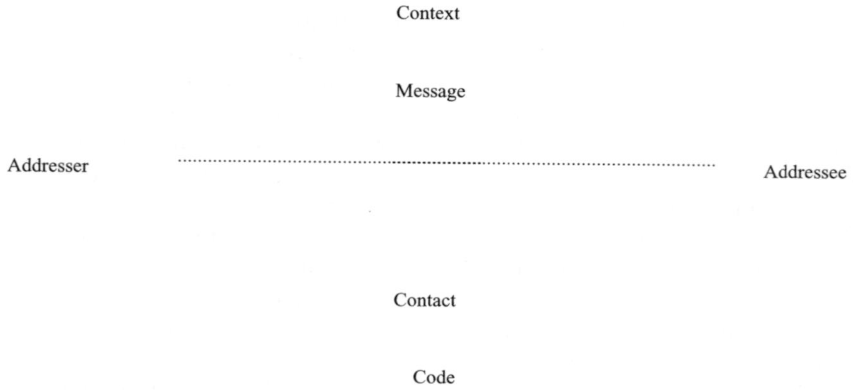

Context

Message

Addresser .... Addressee

Contact

Code

Figure 3   Factors involved in verbal communication.

to indicate their presence in the communication.

The model of factors in verbal communication is complemented by Jakobson with 'a corresponding scheme of the [linguistic] functions' (2002, vol. III: 23: see figure 4).

This conceptual framework was first presented to the community of linguists in Jakobson's presidential address at the annual meeting of the Linguistic Society of America in 1956 (published in 1976), but in general people quote the revised version, 'Linguistics and poetics' (1960). This paper has had significant influence on some kinds of literary studies and semiotics. It also expresses some of the basic views of what is now known as 'functional linguistics', a branch of linguistics that has inherited its notion of 'linguistic functions' from the Prague Linguistic Circle (see *Halliday).

Exactly how these views are expressed in the diagrams, and what difference there is between the 'factors' of the first model and the 'functions' of the second scheme, are still mat-

ters of dispute. Most interpretations conceive of the 'factors' as the external relations of a piece of communication (a text), while the 'functions' can be seen as the internal characteristics of a text (in the wording of Bradford 1994: 85, 'the intrinsic properties of the text itself'). One may also see the 'factors' as the more explicit traits of the text and the 'functions' as the more implicit ones.

There is, for Jakobson, a natural link between these linguistic functions and the linguistic structures utilised by individuals producing linguistic messages. In his 1956 paper 'Two aspects of language' he transfers the analysis of phonemes as 'bundles of features' and as entities in chains of sound to the larger structure of the linguistic sign. Any linguistic sign is said to 'involve two modes of arrangement': 'combination' (or 'contexture') and 'selection' (or 'substitution'). Jakobson invokes both Saussure and *Peirce, but their work is not directly relevant to his interpretation of data from patients suffering from aphasia under the

144

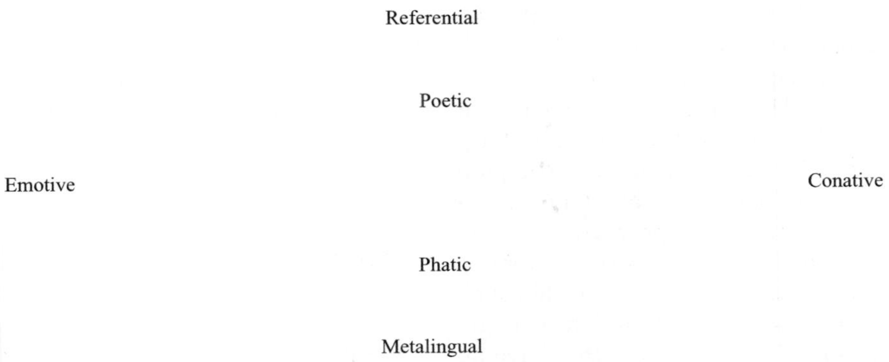

Referential

Poetic

Emotive   Conative

Phatic

Metalingual

Figure 4 The corresponding linguistic functions.

headlines 'similarity disorder' ('selection deficiency') and 'contiguity disorder' ('combination deficiency'). Here Jakobson points to the fact that aphasics with the two types of disorder have different characteristics in their linguistic abilities. Roughly, patients of the first type have difficulties with association between words belonging to the same word classes, while patients of the second type have difficulties putting words together, and this affects the finer details of the subsystems involved.

It is to be expected that Jakobson would draw upon his literary studies, and indeed he points to the obvious correspondence between the 'selection' and 'combination' dimensions and 'the metaphoric and metonymic poles'. Here metaphor is seen as the 'semantic line' when 'one topic in discourse may lead to another through similarity', while metonym does the same by 'contiguity'; and this may be applied to literary texts as well as ordinary discourse. 'Selection' and 'combination' are 'operations' of language use ('encoding-decoding') while 'simi-larity' and 'contiguity' are 'structural relations in code and message', the conceptual framework thereby providing the connection to the theoretical model of communication.

In parallel with this work, Jakobson made contributions to grammatical theory. He also worked on what he called 'shifters', roughly what linguists in general call 'deictic expressions' and philosophers call 'indexicals'. He reflected on the Peircean linguistic sign and contemplated biological structures and functions, but his main contribution as a linguist was his improvements in phonological analysis. In work done with the acoustician C. Gunnar Fant and the linguist Morris Halle, he made acoustic definitions for the phonemic features connected with the articulatory way the sounds were produced. In *Fundamentals of Language* (1956a) Part I: 'Phonology and Phonetics', Jakobson and Halle introduce, for instance, the notion 'redundant feature', used to describe sound properties that are not distinctive but are utilised to support the auditive perception of linguistic expressions.

Jakobson's last major contribution to phonology was *The Sound Shape of Language* (1979), written with Linda Vaugh. His basic claim here is that the sharp distinction between form and substance (that is, the structural relations based on sound properties versus the sound properties *per se*) propounded by the structuralists is hardly tenable because a thorough analysis seems to reveal that there are no sound properties left that have no function in linguistic communication. Therefore phonemes cannot be separated, as an abstract system, from the phonetic properties of their features. Sound properties (substance) and features (form) are entities integrated with each other, and the sound shape of language is a 'cultural artefact' (2002, vol. I: xxxi). From this it follows that the linguistic sign cannot be totally arbitrary, and this perspective can be seen as an encounter with the Saussurian model of the linguistic sign, with Hjelmslev, and with the linguistics tradition of generative phonology (and syntax) that focuses entirely on linguistic form.

The central publication of Jakobson's work is *Selected Writings* (2002), published in eight volumes. *Selected Writings* is special in the sense that the first volume of the first edition was published in 1962, so Jakobson had the opportunity to insert 'Retrospects' in volumes I–IV and VI. It gave him a chance to focus more on his own thinking, and it is characteristic of his self-referential reflections that he does not just sum up his work but continue to contemplate linguistic problems and point to new ones. Jakobson's main legacy is the theoretical clarification of a large number of terms in modern linguistics and semiotics, the consistency and clarity of his reflections on language, and an urge to cross the boundaries of scientific fields. He died in Cambridge, Massachusetts.

Primary works

(1941). *Kindersprache, Aphasie und allgemeine Lautgesetze*. English translation: *Child Language, Aphasia, and Phonological Universals*. A. Kieler (trans.). The Hague: Mouton, 1968.

(1956a) (with Morris Halle). *Fundamentals of Language*. Berlin and New York: Mouton de Gruyter.

(1956b) 'Two aspects of language'. In (as part II) *Fundamentals of Language*. Berlin and New York: Mouton de Gruyter.

(1960). 'Linguistics and poetics'. In *Style in Language*. T. A. Sebeok (ed.). Cambridge, MA: MIT Press.

(1979) (with Linda Waugh). *The Sound Shape of Language*. Berlin and New York: Mouton de Gruyter.

(2002, third edition). *Selected Writings*. Vols I–VIII. Berlin and New York: Mouton de Gruyter, 1962–88.

Further reading

Bradford, Richard (1994). *Roman Jakobson: Life: Language, Art*. London and New York: Routledge.

Fabb, Nigel (1997). *Linguistics and Literature*. Oxford: Blackwell.

Fant, C. Gunnar (1986). 'Features: fiction and facts'. In J. Perkell and D. Klatt (eds), *Invariance and Variability in Speech Processes*. Hillsdale, NJ: Lawrence Erlbaum.

Fischer-Jørgensen, Eli (1975). *Trends in Phonological Theory: A Historical Introduction*. Copenhagen: Akademisk Forlag.

Rudy, Stephen (1990). *Roman Jakobson: A Complete Bibliography of his Writings*. Berlin and New York: Mouton de Gruyter.

Trubetzkoy, Nikolai S. (1937) *Grundzüge der Phonologie: Travaux du Cercle Linguistique de Prague* 7. English translation (1969): *Principles of Phonology*. Berkeley: University of California Press.

Waugh, Linda and Monville-Burston, Monique (1990). 'Introduction to Roman Jakobson'. In *Selected Writings*. Berlin and New York: Mouton de Gruyter, 1962–88.

Hans Götzsche

DANIEL JONES

Jones, Daniel (*b.* 1881, *d.* 1967; British), lecturer, associate professor and then professor at University College London (1912–49), professor emeritus, University College London and president of the International Phonetics Association (1950–67). As the first professor of phonetics in Great Britain, he established himself as the authority on standard English pronunciation (received pronunciation). His greatest influence on phonetics was his universal description and classification of the vowel system as well as his work on the phoneme, based on the study of lesser known languages. (*See also* Bloomfield, Leonard; Jakobson, Roman; Pike, Kenneth; Trubetzkoy, N. S.)

Jones was born in the centre of London and was always proud of being a 'true' Londoner. His father, Daniel Jones senior, was one of the most successful barristers of his time, a founder member of the Wimbledon All England Tennis Club and a gifted musician. His mother Viola (née Carte), a good musician herself, was the sister of Richard D'Oyly Carte, the impresario who managed the Savoy Theatre during the heyday of Gilbert and Sullivan operettas. This may account for Jones's life-long love for music. After his education at Radley College and at University College School, Daniel Jones studied mathematics at King's College Cambridge and took a BA in 1900, the only academic qualification he ever obtained apart from the honorary doctorates awarded to him by the University of Zurich (1936) and the University of Edinburgh (1958). Following in the footsteps of his father, he then prepared for his Bar examination at Lincoln's Inn. But Jones had always been more interested in modern languages than in mathematics and law, and already during his years at Cambridge he had spent his vacations taking language courses in Germany and France. Though it was at the Tilley Institute in Marburg that he was first introduced to phonetics, the turning point in Jones's career was the course of study at Bourg-La-Reine (France) under Paul Passy, the leading phonetician of the time. At the end of the course he took the examinations of the International Phonetics Association (IPA) and achieved such a remarkable result that Passy not only convinced him to take up a career in phonetics, but also helped him get his first job and to establish himself at University College London. The time at Bourg-la Reine was also of importance to Jones's private life, as he later married Cyrille Motte, the daughter of the family he stayed with. They had two children, Oliver Daniel (1917) and Michelle (1922).

The year 1907 was a very important one for Jones. In the same month as he gave his first lecture on phonetics as applied to French, he passed the Bar examination, qualifying him as a trial lawyer. However, it had already become clear to him that his future professional life was not in the law. In fact, he burnt all his law books and devoted himself to phonetics. At the same time he also became a member of the IPA council and assistant editor of *Le Maître Phonétique*. He started writing his own articles for the journal and by the end of the year he had published seven articles and three books: *100 Poésies enfantines*, *Phonetic Transcriptions of English Prose* and *The Sounds of the French Language* (with D. L. Savory). At a vacation course he also first met Henry Sweet, the leading British phonetician of the time, whose work and ideas were the most important inspirations for Jones's own views. Within a very short time Jones had established himself in the field, and his appointment as a temporary lecturer was renewed.

Jones's first major contribution to phonetics was *The Pronunciation of English* (1909), in which he presented a brief outline of phonetics followed by twenty-six transcriptions. The book remains in print almost a century later. It was written for native speakers of English and is very prescriptive in its approach, a stance Jones turned away from in his later work. Though he did not yet use the term 'Received Pronunciation' (RP), but 'Standard Pronunciation', this was the variety he had in mind when stating in the preface that the work was designed for teachers 'whose aim it is to correct cockneyisms or other undesirable pronunciations in their scholars'. On the other hand, the transcripts contained regional and social varieties, showing his awareness that they belonged to a survey of English pronunciation as well. The book became an immediate success. In contrast with Sweet's *The Sounds of English* (1908), it was deliberately written with the aim of popularising phonetics among people who speak in public, such as politicians, barristers, the clergy and teachers. The most important element in the theoretical part of the book is Jones's analysis and description of the vowel system. He described the English vowels from an articulatory (physical) point of view, a major improvement on Sweet's more traditional auditory (sound-based) approach. Though they were not stated explicitly, the book already contained many of the ideas that Jones later developed in *An Outline of English Phonetics* (1918).

In the following years Jones travelled a lot, giving lectures in France, Germany and Scandinavia, and his position in the Simplified Spelling Society even enabled him to embark on a lecture tour to India. At this time he became interested in analysing the sounds of European languages other than English, German and French, as well as African and Asian languages. His publications on spoken language included not only dialectal varieties of English but also phonetic analyses of languages as diverse as Hungarian, Russian, Manx, Cantonese, Chindau, Mono, Tawana, Panjabi, Sechuana and others. Jones himself was very proud of his research and once said that this was the work he had enjoyed most. However, he was to become much better known for his outstanding contributions in the field of phonetic lexicography.

In 1913, with Hermann Michaelis, Jones published *A Phonetic Dictionary of the English Language* as part of a series of pronunciation dictionaries initiated by Passy, who had already published the *Dictionnaire phonétique de la langue française* (1897) with Michaelis as co-author. As the dictionaries in this series were designed as a help for scholars reading phonetic transcripts, the entries were arranged phonetically and not orthographically, which turned out to be counter-productive. The dictionaries were difficult to use, because there is no standard sequence of sounds as there is for spelling, and the market was very small: at the time there existed no dictionary with reliable information on the pronunciation of English words. The phonetic dictionaries of the eighteenth century were outdated and the new dictionaries of the English language – for instance, the *Oxford English Dictionary* – concentrated on written English, and provided either invalid information on the spoken form, or information that was inaccessible to many readers because of the transcription system used.

This situation on the market and the drawbacks of the *Phonetic Dictionary of the English Language* inspired Jones to start work on the *English Pronouncing Dictionary* (*EPD*), published in 1917. It immediately became the standard reference book and has been so ever since. It was not until 1990, when Wells published the *Longman Pronunciation Dictionary,* that the *EPD* received a worthy competitor. With the publication of the *EPD* Jones had taken a big step towards popularising phonetics, which had always been his goal. Although the *EPD* is the most popular phonetics book ever published, it would probably never have achieved such success without the primary work Jones published in *The Principles of the International Phonetics Association* in 1912. This small booklet is undoubtedly the most important contribution to phonetic transcription and a major contribution to phonetics in general.

First of all, Jones removed the hitherto prevalent French bias in phonetics. The knowledge of the sound systems of different languages he had acquired enabled him to follow a general phonetic approach. Apart from four different varieties of English (Southern, Northern, Scottish and American), he took another eighteen languages into consideration, and thus made the phonetic alphabet a truly international one; something it had always claimed to be but had never been. Furthermore, Jones adhered to the principle that phonetic spelling should be easy to read and write. By stating that only distinctive sounds should be indicated in a transcription, he advocated that a broad transcription system should be used in dictionaries. When Jones stated that '[t]he general rule for strictly practical phonetic transcription is therefore to leave out everything that is self-evident, and everything that can be explained once for all. In transcribing any given language it is generally sufficient to represent the distinctive sounds only', he gave a clear definition of the phoneme concept (that spoken language is made up of a sequence of distinct sounds represented by written symbols), although he did not use that term, and hinted too at the concept of allophonic rules (rules governing the realisation of different sounds for the same phoneme) that 'can be explained once for all'. He also claimed that this approach was the best one to use when analysing a language for the first time, stating that '[i]t is necessary to ascertain what are the distinctive sounds in the language, i.e. those which if confused might conceivably alter the meaning of words'. With his revision of the IPA principles, Jones paved the way for his *English Pronouncing Dictionary* (1917a), on which he was to work for the next five years.

The *EPD* was so successful that it had to be reprinted within two years. One reason for this success was surely the fact that because of the phonetic symbols employed it could be used easily even by the non-scientist. Another reason might have been that it did not claim any prescriptive status, but just gave an account of what Jones then called 'Public School Pronunciation'; that is, the forms used by 'the families of Southern English persons whose men-folk have been educated at the great public [non-state funded] boarding-schools'. However, he soon replaced this with Ellis's term 'Received Pronunciation' (1869), and the now commonly used abbreviation 'RP' is Jones's own coinage. From a scientific point of view the *EPD* was seminal. It contained the first full diagram of the primary cardinal vowels, which serves as a reference system by which every vowel sound can be defined. Though the concept of cardinal vowels was not Jones's original idea, he had developed and underlined it substantially by experimental data based on X-ray pictures. This scientific approach had a very positive side-effect in that the work done at the phonetics department was recognised by scholars in other fields.

Also in 1917, Jones gave an address to the Philological Society on 'The phonetic structure of the Sechuana language' (1917b), which is important for two reasons. First, it was there that Jones used the concept 'phoneme' for the first time, and second, his ideas were spread to a wider audience. Although his definition of the phonemes as being 'sounds or families of sounds which are capable of distinguishing one word from another' is not as explicit as his unintentional definitions in his *Principles of the IPA* (see above), and although the phoneme concept was not the focus of this lecture, Jones aroused interest among linguists with respect to the importance of phonetics and its utility to linguistics.

Apart from the *EPD*, *An Outline of English Phonetics* (1918) is Jones's most important contribution to phonetics and linguistics, with its reference to phonetics, phonology and the teaching of English pronunciation alike. In the opening chapters, Jones gives an account of transcription and standards of pronunciation. In explaining the contrast between broad and narrow transcriptions, he introduces his algorithmic approach to phonological problems and devises a method by which different varieties of English can be traced back to an underlying system. He also gives a detailed account of the sound system in general and of every English sound with respect to its articulation as well as the problems the foreign learner is faced with, illustrated with photographs and diagrams. Furthermore, he provides the language teacher as well as the learner with instructions on the training of recognition, articulation, distribution, supra-segmental elements (features such as stress pitch that occur at the same time as distinct phonetic elements), catenation (the way phonemes are connected), and the relationship between spelling and pronunciation, supplemented with respective exercises. Although the book was originally intended as a handbook for the teaching of pronunciations, the phonetician finds a detailed account of the state of the art of theoretical and experimental phonetics. Together with the numerous revised editions between 1922 and 1960, the *Outline of English Phonetics* provides the best account of the development of phonetics in general and of Jones's ideas in particular.

Jones had always dreamed of an Institute of Phonetics, and in the following years most of his energy went into this project. He wanted a world centre of phonetics, at which all the languages of the British Empire could be analysed and spelling systems for hitherto unwritten languages could be developed. Though his dream never came true, mostly for financial reasons, Jones was given the first university chair in phonetics in Great Britain in 1921, although by then he had had a nervous breakdown from which he would never fully recover. Whether it was a result of his illness or bereavements in the family that made Jones turn to Eastern religion and philosophy is not known, but for the rest of his life he was preoccupied with his health and with theosophy, which in his later years became even more important to him than phonetics.

By the early 1920s Jones had written all his major publications with the exception of *The Phoneme* (1950).

However, this does not mean that he was no longer active in the field, but rather that he concentrated on revising and consolidating his own work and supporting his colleagues and students in their research. He toured Europe and the United States, served the IPA first as secretary and then as president for nearly half a century, and was a member of the advisory board on spoken English of the BBC under the chairmanship of George Bernard Shaw, whom he had met previously in connection with Shaw's play *Pygmalion* and with the Simplified Spelling Society. The eagerly awaited book *The Phoneme* appeared a year after Jones's retirement. Although he had hoped it would be a major contribution to phonetics and phonology, it was received very unfavourably. It was considered to be little more than a collection of his work on phonetics, and with respect to the concept 'phoneme', the observations were roughly the same as those stated in *A Colloquial Sinhalese Reader* in 1919. An important side-effect of the negative reception, however, was Jones's answer to his critics in the form of the booklet *The History and Meaning of the Term 'Phoneme'* (1957), in which he summarises the development of his ideas.

The influence of Jones on phonetics and linguistics must be assessed from three different angles: his organisational, practical and theoretical contributions. From an organisational point of view, he was responsible for establishing the first phonetics department in Britain at University College London. Phonetics, which hitherto was an adjunct to philology, became an important discipline in its own right and was soon represented at other universities. This was one element in paving the way for linguistics as an academic subject. Jones's life-long dream of an Institute of Phonetics, however, has never come true. Through his secretarial and presidential work for the IPA, the association established its leading position in the world of linguistics, while his involvement with the Simplified Spelling Society and the BBC made phonetics known outside the academic field. With respect to his practical contributions, the three books *The Pronunciation of English, An English Pronouncing Dictionary* and *An Outline of English Phonetics* have become the major source-books for the teaching of phonetics and of English as a foreign language. They not only deal with methodological problems but also provide the teacher and students with the theoretical background, and they established the IPA principles of transcriptions throughout the world. Jones's analyses of the lesser-known languages were of great importance to linguistics, as they formed the basis for the description and classification of vowels and for his work in phonemic theory with the concept of the phoneme in particular. This remained Jones's main linguistic focus to the end of his life. He died peacefully on 4 December 1967, at his home in London.

Primary works

(1909). *The Pronunciation of English*. Cambridge: Cambridge University Press.
(1912) (with Paul Passy). *The Principles of the International Phonetics Association*. London: IPA. Supplement to *Le Maître Phonétique* 2(27).

(1913) (with Hermann Michaelis). *A Phonetic Dictionary of the English Language*. Hanover and Berlin: Carl Meyer.
(1917a). *An English Pronouncing Dictionary*. Peter Roach and James Hartman (eds). Cambridge: Cambridge University Press, 1997.
(1917b). 'The phonetic structure of the Sechuana language'. *Transactions of the Philological Society*. 1917–20: 99–106.
(1918). *An Outline of English Phonetics*. Cambridge: Heffer and Sons, 1969.
(1919) (with H. S. Perera). *A Colloquial Sinhalese Reader*. Manchester: Manchester University Press.
(1923) (with Michael Trovimov). *The Pronunciation of Russian*. Cambridge: Cambridge University Press, 1969.
(1944). 'Some thoughts on the phoneme'. *Transactions of the Philological Society*.
(1950). *The Phoneme: Its Nature and Use*. Cambridge: Cambridge University Press, 1976.
(1957). *The History and Meaning of the Term 'Phoneme'*. London: IPA.

Further reading

Abercrombie, David (1983). 'Daniel Jones's teaching'. *Works in Progress* 16. Edinburgh: Department of Linguistics.
Abercrombie, David et al. (1964). *In Honour of Daniel Jones*. London: Longman.
Collins, Beverley and Mees, Inger M. (1998). *The Real Professor Higgins: The Life and Career of Daniel Jones*. Berlin: Mouton de Gruyter.
Ellis, A. J. (1869). *On Early English Pronunciation. Part 1*. London: Philological Society.
Juul, H. and Nielson, H. F. (eds) (1985). *Our Changing Speech: Two BBC Talks by Daniel Jones*. Copenhagen: National Institute for Educational Media.
Michaelis, Hermann and Passy, Paul (1897). *Dictionnaire phonétique de la langue française*. Hanover and Berlin: Carl Meyer.
Sweet, Henry (1908). *The Sounds of English: An Introduction to Phonetics*. Oxford: Clarendon Press, 1929.
Wells, John Christopher (1990). *Longman Pronunciation Dictionary*. Harlow: Longman.

Jürg Strässler

IMMANUEL KANT

Kant, Immanuel (b. 1724, d. 1804; German), philosopher, epistemologist and moral philosopher, professor of logic and metaphysics at the University of Königsberg (1770–96). Kant's contribution to the philosophy of language was to take issue with the idea that humans experience reality itself, and thus he was concerned with the truth status of statements about the world. Perhaps the most influential of all German philosophers, Kant brought the classical period of philosophy from *Plato and *Aristotle to *Descartes and *Leibniz to an end and laid the foundations of modern, 'scientific' philosophy. Kant's work induces the 'transcendental turn' in the history of Western thought, thus overcoming the limits of both rationalism and empiricism and giving rise to idealism, the point of departure of modern philosophical thought since the end of the eighteenth century. (See also Ayer, A. J.; Carnap, Rudolf; Derrida, Jacques; Hegel, G. W. F.; Humboldt, Wilhelm von; Husserl, Edmund.)

Kant was born in the town of Königsberg (then in East Prussia, but in the twenty-first century called Kaliningrad and belonging to Russia) into a Pietist family. At the age of 16 he entered the university of his native town to study theology, physics and mathematics. After receiving his doctorate in 1755, Kant earned his living mainly as a private tutor to students. He is said never to have left the area of Königsberg during his entire life. After he was appointed professor at the University of Königsberg in 1770, Kant continued in his secluded life, devoting most of his time to industrious study and reflection. Yet although he lived in many ways an austere and withdrawn life, Kant's influence was widespread even during his lifetime. In the early 1790s, for example, he came into conflict with the Prussian authorities for his liberal religious views, while his work made him well known across Europe.

The result of Kant's preference for work over the pleasures his fame might have offered is a series of epoch-making writings, including his three *Critiques*. The first one, *Kritik der reinen Vernunft* (*Critique of Pure Reason*), which is of most significance to the philosophy of language, is generally considered to be Kant's masterpiece because of its tremendous impact on the history of philosophy. The so-called A-version of this book was published in 1781; the revised and extended B-version was published six years later. This lengthy treatise is the truly breathtaking expression of a mammoth enterprise in philosophy in which Kant had been engaged for more than ten years, since his appointment at the University of Königsberg. The *Critique of Pure Reason* is entirely novel in conception, range and focus. Yet the book's influence was achieved despite the fact that it is very difficult to read. This is largely because of the complex problems discussed, but can also be attributed to the author's peculiar style. Like most texts by Kant published after 1781, the first *Critique* is very detailed, as it aims for comprehensiveness in every respect, an approach that often results in extremely long, complex sentences. Kant himself was aware of this fact and published a somewhat simplified and indeed much more accessible summary in 1783 under the title *Prolegomena zu einer jeden künftigen Metaphysik* (*Prolegomena to Any Future Metaphysics*). The first *Critique* brought about a 'Copernican revolution' (changing the prevailing view of the world) in philosophy, at least according to Kant himself and most of his followers. Kantian and neo-Kantian trends have continued to be influential in philosophy throughout the nineteenth and twentieth and into the twenty-first centuries. Yet the first *Critique* has also encountered resistance among critics who consider its ethereal kind of reasoning futile or its results irrelevant in view of the 'real' problems faced by humankind. The latter assessment, however, is hardly the outcome of an in-depth analysis of Kant's work and does not do justice to the objectives of Kant's transcendental philosophy.

Though his chief interest was in theories of knowledge, Kant's work directly impacts on the philosophy of language through his notion of the transcendental. First, it should be noted that 'transcendental' – in the sense Kant used the term – is not to be confused with 'transcendent'. The latter term refers to what lies beyond all possible experience; saying that something is 'transcendent' means that it is not accessible to rational thinking, for example the concept of God. 'Transcendental' knowledge, on the other hand, is knowledge of the nature of reasoning, and Kant's 'transcendental' turn is, therefore, not so much concerned with the more traditional topics of philosophy as with the way objects of thought are constituted in acts of reasoning. Second, the transcendental turn in philosophy is based on a thorough reassessment of the theory of knowledge, to such an extent that transcendental philosophy became synonymous with epistemology (a core area of philosophy concerning the nature of knowledge). Indeed, Kant's basic idea is that philosophy should clarify as exactly as possible the principles of reasoning in order to determine the conditions (*Bedingungen der Möglichkeit*) of knowledge proper. Such a clarification is considered to be indispensable and basic to all scientific research aiming at a scientifically valid assessment of the objects of knowledge – in physics, mathematics, the humanities and even metaphysics.

According to Kant, the conditions of knowledge cannot be external to the human intellect: this is one feature of his work that locates transcendental philosophy in the eighteenth-century philosophy of Enlightenment. The phrase 'conditions of knowledge' should be distinguished here from 'origins of knowledge': while most knowledge begins in experience, Kant explains that all knowledge, whatever its origins, is conditioned by the human mind. On the one hand, it is clear to Kant that knowledge, including the kind of knowledge that is at issue in the sciences, is only possible because people are able to experience the 'world' (via sensations). On the other hand, it would be self-contradictory to assume that the objects of knowledge are given to us beforehand and that in reasoning the human intellect just mirrors what it experiences through the senses. Rather everything human beings can know about the 'world' presupposes acts of the intellect in which data is experienced in a structured way and according to rules imposed on the data by the intellect itself. Thus to Kant the very concept of knowledge is philosophically inconceivable unless one presumes an intellect 'producing' objects of knowledge proper, which are to be distinguished from the objective world – whatever that 'world out there' may be. For Kant, the 'things' are only present to the mind as appearances (*Erscheinungen*), not as 'things in themselves', and the truth is that the 'thing in itself' (*Ding an sich*) is an empty, albeit logically necessary, construction of the mind.

Evidently the 'Copernican revolution' Kant believed he had triggered resides in the fact that in his philosophical system the world is subsumed under the ideal 'forms' of reason; that is, formal concepts, categories, ideas, mental schemas and so on through which the human intellect 'produces' knowledge about the world in an infinite number of acts of reasoning, rather than the other way around. In fact, Kant's reference to Copernicus is arguably revealing and the comparison well chosen. At the beginning of the sixteenth century, Copernicus proved that the Ptolemaic view, still held at the time, was wrong and that the earth orbits the sun and not the other way around. Needless to say, the Copernican view has profoundly altered the way we human beings conceive the world and our own condition within it. Something similar could be maintained about the influence of Kant's work on the way later generations of philosophers have defined the task of philosophy.

The key question Kant's ideas of knowledge raise about language is that of the status one has to assign to language and linguistic behaviour in general if one is prepared, like Kant, to consider the 'forms' of reason itself as making knowledge possible. The question is legitimate and obvious, yet Kant does not address it explicitly in his *Critique of Pure Reason*, or in any other publication. At first sight this observation is puzzling, indeed almost frustrating. Contemporaries like Johann Georg Hamann and, above all, Johann Gottfried Herder even went so far as to declare that Kant's entire transcendental enterprise was misguided and his arguments fallacious because he failed to recognise language as the most important condition of knowledge. Ever since the publication of the first *Critique*, this claim has been repeated regularly in one way or another by many critics of Kant in the nineteenth and twentieth centuries, including Heidegger and Gadamer. In the more recent history of philosophy, a comparable claim can be found in so-called 'transcendental pragmatism', a philosophical trend that merges Kantian thought with some of the central concepts introduced by the 'linguistic' and 'pragmatic' turns in philosophy represented by Jürgen Habermas and Karl-Otto Apel, among others. Finally, it should be added that Kant has also attracted the attention of scholars working in analytic philosophy and its diverse offshoots, including W. V. O. *Quine,

Hilary *Putnam, Richard Rorty and the Vienna Circle.

Upon closer investigation, the radical claim that the main argument of Kant's *Critique of Pure Reason* is invalid, because it abstracts away from language as the ultimate principle of reason and the allegedly basic condition of human knowledge, proves spurious. As Manfred Riedel (1982) has pointed out, Kant does not explicitly go into the question of whether reason relies on language or vice versa, because the entire *Critique* presupposes the 'transcendental correlation' of both. From a Kantian point of view, it would be equally inconsistent to claim either that reason is conditioned by language or, conversely, that language is a product of reason. The latter view was advocated by the seventeenth-century rationalist school of Port Royal, including Claude Lancelot and Antoine *Arnauld. The view that language and reason are transcendentally correlated with one another emphasises the difference between both without giving priority to either. It could be argued that Kant deliberately refrains from drawing language into his discussion because this would needlessly complicate the enterprise of transcendental philosophy and obfuscate his new theory of knowledge. If one looks at the first *Critique* from this angle, Kant seems to occupy a place right in the middle between rationalist theories of language on the one hand and romanticist views on the other. To Kant, language does not provide the arbitrary or otherwise accidental 'form' to prior thoughts, just as thought itself is not simply the 'matter' of linguistic forms and structures.

At least two important observations can be made in favour of the view that in Kant's transcendental philosophy language and reason are not conditioned by each other. The first one bears upon a central argument expounded in the *Critique of Pure Reason*, that is, Kant's famous account of the so-called categories: *reine Verstandesbegriffe* (pure concepts of understanding) in relation to judgement. The second observation can be drawn from the way Wilhelm von *Humboldt succeeds in integrating Kant's transcendental philosophy into his own coherent and highly sophisticated philosophical theory of language. This is all the more remarkable as Humboldt, whose own linguistic research was ahead of that of his colleagues for generations, did not subscribe to the panlinguistic attack on Kant in Herder's controversial and strangely unproductive *Metakritik der Kritik der reinen Vernunft* (1799).

Kant's adaptation of the Aristotelian theory of categories irrefutably proves the 'transcendental correlation' of language and reason in his philosophy. Unlike 'space' and 'time', considered to be the two non-discursive, pure forms of mental representation (*Anschauung*, traditionally somewhat inaccurately translated as 'intuition'), Kant's categories are directly related to the realm of propositions. The difference between the pure forms 'space' and 'time' on the one hand and the categories on the other is particularly relevant if one attempts to determine the importance of Kant's transcendental philosophy for the philosophy of language. The mind necessarily conceives appearances (which originate in the 'things' one experiences) in spatial and temporal form, yet space and time are neither empirical nor discursive concepts (*Begriffe*). With the categories, however, the case is very different. Kant distinguishes four types of general categorical concepts: quantity, quality, relation and modality. Under each type Kant subsumes three categories, the entire table of categories thus amounting to twelve. It is both significant and remarkable that Kant labels the categories with familiar terms like *Einheit* (unity), *Vielheit* (plurality) and *Allheit* (totality), his three categories of quantity, and *Realität* (reality), *Negation* (negation) and *Limitation* (limitation), the categories of quality, for example. These terms refer not only to the *a priori* concepts the mind selectively applies whenever it performs some act of thought, but simultaneously also to meanings with a propositional value, as these concepts guide the understanding in allowing it to produce and interpret meaningful and communicable propositions. It comes as no surprise, then, that in one of the very few passages in his work where Kant discusses language in any detail (§§38–9 of his 1798 treatise on *Anthropology*), he stresses that natural language is an invaluable tool for referring to thought. Furthermore, he adds that language is the most elaborate means of understanding oneself and others (*das größte Mittel, sich selbst und andere zu verstehen*), and even goes so far as to claim that to think is to speak to and correspondingly to hear oneself. He thus finally explicates the 'transcendental correlation' of language and reason upon which all major works of his 'critical' period seem to be based.

According to Kant, the categories are mutually irreducible abstract concepts emerging from our *Verstand*, that is, our faculty of understanding based on the human intellect. For Kant, the list of twelve categories is exhaustive; they stand for the twelve possible ways of conceiving objects of knowledge. The categories are presented as *a priori* concepts of the understanding, and there can be no doubt that for Kant the categories are both universally valid and immutable. This does not mean, however, that they are 'beyond' language. Although the transcendental correlation in the first *Critique* does not imply any reference to one specific language or another (German as opposed to English or Japanese, for example), Kant is very much concerned with deducing the categories from a 'common principle', and this principle, too, can immediately be linked to a propositional and, consequently, linguistic attitude. According to Kant, the common principle is to be found in the faculty of judgement. To be able to judge means to be able to apply categories to raw data, and to synthesise in a structured way and in terms of concepts what is to Kant a disjointed and heterogeneous input. The human intellect thus transforms the data entering into our experience into discrete objects of knowledge. It is clear throughout the three *Critiques* and the treatise on anthropology that for Kant the linguistic aspect of judgements, in particular the structure of subject and predicate, is a necessary component of the faculty of judgement as such. And when he claims that all judgements are 'functions of unity' among our representations, then this unity is as much based on the universal patterns of the human mind as it is couched in meaningful language structures.

Some passages in the controversial chapter on transcendental 'schemas' in the first *Critique* point in the same direction. Schemas are introduced by Kant as the 'third thing' between the *a priori* concepts on the one hand and the mental representation of data on the other. While the logically irreducible concepts belong to reason and are limited in number, the mental representations are infinite and manifold. A merging of both is necessary to attain true knowledge. This can only be achieved if an intermediate level of intellectual creativity is invoked. This level is called the faculty of imagination (*Einbildungskraft*) by Kant. Thanks to this faculty, he writes, we are able to imagine a dog schematically, without having one or more particular dogs in mind. Obviously, though he himself does not make the link, such a schema is perfectly co-extensive with the general class-meaning of the word *dog* (or any corresponding word in other languages). Interestingly, the work of 'schematism', Kant adds, is 'an art concealed in the depths of the human soul' (*eine verborgene Kunst in den Tiefen der menschlichen Seele*).

Alongside the work on the mental representation of data, Kant's treatment of analytic and synthetic judgements in *Critique of Pure Reason* has been widely discussed by philosophers of language. Analytic judgements are those that are necessarily true. From a linguistic point of view, they are known to be true simply because of the meanings of the words they contain. Kant's own example is 'All bodies are extended'. This is true because the concept of the subject ('bodies') contains the concept of the predicate ('extended'). In a synthetic judgement, however, there is no necessary connection between the subject and predicate (Kant's example is 'All bodies are heavy'). Again, from a linguistic point of view the truth value of a synthetic judgement depends on factors outside the language, so truth cannot be determined by linguistic analysis alone. At the time that *Critique of Pure Reason* was published the received wisdom was that all analytic judgements were *a priori* (known without recourse to experience), while all synthetic judgements were *a posteriori* (dependent on or following from experience). Kant argued that it is possible for judgements to be both synthetic and *a priori*; that is, known to be true neither from experience nor because of the meaning of the words needed to express the judgements. Our knowledge of the truth of such judgements depends on the 'pure reason' in which Kant is interested; it depends on our human system of perception and reasoning. He uses the example of the statements of mathematics. We know that the statement 'seven plus five is equal to twelve' is true, but nothing in the concepts 'seven' and 'five' contains the concept of being equal to 'twelve'. Nor can we imagine any possible evidence that would either confirm our belief in this statement or convince us that it is false. Our knowledge of and belief in this statement depend on the system of mathematics, part of the perceptual structure through which we understand the world.

Although he remained in the town where he was born his whole life, Kant's influence spread quickly. Ever since the first *Critique* appeared in 1781, his transcendental philosophy (also referred to as 'critical philosophy') has been the object of lively debates and intensive research. His ideas have generated huge amounts of secondary literature and have been influential across disciplines as diverse as philosophy, ethics, critical theory, psychology and linguistics. The publication of monographs and articles on Kant has continued almost uninterrupted into the twenty-first century.

Primary works

(1900–) *Kants Gesammelte Schriften (Akademie-Ausgabe)* (29 vols.). Deutsche (formerly Königlich Preußische) Akademie der Wissenschaften (ed.) Berlin: Georg Riemer and Walter de Gruyter.

(1781[A]/1787[B]). *Kritik der reinen Vernunft (Akademie-Ausgabe,* vols. 3 and 4). *Critique of Pure Reason.* N. K. Smith (trans.). New York: St Martin's Press, 1965.

(1783). *Prolegomena zu einer jeden künftigen Metaphysik, die als Wissenschaft wird auftreten können (Akademie-Ausgabe,* vol. 4). *Prolegomena to Any Future Metaphysics.* L. W. Beck (trans.). Indianapolis: Bobbs-Merrill, 1950.

(1788). *Kritik der praktischen Vernunft (Akademie-Ausgabe,* vol. 5). *Critique of Practical Reason.* L. W. Beck (trans.). New York: Garland, 1976.

(1790). *Kritik der Urteilskraft (Akademie-Ausgabe,* vol. 5). *Critique of Judgment.* W. Pluhar (trans.). Indianapolis: Hackett, 1987.

(1798). *Anthropologie in pragmatischer Hinsicht (Akademie-Ausgabe,* vol. 7). *Anthropology from a Pragmatic Point of View.* M. Gregor (trans.). The Hague: Martinus Nijhoff, 1974.

Further reading

Allison, Henry E. (1983). *Kant's Transcendental Idealism: An Interpretation and Defense.* New Haven and London: Yale University Press.

Cassirer, Ernst (1921, second edition). *Kants Leben und Lehre.* Berlin: Verlag Paul Cassirer. (Reprinted Darmstadt: Wissenschaftliche Buchgesellschaft, 1994). English translation: *Kant's Life and Thought.* J. Haden (trans.). New Haven, CI: Yale University Press, 1981.

Guyer, Paul (ed.) (1992). *The Cambridge Companion to Kant.* Cambridge: Cambridge University Press.

Höffe, Otfried (2000, fifth edition). *Immanuel Kant.* Munich: C. H. Beck. English translation: *Immanuel Kant.* M. Farrier (trans.). New York: State University of New York Press, 1994.

Howell, Robert (1992). *Kant's Transcendental Deduction: An Analysis of Main Themes in his Critical Philosophy.* Dordrecht: Kluwer.

Riedel, Manfred (1982). 'Kritik der reinen Vernunft und Sprache: Zum Kategorienproblem bei Kant'. *Allgemeine Zeitschrift für Philosophie.* Vol. 2: 1–15.

Klaas Willems

J. J. KATZ

Katz, J. J. (Jerrold Jacob) (*b.* 1932, *d.* 2002; American), taught at Massachusetts Institute of Technology (MIT) (1961–75) and was distinguished professor of philosophy and linguistics at the Graduate Centre of the City University of New York (CUNY) (1975–2002). Made significant contributions to linguistic semantics, philosophy of language, philosophy of linguistics, philosophy of mathematics, philosophy of science, metaphilosophy and metaphysics. A die-hard *Platonist, Katz advocated intensionalism in semantics. His publications include fourteen books and over seventy published papers. (*See also* Austin, J. L.; Chomsky, Noam; Fodor, Jerry; Frege, Gottlob; Quine, W. V. O.)

Katz was born in Washington, D. C., to parents who had little to do with academic life. His father, son of Lithuanian immigrants, was a butcher and his American-born mother, of Polish extraction, raised the family, having grown up on a farm in upstate New York. As a young boy at school, Katz read a lot but showed no particular academic interests. Instead he dreamed of a career in professional football (American football), despite his below average stature. Katz, who was known as 'Jerry' to his friends and close associates, received his BA from the George Washington University in 1954. After a brief period serving with the United States Army Counter Intelligence Corps, he received his PhD from Princeton in 1960. He began his career under the influence of *Chomsky, but later distanced himself from his mentor.

Katz will long be remembered for his spirited and untiring defence of, among other things, intensionalism in semantics at a time when the whole notion of meaning was under sustained attack from a number of eminent philosophers and linguists. Foremost amongst these scholars was *Quine, who argued against the distinction between analytic and synthetic propositions, a corner-stone of intensionalist semantics. Intensionalism claims that there is a distinct level of semantic structure in natural languages and that it is thanks to the relations existing at this level (including relations such as synonymy, anomaly and entailment) that one can determine the denotation of expressions, the truth condition of declarative sentences, the type of answers required by interrogatives and so on. For example, the meaning of the English word *bachelor* is claimed to be fully explicated by the expression 'adult unmarried human male' and the meaning of a sentence containing the word is to be regarded as a function of this meaning. In his defence of intensionalist semantics, Katz did acknowledge the powerful influence of *Frege. However, he rejected Frege's semantics, especially the idea that sense and reference are entirely independent.

Very early on, Katz set himself to find a way to analyse formally the question 'What is meaning?' His answer was that the task could be addressed in much the same way as the one Chomsky had proposed in his syntactic theory. In 1963 in collaboration with *Fodor, he published an important paper called 'The structure of a semantic theory', and in the following year, a landmark book entitled *An Integrated Theory of Linguistic Descriptions*, co-authored with Paul Postal. The importance of these early works can hardly be overestimated. The Katz-Fodor hypothesis, as it is widely known, paved the way for the integration of syntax and semantics within the framework of Chomsky's transformational generative grammar. The whole approach was summed up in the slogan: 'Linguistic description minus grammar equals semantics.' It was thought that semantics had a purely interpretative role and that its functioning depended on the prior availability of a fully worked out syntactic component. This claim subsequently became a major tenet of the so-called 'Aspects model' of generative grammar, the model elaborated by Chomsky (1965). In the late 1960s and early 1970s it was at the centre of what is often described as a 'civil war' within the generative paradigm, when a group led by George Lakoff, John Ross, James McCawley and others, all former students of Chomsky like Katz, proposed a theoretical alternative referred to in the literature as 'generative semantics'.

Katz's 1972 book *Semantic Theory* had a profound influence on linguistics, philosophy and psychology. With its uncompromising defence of linguistic universality as 'the basis on which the explications of semantic properties and relations in a semantic theory achieve the status of philosophical analyses', the book also provided philosophical support to the then fledgling field of cognitive science. But Katz's interest went far beyond the confines of the generative paradigm in which he had begun his work. Barely two years after the publication of the groundbreaking work with Postal, he published *The Philosophy of Language*. In this book Katz defended a brand-new approach, one that steered clear of what it identified as its two principal rivals: logical empiricism and ordinary language philosophy. Reiterating his position that philosophy of language should engage in the philosophical investigation of conceptual knowledge and, further, that no theory of language could be considered minimally satisfactory unless it offered a clear statement of linguistic universals, Katz faulted the two rival candidates for shunning rationalism and treating concepts as anathema.

Katz's *Propositional Structure and Illocutionary Force* (1977) is a concerted effort to accommodate some of the key insights of the theory of speech acts, as developed by the Oxford philosopher J. L. *Austin, within the theory of generative grammar. Katz's strategy consisted in positing a neat separation of semantics and pragmatics, which none the less did not coincide with the constative/performative divide as many supposed. Drawing on an earlier claim of regarding the meaning of a sentence as 'the utterance meaning of a use of the sentence in a context devoid of anything that might contribute to contextual construal', Katz argued that those aspects of the meaning of a speech act that have to do with contextual construal should be treated by a separate pragmatic component, leaving semantics free to account for the illocutionary potential, now regarded as a property of sentences functioning in the absence of any context whatsoever. He vigorously defended the concept of a 'null context', on which the whole thesis hinged, by comparing it to similar idealisations such as the physicist's notion of perfect vacuum or frictionless plane.

J. J. KATZ

To defend meaning against the systematic onslaught it had been subjected to by logical positivists and ordinary language philosophers, Katz embarked on a full-length defence of both meaning and metaphysics, and the result was his 1990 book *The Metaphysics of Meaning*. In his view, metaphysics had fallen into disrepute because of *Kant's failure to defend synthetic *a priori* as its locus. As an ardent advocate of mathematical realism and traditional rationalism, Katz also contended that past attempts to defend each of these independently of the other had been primarily responsible for disenchantment with both, especially in the second half of the twentieth century.

Katz's unshakeable faith in realism and rationalism put him on a collision course with the 'linguistic turn' in philosophy, which in his view was an attempt to question all possibility of a non-naturalist metaphysics with the help of linguistic arguments. Naturalism insists that in philosophy only 'hard science' can provide valid explanations for the existence or behaviour of things. Rejecting outright all naturalistic explanations, including Chomsky's, Katz advanced the view that language is an abstract object in Plato's sense. The study of language should, in his view, thus be seen as a branch of mathematics and not, for example, of cognitive psychology, as Chomsky claimed.

Katz was an original thinker of open mind but firm convictions; he was such a dynamic character that a friend once said that talking to him was like talking to five people. He was fully aware of the extreme contentiousness

of some of the theoretical stances he took, and was unflinching in the defence of his convictions even when he knew that the views he held were not fashionable in mainstream circles. Katz was married twice and had two children. He suffered for some time with cancer and died on 7 February 2002 in New York. On the day before his death he signed a contract with Oxford University Press for the publication of his final book, *Sense, Reference and Philosophy*, completed a year before.

Primary works

(1963) (with J. A. Fodor). 'The structure of a semantic theory'. *Language*. Vol. 39: 170–210.

(1964) (with Paul M. Postal). *An Integrated Theory of Linguistic Descriptions*. Cambridge, MA: MIT Press.

(1966). *The Philosophy of Language*. New York: Harper and Row.

(1972). *Semantic Theory*. New York: Harper and Row.

(1977). *Propositional Structure and Illocutionary Force*. New York: Thomas Y. Crowell.

(1998). *The Realistic Rationalism*. Cambridge, MA: MIT Press.

(1990). *The Metaphysics of Meaning*. Cambridge, MA: MIT Press.

(2003). *Sense, Reference and Philosophy*. Oxford: Oxford University Press.

Further reading

Chomsky, N. A. (1965). *Aspects of the Theory of Syntax*. Cambridge, MA: MIT Press.

Quine, W. V. O. (1960). *Word and Object*. Cambridge, MA: MIT Press.

Kanavillil Rajagopalan

SAUL KRIPKE

Kripke, Saul (Aaron) (*b.* 1940; American), assistant professor, Harvard (1964–76) and concurrently Rockefeller (1967–76), McCosh professor of philosophy, Princeton (1977–97), emeritus from 1997, visiting professor at City University New York (CUNY) from 2003. Analytical philosopher who from his work on modality and possible worlds went on to make innovative and influential claims about naming and reference, necessity, identity and metaphysics. (*See also* Frege, Gottlob; Putnam, Hilary; Russell, Bertrand; Wittgenstein, Ludwig.)

Saul Kripke was in his teens when, from his home in Omaha, Nebraska, he published his first paper on modal logic. He was the precocious child of Myer Kripke, a rabbi, and Dorothy Kripke, a well-known author of children's books on Judaism. Saul was born in Bay Shore, New York State, and the Kripkes moved to Omaha in 1946. After high school he enrolled at Harvard for a BA in mathematics, his only non-honorary degree. At Harvard, where he later became a fellow, he continued to work on modal logic, but his best-known work, *Naming and Necessity*, is based on three lectures that he delivered at Princeton in 1970, at the age of 30. The published lectures, as Richard Rorty has commented, 'stood analytical philosophy on its ear', and changed the way that philosophy of language was done (Preti 2003). Kripke was appointed at Princeton after the publication of the lectures and remained there until

2003. His next major work, published in 1982, is an exegesis of passages of *Wittgenstein's *Philosophical Investigations*, and while the arguments it expresses have not been as readily accepted, they have commanded no less attention.

Kripke's work in modal logic is rather technical and challenging for the non-specialist. He is credited with providing a means of interpreting, or providing a semantics for, syntactic constructions in modal logic. In modal logic, unlike in non-modal logic, the truth value of a proposition cannot be given as the truth values of its component parts. Kripke suggested that the operators 'possibly' and 'necessarily' should be expressed as the quantifiers 'all' and 'some', which then operate across sets of possible worlds. So, a necessary truth is true across all possible worlds, and a possible truth is true in some possible world. Using such a model, the truth value of complex modal formulae can be assessed.

It is Kripke's use of possible worlds in *Naming and Necessity* that makes the approach interesting to a broader audience. The text, a lightly edited transcription of the lectures (given without notes), is deceptively informal in style, with a number of very memorable examples. Its claims, however, are complex and far-reaching. Setting aside certain differences in *Frege's and *Russell's views on sense and reference, Kripke begins by announcing a challenge to the 'Frege-Russell view' that reference is achieved through associating a name with a description. He demonstrates that even if the property in question turned out not to apply to the referent, these names would still be referring to the same people. For example, if Jonah was not swallowed by a big fish, Aristotle was not the teacher of Alexander, the man who proved the incompleteness of arithmetic was not in fact Gödel but someone called Schmidt, these expressions would still be referring to the same people. Names are 'rigid designators': they apply across all possible worlds or counterfactual situations, that is, situations that are possible but do not apply to what we understand as reality. 'Nixon', for example, is a rigid designator, but 'president of the US in 1970' is not. Rigid designators are in fact what makes it possible for us to talk about counterfactual situations, such as 'Hitler might never have been born'. Kripke reminds us that we do not try to identify particulars and their properties in possible worlds, but that, rather, possible worlds are stipulated by us. The same arguments apply to attempts to rescue the descriptions theory with 'clusters' of descriptions, which hold that a sufficient number of appropriate descriptions make reference possible.

Kripke's alternative positive view, now known as the causal theory of reference, holds that reference works through a 'chain of communication'. Reference is fixed through an initial 'baptism', after which the name is passed on from link to link in the community. A speaker is able to use a name by virtue of his or her membership of a community. In this way it is possible for someone to use a name without knowing very much about the referent at all. One of Kripke's own examples refers to Richard Feynman, a theoretical physicist who would have been well known to most of Kripke's original audience, though perhaps not to the 'man in the street'. Even so, Kripke argues that even the 'man in the street' might ask, when given the name Richard Feynman, 'Isn't he a physicist or something?' In other words, despite not having a unique description for the referent, the 'man in Vre street' can still use the name Feynman correctly. Kripke argues that although 'he may not think that this picks out anyone uniquely, I still think he uses the term "Feynman" as a name for Feynman'. At the initial baptism, reference can be fixed through ostension (by indicating it physically), but also through description. Kripke illustrates the latter case through examples such as 'a metre is the length of stick S', making the point that, when descriptions are used, it is to 'fix the reference' of an expression rather than give its meaning.

Arriving at similar insights to those of Hilary *Putnam, Kripke goes on to claim that the names of certain kinds of natural phenomena are also rigid designators. In the same way as a description may turn out not to apply to a person, it could be discovered that tigers are not quadrupedal but three-legged; we would still call them 'tigers'. Importantly, Kripke sees statements such as 'heat is molecular motion' and 'gold is atomic number 79' as necessary truths (true in all possible worlds), even though they are scientific discoveries and not *a priori*. This challenged a long-held *Kantian distinction between analytic truth (necessary and *a priori*) and synthetic truth (contingent and *a posteriori*). Kripke was thus distinguishing between metaphysical necessity and epistemological necessity.

In his third and last lecture, Kripke examines identity statements that have implications for the mind–body problem. He claims that 'heat is molecular motion' is not the same as 'pain is the stimulation of C-fibers', because the referent of 'pain' cannot be fixed by something that is an external phenomenon of pain, unlike the referent of 'heat', which can be fixed as 'sensation S'. This reasoning presents an ongoing challenge to those who wish to establish identity between mental states and brain states.

In *Wittgenstein on Rules and Private Language*, Kripke continues his pursuit of the nature of meaning. In the *Philosophical Investigations*, Wittgenstein is usually read as explicitly warning against understanding as a mental, inner phenomenon, emphasising the ways in which understanding a sign is about grasping the application of the sign and following a rule. Wittgenstein had not been regarded as a sceptic, but Kripke's reading of Wittgenstein is that he is in fact presenting a 'sceptical paradox': if I appear to be rule following in my use of a sign now, there is no way of telling whether I was following the same rule in the past when I used that sign. I may have been following another rule which produces the same effect. Thus every time a speaker uses a sign it is 'a leap in the dark', and there is nothing at all that determines the meaning of signs. Wittgenstein's solution to this paradox, according to Kripke, is to say that it is in the community of speakers and in their agreement with my use of a sign that meaning lies. According to Wittgenstein's private language argument, it is not possible to determine whether speakers of a private language are appearing to follow a rule or actually doing so. The normativity of language makes a private language impossible, for how could we know if such a speaker was following his or her rules correctly? Just some of the controversy over *Wittgenstein on Rules and Private Language* has centred on the meaning of 'private' in the text, and the question of whether Kripke has imposed an interpretation on Wittgenstein's text that is contrary to Wittgenstein's aims.

In addition to scholars of Wittgenstein, Kripke's work has certainly busied scholars of essentialist metaphysics, while possible worlds semantics continues to be developed. While Kripke clearly changed the terms of the debate on naming and reference, he has not developed his theory of reference further. In *Naming and Necessity* he claims to be simply presenting 'a better picture', but admits that he gives no necessary and sufficient conditions for reference. Historiographers have examined the origins and development, and in some cases questioned the originality, of Kripke's theory (see Fetzer and Humphreys 2000), but Kripke is a formidable philosophical opponent, known for his willingness to make stout defence of his work. He was honoured with the Schock prize in logic and philosophy in 2001, the equivalent of a Nobel.

Primary works

(1959). 'A completeness theorem in modal logic'. *Journal of Symbolic Logic*. Vol. 24: 1–14.
(1963). 'Semantical considerations on modal logic'. *Acta Philosophica Fennica*. Vol. 16: 83–94.

(1972). 'Naming and necessity'. In D. David-son and G. Harman (eds). *Semantics of Natural Language*. Dordrecht: Reidl. Republished (1980) as *Naming and Necessity*. Cambridge, MA: Harvard University Press.

(1982). *Wittgenstein on Rules and Private Language*. Cambridge, MA: Harvard University Press.

Further reading

Devitt, M. and Sterelny, K. (1999).*Language and Reality: An Introduction to the Philosophy of Language*. Second edition. Cambridge, MA: MIT Press.

Fetzer, J. and Humphreys, P. (eds) (2000). *The New Theory of Reference: Kripke, Marcus and its Origins*. Dordrecht: Reidl.

Fitch, G. W. (2003). *Saul Kripke*. Teddington: Acumen.

Preti, Consuelo (2003). *On Kripke*. Toronto: Wadsworth.

Rorty, Richard (1980). 'Kant vs. Kripke: a review of *Naming and Necessity*'. *London Review of Books*. Vol. 2(17): 4–5.

Soames, Scott (2002). *Beyond Rigidity: The Unfinished Semantic Agenda of Naming and Necessity*. Oxford: Oxford University Press.

Claire Cowie

JULIA KRISTEVA

Kristeva, Julia (*b.* 1941; Bulgarian/French), linguist, semiotician, psychoanalyst, literary theorist and critic, cultural theorist and critic, writer. A professor of linguistics at the Université de Paris VII and a practising psychoanalyst, Kristeva was one of the leading French intellectuals to effect the shift from structuralism to poststructuralism. Her main contribution to linguistics and the philosophy of language is the identifica-tion of two modalities in language: the semiotic (pre-verbal, drive-related) and the symbolic (verbal, social). She is also credited with coining the term 'intertextuality', now a key concept in critical discourse analysis and literary criticism. (*See also*: Bakhtin, Mikhail; Barthes, Roland; Benveniste, Émile; Derrida, Jacques; Hegel, G. W. F.; Husserl, Edmund; Lacan, Jacques; Peirce, C. S.; Saussure, Ferdinand de; Todorov, Tzvetan.)

Julia Kristeva was born on 24 June 1941 in Silven, Bulgaria, the daughter of a church accountant. Because her parents were not members of the ruling communist party, Kristeva was excluded from the privileges enjoyed by the children of the communist 'middle class'. Both she and her sister were sent to a school run by Dominican nuns, where she received, as she says, a 'francophile and francophone' education (1997: 6). Being educated in a communist Eastern European setting, however, she had the opportunity to become acquainted with the work of the Russian formalists and the post-formalist Russian theorist Mikhail *Bakhtin. While a postgraduate student at the University of Sofia, she obtained a doctoral research fellowship to study in France and left for Paris in December 1965. Once there, she started working on her thesis on the origins of the novel under the direction of Lucien Goldmann, Roland *Barthes and J. Dubois. She also became a laboratory assistant for Claude Lévi-Strauss and attended seminars with Jacques *Lacan, whose *Saussurian Freudianism had a great impact on her work. Kristeva soon became involved with the avant-garde journal *Tel Quel*, which provided a forum for structuralist and poststructuralist thought. Through her involvement with *Tel Quel* she was introduced to many of the leading French intellectuals of the time: Jacques *Derrida, Michel Foucault, Marcelin Playnet and Jacques Henric, as well as the editor of the journal, Philippe Sollers, who later became her husband. Kristeva shared the preoccupation with the relationship between language and subjectivity evident in the work of many structuralist and poststructuralist theorists of the time, most notably Barthes, Lacan, Derrida and *Benveniste. What set her apart from these theorists, however, was her effort to claim a central role for the speaking subject as a physical entity in the study of language.

Kristeva's first published article appeared in *La Pensée* as early as 1966 and was soon followed by publications in such prestigious journals as *Critique, Langages* and, of course, *Tel Quel*, the editorial board of which she joined in 1970. A number of these articles were published in 1969 in a volume entitled Σημειωτική: *Recherche pour une émanalyse (Sèméiotikè: Research towards a Semanalysis)*. In this collection of essays, Kristeva puts forward her own brand of semiotic analysis, for which she coined the term 'semanalysis' by blending semiotics and psychoanalysis. Although she very rarely uses the term 'semanalysis' in later writings, a substantial body of her work, especially in the 1960s and 1970s, can be seen as an elaboration of the 'semanalytic' project outlined in this collection of essays.

In *Sèméiotikè*, Kristeva combines Saussure's semiology and *Peirce's semiotics with Lacan's interpretation

of Freud and with Benveniste's theory of the subject of enunciation, in order to provide a dynamic theory of language centred on the speaking subject as both a physical and a social entity. The structuralist paradigm, useful though it had been up to that point, had viewed language as a static system of signs, cut off from the subject and its history. Conditioned by the laws of capitalist society, where value is ascribed to the products of processes rather than the processes themselves, structuralism had abstracted away from reality in order to study language as a lifeless object, a product. Even though semanalysis incorporated the techniques and procedures of the Saussurian structuralist paradigm, Kristeva replaced the notion of language as a static product with the concept of language as a dynamic process.

In place of the notion of a unitary subject and a unified, autonomous text central to the discursive practices of the Western world, Kristeva posited a plural subject and a 'plural, plurilinguistic, polyphonic' text. After Freud's distinction between conscious and unconscious, the subject, according to Kristeva, could no longer be seen as unitary. On the other hand, the idea of a polyphonic text derives from the writings of Bakhtin, whose work Kristeva and her compatriot, Tzvetan *Todorov, introduced to Western audiences. Kristeva elaborated Bakhtin's notions of dialogism and ambivalence and coined the term 'intertextuality' to describe the heterogeneous, polyphonic nature of texts. Textual space for Kristeva is three-dimensional, the three co-ordinates being the writing subject, the addressee and exterior texts. This textual space is organised in two intersecting planes: a horizontal plane linking writing subject and addressee, and a vertical plane connecting the text with exterior texts. It is in this sense that the text is polyphonic: it is the locus of an intersection of texts brought to bear by both the writer and the reader.

Textual analysis proceeds in parallel on two levels: the phenotext and the genotext. This distinction is central in Kristeva's semanalytic project. The phenotext is the surface structure of the text, its linguistic structure in terms of phonology, syntax, semantics and so on. Traditional textual approaches have assumed that the meaning of a text is exhausted in an analysis of this surface structure. The genotext, on the other hand, is the underlying structure of the text which is not reducible to language. It is the pre-verbal, instinctual motivation underlying all enunciation. The genotext makes itself visible on the surface structure as a deviation from the grammatical rules of language, and according to Kristeva, it is the level where meaning is produced.

Semanalysis, however, was more ambitious in its scope than providing a theory of language and textual analysis only; it was meant to be a science of the production of models. For Barthes, semiotics was subordinated to the study of language as a sign system; language provided the model through which all other sign systems could be studied. Kristeva, while retaining the 'epistemological dependence' of semiotics on linguistics, argues for a semiotics of signifying systems in general, language being just one such system. Moreover, conscious of the fact that any theory

is determined by and reflects the ideologies of the society within which it is formulated, Kristeva intended semanalysis to be an auto-critical science, constantly questioning the ideological underpinnings of its own practices and assumptions.

The year 1969 also saw the publication of *Langage, cet inconnu* (translated as *Language, the Unknown*, 1989), initially published under the name Julia Joyaux (Philippe Sollers's family name) but reprinted in 1981 under Julia Kristeva's own name. This book, aptly subtitled *An Initiation* (rather than introduction) *into Linguistics*, is unlike most other linguistic textbooks one is likely to encounter. There is no attempt to itemise and describe the various levels of linguistic analysis, such as syntax, semantics or morphology, except in a summary fashion. Rather, Kristeva undertakes a detailed exposition of the history of the study of language in order to demonstrate that there is nothing like a linear accumulation of knowledge regarding the question 'What is language?' Language is the 'unknown' for the *Chomskyan proponents of generative grammar as much as it was for the Sumerians and Akkadians thousands of years ago. What this vast survey of the history of linguistics reveals, however, is that the way language is thought of or theorised is inextricably tied to the social, historical and philosophical circumstances of the day. Tracing the beginnings of the study of language as a science to ancient Greece, Kristeva arrives at a description of twentieth-century linguistics for which language has been objectified and cut off both from the society in which it is practised and from the speaking subject. However, Kristeva argues that the psychoanalytic study of language demonstrates that studying language independently of the subject is impossible: language as a formal system is simply non-existent outside speech. Kristeva also repeats here that the study of language would profit if it were incorporated in a more general semiotic theory of signifying practices.

These books prepared the ground for *La Révolution du langage poétique* (1974), arguably Kristeva's most important work up to that date.This was actually her doctoral thesis, which she defended in 1973 with press coverage from *Le Monde*. *La Révolution du langage poétique* is a massive 600-odd-page volume, only the first part of which (*Theoretical Preliminaries*) has been translated in English as *Revolution in Poetic Language* (1984). The sections omitted from the English translation contain the application of her theoretical framework to the work of the avant-garde nineteenth-century poets Mallarmé and Lautréamont.

The much-quoted opening sentence of *Revolution in Poetic Language* reiterates Kristeva's objection to linguistics as practised throughout the twentieth century: 'Our philosophies of language, embodiments of the Idea, are nothing more than the thoughts of archivists, archaeologists and necrophiliacs.' Kristeva's main concern here, as in *Sèméiotikè*, is with de-objectifying language, recontextualising it in the realm of the social, and viewing it as a dynamic, heterogeneous process in which the speaking subject is engaged.

Unlike the unitary *Cartesian subject posited by Chomskyan linguistics, Kristeva posits a heterogeneous, split subject (analogous here with Chomsky's 'ideal speaker') in process/on trial (*sujet en procès*). The Kristevan subject is split between the physical and the social, the semiotic and the symbolic modalities of language. The semiotic disposition represents the dynamic sum of biological drives in the Freudian sense that precede the acquisition of language as a formal system of rules. These drives are encompassed within the semiotic 'chora', a term Kristeva borrows from *Plato. The semiotic chora designates both a receptacle and the maternal womb and acquires a connotation of the feminine and the maternal. The chora is a pre-social, psychic space, where the symbolic separation from the maternal body has not yet taken place and the subject sounds produced by the young child are the outward manifestation of the biological drives in the semiotic chora. The symbolic, on the other hand, is the realm of the social, presupposing a subject, an addressee, and a conventionalised language as a formal system with its syntax and semantics. The symbolic marks the separation between the subject and objects external to it, which is a precondition of the acquisition of language as a formal system. The child, realising its separateness from the objects surrounding it, also realises that combinations of sounds can be used systematically to refer to those external objects. Borrowing the term 'thetic' from *Husserl, Kristeva maintains that the symbolic is the realm of the thetic, that is, of position, judgement, and hence rationality.

The passage from the undifferentiated semiotic chora to the symbolic realm of position and judgement (that is, language acquisition) takes place during the 'thetic phase', which is evident at two points: the mirror stage and the discovery of castration. Here Kristeva follows Lacan's account of language acquisition. During the mirror stage, the child first becomes aware of its separateness from objects in the world and also from the mother. The fear of castration forces separation from the mother and identification with the father. In this way, the child acquires language as a means of substituting for an absent, desired object: the mother. Once the child enters the realm of the symbolic, the semiotic chora is partially repressed and surfaces in communication as the play of sounds (rhythm, rhyme, intonation) and as a disruption of the rules of conventional grammar.

Even though Kristeva uses *Hegel's dialectic (thesis–antithesis–synthesis) in order to describe the relation of the semiotic to the symbolic, for her synthesis between the two elements never takes place; the semiotic and the symbolic are in constant tension and it is this tension that produces signification. In other words, the semiotic and the symbolic are inseparable. The semiotic provides the motivation to speak in the first place; without it there would be no symbolic communication. But, on the other hand, the symbolic provides the formal means for communication: without it there would only be meaningless sound. It should have become apparent by now that Kristeva's use of the semiotic bears no relation to the science of semiotics. Semiotics as conceived within the structuralist paradigm would have as its object of investigation the symbolic modality rather than the semiotic.

Kristeva draws a parallel between the symbolic and semiotic dispositions and Lacan's imaginary and symbolic realms. But while for Lacan the Imaginary is totally suppressed after the mirror stage and the Symbolic becomes the exclusive realm of language and speech, for Kristeva the semiotic is ever present, energising and at the same time challenging symbolic communication.

In the light of the distinction between the semiotic and the symbolic, Kristeva redefines the terms 'genotext' and 'phenotext' first introduced in *Sèméiotikè*: the genotext includes the semiotic and prefigures the symbolic, while the phenotext is the symbolic language of communication. The degree to which the genotext is allowed to surface in the phenotext is a matter of social and historical circumstances, and the dialectics between genotext and phenotext is used in order to provide a typology of discourses. These range from the pure phenotext ('the narrative'), where meaning is exhausted on the surface syntactic and semantic relations between words, to the predominantly genotext ('the text'), where meaning is produced by the way the semiotic upsets the symbolic through the play of sounds and violation of grammar.

A number of articles Kristeva wrote between 1973 and 1976 were published in 1977 under the title *Polylogue*. Apart from essays on language theory, such as 'The ethics of linguistics', this volume also contained essays of primarily psychoanalytic interest ('Father, love, and banishment'), as well as essays dealing with the semiotics of paintings ('Giotto's joy'). Even though *Polylogue* lacks the striking originality of *Sèméiotikè* and *Revolution in Poetic Language*, it is nevertheless important because it was the first of Kristeva's works on language and semiotics to be made widely available to English-speaking audiences. In fact seven of the essays in *Polylogue* (along with two from *Sèméiotikè*) were translated in English and appeared in *Desire in Language* (1980a).

Three key events from the mid-1970s onwards marked a change of focus in Kristeva's oeuvre. Disillusionment following a *Tel Quel* trip to Maoist China in 1974, the birth of her son David in 1976, and completion of her training as a psychoanalyst in 1979 steered her away from the primarily linguistic and socio-historical concerns of her first decade in France and towards a more psychoanalytic perspective, where the pathology of psychotic discourse, motherhood and the feminine became central preoccupations in her work. This change of focus, already evident in *Polylogue*, is more pronounced in her work in the 1980s, as in *Pouvoirs de l'horreur* (1980b; *Powers of Horror*, 1982) and *Soleil Noir* (1987; *Black Sun*, 1989). Her work in the 1990s and the beginning of the twenty-first century, in addition to an emphasis on psychoanalysis and the feminine, is also characterised by an increasing interest in cultural criticism, dealing with issues such as foreignness and nationalism. She has also published three novels.

Kristeva is a professor of linguistics at the Université de Paris VII, a permanent visiting professor at Columbia University and the University of Toronto, and a practising psychoanalyst. Despite the breadth of her interests, ranging from linguistics and semiotics to psychoanalysis, feminism, fiction and cultural criticism, her oeuvre is characterised by remarkable consistency: a preoccupation with subjectivity, split between the realm of the semiotic/instinctual and that of the symbolic/social, informs her theory of language and her psychoanalytic theorising and practice as well as her social criticism.

Primary works

(1969a). Σημειωτική: *Recherches pour une sémanalyse*. Paris: Éditions du Seuil. Four of the eleven essays in Σημειωτική have been translated in English: 'Word, dialogue, and novel' and 'The bounded text' appear in Kristeva 1980; 'Semiotics: a critical science and/or a critique of science' in Kristeva Reader, 1986; and 'Gesture, practice or communication?' in Polhenus 1978.

(1969b). *Language, the Unknown: An Initiation into Linguistics*. Hemel Hempstead: Harvester Wheatsheaf, 1989.

(1974). *Revolution in Poetic Language*. New York: Columbia University Press, 1984.

(1977). *Polylogue*. Paris: Éditions du Seuil.

(1980a). *Desire in Language: A Semiotic Approach to Literature and Art*. Leon S. Roudiez (ed.). New York: Columbia University Press.

(1980b). *Powers of Horror: An Essay on Abjection*. New York: Columbia University Press, 1982.

(1986). *The Kristeva Reader*. Toril Moi (ed.). New York: Columbia University Press.

(1987). *Black Sun: Depression and Melancholia*. New York: Columbia University Press, 1989.

(1996). *Julia Kristeva: Interviews*. Ross Mitchell Guberman (ed.). New York: Columbia University Press.

(1997; Second edition, 2002). *The Portable Kristeva*. Kelly Oliver (ed.). New York: Columbia University Press.

Further reading

Lechte, John (1990). *Julia Kristeva*. London: Routledge.

Lewis, Philip E. (1974). 'Revolutionary semiotics'. *Diacritics*. Vol. 4(3): 28–32.

McAfee, Noëlle (forthcoming). *Julia Kristeva*. London: Routledge.

Oliver, Kelly (1993). *Reading Kristeva: Unraveling the Double-bind*. Bloomington: Indiana University Press.

Payne, Michael (1993). *Reading Theory: An Introduction to Lacan, Derrida, and Kristeva*. Cambridge, MA, and Oxford: Blackwell.

Polhemus, Ted (ed.) (1978). *The Body Reader: Social Aspects of the Human Body*. New York: Pantheon.

Smith, Anne-Marie (1998). *Julia Kristeva: Speaking the Unspeakable*. London: Pluto Press.

Stavroula-Thaleia Kousta

WILLIAM LABOV

Labov, William (*b.* 1927; American), assistant professor, Columbia University, New York (1961–70), associate professor and full professor, University of Pennsylvania (1970–). Sociolinguist who pioneered the quantitative study of language variation in the early 1960s and is responsible for many key developments in sociolinguistic methodology. He is also noted for his significant contributions to the debate surrounding the linguistic validity of African-American Vernacular English as well as his groundbreaking work towards a theory of language change, particularly sound change. (*See also* Bernstein, Basil; Bloomfield, Leonard; Cameron, Deborah; Chomsky, Noam; Hockett, Charles; Martinet, André; Milroy, Lesley; Tannen, Deborah.)

Labov was born in Rutherford, New Jersey, and attended high school in Fort Lee, on the outskirts of New York City. He majored in English and philosophy at Harvard University (1944–8) and worked afterwards for several years in marketing and journalism, later finding employment as a printing-ink chemist in the laboratory of a small manufacturing company. Labov has frequently linked his rejection of the introspection-reliant theoretical orthodoxies in 1960s North American linguistics to a belief in the reliability and broad applicability of standard empirical method that was reinforced by his experiences in research and development in industrial chemistry. His commitment to the systematic study of 'real language' used by 'real people' is, he claims, grounded in observations he made of language in use during this non-academic period of his career.

Labov returned to academia in 1961 as a postgraduate student in Columbia University's linguistics department, of which Uriel Weinreich was then head. Under Weinreich, Labov began to develop ideas about the observability of language change in progress, ideas that ran against the grain of the doctrine inherited, in diluted form, from the neogrammarians by the twentieth-century American structuralists, notably *Hockett and *Bloomfield. Crucial to the development of methods by which language change could be observed was Labov's refinement of the traditional dialectological concept of the linguistic variable, a unit that may be lexical or grammatical, but which is most often phonological, representing a category of semantically equivalent variants with distributions found to correlate with variations in the social characteristics – gender, social class and so on – of the community's speakers (see Milroy 1992). This tool not only allowed researchers to quantify the distribution of phonological or morphosyntactic variants in the language of a speech community, but was also argued to reflect the variable nature of the grammatical rules of the sociolect or language itself.

Labov and Weinreich (the latter described by Labov as 'the perfect academic' and indubitably Labov's strongest formative influence) worked together on the enumeration of a set of postulates that would underpin an empirical theory of language change. In this they cast the genesis, transmission and adoption of language changes in the form of five 'problems': actuation, constraints, transition, evaluation and embedding (see Labov with Weinreich and Herzog 1968). Much sociolinguistic research since then has been conducted, implicitly or explicitly, within this general framework. But even so it has been argued that Weinreich, Labov and Herzog's formulation of the actuation problem of why a change begins in a particular variety of a particular language at a particular time is intrinsically insoluble (see Milroy 1992).

Labov's seminal MA study (1963) of the social conditioning of phonological variation in the English of Martha's Vineyard, an island off the coast of Massachusetts, set the pattern for his later doctoral work on New York City English (published 1966), and his research on working-class varieties spoken in other American cities (Labov with Yaeger and Steiner 1972d). Labov's focus on vernacular language forms follows what he calls 'the principle of the vocal majority'; that is, vernacular language should be the central object of the linguist's analyses, because 'most of the speakers of any social group have a vernacular style, relative to their careful and literary forms of speech. The most spontaneous, least studied style is the one that we as linguists will find the most useful as we place the speaker in the overall pattern of the speech community' (1972c: 112). In Labov's view, mainstream linguistics suffered from inadequate methodological transparency and rigour. He became dissatisfied with its lack of accountability to systematically collected data samples and with its concentration on standard forms of languages, or worse, on the idiolects of individual researchers themselves. This led him to the view that 'either our theories are about the language that ordinary people use on the street, arguing with friends, or at home blaming their children, or they are about very little indeed' (1972c: 109). In both academic and public spheres, Labov was quick to come to the defence of non-standard vernaculars, particularly African-American Vernacular English, which had long been portrayed as 'deficient' and indicative of cognitive inferiority by the educational theorists of the day, among whom Basil *Bernstein was a central figure.

The methodologies Labov developed during the 1960s for elicitation of spontaneous and unself-conscious language behaviour at one end of the stylistic spectrum, and 'careful', self-monitored speech at the other, were highly innovative and continue to provide models for much contemporary work in sociolinguistics. In fact Labov has called sociolinguistics 'secular linguistics', in reaction to the contention among many linguists working in a broadly *Chomskyan framework that language can be dissociated from its social functions. Labov moved from Columbia in 1970 to found the University of Pennsylvania's sociolinguistics programme, a school that has produced many of the most prominent figures in late twentieth-century sociolinguistics, including Sharon Ash, John Baugh, Penelope Eckert, Gregory Guy, Shana Poplack and John Rickford (see Sankoff 2002).

A significant proportion of the work Labov and his colleagues have produced since the 1970s has focused on investigations of sound change, with a particular emphasis on the vowel systems of varieties of North American English. This work has synthesised techniques in instrumental acoustic analysis borrowed from laboratory phonetics with insights from historical phonology. It has produced a considerable body of empirical evidence in support of the constraints on the directions taken by sound changes that Labov elucidates in his three-volume *Principles of Linguistic Change* (1994, 2001, forthcoming). Labov's principles attempt to account for recurrent patterns of variation and change observed synchronically (at a given moment) and diachronically (over time) in vowel systems of the world's languages, and have their basis to a large degree in the structuralist treatments of chain shift, merger and split propounded by figures such as Hockett and *Martinet. Observations made of

varieties of English in this framework have led Labov to propose a typology of dialects based on the configuration of chain shift patterns in their vowel systems. Much of the research he and his associates are currently conducting for large-scale atlas projects, in particular Labov, Ash and Boberg's *Atlas of North American English*, is situated in the context of this theoretical model.

In statements of his views regarding the relationship of sociolinguistics to other theoretical approaches to the study of language structure, use, acquisition and evolution, Labov has advocated revisiting the parallels drawn by nineteenth- and early twentieth-century linguists between Darwinian natural selection and the paths taken by languages over their histories (2001: 3–34). He has also sought more successfully to integrate the findings emerging from the work of his own circle and from those of the historical linguistic and dialectological traditions with the fundamental tenets (the existence of an innately endowed Universal Grammar, for instance) of the Chomskyan generative paradigm.

The centrality of Labovian method and theory in contemporary sociolinguistics worldwide is unquestionable; in his fifth decade as a researcher and innovator in the field, Labov's influence appears undiminished. He is one of the few linguists to have been elected to the United States' National Academy of Sciences (1993), has been awarded several honorary doctorates by institutions around the world, and for several years was a regular invited plenary speaker at the annual North American NWAVE (New Ways of Analyzing Variation) conference. He co-edits the journal *Language Varia-tion and Change* with David Sankoff and sits on the editorial boards of *Journal of Sociolinguistics*, *Narrative Inquiry* and *Forensic Linguistics: The International Journal of Speech, Lan-guage and the Law*.

Primary works

(1963). 'The social motivation of a sound change'. *Word*. Vol. 19: 273–309.

(1966). *The Social Stratification of English in New York City*. Washington, DC: Center for Applied Linguistics.

(1968) (with Uriel Weinreich and Marvin Her-zog). 'Empirical foundations for a theory of language change'. In W. P. Lehmann and Y. Malkiel (eds). *Directions for Historical Linguistics*. Austin, TX: University of Texas Press.

(1972a). *Sociolinguistic Patterns*. Philadelphia: University of Pennsylvania Press.

(1972b). *Language in the Inner City*. Philadel-phia: University of Pennsylvania Press.

(1972c). 'Some principles of linguistic method-ology'. *Language in Society*. Vol. 1: 97–120.

(1972d) (with Malcah Yaeger and Richard Steiner). *A Quantitative Study of Sound Change in Progress*. Philadelphia: US Re-gional Survey.

(1975). *What is a Linguistic Fact?* New York: Academic Press.

(1994). *Principles of Linguistic Change. Vol. I: Internal Factors*. Oxford: Blackwell. (*Vol. II: External Factors*, 2001; *Vol. III: Cognitive Factors*, forthcoming).

(2002) (with Sharon Ash and Charles Boberg). *Atlas of North American English*. Berlin: Mouton de Gruyter.

Further reading

Guy, Gregory R., Feagin, Crawford, Schiffrin, Deborah and Baugh, John (eds) (1996). *To-wards a Social Science of Language: Essays in Honor of William Labov* (2 vols). Amster-dam: John Benjamins.

Milroy, James (1992). *Linguistic Variation and Change: On the Historical Sociolinguistics of English*. Oxford: Blackwell.

Sankoff, David (2002). 'Labov, William'. In R. Mesthrie (ed.). *Pergamon Concise Ency-clopaedia of Sociolinguistics*. Amsterdam: El-sevier Science.

Dominic Watt

JACQUES LACAN

Lacan, Jacques (Marie Émile) (*b.* 1901, *d.* 1981; French), a doctor of medicine, member of the Société Psychoanalytique de Paris, founding member of the École Freudienne in Paris. A controversial psychoanalyst and a prominent theoretician, he ad-vocated a 'return to Freud', intro-ducing into psychoanalysis ideas from structural linguistics and from phi-losophy. (*See also* Jakobson, Roman; Saussure, Ferdinand de.)

Born in Paris to a Catholic family, La-can was educated in a Jesuit school: his mother was devoutly religious and his younger brother later joined the Benedictine Order. He undertook a medical degree at the Sorbonne and studied psychiatry under Gaëtan de Clérambault. Due to their differences (Lacan opposed Clérambault's theory of 'mental automatism'), he failed his *aggregation* (a final examination). In 1932 he was awarded a *doctorate d'état* for his thesis on paranoia and its relation to the personality, and he became a specialist in that field. His analysis of the 'Aimée case' (the case of a female patient arrested for at-tacking with a knife a well-known actress because she believed that the woman was endangering her son's life) made him famous among the surrealist thinkers, and Lacan contributed some articles to the surrealist magazine *Minotaure*. During the German occupation of France, he worked in a military hospital in Paris and did not take part in official activities. In 1951 the Société Psychoanalytique de Paris, of which Lacan was a member, raised the issue of Lacan's unorthodox short sessions with his patients – Lacan varied the length of his sessions because he believed that the unconscious lacked the notion of time and, therefore, that it did not makes sense to insist upon the standard analytical hour. For some time, Lacan was able to defend his approach and in January 1953 was elected president of the Société. Six months later he resigned to join the Société Française de Psychanalyse, where in the course of time his seminars attracted a large audience of philosophers, critics, psychologists, linguists and mathematicians.

In 1962, Lacan was expelled from the International Psychoanalytic Association for his non-standard practices, and the Société Française de Psychanalyse also banned him as a teacher and instructor. Subsequently he founded the École Française de Psychanalyse, soon to become the École Freudienne de Paris, and continued to train analysts, as well as students of philosophy and other disciplines. He supposedly belonged to the main instigators of the May 1968 French student revolt. In 1974, Lacan became a director of the psychoanalytic department of the University of Vincennes.

Reading Lacan presupposes at least an acquaintance with Freud's work, as well as familiarity with the concepts used in structural linguistics and contemporary philosophy. His writings are difficult to comprehend because of his frequent use of neologisms and linguistic puns and his reluctance to define the terminology he is using, leaving it up to the reader to decipher the intended meaning.

One area where Lacan has been most influential in linguistics and elsewhere is child development. For example, in an unpublished paper from 1936, Lacan introduces the concept of the 'mirror stage', a period in a child's development from 6 to 18 months of age in which the infant is able to recognise her or his own image in the mirror. By identifying with it, the child thus forms his or her *I*, a unified whole that is in opposition to the inner experience of fragmentation. Similarly to Freud's idea of narcissistic identification, Lacan claims that the child's sense of self is always formed via a reference to some 'other'. A revised version of the paper was presented in 1949 and appears in Lacan's *Écrits* (1966).

The year of the *Rome Report*, 1953, can be seen as the year when Lacan broke with the existing analytic establishment. He suggested that psychoanalysts focus on the analysis of the subject's speech as the only medium of access to the analysand's inner world. In the same paper, he introduces in detail the three interacting 'Orders' in the mind, the Symbolic, the Imaginary and the Real. The Imaginary is formed by conscious as well as unconscious images of the world, the Symbolic is concerned with symbols and symbolic systems, and the Real is what is neither imaginary nor symbolic; in other words, what remains beyond the experience of language, since 'the real is the impossible'. Language, itself is located on the symbolic level, at which the subject's reality is constituted.

In an article from 1957 entitled 'L'instance de la lettre dans l'inconscient ou la raison depuis Freud' ('The agency of the letter in the unconscious or reason since Freud'), Lacan discusses *Saussure's concept of the sign as being composed of the signifier and the signified. Lacan abolishes the structural unity of the two components and reverses Saussure's algorithm, such that

$$\frac{S}{s}$$

the signifier 'S', being the primary notion, stands above the signified 's'. Lacan emphasises the presence of the dividing bar: it is important that the signifier bears no relation to its meaning effects; the signified is 'sliding' under the signifier. The function of the signifier (that is, of that which has a meaning effect) is the foundation of the symbolic dimension, a chain of signifiers in which a signifier can represent something only with respect to another signifier. It is the analyst's task to search for the relationships between signifiers, as the subject *is* in the chain of signifiers (she or he is 'running' along the chain). Lacan also appropriates *Jakobson's 'metaphor' (substitution of a word or a discourse topic with a similar word or topic) and 'metonymy' (sequence of contiguous words or topics) and relates them to Freud's 'condensation' and 'displacement'. For Lacan, metonymy and metaphor are two effects of the endless 'chase' of signifiers.

An important concept in Lacan's work is that of *jouissance* (enjoyment, delight, use), the act of enjoying without a purpose or meaning. *Jouissance* can be characterised as different relations to satisfaction that the desiring and speaking subject can experience at the use of a desired, but crucially never appropriated, object. Lacan's *jouissance* has become a seminal notion in the literature of postmodernism (see also Roland *Barthes).

In *Encore*, Lacan returns to his claim that the notion of 'discourse' should be understood as a social link and refers to his earlier distinction of four types of discourses. The Four Discourses (Master's, University, Hysteric's and Analyst's Discourse) are described in terms of power relations in that they serve a certain set of social interests. The Master's Discourse is despotic in that the Master simply expects his students to reproduce it. The University Discourse is regulative; it endows the students with a certain body of knowledge on which they are expected to build. The Hysteric's Discourse is both ignorant and destructive; the hysteric lacks the knowledge of 'the rules of the game' but has the power to influence them; in a sense, she or he 'knows too much'. The Analyst's Discourse is the discourse of the listener who stops himself or herself from 'knowing too soon' and, while listening, modifies her or his own discourse in order to understand the student or patient.

In his work, Lacan was especially concerned with the language relationship between the analyst and the patient. Famously, he claimed that before signifying *something*, language must signify for *someone*; what the patient says to the analyst can never be meaningless because in it there is concealed the wish to establish a relationship: 'all speech is demand'. He coined the term *la linguisterie*, translated into English as 'linguistricks', expressing the erratic nature of language. In this, Lacan distinguished between, on the one hand, the signification of language in psychoanalysis as that in which the unconscious is grounded ('the unconscious is structured like a language') and, on the other, linguists' understanding of language phenomena.

Lacan has sometimes been subjected to criticism for his misuse of logic and mathematics and his disregard for new scientific discoveries in the area of human development and linguistics. Nevertheless, he belongs among the most prominent thinkers of the twentieth century. His ideas are influential in the development of deconstruction and feminism and have had a major influence on French philosophy and cultural theory. In 1980 Lacan dissolved the École Freudienne and created a new society, the Cause Freudienne, a move that was resented by a number of his associates and was going to land him in court. He died before any conclusion could be reached.

Primary works

(1966). *Écrits*. Paris: Seuil.
(1973). *Le séminaire. Livre XI: Les quatre concepts fondamentaux de la psychanalyse, 1964*. Paris: Seuil.
(1975). *Le séminaire. Livre XX: Encore, 1972–1973*. Paris: Seuil.
(1981). *Le séminaire. Livre III: Les psychoses, 1955–56*. Paris: Seuil.

Further reading

Bice, Benvenuto and Kennedy, Roger (1986). *The Works of Jacques Lacan: An Introduction*. New York: St Martin's Press.
Felman, Shoshana (1987). *Jacques Lacan and the Adventure of Insight: Psychoanalysis in Contemporary Culture*. Cambridge, MA: Harvard University Press.
Grosz, Elizabeth (1990). *Jacques Lacan: A Feminist Introduction*. London: Routledge.
Hogan, Patrick Colm and Pandit, Lalita (eds) (1990). *Criticism and Lacan: Essays and Dialogue on Language, Structure, and the Unconscious*. Athens, GA: University of Georgia Press.
Leader, Darian, Groves, Judy and Appignanesi, Richard (2000). *Introducing Lacan*. Totem.
Ragland-Sullivan, Ellie and Bracher, Mark (1991). *Lacan and the Subject of Language*. New York: Routledge.
Roudinesco, Élisabeth (1994). *Jacque Lacan: esquisse d'une vie, histoire d'un système de pensée*. Paris: Fayard.

Marie Šafářová

GOTTFRIED WILHELM LEIBNIZ

Leibniz, Gottfried Wilhelm (*b.* 1646, *d.* 1716; German), lawyer, courtier, diplomat and librarian, who wrote extensively on many subjects. In the philosophy of language he is best known for his account of innate ideas, for work that would later contribute to an understanding of intensional contexts, and for laying the foundations of possible world semantics. (*See also* Arnauld, Antoine; Chomsky, Noam; Frege, Gottlob; Kripke, Saul; Lewis, David; Locke, John; Montague, Richard; Plato.)

Leibniz was from an academic background (his father was professor of moral philosophy at Leipzig, where Leibniz was born) but never held a university appointment. From the age of 20 onwards he was offered a series of professorships, but preferred to remain in public service and employed in the courts of various aristocratic families. For many years he was official historian to the House of Brunswick at Hanover, latterly under the patronage of Duke Georg-Ludwig, who became George I of England. However, Leibniz continued to pursue his diverse interests in fields such as law, theology, mathematics, physics, engineering, etymology, economics and geology, as well as philosophy. He wrote extensively on all these topics, and corresponded with most of the leading thinkers of his day, including *Arnauld and *Locke, but published very little during his lifetime.

This breadth of interests is apparent in his pursuit of the ambitious, but ultimately unfulfilled, goal of producing a 'general encyclopaedia', describing and linking all human knowledge. He saw such knowledge as necessarily derived from the application of reason, a view that led him for a long time to be labelled a 'rationalist'. Recent assessments of his work have tended to see this as a rather restrictive definition (see, for instance, MacDonald

Ross 1984; Adams 1994), but it does nevertheless explain a number of important connections in his vast output. In the only book he published during his lifetime, *Theodocy* (1710), Leibniz argues that religious belief can and should be based on reason, not just on faith, and introduces the notion that ours is the best of all logically possible worlds. His further development of this notion, and much of his other work that has proved most influential in the study of language, is contained in *New Essays on Human Understanding*, published posthumously in 1765.

This book constitutes Leibniz's response to Locke. It takes the form of a dialogue between two characters, Philalethes and Theophilus, who voice the views of Locke and Leibniz respectively. So, for instance, when Philalethes argues that knowledge must be derived from experience of the world, Theophilus responds that knowledge is derived by reason, building on innate ideas. In this Leibniz was reviving ideas dating back to *Plato, and outlining a description of human knowledge that would be one of the sources for *Chomsky's innatist account of language.

In rejecting the notion that the child is born with a soul (or mind) that is a 'blank slate' to be written on by experience, Theophilus draws attention to the properties that make us individuals. If minds were really blank, there would be no way of distinguishing one human mind from another, or indeed a human mind from that of an animal. In this, Leibniz was drawing on a notion he developed from *Aristotle, the principle of the 'identity of indiscernibles', also known as

179

'Leibniz's Law'. Two entities, A and B, are identical if every property that belongs to A also belongs to B, and vice versa. In the study of language this takes the form of the 'law of substitution', which states that if two expressions are extensionally equivalent one can be substituted for another in a sentence, 'salve veritate' (with truth unchanged). This law was used by *Frege to offer support to the distinction between extension and intension, or between reference and sense. In so-called 'intensional contexts' the law of substitution does not hold.

In his own comments on word meaning, Theophilus argues that words stand for things as well as our ideas of things, arguing against Locke's ideational account of meaning, as voiced by Philalethes. Further, words are sometimes used to talk about neither things nor our ideas of things, but about words themselves. Theophilus points out that instances of words being spoken of 'materially' are most common in the discussions of grammarians and lexicographers: occasions when language is used to talk about language. This point is not developed any further by Leibniz, but can be seen as a forerunner to discussions of meaning in the twentieth century that would distinguish between the 'use' and the 'mention' of a word, a distinction most commonly illustrated by pairs of examples such as 'John is tall' and '"John" has four letters'.

Much of the interest in Leibniz's work from philosophers of language and linguists in the twentieth century, however, focused on his notion of possible worlds. For Leibniz himself, this was largely a theological issue. The world we inhabit is in fact just one of an infinite series of possible worlds existing in the mind of God. Each one differs from all the others in terms of the entities it contains or has contained. Yet despite this infinity of variation it is no coincidence that the actual world is as it is. God, being good, could not possibly have created anything other than the best of all possible worlds. Leibniz was drawing on a logical notion of perfection in terms of simplicity; the actual world contains the greatest number of states of affairs for the least number of individual laws, or the maximum of effects for the minimum of causes. Nevertheless this view led to the caricature of Leibniz as the absurdly optimistic Dr Pangloss in Voltaire's *Candide* (1759). Pangloss insists throughout a series of increasingly catastrophic misadventures that everything must be for the best in this, the best of all possible worlds.

Twentieth-century philosophers such as *Kripke, *Lewis and *Montague, however, were less scathing, seeing in Leibniz's idea a potential basis for a 'truth' semantics. The terms 'true' and 'false' should be considered not just in the actual world, but across the range of possible worlds. Among other consequences, this allows for modal expressions such as 'possible' and 'necessary' to be explained using the non-modal terms 'some' and 'all'. Some recent Leibniz scholars have suggested that possible world semantics does not fit very comfortably with Leibniz's original account (see, for instance, MacDonald Ross 1984; Adams 1994). Nevertheless,

Leibniz's idea can certainly be seen as providing the inspiration, and some of the terminology, for this important development in twentieth-century linguistics.

Leibniz's phenomenal written output was the product of an open and inquisitive mind, a voracious appetite for knowledge, and an immense dedication to work. He never married, frequently paid scant attention to his official duties, and is reported to have spent months at a time in his study, working, eating and sleeping in the same chair. Although generally well regarded by both his peers and his employers, he ended his days in Hanover, isolated and rather embittered, George having refused to allow him to accompany him to England on his succession in 1714. Leibniz's dispute with Isaac Newton may have been the cause. Both men claimed to have been the first to discover differential calculus, and George may have felt it tactful not to upset his prestigious new subject. In fact, it seems that both reached the same conclusions, working independently. Newton was the first to make the discovery, but Leibniz the first to circulate it publicly.

Leibniz died in Hanover on 14 November 1716 after a short illness. His chief initial influence was in continental mathematics, where his system of symbolism for calculus was adopted in preference to Newton's. His philosophical ideas took longer to find an audience. They were read and admired by eighteenth-century German philosophers, including *Kant, but were not known more widely until the twentieth century, when Bertrand *Russell (1900) introduced them to an English-speaking audience, and they were subsequently taken up by linguists and philosophers of language. The fact that many of his ideas had to wait for more than two hundred years has been taken as evidence that Leibniz was ahead of his time. Some of his more practical inspirations, too, showed considerable foresight. He was passionate in his desire to produce a mechanical calculating machine, and also worked on designs for a high-speed coach, steam engines and a submarine.

Primary works

(1710). *Theodicy*. E. M. Huggard (trans.). London: Routledge, 1951.
(1765). *New Essays on Human Understanding*. Peter Remnant and Jonathan Bennett (trans.). Cambridge: Cambridge University Press, 1981.
(1998). *Philosophical Texts*. R. S. Woolhouse and Richard Francks (trans. and ed.). Oxford: Oxford University Press.

Further reading

Adams, Robert (1994). *Leibniz: Determinist, Theist, Idealist*. Oxford: Oxford University Press.
Brown, Stuart (1984). *Leibniz*. Brighton: Harvester.
Jolley, Nicholas (1984). *Leibniz and Locke: A Study of the New Essays on Human Understanding*. Oxford: Oxford University Press.
MacDonald Ross, G. (1984). *Leibniz*. Oxford: Oxford University Press.
Russell, Bertrand (1900). *A Critical Exposition of the Philosophy of Leibniz*. Cambridge: Cambridge University Press.

Siobhan Chapman

DAVID LEWIS

Lewis, David (Kellogg) (*b.* 1941, *d.* 2001; American), fellow of the American Academy of Arts and Sciences (1983) and corresponding fellow of the British Academy (1992). Lewis was the class of 1943 university professor of philosophy at Princeton and held honorary degrees from the universities of Cambridge, York and Melbourne. An outstanding analytical philosopher of language renowned for the application of possible worlds semantics to problems of linguistic meaning and mental content. (*See also* Leibniz, Gottfried Wilhelm; Ramsey, F. P.)

Lewis was born in Oberlin, Ohio, where his parents taught at a local college. He began undergraduate studies initially in chemistry but, after spending a term at Oxford, where he attended lectures on metaphysics by Gilbert *Ryle, Lewis changed subjects and graduated with a BA in philosophy from Swarthmore College in 1962. He later received a doctorate from Harvard, working under the supervision of W. V. O. *Quine. Lewis served as assistant professor of philosophy at the University of California at Los Angeles (1966–70), moving to Princeton in 1970, where he taught for the rest of his career.

His first book, *Convention: A Philosophical Study* (1969), earned him the Matchette Prize in Philosophy, a national award for the best book by a young thinker in philosophy. In it, conventions were analysed as the regularities of behaviour that are recognised as solutions to co-ordination problems in a community of actors with a tradition of common goals and shared activities. Lewis also introduced a distinction between the purely formal specification of a language and the empirical question of determining the language of a given speech community.

Lewis's work on conditional sentences and the philosophy of modality has been particularly influential. In his book *Counterfactuals* (1973), he showed the fruitfulness of using possible worlds in the analysis of counterfactual conditionals. According to him, a counterfactual sentence such as 'If kangaroos didn't have tails, they would topple over' is true in the actual world if the consequent is true in that world which is as much like the actual world as possible, but with the antecedent true.

Lewis made signal contributions to the development of possible worlds semantics and related issues in philosophy of language; he was considered by many the most important metaphysician of the twentieth century. However, he has been strongly criticised for his modal realism, the thesis that possible worlds are not just a purely abstract notion useful for explaining concepts of possibility and necessity, but as real as our own universe (Forrest and Armstrong 1984; Stalnaker 1984). On a lighter and more personal note, Lewis was a railway enthusiast who built elaborate model train circuits and was very fond of Australia, a country he and his wife visited frequently. He died suddenly on 14 October 2001 from complications arising from diabetes.

Primary works

(1969). *Convention: A Philosophical Study.* Cambridge, MA: Harvard University Press.
(1973). *Counterfactuals.* Oxford: Blackwell.

Further reading

Forrest, Peter and Armstrong, David M. (1984). 'An argument against David Lewis' theory of possible worlds'. *Australasian Journal of Philosophy.* Vol. 62: 164–8.
Stalnaker, Robert (1984). *Inquiry.* Cambridge, MA: MIT Press.

Iván García-Álvarez

JOHN LOCKE

Locke, John (*b.* 1632, *d.* 1704; English); philosopher, Oxford scholar, economist and political operative, who wrote on a variety of topics. He is best known for his attack on the rationalist doctrine of innate ideas, and is recognised as the establisher of the principles of British empiricism. His work has also had an enormous impact on subsequent study in the nature of human consciousness. (*See also* Berkeley, George; Chomsky, Noam; Descartes, René; Hume, David; Leibniz, Gottfried Wilhelm; Searle, John.)

The son of a country lawyer who served in the parliamentary army during the English Civil War (1642–51), John Locke was born at Wrington, Somerset, on 29 August 1632. He entered Westminster school in 1646, and in 1652 passed to Christ Church College, Oxford, where he received his BA in 1656 and MA in 1658. As a fellow of Christ Church, Locke was lecturer in Greek in 1660, reader in rhetoric in 1663, and censor of moral philosophy in 1664. His friend Robert Boyle aroused in him an interest in experimental science. In 1667, Locke began collaborating in medical research with Thomas Sydenham, and later became personal physician and political adviser of Ashley Cooper, who later became earl of Shaftesbury and one of the lord proprietors of the Carolina colonies. Locke was elected a fellow of the English Royal Society, which went against with the Scholastic tradition and aimed to study nature empirically rather than through books. When Ashley was made lord chancellor in 1672, Locke became his secretary of the Board of Trade and Plantations and secretary to the lords proprietors of the Carolinas.

Locke's life unfolded during a period of great political changes and scientific discoveries, and he was connected with some of the most important events in both areas. The seventeenth century witnessed conflicts between Parliament and the crown as well as between Catholics and Protestants. In those years, Lord Shaftesbury built up a parliamentary majority to secure the passage of an exclusion bill that would prevent Charles II's Catholic brother James from becoming king. The exclusion bill failed, Parliament was thus prorogued, and Shaftesbury, dismissed from office, took refuge in Holland. Although Locke was not concerned in Shaftesbury's political plans, suspicion fell upon him, and he fled to Holland, where he became one of William of Orange's advisers. In England, the turmoil of those years ended with the 'Glorious Revolution' of 1688, which brought William of Orange to the throne. In February 1689, Locke came back to England escorting William's wife, who later became Queen Mary.

Locke's commitments led him to write on a variety of political, philosophical and religious matters. The *Two Treatises of Civil Government* (1690a) offer a theory of natural law and natural rights and argue for the legitimacy of rebellion against tyrannical governments. In *The First Treatise*, Locke rejected the doctrine of the divine right of kings (the idea that monarchs held their position by the will of God) and based his view on a detailed examination of key biblical passages. In *The Second Treatise*, he put forward a claim for the liberty of the citizens and for the existence of natural human rights independent of government and constitutions.

In the *Essay Concerning Human Understanding*, arguably Locke's greatest philosophical contribution, he analyses the mechanisms of human thought. Immediately after its publication in December 1689, the *Essay* was received with great enthusiasm, attracting many written replies both in favour and attacking it. Locke's arguments against the innateness of ideas (a theory dating back to *Plato) were felt as a strong position in favour of the natural law and the liberty of citizens (Yolton 1956), and were seen as a clear attack on the institution of monarchy and the structures surrounding it. The *Essay* was studied in the universities, especially by younger scholars, but many heads of colleges – often aristocrats themselves – realised the implications of the idea that people are not innately equipped for certain stations in life, and tried to devise means for its suppression. Not only had the *Essay* a major impact on Locke's contemporaries, but it also had such a powerful influence on later publications on the topic that most thinkers were incapable of building their social, cognitive or religious philosophical models without relying upon or detracting explicitly from the *Essay*. Locke ascribed the origin of his *Essay* to a conversation about the 'principles of morality and revealed religion' he had in the winter of 1670 with some friends, who later asked him to write down his thoughts on the topic in no more than a sheet of paper (Cranston 1957). Soon Locke realised that the vastness of the question needed time to be investigated, and he devoted his leisure to the question for almost twenty years. What was intended to be a brief essay became a substantial work articulated into four books, with each book highlighting such philosophical issues as the nature of the self, the world, God, and how human beings come to have knowledge of them.

In the first book, Locke attacks the doctrine of innate principles and ideas, thus following on from *Berkeley and *Hume and diverging from *Descartes and *Leibniz. Locke claims that at birth the human mind is a blank tablet with no innate knowledge. Taking a lead from *Aristotle, Locke argues that it is experience that leaves traces on the mind. Nevertheless, according to Locke the mind does have some innate faculties, such as those of perceiving, remembering, and combining ideas. Experience he describes as consisting of two modes: sensation, which grasps objects and processes in the external world, and reflection, the process by which humans become aware of their mental processes. Ideas are not created by the mind, but come from sensation, or from reflection, or from both, depending on their simplicity or complexity. In the second book, Locke describes how the mind passively stores simple ideas coming from experience of objects in the outside world through the windows of sensation and reflection, and how it actively combines them into complex ideas through the processes of combination and abstraction. Locke identifies in the objects two types of material properties that, following the terminology of Boyle (who discovered and gave his name to Boyle's Law, which explains the behaviour of gases), he labels as the primary and secondary qualities. Space, motion, rest and texture are primary qualities possessed by the object independently of human beings, whereas colour, smell and taste are secondary qualities derived from the interaction of the human perceptual apparatus with the primary qualities. From all this, Locke claims that the human being has access to the material world not directly but only through the mediation of secondary qualities, among which is included language. These mediated ideas are the building blocks of all human thought.

Locke's classification of ideas was influenced by mechanical philosophy and the corpuscular hypothesis, which claimed that everything in the world is composed of particles and of the space where the particles move, a distinction that dates back to the Greek atomists and was revived by Galileo, Descartes and Boyle. In this hypothesis, all material phenomena can be explained in terms of matter in motion and of the impact one body has on another. Strictly dependent on the classification of ideas delineated in book two, the third book discusses the nature of language along with the relation with ideas and its importance in attaining knowledge. In his discussion of language, Locke states that words stand for ideas, and distinguishes words mirroring the categories of ideas established in book two. In other words, Locke presents an 'ideational' account of meaning in the tradition of Aristotle, but he differs in seeing our ideas as necessarily private and individual. We need language to transfer these ideas to other minds because we are essentially social beings. So for Locke language is a means of communication, a vehicle for encoding ideas. Perhaps as a result of this, Locke has often been accused of proposing a misleading semantic theory that sees words as means for signifying ideas and ignoring the distinction between reference and meaning. But in fact Locke does explain that distinction clearly and puts forward the argument that ideas provide the meaning of words, not the reference (Kretzmann 1977). The fourth and last book discusses the limits of knowledge and the interconnection between reason and faith with knowledge.

The *Epistola de Tolerantia*, published in Holland in 1689 and translated by Popple as *A Letter Concerning Toleration* (1690b), argues for a separation between church and state, and proposes a principled account of religious toleration, an issue Locke had pondered upon together with Shaftesbury and included in their *Fundamental Constitution of the Carolinas.*

One of the most influential people of the seventeenth century in the fields of philosophy, politics and religion, John Locke is considered of great interest in the twenty-first century for both linguists and philosophers of language. His empiricism paved the way towards current studies on the strict relationship between the mind and the external world, though his attacks on innateness are once again meeting opposition, this time from evolutionists and proponents of genetics. Yet his way of comparing external sensible objects and the internal operations of mind perfectly complies with twenty-first-century views of conceptual metaphors in both philosophy and cognitive linguistics with a focus on the notion of the 'embodied mind' (Lakoff and Johnson 1999). John Locke spent the last years of his life at Oates, in Essex, home of Sir Francis Masham and his wife Damaris, the daughter of Cudworth, the Cambridge Platonist, and a philosopher in her own right. He died on Sunday 28 October 1704 in Oates. He was buried in the churchyard of High Laver.

Primary works

(1689). *Essay Concerning Human Understanding.* Peter N. Nidditch (ed.). Oxford: Clarendon, 1989.
(1690a). *Two Treatises of Government.* Peter Laslett (ed.). Cambridge: Cambridge University Press, 1988.

(1690b). '*Epistola de Tolerantia*', *A Letter on Toleration.* John W. Gough and Raymond Klibansky (eds). Oxford: Oxford University Press, 1968.

Further reading

Cranston, Maurice (1957). *John Locke: A Biography.* Oxford: Oxford University Press.
Kretzmann, Norman (1977). 'The main thesis of Locke's semantic theory'. In I. Tipton (ed.). *Locke on Human Understanding: Selected Essays.* Oxford: Oxford University Press.
Lakoff, George and Johnson, Mark (1999). *Philosophy in the Flesh: The Embodied Mind and its Challenge to Western Thought.* New York: Basic Books.
Yolton, John (1956). *John Locke and the Way of Ideas.* Oxford: Oxford University Press.

Annalisa Baicchi

BRONISLAW MALINOWSKI

Malinowski, Bronislaw (*b.* 1884, *d.* 1942; Polish, naturalised British), influential British anthropologist and founder of Functionalism. His two major concepts of ethnographic theory of language are the context of situation and the view of language as a mode of action. (*See also* Austin, J. L.; Sapir, Edward; Wittgenstein, Ludwig.)

Malinowski was born in Krakow, Poland, on 7 April 1884 to Lucyan and Jozefa Malinowski; his father was an academic linguist. He attended King John Sobieski public (fee-paying) school, then in 1902 went to Jagellonian University, Krakow, where he received his PhD in philosophy, physics and mathematics (1908). He was registered as a student at the London School of Economics (LSE) between 1910 and 1916, but first joined the faculty between 1913 and 1914. He returned in 1921 as an occasional lecturer and was appointed to the first chair in social anthropology at LSE in 1927. It was there that he read *The Golden Bough* by Sir James Frazer and sparked his interest in anthropology. He later lectured at Cornell (1933), Harvard (1936) and Yale (1939), where he was visiting professor, though fieldwork occupied much of his time.

During his expeditions to the Trobriand Islands (1915–16 and 1917–18), Malinowski sought to understand the islanders' language, concluding that literal translation of linguistic expressions did not reveal the way in which a native speaker would understand them. To deal with these cases, he devised the concept of 'context of situation', broadening the idea that the context and situation in which words are uttered can never be passed over as irrelevant to the linguistic expression. The methods used for the study of dead languages are inappropriate to approach living languages; instead, one needs a description of the social activities, symbolic and material resources, and interpretative practices of a particular group of people. Malinowski's writings on ethnographic approaches to language contributed to the development of modern pragmatics. For him, the function of language is not to express thought, but rather to play an active part in human behaviour. His notion of a 'verbal act' is akin to *Austin's notion of 'speech act'. The notion of whole contexts is reminiscent of the embedding of individual words in language games described by *Wittgenstein.

For linguists building on Malinowski's work, speaking is a mode of action and words must be understood in their context. His work also constituted the point of departure for the analysis of language which found expression in the work of later linguists such as *Firth and *Halliday. Malinowski died on 14 May 1942 in New Haven, Connecticut. The *New York Times* obituary named him an 'integrator of ten thousand cultural characteristics'.

Primary works

(1922). *Argonauts of the Western Pacific*. New York: Dutton

(1923). 'The problem of meaning in primitive languages'. In C. K. Ogden and I. A. Richards (eds). *The Meaning of Meaning*. New York: Harcourt, Brace and World.

Further reading

Kottak, Conrad Phillip. (1997). *Anthropology: The Exploration of Human Diversity*. Seventh edition. New York: McGraw Hill.

John Williams

ANDRÉ MARTINET

Martinet, André (*b.* 1908, *d.* 1999; French), an important representative of European structuralism, to which he applied functionalist ideas, and best known for his works in the area of diachronic phonology. He contributed fundamentally to the development of Interlingua, a constructed language. From 1938 professor at the École Pratique des Hautes Études in Paris, director of the International Auxiliary Language Association (IALA, 1946–8) in New York, held the chair of general and comparative linguistics at Columbia University (1947–55), then professor for general linguistics at the Sorbonne. (*See also* Bloomfield, Leonard; Hjelmslev, Louis; Jakobson, Roman; Saussure, Ferdinand de; Trubetzkoy, N. S.)

Born in Saint-Albans-des-Villards as a son of primary school teachers, Martinet grew up in the bilingual Savoy, where a French-Provençal patois is spoken alongside regular French. He studied English and German philology as well as general linguistics in Paris and Berlin. Through *Trubetzkoy, Martinet came into close contact with the Prague school, from which he later dissociated himself. He also met *Sapir's students and followers of *Bloomfield in the United States.

During imprisonment in World War II, Martinet carried out a survey on the pronunciation of current French. As director of the International Auxiliary Language Association (IALA), he became one of the founders of Interlingua, a constructed language intended to be a language of passive use for speakers of Romance languages, thus based almost exclusively on Romance models.

In 1955, Martinet returned to France and his *Économie des changements phonétiques* appeared, being a considerable contribution to diachronic phonology (comparing sound systems in different periods of a language's development) from a functional structuralist perspective. According to Martinet, the principle of economy takes a key position in language. In his works, this economy is understood as the permanent tension between the two contradictory forces of the communicative needs of the speaker and hearer on the one hand, and the tendency to articulatory and memorial laziness on the other. This permanent contradiction constitutes for Martinet the central motive for language change.

Martinet's lasting impact in Romance linguistics is also due to the precise but still pleasant style of his book *Elements of General Linguistics* (1960). In this introduction to general linguistics, since translated into several languages, the different linguistic units are classified according to the role they play in the communication. A statement attributed to Martinet is that language is a communication instrument with a double articulation. This term refers to the fact that verbal languages are articulated into meaningful units, morphemes, and also smaller non-meaningful units, phonemes. With honorary doctorates from several universities and honorary membership of many different linguistic societies, Martinet died in Châtenay-Malabry on 16 July 1999, at the age of 91.

Primary works

(1955). *Économie des changements phonétiques*. Bern: A. Frank.

(1960). *Elements of General Linguistics*. Elisabeth Palmer (trans.). Chicago: University of Chicago Press.

Further reading

Anderson, Stephen (1985). *Phonology in the Twentieth Century: Theories of Rules and Theories of Representations*. Chicago: University of Chicago Press.
Gode, Alexander and Blair, Hugh E. (1951). *Interlingua: A Grammar of the International Language*. New York: Storm.

Eva Herrmann-Kaliner

KARL MARX

Marx, Karl (Heinrich) (*b*. 1818, *d*. 1883; German), journalist, historian and philosopher, who wrote and published on politics, social theory and economics. In the philosophy of language, he is well known for his views concerning the fundamental nature of language and the relationship between social class and linguistic customs. (*See also* Chomsky, Noam; Firth, J. R; Halliday, M. A. K.; Hegel, G. W. F.; Labov, William.)

Karl Marx was born into a middle-class Jewish family in Trier, Germany. His mother, Henrietta Pressburg Marx, was originally from Holland, and his father, Herschel Marx, was a lawyer known for his enlightened political and social views. To escape the discrimination that Jews experienced at the time, Marx's father, who changed his first name to Heinrich, had the whole family baptised. They also joined the Lutheran church. Marx received a well-rounded educa-tion at the Friedrich Wilhelm Gymnasium in Trier and then began his university studies in Bonn and Berlin. He was influenced by the philosophy of *Hegel, and he eventually joined the Young Hegelians, a group of students who admired Hegel but who had more radical social and political objectives. Marx originally wanted to find a position teaching philosophy at a German university, but his political views and activities made it impossible for him to teach within the existing university system. Instead, he wrote for magazines and newspapers to earn a living. From 1840 to 1883 Marx authored numerous articles, pamphlets and books advocating political, economic and social activism, and he lived in a variety of cities, including Cologne, Paris, Brussels and finally London. Marx married Jenny von Westphalen in June 1843; they had seven children.

Marx's most famous publications include *Manifesto of the Communist Party* (1848), *Grundrisse: Foundations of the Critique of Political Economy* (1859) and *Capital: A Critical Analysis of Capitalist Production* (1867), the first volume of the three-volume work *Capital: A Critique of Political Economy* (1867–94). While researching and writing, he frequently collaborated with Friedrich Engels, the son of a wealthy textile manufacturer from Wuppertal, Germany. As Marx developed his various theories, he combed written accounts of history and grew to understand the past as a continuous struggle between the working class and those individuals who controlled a country's financial system and manufacturing infrastructure. He believed that this struggle manifested itself in all aspects of life, including cultural and linguistic matters. Unlike many other philosophers, Marx did not express his linguistic theories in one or two central works; instead, he made reference to language – sometimes very briefly – in various essays, articles and books. He also wrote about language in many different contexts. His speculations range from discussions concerning the relationship between language and the human thought process to a description of the development of national languages; he also commented on the appearance and disappearance of languages. Marx wrote most extensively on the origin and class character of language. Much of his work pertaining directly to the study of language is contained in *Economic and Philosophic Manuscripts* (1844; first published in 1959) and *The German Ideology* (1846; first published in 1932).

In his writings, Marx addresses the issue of the nature or character of language. He clearly states that the origin, function and goal of language are successful, efficient communication between human beings. In *The German Ideology*, he voices the opinion that 'language, like consciousness, only arises from the need, the necessity, of intercourse with other men' (1932b: 44). According to Marx, human beings enter into social and political relationships with other human beings in order to acquire food, clothing and shelter. Over the course of time, a community or communal consciousness forms. As the community reinforces relationships and fosters new associations, community structures, such as a common language, arise. Language is, therefore, a communal possession and should be viewed as a social phenomenon. As Marx states in *Economic and Philosophic Manuscripts*, language is 'social activity' (p. 298).

This emphasis on the social nature of language and its relation to the external world separates the Marxist idea of language from claims that linguistic analysis can be done without considering the culture, society or beliefs of the language's speakers. *Chomsky, for example, has argued that language is a human-specific competence of the mind, and he believes that this innate ability, working according to abstract rules, can best be studied using the methods and techniques of the natural sciences. Marx's statements concerning language have also been interpreted as an attempt to discourage efforts to produce and popularise an artificially created international language, for example Esperanto. Marx is known to have criticised the desire to create a universal language, labelling such efforts as utopian; both Lenin and Stalin remained in agreement with his views. Although proponents of languages like Esperanto have claimed that a universal or international language would hasten the attainment of socialist goals, such as the promotion of international understanding among workers and the elimination of nationalism and cultural elitism, many Marxist theorists throughout the twentieth century felt that these individuals were looking for a quick panacea and were being distracted from developing realistic means to carry out the class struggle.

In his philosophical works, Marx describes how language reflects the socioeconomic structure of a country at a given period of time. According to Marxist views, language enables human beings to interact with one another; however, while allowing communication with others, language is also a means by which one individual or group might exercise authority or influence over another. Marx points out that language and the ideas of the dominant class are inextricably linked. Language mirrors power relations and ideology, and the dominant class determines linguistic conventions. Moreover, the dominant class uses language to further its causes. One can conclude that to change language, one must transform class relations.

Marx's main concern was not the philosophy of language or linguistics, and consequently, many questions remained unanswered in his writings concerning the relationship of society, language and thought. In the twentieth century, sociolinguists, such as *Firth, *Halliday and *Labov, worked to explore the social influences on language and the role of language in society by examining such areas as style shifting, language change and linguistic variation within a speech community. Marxist linguists, including Marcel Cohen, Georg Lukács, N. Ja. Marr, Oskar Negt and Ferruccio Rossi-Landi, sought to supplement existing explanations concerning the relationship between language and the economic structure of society.

During his lifetime, Marx earned the reputation of being a conscientious scholar who wrote convincingly and with enthusiasm. He was also a loving husband, a devoted father and a faithful friend. Furthermore, he exhibited an inexhaustible reserve of energy for promoting revolutionary causes. When the International Working Men's Association was founded in London in 1864, Marx became an intellectual leader in the organisation, authoring many of the group's important documents. His health suffered as a result of his tireless dedication to the International, and during the 1870s and 1880s, he was not able to complete much noteworthy scholarly work.

Plagued by numerous ailments in the latter years of his life, Marx died in London on 14 March 1883. His wife Jenny had succumbed to illness in 1881 and he had outlived five of their seven children. At his funeral at Highgate Cemetery in London, with only eight people in attendance, Engels delivered the eulogy, in which he gave voice to the contradictory emotions surrounding Marx and his writings: while some people detested and feared Marx, many more admired and respected his revolutionary zeal. Marx's chief influence was in economics and politics, but his impact on the study of language has been impressive. He quite forcefully pointed out the need to study the social role and class character of language. Indeed, a basic tenet of sociolinguistics relies heavily on his view that language and society influence and depend on each other.

Primary works

(1848) (with Friedrich Engels). *Manifesto of the Communist Party*. Samuel Moore (trans.). In *Karl Marx and Friedrich Engels: Collected Works*. New York: International Publishers, vol. 6, 1976.

(1859). *Grundrisse: Foundations of the Critique of Political Economy*. Martin Nicolaus (trans.). Harmondsworth: Penguin, 1973.

(1867). *Capital: A Critical Analysis of Capitalist Production*. Samuel Moore and Edward Aveling (trans.). In Friedrich Engels (ed.), *Capital*. Moscow: Foreign Languages Publishing House (3 vols), 1963.

(1932a). *Economic and Philosophic Manuscripts of 1844*. Martin Milligan and Dirk J. Struik (trans.). In *Karl Marx and Friedrich Engels: Collected Works*. New York: International Publishers, vol. 3, 1975.

(1932b) (with Friedrich Engels). *The German Ideology*. Clemens Dutt, W. Lough and C. P. Magill (trans.). In *Karl Marx and Friedrich Engels: Collected Works*. New York: International Publishers, vol. 5, 1976.

Further reading

Adler, Max K. (1980). *Marxist Linguistic Theory and Communist Practice: A Sociolinguistic Study*. Hamburg: Helmut Buske.

Berlin, Isaiah (1939; fourth edition, 1978). *Karl Marx: His Life and Environment*. Oxford: Oxford University Press.

Rossi-Landi, Ferruccio (1982). *Marxism and Ideology*. Roger Griffin (trans.). Oxford: Oxford University Press, 1990.

Vološinov, V. N. (1930). *Marxism and the Philosophy of Language*. Ladislav Matejka and I. R. Titunik (trans.). New York: Seminar Press, 1973.

Wheen, Francis (2000). *Karl Marx: A Life*. New York: W.W. Norton.

David V. Witkosky

J. S. MILL

Mill, J. S. (John Stuart) (*b.* 1806, *d.* 1873; British), philosopher, political economist and administrator. Mill was the most prominent advocate of empiricism in nineteenth–century Britain. His analysis of names and their meaning, and his emergentist associationism, constitute his main contributions to the philosophy of language. (*See also* Frege, Gottlob; Kant, Immanuel; Kripke, Saul; Locke, John; Russell, Bertrand; Searle, John.)

John Stuart Mill was born in London on 20 May 1806, the eldest son of the philosopher and political economist James Mill. While his mother, Harriet Barrow, played no part in his formal education, his father determined both his education and later professional career. Under his guidance John Stuart started learning ancient Greek at the age of 3 and Latin at 8, and by the age of 14 he was widely read in philosophy, history, mathematics and literature. One result of this rigorous education was a mental breakdown at the age of 20, which changed his outlook on life. In 1823 he became a clerk at the East India Company, where his father was chief examiner. He became chief examiner himself in 1856, shortly before the Company's dissolution, and was also a Liberal Member of Parliament from 1865 until 1868.

In his first major work, *A System of Logic* (1843), Mill provides the first systematic treatment of induction as the only form of ampliative reasoning and a thoroughgoing defence of empiricism against the so-called *a priori* school, as represented in Britain at the time by Whewell and Hamilton. Even though a comprehensive analysis of language was never Mill's intention, he devotes the first book of *A System of Logic* to it, mainly because an analysis of language is instrumental in the distinction he intends to draw between verbal and real propositions.

Mill follows traditional logic in assuming that propositions consist of a subject and a predicate linked by the copula. Before analysing the meaning of propositions, he devotes a long portion of his exposition to names. In his view, a name is a word or word-string that can appear as the subject or predicate of a proposition. Contra *Locke, Mill assumes that names are not names of our ideas of things but of the things themselves. He puts forward six main distinctions regarding names: general/singular; concrete/abstract; connotative/non-connotative; positive/negative; relative/absolute; and univocal/æquivocal. The most important of these distinctions, both for Mill himself and for later philosophers of language, is the distinction between connotative and non-connotative names, first introduced in his review of Whately's *Elements of Logic* (1828).

According to Mill all general names, that is, names that can be 'truly affirmed of each of an infinite number of things', have both connotation and denotation; they denote a subject and connote an attribute or set of attributes. For instance, the general name 'white' denotes white things and connotes the attribute of whiteness. Translated in contemporary linguistic terminology, connotation is roughly equivalent to intension and denotation is equivalent to extension. Unlike general names, not all singular names are connotative; certain abstract names, such as 'virtue', and – importantly – proper names are non-connotative. These names denote an attribute or thing but do not connote anything. Mill assumes that the meaning of connotative names is their connotation, whereas the meaning of non-connotative abstract names is their denotation. Proper names lack any meaning whatsoever. They are just 'unmeaning marks'.

Turning to the meaning of propositions, in the case of propositions where both subject and predicate are connotative, meaning is determined on the basis of the connotation of those terms. A proposition in which the subject is a proper name and the predicate a connotative name means that what the subject denotes has the attributes connoted by the predicate. When both terms of a proposition are proper names, its meaning is determined by the denotation of the proper names.

Mill was not concerned with the problems raised by identity statements such as 'Cicero is Cicero' versus 'Cicero is Tully'. Whereas the first statement is uninformative, the second adds to our knowledge, even though both 'Cicero' and 'Tully' denote the same individual. Nor did he deal with the contribution to sentence meaning of empty names, that is, proper names lacking denotation, such as 'Pegasus'. These problems led *Frege, *Russell and later *Searle to reject Mill's position and claim that proper names have sense (connotation) and, only contingently (that is, not necessarily), reference (denotation). Mill's position became prominent again with *Kripke, who argued against Frege, Russell and Searle that Mill was right in assuming that proper names are non-connotative. Kripke, however, disagreed with Mill concerning general names: he claimed that certain general names, those for natural kinds ('cat', 'gold'), are akin to proper names. The status of proper names is one of the most recalcitrant questions in the philosophy of language and is still hotly debated between contemporary Fregeans and Millians. The latter have proposed solutions to the main areas identified as problematic for Mill's account, including the identity problem and the emptiness problem referred to above, that cannot be easily dismissed.

As was mentioned earlier, Mill analysed language in order to be able to distinguish with formal criteria between verbal and real propositions. This distinction parallels *Kant's distinction between analytic and synthetic judgements. According to Mill, verbal propositions are those where the meaning of the predicate is contained in the meaning of the subject. These propositions for Mill are neither true nor false; rather, they are either 'correct' or 'incorrect', since they only depend on correct linguistic usage and do not correspond to any facts in the world. On the other hand, real propositions are propositions which assert matters of fact and are therefore susceptible of truth and falsity. Mill's aim in A System of Logic is to demonstrate that all real propositions, including the statements of mathematics, are a posteriori, the products of experience.

Mill has also influenced contemporary theories of language through his brand of associationist psychology. Even though none of his works is exclusively on psychology, Mill edited the second edition of his father's Analysis of the Phaenomena of the Human Mind 1869, adding detailed notes and reworking James Mill's ideas. John Stuart espoused most of the basic tenets of his father's associationist psychology. The main idea behind associationism, which was originally conceived by *Aristotle, is that entities which co-occur in experience also co-occur in thought. Mental operations are determined by the principles of contiguity and resemblance: entities that are contiguous in space or time are similarly linked by association. In Mill's view, the associationist principle of resemblance can explain, for instance, how general terms in language come about. For example, a general term g starts off by being associated with a single instance a. But if a stands in a resemblance relation with b, each time a is evoked in the mind, both b and the term g are evoked. In this way, the term g comes to be associated not only with a but also with b, and this is the case for all entities with which a stands in a resemblance relation.

The crucial difference between James Mill's associationism and that of John Stuart Mill is that, while the elder Mill maintains that the properties of complex associations are nothing more than the sum of the properties of the antecedent simple associations, the son Mill claims that complex associations exhibit properties that are not reducible to the properties of the simple associations that compose them. The former type of properties are purely mechanistic while the latter are 'emergent', a term coined by George Henry Lewes. This distinction, which Mill first introduced in A System of Logic, underlies contemporary emergentist approaches to language, whereby language is assumed to emerge as a result of the complex interaction between biology and environment. In this view, the properties of complex linguistic representations are not reducible to their causal antecedents.

In 1830, roughly at the same time as he was writing the first book of *A System of Logic*, Mill met and became platonically involved with Harriet Taylor, who was then married. Mill's family strongly disapproved of the relationship, and when eventually they married in 1851, after the death of Harriet's husband, Mill became totally estranged from his mother and sisters. Harriet's unexpected death in 1858 left Mill inconsolable. He died in 1873 and was buried next to his wife at Avignon. Even though Mill is best known for his Utilitarian moral and social philosophy and his work on political economy, his analysis of language has had a lasting influence well into the twenty-first century. Gilbert *Ryle, although highly critical of Mill's analysis of language, acknowledged him as one of the first to attempt a formulation of a theory of meaning.

Primary works

(1828). *Whately's 'Elements of Logic'*. In J. M. Robson (ed.), *Collected Works of John Stuart Mill. Vol. XI*. Toronto: University of Toronto Press, 1978.

(1843). *A System of Logic, Ratiocinative and Inductive*. In J. M. Robson (ed.), *Collected Works of John Stuart Mill. Vols VII and VIII*. Toronto: University of Toronto Press, 1974.

(1869; ed.). *Analysis of the Phaenomena of the Human Mind*. James Mill. New York: A. Keley, 1967.

Further reading

Jong, Willem Remmelt de (1982). *The Semantics of John Stuart Mill*. Dordrecht: Reidel.

Ryan, Alan (1974). *J. S. Mill*. London: Routledge and Kegan Paul.

Ryle, Gilbert (1966). 'The theory of meaning'. In C. A. Mace (ed.), *British Philosophy in the Mid-Century: A Cambridge Symposium*. London: Allen and Unwin.

Skorupski, John (1989). *John Stuart Mill*. London and New York: Routledge.

Stavroula-Thaleia Kousta

LESLEY MILROY

Milroy, (Ann) Lesley (*b.* 1944; British), research fellow, University of Manchester (1982–83); lecturer and professor, University of Newcastle upon Tyne (1983–94); Hans Kurath collegiate professor of linguistics, University of Michigan (1994–). Sociolinguist noted for her major contributions to theory and method in the quantitative and qualitative study of language variation, bilingualism and language ideology. (*See also* Cameron, Deborah; Labov, William; Tannen, Deborah.)

Born in Newcastle upon Tyne, England, Lesley Milroy was raised near Glasgow and attended school in Darlington. She obtained a BA (1965) and MA (1967) from the University of Manchester, and her PhD from Queen's University Belfast (1979). Between 1972 and 1988 she held research and teaching positions at Ulster Polytechnic (now University of Ulster), Manchester and Newcastle. She was promoted to a personal chair at Newcastle in 1988, and in 1994 took up her position at the University of Michigan.

Milroy is probably best known for the research she conducted in Belfast in collaboration with her husband James Milroy. Lesley, who carried out the fieldwork, used participant observation as a means of gaining access to three close-knit working-class communities in the city. A particularly innovative aspect of this study, which combined an ethnographic approach to fieldwork with rigorous quantitative data analysis methods, was the adoption from sociological research of the social network model. This, the Milroys argued, more appropriately characterised the structure of the Belfast communities than did conventional means of delineating sample populations, such as the socioeconomic class indices employed by *Labov and the British sociolinguist Peter Trudgill. A crucial insight emerging from the Belfast study concerned the centrality of the role of vernacular (versus institutional or middle-class) norms in the mechanisms underlying language variation and change. Such norms, the Milroys contended, compete against normative pressures from beyond the immediate locality, and depend for their perpetuation on the 'density' and 'multiplexity' of the network ties binding the community's individual members. The persistence and stability of non-standard forms used as markers of local affiliation, in spite of the influence of externally imposed forces such as standardisation and levelling resulting from societal homogenisation, continue to be a principal theme in Lesley Milroy's

work. Her research since the 1990s has investigated patterns of variation in urban varieties of English in the UK (Newcastle, Derby) and the US (notably Detroit). She has also published on bi- and multilingualism (1995, with Muysken) and language disorders (1993, with Lesser), and is considered a leading authority on sociolinguistic methodology. In this area her *Observing and Analysing Natural Language* (1987) and its successor volume (2003, with Gordon) are canonical texts.

Lesley Milroy sits on the editorial boards of several major journals, including *Journal of Linguistics*, *Journal of Sociolinguistics*, *Language in Society* and the *International Journal of Bilingualism*, and since 2000 has been honorary visiting professor of linguistics at the University of York.

Primary works

(1980; second edition, 1987). *Language and Social Networks*. Oxford: Blackwell.

(1985; third edition, 1999) (with James Milroy). *Authority in Language: Investigating Standard English*. London: Routledge.

(1987). *Observing and Analysing Natural Language*. Oxford: Blackwell. Rev. edition (2003) (with Matthew Gordon). *Sociolinguistics: Method and Interpretation*. Oxford: Blackwell.

(1993a) (with Ruth Lesser). *Linguistics and Aphasia: Psycholinguistic and Pragmatic Aspects of Intervention*. London: Longman.

(1993b, ed.) (with James Milroy). *Real English: The Grammar of English Dialects in the British Isles*. London: Longman.

(1995, ed.) (with Peter Muysken). *One Speaker, Two Languages: Cross-Disciplinary Perspectives on Code-Switching*. Cambridge: Cambridge University Press.

Further reading

Li Wei (2001). 'Milroy, Lesley'. In R. Mesthrie (ed.). *Pergamon Concise Encyclopaedia of Sociolinguistics*. Amsterdam: Elsevier Science.

Dominic Watt

RICHARD MONTAGUE

Montague, Richard (Merritt) (*b.* 1930, *d.* 1971; American), logician, philosopher of language and mathematician, whose original works laid the foundation for the theory known after his death as 'Montague Grammar'. Montague was a member of the United States National Committee for the International Union of the History and Philosophy of Science, and chairman of the National Subcommittee for Logic, Methodology, and Philosophy of Science (1966–7). He revolutionised the field of linguistic semantics by pioneering a completely rigorous formal analysis of natural languages, which allowed them to be treated in the same way as artificial languages described by logicians. (*See also* Carnap, Rudolf; Davidson, Donald; Frege, Gottlob; Lewis, David; Tarski, Alfred.)

Montague was born in Stockton, California. His studies were at the University of California at Berkeley, where he received an AB in philosophy in 1950. As an undergraduate, he was particularly interested in Semitic languages, philosophy and mathematics, subjects he pursued to an advanced level. He remained at Berkeley for his postgraduate studies. He worked under the supervision of Alfred *Tarski and formally defended his dissertation in 1957. Montague held the Howison Fellowship in Philosophy between 1950 and 1953 and served as a teaching assistant in mathematics for two consecutive years. In the spring of 1955, he joined the faculty of the University of California at Los Angeles, where he taught until his death.

Montague's most important contribution to linguistics and the philosophy of language was the development of a philosophically satisfactory scientific account of natural language. From the mid-1960s, he authored a number of papers in which he pursued this very ambitious goal. Montague's work was guided by the controversial thesis, stated explicitly in the opening paragraph of his paper 'English as a formal language' (1970a), that there is no fundamental theoretical difference between the syntax-semantics relation in a natural language like English, and that of a formal language such as first-order predicate logic. Before Montague, most linguists and philosophers of language believed that natural languages were too full of idiosyncrasies, ambiguities and vagueness to be directly amenable to formalisation, but Montague's revolutionary ideas were soon to change that widely held point of view.

The paper 'Universal grammar' (1970b) is the most general presentation of Montague's semiotic programme. In it, he laid out the bases of a general theory of language that he hoped would encompass the syntax and semantics of natural and artificial languages alike, and it is in this sense that the term 'universal grammar' should be understood. In modern linguistics, the phrase 'universal grammar' customarily refers to the problem of characterising just the class of possible human languages (see *Chomsky), but Montague was not really concerned with this goal. He believed that the syntax, semantics and pragmatics of natural languages were branches of applied mathematics rather than of cognitive psychology, and thus he placed full generality and mathematical elegance in his work over concern for empirical claims about linguistic universals. Nevertheless, Montague's approach has been in fact quite relevant to the aims of modern linguistics, because it provided an outstanding reference framework within which to formalise, investigate and compare various linguistic theories of possible human languages.

An important methodological feature of Montague's work in natural language is the assumption that there exists a one-to-one correspondence between the syntax that determines recursively how sentences are constructed out of smaller syntactic parts, and the semantic rules that determine how the meaning of a sentence is a function of the meaning of its parts and their mode of syntactic combination. This is the principle of compositionality of meaning, sometimes referred to as '*Frege's principle', which logical languages characteristically satisfy.

Another key aspect of Montague's enterprise was a focus on the truth-conditional aspect of sentence meanings. For him, the meaning of a sentence in a natural language amounts to a specification of the necessary and sufficient conditions for the truth of that sentence, where 'truth' is to be understood here as correspondence to the way the world is. Thus to know the meaning of a declarative sentence such as 'London is the capital of the United Kingdom' is to know what the world would have to be like for this sentence to be true.

The general theory of language Montague formulated in his treatise 'Universal grammar' was subsequently developed in the papers 'English as a formal language' (1970a) and 'The proper treatment of quantification in ordinary English' (1973), which can be regarded as particular instances of his theory. In these papers, he did not analyse the whole English language, but instead gave a complete syntax and semantics of a formal language that could reasonably be considered a subset, or fragment, of ordinary English. The fragment illustrated what Montague considered were the most interesting and challenging syntactic constructions of English. This method of providing a rigorous semantics for a formal system that resembles a fragment of a natural language is yet another methodological feature of Montague's work, and much fruitful work in theoretical and computational linguistics has been pursued within this tradition.

'The proper treatment of quantification in ordinary English' is perhaps Montague's most influential paper among linguists; So much so, in fact, that the expression 'Montague Grammar' often refers to the style of logical grammar he formulated in this paper. But what does a Montague Grammar consist of? The grammar formulated in 'The proper treatment of quantification in ordinary English' has four basic components: the specification of the set of well-formed sentences of a fragment of English; the specification of the set of well-formed formulae of a logical language; a set of explicit translation rules mapping English sentences onto formulae of the logical language; and a complete model-theoretic interpretation of the formulae of the logical language. Crucially, the translation procedure of the grammar is meaning-preserving and, as a result, the meaning assigned to a well-formed formula of the logical language by the semantics is precisely the same meaning assigned to the English sentence that the formula translates. Although Montague relied on an intermediate, or auxiliary, formal language in 'The proper treatment of quantification in ordinary English', he did so only for clarity; in other work, he provided a grammar with direct interpretation of English.

Montague made use of very powerful logical tools in his formalisation of natural language. Standing on the shoulders of Alfred Tarski and Rudolf *Carnap, who pioneered model-theoretic semantics of logic, Montague developed an intensional logic with a rich type theory and a possible worlds model-theoretic semantics that even tried to incorporate some aspects of pragmatics. Of course, Richard Montague was not the only one to employ logical and mathematical techniques in the description of the meanings of natural language expressions. David *Lewis and Donald *Davidson, for exam-

ple, made proposals that went in the same general direction. But Montague Grammar remains by far the most influential theory of the interpretation of natural languages in the tradition of model-theoretic semantics. Montague's work has been extended and subsequently modified by linguists and logicians (See Dowty et al. 1981; Partee 1996; Partee with Hendriks 1997.)

Although his most influential work lies without doubt in the semantics of natural language, Montague also made significant contributions to the fields of mathematics and mathematical logic. These include work in Boolean algebra, model theory, proof theory, recursion theory, axiomatic set theory and higher-order logic. He was an outstanding teacher too. In 1964, he co-authored a successful logic textbook entitled *Logic: Techniques of Formal Reasoning*, and in 1966, he was nominated by the Los Angeles graduate students in philosophy for a distinguished teaching award. Montague died tragically at the hands of unknown persons in his home in Los Angeles on 7 March 1971.

Primary works

(1964) (with Donald Kalish). *Logic: Techniques of Formal Reasoning*. New York: Harcourt, Brace, and World.

(1968). 'Pragmatics'. In R. H. Thomason (ed.), *Formal Philosophy: Selected Papers of Richard Montague*. New Haven, CT, and London: Yale University Press, 1974.

(1970a). 'English as a formal language'. In R. H. Thomason (ed.), *Formal Philosophy: Selected Papers of Richard Montague*. New Haven, CT, and London: Yale University Press, 1974.

(1970b). 'Universal grammar'. *Theoria*. vol. 36: 373–98.

(1973). 'The proper treatment of quantification in ordinary English'. In R. H. Thomason (ed.), *Formal Philosophy: Selected Papers of Richard Montague*. New Haven, CT, and London: Yale University Press, 1974.

(1974). *Formal Philosophy: Selected Papers of Richard Montague*. R. H. Thomason (ed.). New Haven, CT, and London: Yale University Press.

Further reading

Dowty, David (1979). *Word Meaning and Montague Grammar*. Dordrecht: Reidel.

Dowty, David R., Wall, Robert E. and Peters, Stanley (1981). *Introduction to Montague Semantics*. Dordrecht: Kluwer Academic.

Halvorsen, Per-Kristian and Ladusaw, William A. (1979). 'Montague's "Universal Grammar": an introduction for the linguist'. *Linguistics and Philosophy*. vol. 3: 185–223.

Partee, Barbara H. (1975). 'Montague Grammar and transformational grammar'. *Linguistic Inquiry*. vol. 6(2): 203–300.

Partee, Barbara H. (1996). 'The development of formal semantics in linguistic theory'. In S. Lappin (ed.), *The Handbook of Contemporary Semantic Theory*. Oxford: Blackwell.

Partee, Barbara H. with Hendriks, Herman L. W. (1997). 'Montague Grammar'. In J. van Benthem and A. ter Meulen (eds), *Handbook of Logic and Language*. Amsterdam and Cambridge, MA: Elsevier and MIT Press.

Iván García-Álvarez

G. E. MOORE

Moore, G. E. (George Edward) (*b.* 1873, *d.* 1958; British), a founding figure in the British analytic tradition of philosophy, perhaps most famous for his defence of 'common sense' in philosophical analysis. In the philosophy of language, his most influential ideas were his theory of perception, introducing the terminology 'sense data', and his discussion of 'Moore's paradox'. From 1918, Moore was a fellow of the British Academy, and he was editor of the leading philosophy journal *Mind* from 1921 to 1947. In 1951 he was awarded the Order of Merit. (*See also* Austin, J. L.; Ramsey, F. R. Russell, Bertrand; Wittgenstein, Ludwig.)

Born in Upper Norwood, a suburb of London, into a wealthy family, Moore attended Dulwich College and entered Trinity College, Cambridge, in 1892. Although he started out reading classics, he finally completed the 'moral science' tripos in 1896. After he wrote a dissertation on *Kant's ethics, he was made a fellow of Trinity College, a position he held between 1898 and 1904. For the next seven years Moore lived on a private income, studying philosophy independently until in 1911 he became a university lecturer at Cambridge, a position he held until 1925, when he was awarded his professorship. Moore retired in 1939 and spent World War II lecturing in the United States.

Although Moore's early papers (those up to 1903 are published) used methods and views that had been familiar from the philosophical works of Kant, Reid and Bradley, his later papers and books, together with related works by *Frege, *Russell and *Wittgenstein, created methods and views that form the historical and philosophical grounds of analytic philosophy. Moore's philosophy was taken by him to consist of conceptual analysis. Concepts, which are objects of thought, are associated with but distinct from both the related linguistic expressions and the related entities. Concepts are either simple or amenable to analysis, which is a philosophical activity. Among the tools used in philosophical enquiry, Moore included logical principles and certain empirical methods he considered justified. Perhaps his most important and influential positions were his meta-ethical theory and his theory of perception.

Moore held ethics to be the study of goodness, and the quality of being good he took to be simple. Any attempt at defining the good in terms of natural qualities involves what he dubbed 'the naturalistic fallacy'. Ethical sentences express propositions, asserted on grounds of appropriate 'intuitions', but they do not lend themselves to any reduction to non-ethical sentences. Among the greatest goods we have, according to Moore, are personal affection and aesthetic enjoyments.

Moore's theory of perception introduced the notion of 'sense data'. The philosophical motivation for it was the apparent variety of perceptions related to one and the same object when viewed from different perspectives. The exact nature of the sense data remained unclear. He also raised the problem of sentences of the form 'p but I do not believe that p' being considered paradoxical but not self-contradictory. 'Moore's paradox', as it is known, has attracted much attention in the fields of epistemic logic and the philosophy of language.

Moore's philosophy was most influential in the early to mid- twentieth century. Russell said, with respect to his book *The Principles of Mathemat-*ics, that 'on fundamental questions of philosophy, [the book's] position is derived from G. E. Moore'. Later on the importance of Moore's meta-ethics and the interest in his theory of perception diminished, but his contribution to the very creation of mainstream analytic philosophy remains significant in the twenty-first century. Moore was generally well liked and respected by his colleagues and died in old age.

Primary works

(1903). *Principia Ethica*. Cambridge: Cambridge University Press.
(1912). *Ethics*. London and New York: H. Holt.
(1922). *Philosophical Studies*. London and New York: Kegan Paul, Trench, Trubner.
(1953). *Some Main Problems of Philosophy*. London and New York: George Allen and Unwin.
(1959). *Philosophical Papers*. London and New York: George Allen and Unwin.
(1962). *The Common Place Books, 1919–1953*. Casimir Lewy (ed.). London: George Allen and Unwin.

Further reading

Ambrose, A. and M. Lazerowitz (eds) (1970). *G. E. Moore: Essays in Retrospect*. London and New York: George Allen and Unwin.
Ayer, A. J. (1971). *Russell and Moore: The Analytical Heritage*. Cambridge, MA: Harvard University Press.
Baldwin, Thomas (1972). *G. E. Moore: The Arguments of the Philosophers*. London: Routledge, 1999.
Hutchinson, Brian (2001). *G. E. Moore's Ethical Theory: Resistance and Reconciliation*. Cambridge: Cambridge University Press.
Klemke, E. D. (2000). *A Defense of Realism: Reflections on the Metaphysics of G. E. Moore*. Amherst: Humanity Books.
Levy, Paul (1988). *Moore: G. E. Moore and the Cambridge Apostles*. Oxford: Weidenfeld and Nicholson.

Regan, Tom (1986). *Bloomsbury's Prophet: G. E. Moore and the Development of his Moral Philosophy*. Philadelphia: Temple University Press.

Schilpp, P. A. (ed.), (1942). *The Philosophy of G. E. Moore*. New York: Tudor. Rev. edition 1952.

Soames, Scott (2003). *Philosophical Analysis in the Twentieth Century*. Princeton, NJ: Princeton University Press.

Sylvester, Robert Peter (1990). *The Moral Philosophy of G. E. Moore*. Ray Parkins, Jr, and R. W. Sleeper (eds). Philadelphia: Temple University Press.

White, Alan R. (1958). *G. E. Moore: A Critical Exposition*. Oxford: Blackwell.

Cambridge University Library has a catalogued archive of Moore's personal papers, including his lecture notes (1911–39), notes taken in lectures by Russell and Wittgenstein, and correspondence with McTaggart, Russell, Sidgwick, Wittgenstein, Ramsey, Austin and many others.

Asa Kasher

CHARLES MORRIS

Morris, Charles (William) (*b*. 1901, *d*. 1979; American), associate professor, lecturer and then research professor, Chicago (1931–58), research professor, Florida (1958–71). Semiotician. His greatest influence on linguistics was his division of the study of signs into three branches: syntactics, semantics and pragmatics. (*See also* Bloomfield, Leonard; Carnap, Rudolf; Jakobson, Roman; Peirce, C. S.; Sapir, Edward.)

Born in Denver, Colorado, Morris was educated and employed within the United States, and belonged to an American empirical tradition inherited from his teacher George H. Mead and shared with associates such as *Sapir, *Bloomfield and *Jakobson. However, touring Europe during the early 1930s, he also met many of the leading European thinkers of the day, including Rudolf *Carnap. In his subsequent writings Morris sought to integrate the ideas of logical positivism with those of his own philosophical background.

Within this framework, Morris's aim was to develop a unified theory of signs, or a 'semiotic', a term he adopted from the work of John *Locke. Morris's semiotic drew heavily on *Peirce's account of the role of signs in human cognition, but took a more behaviourist approach (for Morris, the significance of a sign is determined by the disposition to respond it promotes in an interpreter). It was also more inclusive; Morris's aim was to integrate subjects studied in logic, aesthetics, sociology, anthropology, psychology and linguistics, together with studies of animal communication systems. In 'Foundations of the theory of signs' (1938) he described the necessary components in the study of any system of signs: syntactics (the structural relationships of signs to one another), semantics (the meaning relationships of signs to what they signify) and pragmatics (the contextual relationship of signs to their users and uses).

Outside of his professional philosophy, Morris took an active interest in education policy and reform, studied Zen Buddhism, and enjoyed literary and visual arts, publishing a book of poems in 1966. He attributed his desire to develop a theory of signs of all types to the fact that his own interests were so broad.

Morris's goal of a fully integrated behavioural account of signs was never fully achieved and is generally no longer sought. However, his distinction between structure and meaning laid important foundations for the subsequent development of linguistics, and has particularly informed work within a generative framework (see *Chomsky). He is also credited with coining the term 'pragmatics', and with drawing attention to the distinction between this and semantics, although present-day pragmatics generally has a narrower focus than he envisaged. Morris was made emeritus professor of the University of Florida in 1971, and died in Gainsville, Florida, in 1979.

Primary works

(1938). 'Foundations of the theory of signs'. In O. Neurath, R. Carnap and C. Morris (eds), *International Encyclopaedia of Unified Science*. Chicago: University of Chicago Press.
(1946). *Signs, Language and Behavior*. New York: Prentice Hall.

Further reading

Black, Max (1947). 'The limitations of behaviorist semiotic'. *Philosophical Review*. vol. 56: 258–72.
Clarke, D. S., Jnr (1987). *Principles of Semiotic*. London: Routledge and Kegan Paul.

Siobhan Chapman

C. S. PEIRCE

Peirce, C. S. (Charles Santiago Sanders) (*b.* 1839, *d.* 1914; American), philosopher, logician, scientist, member of the National Academy of Sciences (1977). Founder of pragmatism, who introduced signs as the centrepiece of philosophical thought and held that logic and language ought to be studied in the manner of exact sciences. (*See also* Kant, Immanuel; Morris, Charles; Wittgenstein, Ludwig.)

The second son of noted Harvard University mathematics and astronomy professor Benjamin Peirce, Charles S. Peirce was born in Cambridge, Massachusetts, and was educated as a chemist in the Lawrence Scientific School at Harvard, from which he graduated at the age of 20. In 1861 he began working for the United States Coastal and Geodetic Survey as scientific assistant and consultant, a position he held until 1891. From 1879 to 1884 he was employed by the Johns Hopkins University as a lecturer in logic. In 1888 he retired with his second wife Juliette Froissy to Arisbe, Milford, Pennsylvania, never to return to academia other than to deliver the occasional lecture. From 1891 onwards he worked as a private and independent researcher, employed, among others, by William Dwight Whitney, the editor of *The Century Dictionary* (1889), for which Peirce wrote over 1,600 definitions on all aspects of science, and by James Mark Baldwin, the editor of the *Dictionary of Philosophy and Psychology* (1901–2).

Peirce's literary output was prodigious, as many as 800 published items, and his manuscripts comprise roughly 100,000 pages. The project of publishing a critical edition of his output in thirty-odd volumes is underway (1980–), but the *Collected Papers* in eight volumes provides a decent overview (1931–66). Peirce is best known for his triadic theory of signs and semiotics (see *Morris), which divides signs into index, icon and symbol, this last explaining how language works. He also advocated a broad conception of language and logic based on the communicative and dialogic character of thought, in which signs function as mediators between parties (not necessarily real) that he termed the utterer and the interpreter. Peirce anticipated many topics in pragmatics, including the force of assertions, speech acts, speaker's meaning versus literal meaning, and the evolutionary core of meaning. To account for these, he used his tripartite divisions of the notions of interpretants, which he took to arise in interpreters upon encountering signs.

Peirce claimed poor proficiency in spoken and written language and came to propose a novel diagrammatic and graphical method of representing propositions and of reasoning about them. Except in accounting for proofs and necessary reasoning, his diagrammatic approach and method of interpretation prefigured model-theoretic ways of looking at logical meaning. His claim of poor language abilities should not be taken too seriously, however, since apart from the numerous languages and calculi he devised for logical purposes, he knew or was familiar with French, Latin, ancient Greek, Italian, Spanish, Arabic, Japanese, Tibetan, Dravidian, Inuktitut, Hebrew, Adelaide, Tagalog, Gaelic, Welsh, hieroglyphs and cuneiform.

Not only improving on *Kant's concept of logical analysis, Peirce's pragmatism, which relates meaning of concepts to their practical consequences, along with his dauntingly rich logical and semiotic system, are extraordinarily resistant to both scientific and philosophical classifications. Disdaining as he did all ordinary schools of thought, he is perhaps best regarded as a grand promoter of positive knowledge of the highest ethical, logical and normative standards. His legacy grows steadily as the details of his works become better known. Beyond philosophy, logic and linguistics, Peirce attracts the attention of people in such diverse fields as literary studies, aesthetics, informatics and artificial intelligence. He died of cancer in Arisbe in 19 April 1914, before gaining wide international acclaim.

Primary works

(1931–66). *Collected Papers of Charles Sanders Peirce* (8 vols). Charles Hartshorne, Paul Weiss and A. W. Burks (eds). Cambridge, MA: Harvard University Press.
(1980–). *The Writings of Charles S. Peirce* (The Peirce Edition Project) (6 vols as of 2003). Bloomington: Indiana University Press.

Further reading

Peirce Edition Project [Online]: www.iupui. edu/~peirce/web (accessed on 23 September 2003).

Ahti-Veikko Pietarinen

JEAN PIAGET

Piaget, Jean (*b.* 1896, *d.* 1980; Swiss), malacologist, child psychologist, epistemologist, director of the International Bureau of Education (1929–67), founder and director of the International Center for Genetic Epistemology (1955–80). An influential researcher of cognitive development in children. (*See also* Chomsky, Noam; Skinner, B. F.)

Having published his first paper by the age of 11 Piaget made an early impression in his native Neuchâtel, Switzerland, as a budding scientist. His father, Arthur Piaget, a professor of medieval literature, instilled in him an ability to work independently and systematically, while his mother, Rebecca Jackson, influenced his interest in psychology through her own mental instability. Later in life Piaget's family continued to be integral to his studies; his own son and two daughters served as behavioural subjects of his innovative research in learning and language in children.

After having started his intellectual career studying molluscs, Piaget's interests turned to child cognitive development while working to standardise tests for schoolchildren. At this time, he witnessed a pattern among children's correct and incorrect answers, leading him to develop a theory of the stages of understanding through which a child's cognition passes. He quickly established a clinical method of study, involving not only observation but also verbal interaction with the child subjects of his research. Piaget's writings on the subject attracted much attention initially and then fell into obscurity for many years. Upon publishing detailed analyses of his work involving his three children, his work once again received wide recognition in the field.

Piaget's approach to epistemology included an examination of the role of language in learning. While many voices of the time argued for language as the basis for cognitive development, Piaget showed that, on the contrary, logical organisation precedes language in the mind. As evidence, he turned to studies that showed that deaf children develop the same ability for logical thought as do hearing children. Through these studies and particularly through those he performed with his own children, he showed that logic in action precedes logic in language. In other words, knowledge and understanding form the basis from which language can develop as a semiotic function. Language – like gestures, imitation and drawing – serves to represent externally knowledge that resides internally.

From his development of the clinical method to his prolific work with children of various ages, Piaget's impact on our understanding of a child's ability to learn and understand has been indisputable. His theories have influenced teaching methodology in the classroom while inspiring interest in the field as a whole. In 1955, Piaget founded the International Center for Genetic Epistemology in Geneva, and thereafter continued to publish prolifically until his death in 1980.

Primary works

(1926). *The Language and Thought of the Child*. London: Routledge and Kegan Paul.
(1936). *The Origin of Intelligence in Children*. London: Routledge and Kegan Paul.

Further reading

Evans, Richard I. (1973). *Jean Piaget: The Man and his Ideas*. New York: E. P. Dutton.
Modgil, Celia and Modgil, Sohan (eds) (1982). *Jean Piaget: Consensus and Controversy*. New York: Praeger.

Jennifer A. Baldwin

KENNETH PIKE

Pike, Kenneth (Lee) (*b*. 1912, *d*. 2000; American), associate professor, then full professor of linguistics, University of Michigan (1948–79); adjunct professor, University of Texas at Arlington (1979–2000); president (1942–79), then president emeritus (1979–2000), at the Summer Institute of Linguistics. General linguist and phonetician, best known for his expertise as a field linguist, performing numerous monolingual demonstrations, and for 'tagmemics', defined as 'a theory of theories that tells how the observer universally affects the data and becomes part of the data' (Pike 1982: 3). (*See also* Bloomfield, Leonard; Hockett, Charles; Jakobson, Roman; Sapir, Edward.)

Pike was the seventh of eight children and was born on 9 June 1912 in Woodstock, Connecticut, where his father, Ernest R. Pike, was a country doctor. Although Kenneth initially wanted to go to China as a missionary, when that didn't work out he began his study of linguistics in 1935 with W. Cameron Townsend, and enjoyed 'ten days of phonetics' at Townsend's Summer Institute of Linguistics (SIL), instructed by Elbert McCreery. The goal of SIL was and is to prepare translations of the Bible into various preliterate languages. The only way to accomplish this task was to research the target language through intensive linguistic fieldwork and analysis in order to devise an optimal orthography for it. Such work required a detailed knowledge of phonetics and phonology, and Pike learned his skills in part through working on this project in Mexico. Pike's Christian faith was a powerful driving force throughout his life and work. He was nominated many times for the Nobel Peace and Literature prizes because of his work at the SIL. He married in 1938 and had three children; he and his wife Evelyn also wrote and published together.

The aim of Pike's 229-page Michigan doctoral dissertation, subsequently revised and published as *Phonetics* (1943), was to describe all the sounds of the world's languages. *Phonetics* further contributed to Pike's international reputation in phonetics and in fact has remained in print since its first publication. But by 1949 Pike seemed to have tired of phonetics and began to research the idea of a unit of grammar analogous to the phoneme. Originally calling it a 'grammeme', Pike later adopted the *Bloomfieldian term 'tagmeme', but with different meaning and application (Pike

1954–60). In the twenty-first century, Pike's phonological work has proved to be more valuable than tagmemics, which remains of interest largely for historical reasons.

Pike's most famous contribution to terminology are the words 'emic' and 'etic', which have influenced many of the disciplines in humanities and social sciences. Stemming from his work in phonemics, the terms resulted from the shortening by Pike in 1954 of phonemic and phonetic to explain aspects of human behaviour besides language. He was one of the first major theoreticians to view language and the total human behavioural system as one composed of multiple systems.

Pike was a popular and well-regarded scholar whose linguistic abilities earned him widespread admiration. In fact, he became so proficient at analysing tone languages that he gave demonstrations in which he would learn to converse with native speakers of languages that were new to him simply by listening to them speak and mimicking the sounds they made. Several recordings of these demonstrations are available. Pike received numerous honorary degrees from universities and colleges such as Huntington College (1967), University of Chicago (1973), Houghton College (1977), Université René Descartes (1978), Gordon College (1982), Georgetown University (1984) and Albert Ludwig University, Freiburg (1993). A list of other awards and accomplishments may be found, along with Pike's own reflections on a long and distinguished career, in Kaye (1994). Pike died in Fort Worth, Texas, on 31 December 2000 after a brief illness.

Primary works

(1943). *Phonetics: A Critical Analysis of Phonetic Theory and a Technic for the Practical Description of Sounds*. Ann Arbor: University of Michigan Press.
(1948). *Tone Languages: A Technique for Determining the Number and Type of Pitch Contrasts in a Language, with Studies in Tonemic Substitution and Fusion*. Ann Arbor: University of Michigan Press.
(1954–60). *Language in Relation to a Unified Theory of the Structure of Human Behavior*. Second edition. The Hague: Mouton, 1967.
(1977). 'Into the unknown'. *Pike on Language*, program 5. On 3.4-inch video-cassettes (NTSC standard) and 16-mm kinescopes. Ann Arbor: University of Michigan Television Center.
(1982). *Linguistic Concepts: An Introduction to Tagmemics*. Lincoln, NE: University of Nebraska Press.

Further reading

Brend, Ruth M. (ed.) (1972). *Kenneth L. Pike: Selected Writings*. The Hague: Mouton.
Brend, Ruth M. (1987). *Kenneth Lee Pike Bibliography*. Bloomington: Eurolingua.
Brend, Ruth M. (2001). 'Kenneth L. Pike'. *Language*. vol. 77 (3): 562–6.
Kaye, Alan S. (1994). 'An interview with Kenneth Pike'. *Current Anthropology*. Vol. 35: 291–8. Also available at: [online] www.sil.org/klp/kayeint.htm (accessed 22 September 2003).

Alan S. Kaye

PLATO

Plato (*b*. c. 427 BC, *d*. 347 BC; Greek), founder of the Academy, the longest-running institution of learning in the Western world, identified with the Theory of Forms, speculating that we recognise specific, real-world objects through referring to built-in knowledge of what the 'ideal' form of the object should be. Plato was also author of some of the earliest surviving speculations on language. (*See also* Aristotle; Chomsky, Noam; Katz, J. J.)

The most generally accepted date for Plato's birth is around 427 BC. He was born into an old, aristocratic Athenian family, and a career in politics would have been the expectation of someone of his station. His family had a particularly strong political tradition and history. His father Ariston was said to have been descended from Kodros, the last of the legendary kings of Athens, and his mother Perictione was distantly related to Solon, the famous Athenian statesman and lawgiver of the sixth century BC. When Plato was still a child his father died and his mother remarried Pyrilampes, who was said to be a close associate of another famous Athenian statesman, Pericles. Plato's given name was Aristocles, after his grandfather. However, he acquired the nickname Plato (which translates as 'the broad'), and ancient biographers suggest several possible sources, including a comment on his physique from his wrestling coach, the breadth of his style or the breadth of his forehead.

Despite his background Plato initially started not with political ambitions, but with literary ones. Various writers in antiquity suggested that in his youth he had been a writer of poetry and drama. Indeed, from a literary point of view the dialogues show him to be an excellent writer. Upon meeting Socrates, however, he became convinced that a literary career was of no value, burned a tragedy he had written, and turned instead to philosophy.

The early years of Plato's life came at a turbulent time in Athens' history. He saw military service during the latter stages of the Peloponnesian War, which ended in 404 BC with the defeat of Athens. Shortly thereafter his great-uncle Critias became the leader of the Thirty Tyrants, an oligarchical junta who ruled Athens for eight months in the immediate aftermath of the war. Plato describes being involved in this junta for a very short period, but leaving after quickly becoming disillusioned with their corruption and injustices. Democracy was restored and he again had some hope of political service to Athens. However, because of the prevailing atmosphere of retribution and injustice, he remained ambivalent about entering politics. Worse was to come in 399 BC when his mentor and teacher Socrates was brought to trial and then executed by the democratic government, the charge being impiety and corrupting the youth of Athens.

It was shortly after the execution of Socrates that Plato began his philosophical writings, at the age of about 29. They are traditionally divided into the early, middle and later periods. One of their most notable aspects is their form: all of Plato's works consist of dialogues between various participants. He himself never appears, however. Instead the protagonist is normally his teacher Socrates. In the dialogues of the early period, it is claimed that Plato is more faithfully recording Socrates' own views rather than putting forward his own, and that these dialogues were written as a form of tribute to his teacher. Some evidence for this view can be taken from the fact that three of the early dialogues, the *Euphythro*, the *Apology* and the *Crito*, concern the period immediately surrounding Socrates' trial (before, during and after, respectively).

The early dialogues have a recurring structure. Socrates, professing ignorance about a particular subject, usually a moral or ethical one, encounters someone who claims to be knowledgeable about it. In the *Laches*, for example, the subject is 'courage'; in the *Euphythro*, it is 'piety'. Socrates proceeds to ask the person questions about the topic, in an attempt to draw out a general answer to questions such as: 'What is virtue, in essence?' Over the course of the discussion, what Socrates' questioning reveals is that, although his interlocutor can provide examples or instances, he is unable to provide the requisite general answer. These early dialogues tend not to go any further than that, however, and are thus generally inconclusive. Various definitions are suggested and rejected as being too narrow or too broad, but with no positive conclusion being reached.

In 387 BC, at the age of around 40, Plato founded the Academy, an institution of learning that operated for over 900 years. It is at this point that his middle period begins. In contrast to the early period, he now begins to use Socrates to advance more positive doctrines. Plato's work begins to branch out into other areas, such as politics and metaphysics. Running through various middle-period dialogues (including the *Phaedo*, the *Symposium* and the *Republic*) is one

of his most important contributions to philosophy: the Theory of Forms.

The 'Theory of Forms' (also sometimes called the 'Theory of Ideas') is Plato's answer to one of the most important philosophical questions: what is real? It claims that there are entities that exist in a realm beyond the world of ordinary senses. The entities in this realm are objective, changeless and eternal. They would exist even if there were no intelligent life in the universe to discover them. In a Platonist interpretation of mathematics, for example, the number three genuinely exists independently of any particular mind. Its properties are not contingent properties of human beings and it would exist even if there were no intelligent life to discover its properties. However, by reasoning (consulting our faculty of intuition), we can none the less come to discover properties of the number three. This transcendental realm contains not only entities such as numbers, but also (more famously) the entities that general or universal concepts denote, such as the Good, the Beautiful and so on. This has obvious implications for the study of language and meaning, especially since it implies that meaning exists independently of human life.

The later dialogues are characterised by a development in the way that Plato thinks philosophy should be done. In the early and middle dialogues, we see the familiar 'question-and-answer' mode led by Socrates and the search for general definitions. However, in the later dialogues Plato develops a 'collection-and-division' method, in which all instances of something that seem to possess a common characteristic are collected together and then sub-divided further and further into different sub-categories until nothing remains. In addition, Socrates the character becomes marginalised. Although he takes his traditional central role in the *Theataeus* and the *Philebus*, he contributes very little in the *Sophist* and the *Politicus* and does not appear at all in Plato's final work, the *Laws*.

The traditional form for the citation of Plato's works is by 'Stephanus number'. Running down each page of the complete 1578 edition by Henri Estienne ('Stephanus' in its Latinised form) were the letters 'a' to 'e', sub-dividing each page into five sections. Thus a citation of *Meno* 82b refers to a quotation which appears in section b of page 82 of the original Stephanus edition: almost all subsequent editions indicate the Stephanus numbers in the margin. With the exception of the *Timaeus*, all of Plato's works were lost to Western civilisation until medieval times. Like much of the ancient Greek culture, they were preserved only by Muslim scholars in the Middle East.

The study of Plato and his works raises a number of interesting issues relating to language and linguistics. For example, it has been suggested that there are aspects of the Greek language itself which influenced the direction of Plato's philosophy, particularly regarding the Theory of Forms. As Hare (1982) notes, for example, the various verbs 'to know' in Greek were very often used as complex transitive verbs, similar to the English 'I know him to be here'. Given that the subject of the embedded clause appeared in the accusative case (as in English), it is easy to imagine this con-struction leading one to a view of knowledge as a relation between a knower and a tangible thing (the direct object of the verb). Additionally, one of the verbs 'to know' that Plato uses very commonly is also cognate with the verb 'to see'. This could also have influenced Plato to view knowledge as a kind of mental 'seeing'.

Hare also notes that a further potential source of confusion comes from the Greek word *alēthes*. This is generally translated as 'true' or 'real', but it also means 'true' in the sense of true and false propositions. There is therefore a potentially tempting line of argumentation that says that because we cannot be said to know something if it is false (that is, it is not '*alēthes*'), then things that we *do* know are '*alēthes*', both true and genuinely (even necessarily) existing. The problem is compounded by the fact that Greek rather freely created abstract substantives by adding a definite article to the neuter form of the adjective. Thus it becomes easy to talk about knowing the Beau-tiful, as opposed to knowing what 'beauty' is or what the word 'beautiful' means. The dialogues themselves also contain some speculation about language and linguistic issues. The one dialogue in which Plato deals directly with these issues is the *Cratylus*. More so than some of the other dialogues, the *Cratylus* has been the subject of a lively debate, in terms of both its dating and its significance.

Until the mid-twentieth century, there was a general consensus that the *Cratylus* represented a relatively early dialogue, written just before Plato's founding of the Academy. However, since that time, critics have noted affinities with some of the later dialogues such as the *Parmenides* and the *Politicus*, and its precise place is now less clear. The Theory of Forms, for example, seems to be in a relatively early state in general, but then is unexpectedly advanced with respect to certain specific aspects.

The debate concerning its significance arises because the *Cratylus* is a relatively self-contained whole, treating a subject that is seemingly tangential to Plato's general philosophical programme and the Theory of Forms. The *Cratylus* concerns the nature and origin of 'names', by which are meant both personal names and natural kind terms, such as 'man', 'horse' and so on. In fact, the word *onoma* in Greek did not distinguish between the two and could even refer to adjectives and adverbs. However, the concern with nature versus convention with respect to names can be seen as connected with Plato's concern for the natural/conventional debate in other areas such as laws. This interest probably stemmed from the moral relativism, prevalent in Athens at the time, which Plato found so objectionable.

The three participants in the *Cratylus* dialogue are Cratylus, a Sophist teacher with whom Plato had been acquainted in his youth; Hermogenes, a young associate of Socrates; and Socrates himself, who agrees to explore the issue with them. The dialogue opens with a frustrated Hermogenes, who has been attempting to elicit from Cratylus some information regarding his theory of names. Cratylus' view is that names are not merely conventional agreements to use certain sounds to refer to certain things. Rather, each thing has a true and correct name for it, irrespective of any particular language. However, when Hermogenes pushes him to explain further, Cratylus replies only by teasing him, saying that although 'Cratylus' is his true name, and 'Socrates' is the true name of Socrates, Hermogenes' true name isn't 'Hermogenes'. The joke here is that 'Socrates' parses transparently as 'sound ruler' and 'Cratylus' also contains the root *krat-* meaning 'strength'. Hermogenes (transparently 'born of Hermes') is not well named because Hermes is the patron of the wealthy, but as we learn Hermogenes' financial ventures always end in failure.

Hermogenes asks Socrates to help him unravel Cratylus' theory or, alternatively, to put forward his own proposal about the correctness of names. Socrates replies, as usual, by professing ignorance on the matter. However, he suggests that Hermogenes put forward his view, which is that there is no principle of correctness regarding names other than convention and agreement. The dialogue thus contains two discussions, carried on with Hermogenes and Cratylus respectively.

The first discussion concerns Hermogenes' conventionalism. In his view, either lone individuals or communities can have naming conventions, and those conventions are as right for the speaker or community as any other conventions. A person may choose to refer to human beings as 'horses' and vice versa; there is no question of rightness or wrongness. Many though not all commentators take Hermogenes to task for espousing an 'anything goes' or 'Humpty-Dumpty' view of conventionalism. (See Barney 1997 for more background and an alternative interpretation.)

However, Socrates counters by suggesting that naming is just another type of action, such as weaving or lighting a fire. It requires an instrument, which is in this case the name. And just as there are instruments that are more or less useful, and therefore more or less proper, so there are names that are more or less proper and therefore more or less correct. When pressed by Hermogenes, Socrates proposes that a correct name reveals something about the nature of its object. For example, Iatrokles ('famous physician') or Akesimbrotos ('healer of men') would be appropriate names for a doctor.

The conclusion that a correct name reveals something about its object becomes the jumping-off point for a substantial and controversial part of the dialogue, in which Socrates argues that the gods, the stars, elements, the virtues and other terms are all correctly named, and that their names therefore reveal something about their nature. Although there is some dispute, most commentators agree that Socrates does not in general intend the etymologies proposed to be taken seriously. Under this interpretation, the section becomes a thinly veiled attack on the Sophists, for whom etymological examination was a central intellectual activity. Whatever the status of the investigation, however, some of the principles appealed to during Socrates's etymological exploration do have some modern resonance, such as the effect of euphony on sound change (404d) and the need to seek out the oldest forms (418e).

Having examined various etymologies, Socrates moves on to the question of 'primary' names: those that are not derived from others. In order for primary names to be correctly given, the letters that they are composed of must give some insight into their nature. Socrates suggests, for example, that the letter rho expresses motion, since it appears in words such as *rumbein* 'whirl' and *tromos* 'trembling'. The letter lambda indicates smoothness and softness (*liparon* 'sleek' and *leios* 'level'). As for vowels, the letter omicron, for example, indicates roundness, while eta indicates length.

This discussion naturally leads to a reintroduction of Cratylus into the debate, and Socrates therefore turns to problems with the position that he has just argued, namely that there is a natural connection between names and things. He points out that there are at least some names, the names of numbers for example, which could not possibly resemble the things themselves. However, Socrates' central aim in this final section of the dialogue is to argue against the Sophist position that an investigation into things themselves can be accomplished by investigating names. He notes that there are various potential problems. For example, the original name-givers might have been mistaken about a thing; they could not have had knowledge of the things they were naming if, as Cratylus claims, names are the only paths to knowledge about the thing. More importantly, since names can only be images or copies of the things, we are more likely to arrive at the truth if we examine the things themselves, rather than the copies.

In addition to having a dialogue devoted to linguistic issues, Plato's more general metaphysical ideas have also informed the views of some philosophers of language. The most direct example is *Katz, whose work from the 1980s onward is directly informed by Plato's Theory of Forms. In Katz's view, sentences and languages are abstract objects that are part of a Platonic transcendent reality: they are timeless, changeless entities. Just as with forms more generally, we gain access to their properties through the faculty of intuition. In this way, Katzian Platonic linguistics draws a sharp distinction between the objects of linguistic knowledge and the objects themselves.

The works of Plato have also provided indirect, rather than direct, inspiration for ideas surrounding language. *Chomsky identifies what he calls 'Plato's problem' in the context of our knowledge of our language. Simply put, there are things that we know about our language (for example, the grammaticality or ungrammaticality of certain strings, possible interpretations and so on) that go beyond what it is plausible to assume we could have picked up from the acquisition data that we were exposed to. Chomsky claims that Plato addresses a similar problem in the *Meno*. At one point in this early dialogue, Socrates demonstrates that an untutored slave boy knows truths about geometry. The question then arises as to where this knowledge could have come from. Chomsky claims that Plato's answer (that the knowledge was remembered from a previous existence) can be recast in a modern form by appealing to genetics, specifically to a species-specific language acquisition device.

It is impossible to overstate the influence that Plato has had on modern Western philosophy. The philosopher and mathematician Alfred North Whitehead famously described the history of Western philosophy as 'footnotes to Plato'. Plato has something to say on almost every topic imaginable, from the nature of politics to the immortality of the soul, and the dialogue as a way of presenting philo-. sophical arguments was picked up by philosophers such as *Leibnitz and *Berkeley. After his death in 347 BC, Plato's body was buried in the grounds of his Academy.

Primary works

(1953). *The Dialogues of Plato, with Analyses and Introductions*. Fourth edition. Benjamin Jowett (trans.). Oxford: Clarendon Press.
(1995). *Plato Opera*. Vol. I. E. A. Duke et al. (eds). Oxford: Oxford University Press.

Further reading

Barney, Rachel (1997). 'Plato on conventionalism'. *Phronesis*. Vol. XLII (2): 143–62.
Guthrie, W. K. C. (1975–8). *A History of Greek Philosophy*. Vols 4 and 5. Cambridge: Cambridge University Press.
Hare, R. M. (1982). *Plato* (Past Masters Series). Oxford: Oxford University Press.

Joseph, John E. (2000). *Limiting the Arbitrary: Linguistic Naturalism and its Opposites in Plato's 'Cratylus' and Modern Theories of Language*. Amsterdam: John Benjamins.

Geoffrey Poole

KARL POPPER

Popper, Karl (Raimond) (*b*. 1902, *d*. 1994; Austrian, naturalised British), principally known as a philosopher of science, Popper spent most of his academic career in England, at the London School of Economics (LSE), where he became professor of logic and scientific method in 1949. He received a knighthood in 1965. Although he did publish some reflections on human language, it is Popper's more general ideas concerning the philosophy of science and ontological pluralism that have influenced linguists. Popper was also well known for his critique of Marxism and as an advocate of gradual, piecemeal social change (as opposed to top-down revolutionary change). (*See also* Kant, Immanuel; Russell, Bertrand; Wittgenstein, Ludwig.)

Popper's father was Simon Siegmund Carl Popper, a doctor of law at the University of Vienna who also worked as a trial lawyer and solicitor; his mother was Jenny Popper, née Schiff, a talented amateur pianist from a musical family. The family owned an extensive library of history and philosophy books, though Popper's father was reluctant to influence the direction of his son's thought. By the age of 10 Popper had come under the influence of Arthur Arndt, then 30 years old, and an anti-nationalist and socialist; Arndt became a life-long friend. When World War I began, Popper was dismayed by the way former pacifists had abandoned their positions to support the Austrian and German cause; he soon came to believe that Austria deserved to be defeated. He left school aged 16 when the war ended, claiming that his formal education up to that point had been a waste of time. He finally matriculated at the University of Vienna in 1922, having studied there as a non-matriculated student for almost five years. He qualified to teach mathematics and physics in secondary schools, but while studying he had begun an apprenticeship as a cabinet maker, and when he was unable to find a teaching job he finished his apprenticeship. Popper was awarded a PhD by the University of Vienna in 1928, though he believed he did not deserve it.

Before examining Popper's influence on linguistics and the philosophy of language, it is worth considering his work in the philosophy of science. He set out to provide a set of criteria that would allow for a demarcation between scientific and non-scientific knowledge. In doing so he stressed the fallibility of scientific knowledge, denying that absolutely certain knowledge can ever be attained. In making this claim he opposed the verificationism of the logical positivists (see *Ayer). Verificationism is the idea that scientific knowledge is knowledge that has been conclusively proven to be true, since it is, the logical positivists claimed, based on infallible observation statements. In contrast, Popper stressed that all observation statements are grounded in sets of assumptions and theoretical concepts that are fallible and subject to change over time. This is his widely cited claim that there is no such thing as theory-free observation. Rather than stressing proof of the truthfulness of scientific theories, Popper stressed falsifiability as the hallmark of scientific hypotheses: if a statement about the world is framed so as to exclude certain states of affairs, then it admits of counter-evidence, is falsifiable in principle and is thus scientific. Popper thus proposed a link between falsifiability and content. The more a conjecture excludes, the more content it has and the more it is claiming about the world. Hypotheses that exclude nothing are not scientific, for Popper, since they are unfalsifiable.

Unlike the logical positivists, Popper denied that non-scientific statements are necessarily meaningless. On the contrary, he pointed out that scientific theories may emerge from non-scientific stories about the world, such as myths. An example of this is the heliocentric theory (the idea that the sun is at the centre of our planetary system), which existed in myth before it came to be framed in falsifiable, scientific terms. Popper also stressed that a given scientific theory is usually embedded within a general picture of the world, a metaphysical research programme, which is not itself refutable. Central to Popper's thinking are the twin notions of conjecture and refutation: scientific theories are fallible conjectures about the world, but conjectures that are capable of refutation. While Popper denied that we could ever prove, once and for all, the truth of our scientific theories, he did believe that those theories are attempts at describing reality. He advocated scientific realism and opposed instrumentalist interpretations of scientific theories according to which our theoretical constructs are seen merely as tools for systematising observable data and making ever-more accurate predictions about observable phenomena.

Popper believed that the world is open-ended and that new kinds of reality can emerge. He believed that our scientific theories constitute a novel kind of reality, a reality that has emerged over evolutionary time. He referred to this as world three, the world of our theoretical and cultural constructs, as distinct from the purely physical world (world one) and the world of mind-internal states and events (world two). This three-way distinction was important for Popper, since he opposed subjectivism in the philosophy of science (the idea that scientific knowledge consists in the mental states of scientists). For Popper, scientific knowledge was objective knowledge: scientists can come to discover facts about theories, such as the consequences of our theoretical constructs. Such consequences, he believed, exist independently of our internal, subjective states. This three-way distinction led Popper to adopt a version of Cartesian (see *Descartes) dualism (distinguishing mind from brain), reflected in his work with neuroscientist John Eccles. This aspect of Popper's ontological pluralism flew in the face of mainstream late-twentieth-century thinking about the nature of mind, which has been physicalistic since at least the appearance of *Ryle (1949).

Popper was unusual among twentieth-century British philosophers in having considerable influence outside of the narrow world of academic philosophy. His thinking influenced both politicians and working scientists such as John Eccles and Peter Medawar. His influence on linguistics was both direct and indirect. The most obvious indirect influence is the widespread awareness among working linguists of the notion that falsifiability is the hallmark of scientific hypotheses, and the proposed relation between the explicitness of an hypothesis, its falsifiability and its empirical content. For many linguists who wish to presuppose, or claim overtly, that their work is scientific in nature, it suffices to demonstrate that their hypotheses are falsifiable, and many, in particular generative linguists, believe that this is self-evidently the case. Such linguists may or may not have read Popper, but they have certainly taken on board his demarcation criterion. Popper's scientific realism is also arguably present in Noam *Chomsky's (2000 and elsewhere) realist approach to linguistic enquiry.

More direct influences can be seen in the explicit application to linguistics of Popper's ideas concerning ontological pluralism and the putative central role of conjectures and refutations in scientific theorising. An early attempt to claim specifically that Popper's notion of world three objects applied to linguistic objects was made by

Lass (1976), later elaborated by Carr (1990). Perhaps the most explicit application of Popper's ideas to linguistic enquiry is that of Geoffrey Sampson. He seeks to defend an empiricist account of linguistic knowledge in the face of the prevailing rationalist approach adopted by Chomsky, and the version of empiricism that Sampson defends is overtly based on Popper's work. Sampson (1997) argues against the Chomskyan rationalist claim that human beings are equipped at birth with innate linguistic knowledge (referred to by many as Universal Grammar, or UG). Instead, Sampson argues that human beings come to have linguistic knowledge because they are good learners, capable of devising novel (if fallible) conjectures and testing these: they come to have knowledge of language in the same way that they come to have any other kind of knowledge of the world.

Challenging the late-twentieth-century consensus view of the mind, Sampson also explicitly adopts Popper's mental/physical dualism, the view that human minds are not physical objects, and thus not open to scientific enquiry. This view runs into exactly the same problem as Descartes ran into: if the mind is distinct from the body, how can the two possibly interact? Sampson seems to have no more of an answer to this question than Descartes did. It is arguable that Popper's advocating of Cartesian dualism towards the end of his career was a mistake. But it is possible to adopt an empiricist approach to linguistic knowledge of a Popperian sort without resort to dualism. An example of this is

Gopnik's (2001) work on the 'theory theory' of child language acquisition, which sees the child as a little scientist, testing out hypotheses in different cognitive domains as the main means of acquiring language.

Like those of many of his contemporaries, Popper's early life and career were disrupted by world events. Popper was a socialist of long standing and although he had been baptised at birth he realised in the 1930s that this, combined with his Jewish origins, made Vienna a dangerous place to live. In 1937 he and his wife Hennie left for New Zealand. They finally settled near London when Popper was offered a readership at the LSE in 1945. The couple bought an isolated house near Penn, Buckinghamshire, where they had few visitors; it has been argued that this isolation had a profound effect on Popper's subsequent thinking and world view. Popper died on 17 September 1994.

Primary works

(1935). *Logik der Forschung: Zur Erkenntnistheorie der Modernen Naturwissenschaft*. Vienna: Springer.
(1945). *The Open Society and its Enemies* (2 vols). London: Routledge and Kegan Paul.
(1957). *The Poverty of Historicism*. London: Routledge and Kegan Paul.
(1959). *The Logic of Scientific Discovery*. London: Hutchinson.
(1963). *Conjectures and Refutations*. London: Kegan Paul.
(1972). *Objective Knowledge: An Evolutionary Approach*. Oxford: Clarendon Press.
(1976). *Unended Quest: An Intellectual Autobiography*. London: Fontana.
(1977) (with J. C. Eccles). *The Self and its Brain*. Berlin: Springer.
(1982–3). *Postscript to the Logic of Scientific Discovery*. Vols 1 and 2, London: Hutchinson; Vol. 3, Totowa, NJ.: Rowan and Littlefield.

Further reading

Carr, P. (1990). *Linguistic Realities*. Cambridge: Cambridge University Press.
Chomsky, N. (2000). *New Horizons in the Study of Language and Mind*. Cambridge: Cambridge University Press.
Gopnik, A. (2001). 'Theories, language and culture: Whorf without wincing'. In M. Bowerman and S. Levinson (eds), *Language Acquisition and Conceptual Development*. Cambridge: Cambridge University Press.
Lass, R. (1976). *English Phonology and Phonological Theory*. Cambridge: Cambridge University Press.
Ryle, G. (1949). *The Concept of Mind*. London: Hutchinson.
Sampson, G. (1997). *Educating Eve: The 'Language Instinct' Debate*. London: Cassell.

Philip Carr

HILARY PUTNAM

Putnam, Hilary (b. 1926; American), professor of philosophy at Princeton (1953–60), MIT (1960–5) and Harvard (since 1965). Analytic philosopher who made groundbreaking contributions to the philosophy of science, the philosophy of mathematics, the philosophy of mind and language and metaphysics. (*See also* Kripke, Saul; Quine, W. V. O.)

Born in Chicago, Putnam spent the first eight years of his life in Paris, where his father (who later joined the communist party) worked as a writer and translator. During his university studies (he specialised in philosophy of science and logic) in the 1940s, Putnam was influenced by the two currents that marked American academic philosophy at the time, pragmatism and logical positivism, as well as by *Quine. During the Vietnam War, Putnam founded an anti-war committee and gave lectures on Marxism.

Putnam's work spans a broad range of philosophical topics. At first he focused mainly on the philosophy of science, logic and the philosophy of mathematics. From the late 1950s to the early 1970s, he gave the philosophy of mind a new direction by developing the computer model of the mind (known as functionalism), according to which functional organisation rather than physical makeup is essential for mentality.

In the 1970s, he argued for a radically new view about the nature of meaning, known as semantic externalism. Until then the orthodox view in the philosophy of language, dating back to *Frege, was that the meaning of an expression determines what the expression refers to, where meanings are the kind of thing competent speakers of a language can fully grasp. In 'The meaning of meaning' (first published 1975), Putnam developed a famous thought experiment he called 'Twin Earth' to show that meanings (what determines reference) are not 'in the head' as such. What is in the head, the descriptions associated with the expression in question, is stereotypes such as 'tigers are big cats with stripes'. Speakers have to know these stereotypes to be credited with full understanding of the expression, but the stereotypes themselves do not determine reference. Rather, Putnam argued, both the speech community as a whole, and the environment in which users of the language are embedded, contribute to fixing the reference of many expressions. Independently from Saul *Kripke, Putnam developed the causal theory of reference to account for how reference mechanisms work.

In his article 'Models and reality' (first published 1980), Putnam employed results from mathematical logic to draw far-reaching metaphysical conclusions. His 'model-theoretic argument' was designed to show that some metaphysical-realist positions, of the kind he sympathised with earlier in his life, are untenable. Since 2000, Putnam has been professor emeritus at Harvard University and continues to be extremely productive. His functionalist theory of the mind was a major contributor to the development of cognitive science, while his work on semantic externalism has opened up new areas of enquiry in the philosophy of mind, the philosophy of language, metaphysics and epistemology.

Primary works

(1975a). *Mathematics, Matter and Method: Philosophical Papers. Vol. 1.* Cambridge: Cambridge University Press.

(1975b). *Mind, Language and Reality: Philosophical Papers. Vol. 2.* Cambridge: Cambridge University Press.

(1983). *Realism and Reason: Philosophical Papers. Vol. 3.* Cambridge: Cambridge University Press.

Iris Einheuser

W. V. O. QUINE

Quine, W. V. O. (Willard Van Orman) (*b*. 1908, *d*. 2000; American), the Edgar Pierce professor emeritus at Harvard, a renowned philosopher of language and a logician. He was influenced by logical positivism but famously rejected some of its characteristic semantic doctrines. In his work, he focused mainly on ontological and epistemological questions. (*See also* Carnap, Rudolf; Davidson, Donald; Kant, Immanuel.)

Born in 1908 in Akron, Ohio, to an owner of a heavy-equipment company and an elementary school teacher, Quine grew up in a safe family environment. From his early childhood he had a zest for travelling and in his lifetime managed to visit 118 countries and all the states of his native country. Apart from philosophy, his early interests included cartography and language (especially etymology); later in his life he wrote several reviews of dictionaries and cartography books. He was reported to speak six languages and gave lectures in English, French, Italian and Spanish; one of the more than twenty books he published during his life was written in Portuguese. He graduated from Oberlin College in 1930 with a major in mathematics and, driven by economic needs, earned his doctorate from Harvard only two years later. He started teaching at Harvard in 1936 and never left the institution, apart from the war years 1942–5, which he spent in the United States Navy, where he worked with cryptanalysts in the Atlantic anti-submarine campaign. In 1953 he was awarded the Eastman Professorship at Oxford, where his interest in the philosophy of language deepened. His encounters with famous philosophers are described in his autobiography *The Time of My Life* (1985), a mixture of witty personal observations, technical points and gossip. While at Oxford he had contact with Michael *Dummett, Jonathan Bennett and W. Stegmüller, as well as discussions with P. F. *Strawson and H. P. *Grice in the seminar they ran together. He was also acquainted with Peter *Geach (with whom he previously had some 'discouraging exchanges on logical matters') and J. L. *Austin; he repeated his visit to Oxford in 1973–4. Among his famous pupils were Donald *Davidson, Daniel C. Dennett, David *Lewis, Charles D. Parsons and Theodore J. Koczynski, who later became known as the 'Unabomber' (a mathematics PhD who planted home-made bombs in aircraft and universities between 1978 and 1985, injuring and killing many people): 'although I don't remember him', Quine supposedly told an interviewer in 1996, 'he tied for top, ninety-eight point nine percent'.

Quine's initial career choice to become a mathematical logician grew out of his interest in Bertrand *Russell's work and the attractive combination of mathematics and philosophy. Quine's unusually long dissertation was entitled 'The logic of sequences: a generalization of *Principia Mathematica*' and concerned, in his own words, 'cleaning up' Whitehead and Russell's famous work. Unaware of the work of Gottlob *Frege, Rudolf *Carnap or the Polish logicians, Quine proposed to resolve the confusions of 'use' and 'mention', an idea that he further developed in the book *Mathematical Logic*. Soon after his PhD he was able to travel to Europe, where he spent five months attending the meetings of the Vienna Circle. In Prague he finally met Carnap, and in Warsaw he communicated with Alfred *Tarski and others. In 1939 he pressed Tarski to accept an invitation by Harvard, which probably turned out to save Tarski's life: not long after, Poland was invaded by Nazi Germany.

Many of Quine's philosophical views are a response to the form of empiricism advocated by the Vienna Circle, in particular by Carnap. According to the Viennese positivists, knowledge could only be scientific with physics as its basis: metaphysics, ethics, aesthetics or religious studies were meaningless because they could not be pursued as a scientific activity. For the positivists, the meaning of expressions/sentences involves a connection with reality; understanding a sentence means knowing under what circumstances it is true. Although Quine attacked a number of positivist dogmas, he remained committed to the empiricist idea that our knowledge must be based on scientific claims. Philosophy itself is not privileged in having some special tools and methods at its disposal by means of which it could supply foundations for natural science.

Quine once noted that he found philosophical thought almost inseparable from its expression, and his opinions remain in the general philosophical consciousness partly thanks to the pithy slogans and lively

metaphors he used. In 'On what there is', the first of the nine essays published in the collection *From a Logical Point of View* (1953), Quine expresses his view of logic as the language we use to capture the ontology of our theory (that is, things that must exist if the theory is true) in his slogan, 'to be . . . is . . . to be reckoned as the value of a variable' (1953: 13). Here Quine is concerned with the ontological commitments reflected in our use of language. Are we committed to the existence of Pegasus by using the word? And if the answer is yes, what then of sentences like 'Pegasus is/is not'? Quine suggests applying Russell's argument for definite descriptions; we can rephrase the proper name as a definite description; for example, 'the winged horse that was captured by Bellerophon' or, somewhat less poetically, 'the thing that pegasises'. From there we can analyse the statement as 'There is a thing that pegasises' for the positive proposition, or 'Either each thing fails to pegasise or two or more things pegasise' for its negation.

Another of Quine's arguments concerns attributes and the existence of abstract entities. We can say 'Redness is a colour', yet 'redness' is a singular term that does not have an extension in the real world. Similarly we understand and consider meaningful a sentence like 'The bus is red'; the predicate 'red' is meaningful to us even though it is not clear what it refers to in the real world. We also use expressions like 'the average man', as in 'The average man lives seventy-two years'. Does our usage of the terms/attributes commit us to the existence of such abstract entities?

According to Quine, we should be reluctant to take this step. In fact, it is not necessary if we accept the primacy of sentence meaning over word meaning; that is, the idea that the meaning of a sentence is not, in general, derived from the meaning of the words it contains, but can be used and understood as a whole (although Quine does not suggest that all sentences are learned as wholes – most sentences are, according to him, learned from parts by 'analogical synthesis'). Since a sentence like 'Redness is a colour' can be paraphrased into a sentence that lacks the term 'redness', for example 'Anything red is coloured', there is no need to assume the existence of the abstract entity. Likewise, the sentence 'The average man lives seventy-two years' can be paraphrased as 'If we divide the sum of the ages at which a given number of men died and divide it by the number of men, we get the number seventy-two'; there is no need to postulate the existence of an entity to which the expression 'the average man' would refer.

The main topic of 'Two dogmas of empiricism', probably the most widely discussed essay in *From a Logical Point of View*, is the dichotomy between two kinds of statements, 'analytic' and 'synthetic', as it had been formulated by *Kant. For the positivists, analytic statements can be verified without any observation because they hold in all states of the world. A typical example of an analytic statement is a sentence relating two synonymous expressions or expressions where the concept of the predicate is contained in the concept of the subject; for example, 'All bachelors are unmarried' or 'We are our cousins' cousins'. All mathematical and logical statements are assumed to be analytic. Synthetic statements, on the other hand, are only contingently true. We decide whether they hold or not on the basis of empirical evidence. Quine attacks the view that analytic statements are true by virtue of their meaning. He rejects the idea that the meaning of a sentence could be fixed; for him, there are no analytic truths in Kant's sense. The notion of synonymy, which is crucial for the description of analyticity, cannot be adequately defined in the context of this world, that is, in terms of *salva veritate* interchangeability ('saving the truth'; when two statements mean exactly the same thing); it requires using the notion of 'necessity' or 'analytic', thus leading to circularity.

Quine argues that all our beliefs are in fact intertwined in a single holistic system that shapes our acceptance of evidence, as each new fact has to be accommodated with the rest of our beliefs. Everything can be subjected to revision: 'Having re-evaluated one statement we must re-evaluate some others, which may be statements logically connected with the first or may be the statements of the logical connections themselves. But...there is much latitude of choice as to what statements to re-evaluate in the light of any singular contrary experience' (1953: 42–3). Even logical and mathematical statements could thus be rejected in principle. As for philosophy, since it is equally a part of our system of beliefs, practising it is, in a sense, impossible: it is as if we were trying to rebuild a sailing ship at sea from scratch. In other words, there is no independent position from which we can judge our beliefs. Instead of searching for *a priori* foundations of meaning, philosophers should instead pursue naturalistic explanations of how theories are the product of the human sensory system, a position that Quine calls 'naturalized epistemology' and develops further, for example, in *From Stimulus to Science* (1995).

Throughout his work, Quine argues in favour of the view that a purely extensional (tenseless) language is sufficient for any serious scientific endeavour. He admits that in ordinary language, we often use adverbs like 'necessarily' and 'possibly', which seem to require an intensional description. It is possible, however, to explain their use without having to burden ourselves with modal logic, which he considered a 'pseudo-logic': it is a fact that when we communicate, we mutually agree on the truth of some statements, while other issues stand under discussion. Perhaps we use the predicate 'necessary' not for universal truths but for truths that logically follow from the accepted statements. A similar point can be made with respect to 'essence'. Quine is opposed to the idea that some properties necessarily hold of an object and thus are 'essential'; rather, some properties of an object stand under scrutiny at a given point, while others do not. The logic and semantics of necessity is, according to him, of interest only as a study in linguistics and psychology; it does not reflect broad structures of reality. Unlike modalities, however, propositional attitudes, as in 'Ralph believes that Ortcutt is a spy', cannot be entirely dispensed with. For example, *de dicto* beliefs ('of what is said'; one believes because it is said), where Ralph believes that there is someone called 'Ortcutt' and that someone is a spy, are just instances of quotation. But *de re* beliefs ('of the thing'; one believes because of what the thing is), where Ralph has a specific individual in mind, remain problematic. It is in relation to propositional attitudes that Quine adopts Davidson's anomalous monism: our mental states cannot be reduced to brain activity and subjected to physical laws.

In *Word and Object* (1960), possibly Quine's best-known book, he discusses the notion of 'stimulus synonymy', which he sets out to explore as relating longer segments of discourse than single words or phrases, and 'stimulus analyticity'. Stimulus analyticity can be said of sentences to which (almost) every speaker is disposed to assent after every stimulus. His understanding of analyticity is given further precision in *The Roots of Reference* (1974): language is a social construct and analyticity – as a truth that is grounded in language – depends on social uniformity among native speakers. A sentence is analytic when they all agree that it is true because they learned its words in a uniform way.

In chapter two of *Word and Object*, Quine discusses a frequently cited thought experiment in radical translation, illustrating what he calls 'the indeterminacy of translation'. A field linguist facing an unknown language may, in the absence of bilingual speakers, assume through observation that the expression 'Gavagai' refers to a rabbit because the natives use it when a rabbit scurries by. By asking 'Gavagai?' in various stimulus situations, the linguist can confirm her or his hypothesis by noting the conditions under which the natives would assent to the use of the expression. It is possible, however, that they are using a frame of reference slightly different from that of the linguist and 'Gavagai' actually refers to 'an undetached rabbit part', 'a rabbit-stage' or 'an instance of rabbithood', as all these would account for the stimulus situations. 'The only difference is how you slice it. And how you slice it is what ostension, or simple conditioning, however persistently repeated, cannot teach' (1960: 32). There is not one right answer concerning the extension of a term – a thesis also known as 'the inscrutability of reference'. The translation from one language scheme into another may be in accordance with the linguist's empirical observations and yet be at odds with the original language, or even another empirically adequate translation of it, because there is no unique 'meaning' of the term independent of its use in context. In principle, we cannot even exclude the possibility that an utterance expressing a positive proposition in one language would get translated into its negation.

As it is, the theory of 'the indeterminacy of translation' is valid also for our own idiolect compared to someone else's language:

> On deeper reflection, radical translation begins at home...we can systematically reconstrue our neighbor's apparent references to rabbits as really references to rabbit stages, and his apparent references to formulas as really references to Gödel numbers and vice versa. We can reconcile all this with our neighbor's verbal behav-ior, by cunningly readjusting our translations of his various connecting predicates so as to compensate for the switch of ontology. (1960: 46–7)

Therefore, Quine argues, there are no determinate meanings: every ontology is relative. He postulates the thesis of 'under-determination of theories', which he distinguishes from the 'indeterminacy of translation' thesis: it is possible to formulate empirically equivalent but logically incompatible scientific theories.

Comparably to John Dewey or the later Ludwig *Wittgenstein, Quine repeatedly purported the view that there is no more to the meaning of an expression than the overt way in which we use it. Meanings are not 'specimens in a museum of ideas, each labelled with the appropriate expression' (1987: 130); they are not special entities, mental or otherwise. 'Being meaningful' can only consist in having the same meaning as another expression, but there is no precise answer (or the need of one) to the question of what 'sameness of meaning' is.

In his philosophising, Quine is sensitive to the task of a linguist, which, according to him, should be performed with 'little theoretical commitment', and to linguistic issues in general, since conceptualisation is inseparable from language. Our theory of the world is basically a system of sentences, and when we are judging the truth of a sentence, we are influenced by our sensory experiences as well as by our knowledge of language; this is known as 'the doctrine of inextricability'. Our beliefs are thus fundamentally determined by our theory of the language; nothing we know lies outside of its realm. In a number of places, Quine discusses language acquisition: we learn many words through direct association with certain sensory stimuli, but it would be incorrect to call this mechanism 'objective reference'. A child that learns the word 'milk' by ostension learns the sentence 'it's windy' or 'it's cold' by the same principle (see Quine 1981). As an explanation of language acquisition, this description is incomplete: a number of non-observation sentences/expressions in a language lack a distinctive stimulus meaning. Quine's answer to this problem is anchored in the naturalistic-behaviouristic thesis: we learn language through social emulation and feedback. Unlike in psychology, behaviourism is necessary in linguistics (see Quine 1990). We become adequate language users through observing other people's verbal behaviour and through having our own verbal behaviour reinforced or corrected by them.

Quine's *Quiddities: An Intermittently Philosophical Dictionary* (1987) is a collection of popular essays (some of which are rather technical), modelled on Voltaire's *Philosophical Dictionary*. Somewhat characteristically for Quine, at the end of the entry for 'Ideas', he earnestly suggests to the reader that in science there is no place for ideas, under 'Knowledge' that the theory of knowledge is better off without the notion of 'knowledge', and under 'Meaning' that the theory of meaning should abandon 'meanings'. In his view, when 'cleared of encumbrances, [these theories] thrive the better' (1987: 131).

W. V. O. Quine integrated his interests in logic, language and philosophy to investigate what humans know and how it is that they know it. Although many of his views were controversial and he was called 'a philosopher's philosopher', he had an undeniable influence on American neo-pragmatism and is generally considered to be one of the most prominent analytical philosophers of the twentieth century. Quine was awarded a number of honorary degrees: in 1993 he received the first Rolf Schock Prize in Stockholm and in 1996 the Kyoto Prize in Tokyo. He formally retired in 1978 but remained active almost until his death at the age of 92.

Primary works

(1950; rev. enlarged edition 1982). *Methods of Logic*. Cambridge, MA: Harvard University Press, 1982.

(1953; rev. edition 1961). *From a Logical Point of View*. Cambridge, MA: Harvard University Press, 1980.

(1960). *Word and Object*. Cambridge, MA: MIT Press, 1964.

(1966; rev. enlarged edition 1976). *The Ways of Paradox and Other Essays*. Cambridge, MA: Harvard University Press, 1976.

(1968). *Ontological Relativity and Other Essays*. New York: Columbia, 1969.

(1970; rev. edition 1986). *Philosophy of Logic*. Cambridge, MA: Harvard University Press, 1986.

(1974). *The Roots of Reference*. La Salle, IL: Open Court, 1974.

(1981). *Theories and Things*. Cambridge, MA: Harvard University Press.

(1985). *The Time of My Life: An Autobiography*. Cambridge, MA: MIT Press.

(1987). *Quiddities: An Intermittently Philosophical Dictionary*. Cambridge, MA: Harvard University Press.

(1990). *Pursuit of Truth*. Cambridge, MA: Harvard University Press.

(1995). *From Stimulus to Science*. Cambridge, MA: Harvard University Press.

Further reading

Barrett, R. and Gibson, R. F. (eds) (1993). *Perspectives on Quine*. Oxford: Blackwell.
Davidson, D. and Hintikka, J. (eds) (1969). *Words and Objections: Essays on the Work of W. V. O. Quine*. Dordrecht: Reidel.
Gibson, R. F. (1986). *The Philosophy of W. V. O. Quine: An Expository Essay*. Gainesville: University Press of Florida.
Hahn, L. E. and Schilpp, P. A. (eds) (1986). *The Philosophy of W. V. O. Quine: The Library of Living Philosophers. Vol. XVIII*. La Salle, IL: Open Court.
Hookway, C. (1988). *Quine: Language, Experience and Reality*. Cambridge: Polity.
Orenstein, A. (2002). *W. V. Quine*. Princeton, NJ, and Oxford: Princeton University Press.

Marie Šafářová

F. P. RAMSEY

Ramsey, F. P. (Frank Plumpton) (*b.* 1903, *d.* 1930; British), fellow in mathematics at King's College Cambridge (1924–30). An influential thinker whose ideas had a significant effect on a number of disciplines including mathematics, logic, probability, economics and the philosophy of science. In the philosophy of language, his most important ideas relate to the nature of truth and belief. (*See also* Moore, G. E.; Russell, Bertrand; Wittgenstein, Ludwig.)

Ramsey was born on 22 February 1903 in Cambridge, England. His father, Arthur Stanley Ramsey, was president of Magdalene College and tutor in mathematics, and his younger brother Michael was later to become archbishop of Canterbury, although Frank Ramsey himself was a staunch atheist. He attended Winchester College, from where he won a scholarship in mathematics to Trinity College, Cambridge, in 1920. On graduating in 1923 he travelled to Austria to visit *Wittgenstein, then living as a reclusive school teacher. Wittgenstein later acknowledged Ramsey's role in helping him realise the errors in his own earlier philosophy, and hinted that his return to Cambridge was in part prompted by the chance of further discussion with Ramsey. Indeed, Ramsey was influenced by, and in turn influenced, the work of many contemporary thinkers, including John Maynard Keynes, G. E.*Moore and Bertrand *Russell.

In his 1927 paper 'Facts and propositions' (reprinted in 1990), Ramsey argues that 'p is true' is simply equivalent in meaning to 'p'. Hence to believe, or be prepared to assert, that 'p is true' is simply to believe that 'p'; truth can be defined in terms of belief. This still leaves the question of what it means to have a true belief, or how to define the meaning of any declarative sentence that can form the content of a belief. Ramsey's suggestion is that the content of a belief can be defined by reference to the actions it prompts, or more generally that meaning can be defined in terms of causes and effects. According to 'Ramsey's Principle', the truth of a belief is established by the success of the actions that result from it. This account was in part prompted by Ramsey's interest in American pragmatism, such as that advocated by *Peirce, and has itself been significant in the subsequent development of pragmatic theories of truth and belief. It has also informed speech act theory (see *Searle and *Strawson).

Ramsey married Lettice Baker in 1925 and the couple had two daughters. He was valued by colleagues and students for his engaging lecturing style, his unassuming personality and his infectious sense of humour. He underwent an operation for a liver complaint and died shortly afterwards on 19 January 1930 in Guy's Hospital, London

Primary works

(1931). *The Foundations of Mathematics and Other Logical Essays*. R. B. Braithwaite (ed.). London: K. Paul, Trench, Trudner.
(1990). *Philosophical Papers*. David Hugh Mellor (ed.). London: Hutchinson.

Further reading

Dokic, Jerome and Engel, Pascal (2002). *Frank Ramsey: Truth and Success*. London: Routledge.
Mellor, David Hugh (ed.) (1980). *Prospects for Pragmatism: Essays in Memory of F. P. Ramsey*. Cambridge: Cambridge University Press, 1986.
Sahlin, Nils-Eric (1990). *The Philosophy of F. P. Ramsey*. Cambridge: Cambridge University Press.
'Better than the stars': www.dar.cam.ac.uk/~dhm11/RamseyLect.html/(accessed 20 April 2004), recording of a programme on Ramsey broadcast on BBC Radio 3 on 27 February 1978, and the text of a lecture by D. H. Mellor.
'Frank Ramsey': www.fil.lu.se/sahlin/ramsey/ (accessed 20 April 2004).

Siobhan Chapman

RASMUS RASK

Rask, Rasmus (Christian) (*b.* 1787, *d.* 1832; Danish), together with *Bopp and *Grimm, Rask is generally acknowledged as one of the founders of the genealogical study of languages, known as comparative historical linguistics. The basis of his ideas was his detailed study of the Nordic languages and their origin in Old Icelandic, a language he called Old Norse (*oldnordisk*). It is also generally acknowledged that Rask was the first to describe the so-called Grimm's Law (explaining the first Germanic consonant shift). (*See also* Bopp, Franz; Grimm, Jacob; Hjelmslev, Louis.)

Born on the island of Funen (Fyn) in Denmark, in his early years Rask studied his father's extensive collection of books. He began his school education in 1801, and this environment had a major influence on his later career. In school he put together his own lexicon and grammar of Old Icelandic, and in 1811 he published his first book, a grammar on that language. Rask engaged in describing all the languages he came across, and in 1817 he published, in Stockholm, a grammar of Anglo-Saxon written in Danish (English translation 1830). As a result he may be regarded as one of the founders of the study of Old English. After leaving school in 1807, Rask studied at the University of Copenhagen. In 1813–15 he made a voyage to Iceland, and in 1816 he set out for his great voyage via Sweden, through Finland to St Petersburg, then through the Caucasus and Persia to

India. He returned to Denmark in 1823. In 1831 he was appointed professor in Oriental languages at the university of Copenhagen.

Rask contributed to many linguistic subjects, including Danish orthography: he also wrote *A Grammar of the English Language for the Use of Englishmen* (1830). His primary ambition, however, was to uncover the systems of the languages in order to understand the relations between them, even though, like his contemporaries, he did not always clearly make the distinction between typological sameness and genealogical relationship.

When he embarked on his great voyage in 1816, his explicit purpose according to his records was to compile reports from his journey in the exotic landscapes he went through. But his private agenda was to collect as much linguistic evidence as possible to support his initial hypothesis about the genealogy of the Nordic, the Germanic and ultimately the Indo-European languages. To him, the hypothesis was confirmed, and most of the studies of his 'selected works' published by Hjelmslev in 1932–35 illustrate the way Rask justifies his views.

Rask had good language proficiency in Swedish, Icelandic and English, and he is presumed to have had relevant knowledge of about fifty-five languages. After his great voyage he was in poor physical and mental health. His last years were in many ways not the happiest of his life. When he was appointed professor in 1831, an anecdote tells us that his spontaneous reaction was 'I'm afraid it's too late': he died in 1832. Formal acknowledgement of his achievement may have come to Rask belatedly, but his ingenious achievements in linguistics make him a model for twenty-first-century linguists.

Primary works

(1818). *Undersøgelse om det gamle Nordiske eller Islandske Sprogs Oprindelse.* Copenhagen: Det Kongellige Danske Videnskabers-Selskab.
(1932–5). *Udvalgte Afhandlinger* (3 vols). Louis Hjelmslev (ed.). Copenhagen: Det Danske Sprog Litteratureselskab.

Hans Götzsche

BERTRAND RUSSELL

Russell, Bertrand (Arthur William) (*b.* 1872, *d.* 1970; Welsh); philosopher, mathematician, logician, outspoken pacifist, fellow of the Royal Society, and Nobel laureate in literature, one of the most influential thinkers of the twentieth century. In the philosophy of language, he contributed to the development of contemporary formal logic and is regarded as one of the founding fathers of modern analytic philosophy. He was one the world's most influential critics of nuclear weapons and spent considerable energy campaigning for world peace. He published extensively (more than ninety books) in the fields of logic and mathematics, but also on social life, politics, education and religion. (*See also* Ayer, A. J.; Carnap, Rudolf; Frege, Gottlob; Hegel, G. W. F.; Hume, David; Leibniz, Gottfried

Wilhelm; Locke, John; Mill, J. S.; Moore, George; Strawson, P. F.; Wittgenstein, Ludwig.)

Bertrand Russell was the grandson of Lord John Russell, who had twice served as Liberal prime minister under the reign of Queen Victoria, and the godson of the Utilitarian philosopher J. S. *Mill. Russell was born in Trelleck, Gwent, the second son of Viscount Amberley and Katherine, daughter of the second Baron Stanley of Alderley. The descendant of one of the greatest families of the Whig aristocracy, Bertrand, third Earl Russell, was left an orphan at the age of 3 and, against his father's wish to grant custody of Russell and his brother to two atheists, was brought up by his grandmother, Lady Russell. Educated privately by governesses and tutors, Russell acquired a perfect knowledge of French and German before going up to Cambridge in 1890, where he entered Trinity College. There his keen aptitude for pure mathematics soon came to the fore, and he obtained first class degrees with distinction in mathematics and in the moral sciences. He left Cambridge in the summer of 1894 and moved to Paris, where he was honorary attaché at the British embassy, and in December the same year married Alys Pearsall Smith, an American Quaker. After some months in Berlin studying social democracy the Russells moved to live near Haslemere, where Bertrand devoted most of his time to the study of philosophy. He was elected fellow of Trinity College in 1895. Inspired by Euclidean geometry, he published his fellowship dissertation, *Essay on the Foundation of Geometry*, in 1897. But despite these promising beginnings Russell's academic career stalled in 1916, when he published an anti-conscription leaflet and was deprived of his lectureship as a result of the ensuing political arguments.

In the first half of August 1900, two international conferences, one in philosophy, the other in mathematics, took place in Paris. These events proved not only to be a turning point in Russell's life, but changed the texture of the intellectual world of that time. Russell visited the philosophy conference, where he was impressed by the Italian logician and mathematician Giuseppe Peano, one of the pioneers in mathematical logic and axiomatisation of mathematics. The logicalisation of mathematics, an idea raised over a century earlier by *Leibniz, proposed a symbolic language replacing words, which allowed equations to be written in a simplified manner so as to be understood easily by anyone, regardless of their native language. Peano derived the arithmetic of natural numbers from the principles of logic, together with a set of logical postulates about numbers, thus taking an important step towards the twentieth-century logicalisation and axiomatisation of arithmetic. Peano's major project, known as the *Formulario Mathematico*, was presented in part at the International Conference of Mathematics in Paris. It attempted to collect mathematical formulae and theorems and to write them utilising a standard notation invented by Peano himself. When the project was finished in 1908, the *Formulario* contained over 4,200 symbolised formulae and theorems with proofs in only 516 pages.

At the First International Conference in Philosophy, Peano presented a paper in which he addressed the question of the nature of definitions. Russell was impressed by Peano's brilliant and innovating method of logic symbols. Peano presented Russell with a draft of his ongoing *Formulario*, and after Russell left Paris he immediately began studying Peano's formalism in more detail. Russell himself claimed in his *Autobiography* (1967–9) that Peano's system represented the tool for logical analysis he had sought for years. Russell understood that mathematics could be stated in terms of the concepts of general logic, such as class and membership in a class. Following the example of the German mathematician Gottlob *Frege, who had tried to show that all mathematical propositions could be stated in the language of logic, Russell hoped to formalise, in the light of Peano's example, the foundations of mathematics from a set of logical axioms, thus creating a link between the English analytic philosophy and the Vienna Circle of logical positivists, a group of scientifically minded philosophers including Rudolf *Carnap, Otto Neurath and Moritz Schlick, whose ideas were introduced to an English audience by A. J. *Ayer. Russell aimed to insulate logic from ambiguity and contradiction, both weaknesses of the system proposed by *Hegel. Logic could be rescued from the ambiguities of language and framed in arithmetical and algebraic symbols. Such a symbolic system would provide the model to lay out the foundations of mathematics in a new form.

Russell greatly influenced the discipline of logic through his discovery of a contradiction in the foundations of set theory. Set theory developed at the end of the nineteenth century to enable mathematicians to handle infinite sets. It deals with the nature and relationships between objects (called the members of the set) and sets (membership) or between sets and other sets (subsets). Sets are entirely individuated by their members, but sets are not themselves those members. Russell's paradox, as it is known, may be summed up as follows: if every description determines a set, then so does the description 'the set of all those sets that do not contain themselves'. If such a set exists it will be a member of itself if and only if it is not a member of itself. With recourse to classical logic, the paradox is significant because a logical contradiction entails all (possible) sentences.

Russell's paradox was a challenge to the heart of the logical system, and set theory was completely rebuilt several times in the next few years. Previous set theory came to be called 'naive set theory'. Russell's paradox laid the foundations of modern axiomatic set theory, regarding as sets only those that satisfy axioms. Since, in an effort to avoid paradoxes, set theory is not allowed to perform operations on sets without axioms, it is the task of axiomatic set theory to determine what operations are allowed.

Russell's own attempt at resolving the paradox developed from his 'theory of types', published in 1903 in his *Principles of Mathematics*, the book that paved Russell's way in the philosophical world. There he advanced the proposal of a strict relationship between mathematics and logic, to the extent that the foundations of mathematics could be deduced from a few logical ideas. Recognising that self-reference is the pivot of the paradox, Russell proposed to arrange all sentences into a hierarchy, beginning with sentences about individuals at the lowest level, sentences about sets of individuals at the next level up, sentences about sets of sets of individuals at the next level, and so on. This method would be sure to refer to all objects for which a predicate holds only if they are all at the same level or of the same 'type'.

Type theory and mathematical logic found their mature expression in the three volumes of *Principia Mathematica* (1910, 1912, 1913), the book Russell co-authored with Alfred North Whitehead. It was a masterpiece of rational thought and had a major influence on twentieth-century symbolic logic, set theory in mathematics and logical positivism, especially through the work of Russell's student Ludwig *Wittgenstein. Russell and Whitehead tried to show that the laws of mathematics could be deduced from the basic axioms of logic and proved that numbers can be defined as classes of a certain type. In the process, they developed logical concepts and a logical notation that established symbolic logic as an important specialisation within the field of philosophy. Russell and Whitehead claimed that the task of philosophy should be limited to objective accounts of phenomena, since only empirical knowledge is the path to truth: all other knowledge is subjective and thus misleading. This research established Russell as one of the founding fathers of modern analytical philosophy.

Russell aimed to use logic not only to clarify issues in the foundations of mathematics, but also to shed new light upon philosophical issues. At that time, English Hegelianism identified the forward march of the British Empire with the progression of reason. Russell doubted this identification. Together with G. E. *Moore, Russell embraced the non-conformist tradition of English liberalism that was developing at Cambridge University, and began to propose an alternative view in the group called 'The Apostles', a forerunner of the so-called Bloomsbury Group, which included the economist John Maynard Keynes, Lytton Strachey, Leonard Woolf and Wittgenstein. Eschewing moral or natural foundations of the good and the true, this group of analytic philosophers tried to plan their conceptions upon logic alone.

Russell's analytical philosophy rejected the tenets of idealism, the dominant philosophical school of the period, which held that all objects and experiences are the product of the intellect. He was a rationalist who was convinced that individual facts perceived by the senses have an inherent reality independent of the mind, and that knowledge depended on data from original experience. Russell regarded logical analysis as the core method for philosophy, and he believed that the application of analytical methods to philosophical problems could provide an adequate account of human experience.

Russell's analytical philosophy aimed to uncover logical and philosophical suppositions concealed beneath the superficial structure of statements in ordinary uses of language. In other words, for Russell language was also best treated in logical terms – places where natural language diverged from logic were evidence of the imperfection of natural language, which made it an unfit tool for philosophy. In the philosophy of language, Russell's most important contribution is represented by his theory of descriptions, put forward in 'On denoting' (1905). Russell argued that proper analysis of denoting phrases, such as descriptions and proper names, enables us to represent all thought symbolically, thus avoiding philosophical difficulties about non-existent objects. He used first-order logic to show how a broad range of denoting phrases could be recast in terms of predicates and quantified variables. The theory is generally exemplified by the phrase 'The present King of France', as in Russell's own example 'The present king of France is bald'. 'Definite descriptions', a phrase coined by Russell himself, seem to be like names that by their very nature denote exactly one thing. The problem arises when we focus upon the object to which the above sentence refers, since in 1905 there was no king of France. The problem this raises involves the logical form of definite descriptions, or in Fregean terms, how it is possible to paraphrase them so as to show how the truth of the whole depends on the truths of the parts. What happens when one part of them apparently is not true? Russell proposed to solve the problem by analysing the whole sentence containing a definite description and not the single phrase. Thus, 'The present king

of France is bald' could be rewritten as 'There is an x such that x is a present king of France, nothing other than x is a present king of France, and x is bald'. For Russell the sentence as a whole, in the absence of a king of France, is false. Each definite description, Russell stated, contains a claim of existence and a claim of uniqueness that give this appearance, but these can be broken apart and treated separately from the predication that is the obvious content of the sentence in which they appear. Put in these terms, the whole sentence states three things about the object and the definite description contains two of them, while the rest of the sentence (the predicate) contains the other. If the object does not exist, or if it is not unique, then the whole sentence, as in classical logic, turns out to be false, but crucially not meaningless (see *Aristotle). The problem was later addressed in a different manner by *Strawson, who underlined that definite descriptions do not assert that their object exists, but simply presuppose that it does.

Russell's interest in logical analysis was not limited to philosophy and mathematics, but also had influences upon his epistemology. Convinced that human beings can only perceive their own sense data and that objective phenomena can be known only by inference, Russell drew a distinction between two ways of knowing: 'knowledge by acquaintance' and 'knowledge by description'. Only the objects of immediate experience are known through our direct awareness of them, that is, by acquaintance. Other things are known only through the mediation of our apprehension of true propositions about them, in other words, by description. Knowledge by acquaintance is supposed to provide the foundation for knowledge by description. Thus only sense data is known non-inferentially. In his 1918 lectures on logical atomism, Russell took this further by stating that the world consists of a complex of logical atoms and their properties. Taken together, these form the atomic facts that, in turn, combine to form logically complex objects.

In 1938, Russell moved to the United States as visiting professor at the University of California at Los Angeles and at the College of the City of New York, where he was debarred from teaching because of his libertarian views on morality. He then accepted a five-year contract as a lecturer at the Barnes Foundation at Merijon near Philadelphia. In that period, he wrote one of his most popular books, *A History of Western Philosophy* (1945), which contributed to his winning the Nobel Prize for literature in 1950 'in recognition of his varied and significant writings in which he champions humanitarian ideals and freedom of thought'.

Russell was born at the height of Britain's economic and political ascendancy and died when Britain's empire had all but vanished and its power had been drained in two debilitating world wars. From an early age, he developed a strong sense of social consciousness. He was a strong moralist in the rationalist tradition of *Locke and *Hume, and wrote his reflections on psychological and moral topics in many essays. As one of the founders of the most important anti-war organ-

isation during World War I, the Union of Democratic Control, he demanded immediate peace negotiations. As the editor of the weekly newspaper the *Tribunal*, he wrote an article criticising the United States Army and was jailed for six months in Brixton Prison for making statements 'likely to prejudice His Majesty's relations with the United States of America'. He spent those six months writing his *Introduction to Mathematical Philosophy*. At the outbreak of World War I he declared himself a pacifist and opposed Great Britain's participation in the war. More than this, he collected the signatures of a group of fellow professors to induce his country to declare neutral in the imminent war. This cost him his professorship at Trinity. When he succeeded his elder brother to the earldom in 1931, he utilised his privilege to promote his views on pacifism at the House of Lords. In fact he considered himself a 'relative pacifist'; although he rejected war in principle, he accepted the recourse to fight in some disastrous circumstances, like the threat of Hitler to the whole of Europe. This gained him his re-election as fellow at Trinity in 1946.

From the beginning of the 1950s, Russell became an outspoken opponent of the nuclear weapons. In 1955 he released a manifesto together with Albert Einstein favouring nuclear disarmament. In 1957 Russell was one of the main organisers of the Pugwash Conference, which gathered scientists from all over the world against the proliferation of nuclear weapons, while as president of the Campaign for Nuclear Disarmament (CND), he strove for the removal of American missile bases from Great Britain. He condemned the Bikini test of the H-bomb, opposed the Vietnam War and went on defending peace until the end of his life. In 1963 the Bertrand Russell Peace Foundation was constituted.

Russell was a man of strongly held views, high moral principles and passionate beliefs. But his personal life was often tempestuous and troubled. Besides many well-publicised, and at the time scandalous affairs, he was married a total of four times, to Alys Pearsal Smith, Dora Black (1921), Patricia 'Peter' Spence (1936) and Edith Finch (1951). He had two sons and one daughter. Russell spent his last years in North Wales, where he wrote his *Autobiography*, in which he states that 'Three passions, simple but overwhelmingly strong, have governed my life: the longing for love, the search for knowledge, and unbearable pity for the suffering of mankind.' He died of influenza on 2 February 1970. His ashes were scattered over the Welsh mountains.

Primary works

(1903). *The Principles of Mathematics*. Cambridge: Cambridge University Press.
(1905). 'On denoting'. *Mind*. Vol. 14: 479–93. Reprinted in *Essays in Analysis*. London: Allen and Unwin, 1973.
(1910–13) (with Alfred North Whitehead). *Principia Mathematica* (3 vols). Cambridge: Cambridge University Press.
(1918). 'The philosophy of logical atomism'. *Monist*. Vol. 28: 495. Reprinted in *Logic and Knowledge*. London: Allen and Unwin, 1956.
(1945). *A History of Western Philosophy*. New York: Simon and Schuster.
(1967–9). *The Autobiography of Bertrand Russell* (3 vols). London: Allen and Unwin.

Further reading

Clark, Ronald (1981). *Bertrand Russell and his World*. London: Thames and Hudson.
Eames, Elizabeth (1989). *Bertrand Russell's Dialogue with his Contemporaries*. Carbondale, IL: Southern Illinois University Press.
Irvine, Andrew (1999). *Bertrand Russell: Critical Assessment*. London: Routledge.
Monk, Ray and Palmer, Anthony (eds) (1956). *Bertrand Russell and the Origins of Analytic Philosophy*. Bristol: Thoemmes Press.
Pears, David (1967). *Bertrand Russell and the British Tradition in Philosophy*. London: Collins.
Rodriguez-Consuegra, Francisco (1991). *The Mathematical Philosophy of Bertrand Russell: Origins and Development*. Basel: Birkhauser Verlag.

Annalisa Baicchi

GILBERT RYLE

Ryle, Gilbert (*b*. 1900, *d*. 1976; British), lecturer in philosophy at Christ Church College (1924–45) and Waynflete professor of metaphysical philosophy (1945–68) at Oxford. Leading figure in British analytic philosophy, instrumental in establishing Oxford as a centre for the branch of the movement known as 'ordinary language philosophy'. (*See also* Austin, J. L.; Ayer, A. J.; Grice, H. P.; Moore, G. E.; Russell, Bertrand; Strawson, P. F.; Wittgenstein, Ludwig.)

Ryle was born in Brighton, England. He gained two first class degrees from Oxford: one in classics and then one in PPE (politics, philosophy and economics) when he was invited to sit the finals of this new degree in order to establish a bench-mark for a 'first'. He was an officer in the Welsh Guards during World War II, but otherwise stayed at Oxford throughout his career. His early interests included classical philosophy and, much more unusually, recent continental philosophy; he wrote on *Frege and *Husserl, among others. During the 1930s he was increasingly influenced by contemporary British philosophy, particularly the work of G. E. *Moore, Bertrand *Russell and Ludwig *Wittgenstein, the last of whom became a personal friend.

In 1949 Ryle published *The Concept of Mind*, an attack on the 'dualistic' view of mind and body. Ryle dates back to *Descartes the erroneous understanding of the mind as an entity separate from but inhabiting the body, for which he coins the phrase 'the ghost in the machine'. He sees this as a category mistake, stemming from the vocabulary used in the discussion of mind. Differences between the physical and the mental have been 'represented as differences inside the common framework of the categories of "thing", "stuff", "attribute", "state", "process", "change", "cause" and "effect" ' (1949: 19). All that can legitimately be discussed are dispositions to act in certain ways in certain situations. This led to Ryle being labelled a 'philosophical behaviourist'.

The Concept of Mind was significant in the development of 'ordinary language philosophy' at Oxford under the leadership of J. L. *Austin. Ryle had been appointed editor of the philosophy journal *Mind* in 1947, and published many articles by Oxford philosophers. He also wrote several papers during the 1950s championing the cause. For instance, in 'Ordinary language' (1953) he argues that philosophers must pay attention to the 'stock', rather than any specialist or 'non-standard', uses of words. Here, and in 'The theory of meaning' (1957), he emphasises that the proper focus of study is the use of a word, not some abstract notion of meaning. In his later writings Ryle worked further on logic and on thought, renewing his early interest in classical philosophy.

Ryle was known as an energetic, inspiring and humorous lecturer. Despite his challenging and innovative approach to philosophy, his personal tastes were conservative and his private life apparently uneventful. He lived in college and never married. He retired in 1968 but oversaw the publication of his *Collected Papers* (including 'Ordinary language' and 'The theory of meaning') in 1971. He continued working and writing almost until his death.

Primary works

(1949). *The Concept of Mind*. London: Hutchinson.
(1971). *Collected Papers*. London: Hutchinson.

Further reading

Lyons, William (1980). *Gilbert Ryle: An Introduction to his Philosophy*. Brighton: Harvester Press.
Magee, Bryan (1971). *Modern British Philosophy*. Oxford: Oxford University Press, 1986.
Wood, Oscar P. and Pitcher, George (eds) (1970). *Ryle: A Collection of Critical Essays*. Garden City, NY: Anchor Books.

Siobhan Chapman

HARVEY SACKS

Sacks, Harvey (*b.* 1935, *d.* 1975; American), early researcher in conversation analysis and the ethnography of spoken language. From 1963 to 1968 taught in the Department of Sociology, University of California at Los Angeles, and (1968–75) in the Department of Sociology at the University of California at Irvine. (*See also* Austin, J. L.; Grice, H. P.; Searle, John; Wittgenstein, Ludwig.)

Sacks was born in 1935. He received a BA in 1955 from Columbia College and an LLB in 1959 from Yale Law School. In the latter year he went to the University of California at Berkeley, where he obtained his PhD in sociology in 1966. He was employed at the University of California at Los Angeles, first as acting assistant professor of sociology in 1963, and then from 1964 as assistant professor, until he was appointed associate professor at the University of California at Irvine in 1968. He became full professor in 1974.

Even though Sacks's publications amount only to ten journal articles or chapters in a book, his inspiring lectures earned him deep respect from his colleagues and students. His lectures during the last eleven years of his life were recorded and later transcribed and also circulated for a wider public. These are now available in a definitive edition entitled *Lectures on Conversation* (1992), which bears Sacks's name as author but were put together and edited by Gail Jefferson, who had transcribed practically all the material. This work contains a valuable in-troduction by Emanuel Schegloff. The lectures reveal Sacks's original and genial mind and include ideas that cut across disciplines in the study of language in human interaction. They are key works in the development of a new discipline, known ever since as conversation analysis.

During his graduate studies, Sacks was already interested in conversational exchange as a basis for the understanding of the social organisation through which people communicate. Unlike many practitioners of social sciences, who explain human behaviour in terms of concepts like 'culture' or 'social structure', Sacks began inductively from human actions themselves. To be precise, he studied the actions that build communication, namely, conversation. Sacks's endeavours gained momentum when he was working at the Center for the Scientific Study of Suicide in Los Angeles. There he began to analyse telephone calls made to the centre and demonstrated how the caller's problems became gradually manifest in the interaction between the caller and the centre's staff. He investigated the mechanism of conversational turn taking, its units and patterns. This method was later applied to a larger corpus by including other kinds of telephone conversations. Further collaboration with Jefferson and Schegloff sharpened the focus of the analysis and refined the procedures. The topics investigated include conversational openings and closing, topic organisation, sequence in conversation, 'repairs' of misunderstanding or unclarities, the organisation of person-reference, the use of pronouns, performatives, and speaker selection preferences. A fuller account of conversation analysis as a method is found in Levinson (1983), while a systematic reconstruction of Sacks's thought is given by Silverman (1998), with quotations from the original works. Within the scope of the present entry, it is best to see Sacks's manifold contributions to conversation analysis under three headings: turn taking, adjacency pairs and preferences.

Like other practitioners of conversation analysis, Sacks starts with the assumption that an interactive activity like conversation is fundamentally the product of both speaker and addressee. Thus, for example, speaker A starts a conversation with a greeting like 'How are you?' The short pause after this leads B to reply, "I'm OK, thank you, and you?", which in turn elicits a response from A 'We are fine'. This conversation takes place at the entrance of A's house, where he and his wife are expecting B for dinner. At the outset A is addressing B. In producing the response B is addressing both A and his wife, but only A is selected to take the next turn, since B's words are responding to A's greeting. Interestingly, A's reply, judging from the use of the pronoun 'we', makes it clear that A understands that B is addressing him and his wife even if the next turn is meant only for him. In this situation A's wife is not expected to join in, simply because she is not selected for this turn taking. But she may take the turn when she is selected; for example, when B produces a bottle of wine saying 'I brought something', perhaps making eye contact with her, and this hint will make her take the bottle and utter some appreciation. At this point she is selected by B. Selecting a new participant is part of turn-taking management, sometimes involving body language and other hints. It is important to realise that turn taking is locally managed; that is, it is regulated by the situation itself rather than by any universal rules of conversation.

The exchange of greetings above makes sense if taken together as a sequence of utterances that are closely related to one another. This is what Sacks calls adjacency pairs. Besides exchange of greetings like A–B–A above there are other pairs such as question–answer (A: 'What's your first name?', B: 'Marc, spelled with a "c"', A: 'OK, with a "c"'), offer–acceptance (A: 'How about dinner tomorrow?', B: 'That'll be great!'), apology–minimisation (A: 'Oh, I'm sorry for calling you at this hour!', B: 'That's fine – we are still watching TV') and so on. The notion of pair is not limited to two parts, as is obvious from the exchange of greetings and question–answer above. Yet once somebody produces the first part of some pair, another person has to continue in the same pair. Because of this, adjacency pairs are the fundamental unit of conversational organisation. But pairs do not work mechanically. For example, some questions may be followed by questions before the answer is given. This happens when A makes a request to B: 'Can I borrow your car?' But before giving the answer to that question, B asks 'When?', to which A answers 'This afternoon', which leads to B's next question 'For how long?' and A's answer 'For a couple of hours'. At this point B says, 'OK', thus agreeing to A's initial request to borrow B's car. The exchange about when and how long is an insert in a request–answer pair.

In conversations, the first turns can be taken to imply 'preferred' second turns. A question may elicit what Sacks calls a preferred answer, as in 'So you're quite happy now', which suggests that the expected answer will probably simply be a quick 'Yes'. That is, the second turn that meets the expectation implicit in the first turn tends to be short and almost immediately given. Different from this is what Sacks labels a 'dispreferred' answer, which normally comes after a longer pause and contains more words; for example, (after a deep breath) 'I wish I were. Things are not always the way we'd like them to be'. Besides the significant pause mentioned above, a dispreferred answer gives something more than just the negative answer and contains particles (sounds such as 'er' and 'um' indicating hesitation) or an expression that indicates its dispreferred status or offers further elaboration as to why a preferred reply cannot be given. It is important to note that the mechanism of preference above does not relate to what people feel or think but to what the rules of turn taking imply. Agreements or disagreements with an implied expectation are basic to human sociality, and in this way conversation analysis reveals a lot about how human society is organised.

Sacks's works have enriched both sociology and linguistics with a remarkable inventive account of how to study human interaction through language. But as often happens with original thinkers, it is one thing to understand how they proceed, but another to try to apply their thoughts.

Sacks is reported as saying 'I can tell you something, but you have to be careful what you make of it.' In November 1975, he died in a car accident on his way to the campus at Irvine.

Primary works

(1972). 'An initial investigation of the usability of conversational data for doing sociology'. In D. N. Sudnow (ed.), *Studies in Social Interaction*. New York: Free Press.

(1974) (with E. A. Schegloff and G. Jefferson). 'A simplest systematics for the organization of turn-taking for conversation'. *Language*. Vol. 50: 696–735.

(1977) (with E. A. Schegloff and G. Jefferson). 'The preference for self-correction in the organization of repair in conversation'. *Language*. Vol. 53: 361–82.

(1979) (with E. A. Schegloff). 'Two preferences in the organization of reference to persons in conversation and their interaction'. In G. Psathas (ed.), *Everyday Language Studies in Ethnomethodology*. New York: Irvington.

(1984) 'Notes on methodology'. In J. M. Atkinson and P. Drew (eds), *Order in Court: The Organization of Verbal Interaction in Judicial Settings*. London: Macmillan.

(1992). *Lectures on Conversation*. G. Jefferson (ed.), E. A. Schegloff (intro.) (2 vols). Oxford: Blackwell.

Further reading

Levinson, S. C. (1983). *Pragmatics*. Cambridge: Cambridge University Press.

Silverman, D. (1998). *Sacks: Social Sciences and Conversational Analysis*. New York: Oxford University Press.

Ten Have, P. (1988). *Doing Conversation Analysis: A Practical Guide*. London: Sage.

Agustinus Gianto

EDWARD SAPIR

Sapir, Edward (b. 1884, d. 1939; American), investigator of North American indigenous languages, grammarian, phonologist and an especially influential theorist on the relation between culture, language and thought. The ideas of Sapir and his student *Whorf are often referred to as the Sapir-Whorf hypothesis or 'linguistic relativity'. Sapir was first chief anthropologist in the Division of Anthropology, Ottawa, working for the Geological Survey of Canada (1910–25), then professor of anthropology and general linguistics at the University of Chicago (1925–31) and Sterling professor of linguistics and anthropology at Yale University (1931–9). (See also Boas, Franz; Malinowski, Bronislav; Whorf, Benjamin Lee.)

Sapir was born in Prussia to a family of Lithuanian Jews, his father being a cantor in the synagogue: the family spoke German and Yiddish. When Sapir was very young his father arranged for them to emigrate to the United States. Sapir's first school, on his way to America, was a kindergarten in Liverpool. He attended the University of Columbia, where he studied German and Indo-European linguistics and met Franz *Boas, who was teaching there as a specialist in indigenous languages. Sapir took his BA in three years (instead of the usual four) and then proceeded to an MA in German.

However, he did his PhD on the Takelma language of Southwest Oregon. This is because studying un-der Boas meant fieldwork, collecting data on hitherto unanalysed languages in various states including Washington, Oregon and California. Sapir's numerous ethnographic, linguistic and anthropological expeditions were to provide him with an excellent research background. From 1907 he was carrying out fieldwork as a research assistant at the University of California at Berkeley, applying the methods he had learned as a specialist in German to these languages. This gave him the incentive and the means to use comparative methods to trace patterns of similarity and relations between them. At the same time, it meant learning a variety of languages using tribal informants, and he was fortunate in meeting informants who were helpful for this purpose. He found Tony Tillohash, a speaker of Southern Paiute, particularly helpful.

With a PhD already under his belt at the age of 25, and with the training he had received in linguistics and anthropology (the two at that time much more closely connected than they later became, especially at Columbia under Boas), Sapir moved in 1910 to Ottawa, Canada, where he obtained a job as first chief anthropologist in the Division of Anthropology, working for the Geological Survey of Canada. There he developed his research methods and a museum, the Canadian National Museum of Anthropology, of which he was the director.

Sapir stayed in Canada until 1925. During World War I he married his first wife, Florence, and they had three children, but sadness and frustration were to follow. Florence suffered from mental problems and died in 1924, while Sapir suffered for his pacifism during the war and found he had not enough time to analyse the data he had collected. His next career move came soon after Florence's death, when he became professor of anthropology and general linguistics at the University of Chicago, where he stayed from 1925 to 1931. There his research was funded with money from the Rockefeller foundation. Sapir married again in 1927 and had two more children.

In 1931 he became Sterling professor of linguistics and anthropology at Yale, where he was a founding member of the school of structuralism along with his colleague *Bloomfield. But where Bloomfield argued that meaning could not be used in the scientific study of language, Sapir found meaning essential. Like *Malinowski's, Sapir's work and theories combined several areas – linguistics, anthropology, sociology and psychology – under a general heading of culture, but Sapir shared a particular concern with later phenomenologists that any general cultural pattern must not be imposed to the detriment of individual perceptions.

Sapir was a very influential member of a set of linguists who altered thinking in a number of areas in the early twentieth century, a time when linguistics had not yet become a separate discipline recognised with its own departments in universities. Perhaps his chief contribution was the Sapir-Whorf theory of linguistic relativity, largely created by his student Whorf and often called the 'Sapir-Whorf hypothesis'. This term is somewhat controversial: it seems not to have been invented by either of them, but has become widely known as a shorthand for ideas held for a time by Sapir and divulged and popularised by Whorf.

To get a grasp of Sapir's contribution to cultural studies in general, it is important to situate his work in the early twentieth-century intellectual landscape. This was a time when Western European culture dominated large sections of the rest of the world. Combined with exploration and imperialist tendencies, Western science and other Western European categories of thought (such as Christianity, rationalism, economic liberalism, Communism, Darwinism, psychology) had become the dominant if often conflicting modes of thought across the globe: there was little awareness of other traditions. In language, the patterns of development of the Indo-European tongues were beginning to be understood and had been worked on for well over a hundred years, but the languages studied were the classical languages, which preceded this Western European domination, and the Standard Average European (SAE; see Whorf) languages themselves, especially German, French and English. Now place this in the context of a rapidly rising and increasingly self-confident North America, where the dominant classes still looked to Europe for their ideas but expressed at the same time a strong wish to establish their own understandings and interpretations based on American facts. Place it further in the individual context of the young Sapir, who had learned Yiddish and Hebrew, German and English, and was studying indigenous languages of the Americas.

It is in this atmosphere that Sapir learned the Native American languages Wishram, Takelma, Southern

Table 1 Some American Indian grammatical categories

Language	Representation using English roots
English	he will give it to you
Wishram	will he him thee to give will
Takelma	will give to thee he or they in future
Southern Paiute	give will visible thing visible creature thee
Yana	round thing away to does or will done unto thou in future
Nootka	that give will done unto thou art
Navaho	thee to transitive will round thing in future

Paiute, Yana, Nootka and Navaho, and began to notice differences between them and the more widely studied European languages such as English. In 1929 Sapir wrote a study, published later with his colleague Morris Swadesh, on 'American Indian grammatical categories', in which he shows the table (1929: 103) shown here in simplified form as table 1.

Sapir points out three main implications of his study of indigenous languages. First of all, clearly there is grammar and it is complex (no native language spoken by poor people is itself primitive). Second, these different languages use varied grammars. Third, these grammars use some categories and concepts which are typically found in Western European languages (futurity, transitivity) and some that are not (classification of objects by shape, by whether they are within eyeshot or not).

He points out at the same time that studying these languages can give rise to inferences about Western European languages, giving the example of plurality, which is typically marked in grammar on nouns:

> Sometimes it is the verb rather than the noun which is inherently singular or plural. A vague idea of this *apparently illogical and yet perfectly natural classification* may be obtained by looking upon such English verbs as 'to massacre' and 'to troop' as inherently plural forms meaning 'to kill several' and 'to run (used of several subjects)', respectively. (1929: 102, emphasis added)

Clearly Sapir was immensely impressed by the differences as well as by the subtlety of the languages he studied. At first sight the grammar is 'illogical', but his contribution is to make us see that any grammatical constraint or category, in any language under the sun, will appear 'natural' if it chimes in with the languages with which we are familiar, and 'illogical' otherwise. In the same paper, Sapir argues that 'a small and devoted band of students, working far from the market place of science, have already rescued so much of these exceptionally difficult languages that general linguistic theory would be a quite different thing without their labors' (1929: 100).

Through this work and by generating these insights, Sapir thus laid the foundations for linguistic relativity, arguably one of the most influential linguistic theories of the mid- to late twentieth century. It has impacted on areas as diverse as critical discourse analysis, feminism, cultural studies, anthropology and critical theory. His only book, *Language: An Introduction to the Study of Speech* (1921), was written for the educated general reader and was significant in popularising the study of language at the time.

Sapir's appointment at Yale proved to be his last. He suffered from a heart condition and had his first heart attack in 1937. He eventually died from a heart attack in 1939.

Primary works

(1921). *Language: An Introduction to the Study of Speech*. New York: Harcourt Brace.
(1929). 'The status of linguistics as a science'. *Language*. Vol. 5 (4): 207–14.
(1964) (With Morris Swadesh). 'American Indian grammatical categories'. In Dell Hymes (ed.), *Language in Culture and Society: A reader in Linguistics and Anthropology*. New York: Harper Row.
(1989–). *The Collected Works of Edward Sapir*. William Bright (ed.). Berlin: Mouton de Gruyter.
(1997). *Biographical Memoirs*. National Academy of Sciences, Washington DC.

Mike Scott

FERDINAND DE SAUSSURE

Saussure, Ferdinand de (*b.* 1857, *d.* 1913; Swiss), instructor at the School of Advanced Studies in Paris (1881–91), professor of Indo-European linguistics and Sanskrit (1901–13) and of general linguistics (1907–13) at the University of Geneva. Widely considered to be the father of modern linguistics because of his definition of linguistic units as arbitrary signs and his distinction between *langue* (language system) and *parole* (speech). His ideas have influenced a variety of disciplines including linguistics, structuralism and literary criticism.

(*See also* Barthes, Roland; Bloomfield, Leonard; Boas, Franz; Chomsky, Noam; Hjelmslev, Louis; Jakobson, Roman; Pike, Kenneth; Sapir, Edward.)

Saussure's parents were French refugees and he was born in Geneva. His father was a prominent naturalist. Saussure's keen interest in languages and linguistics started at an early age: in addition to French, his native language, he had learned German, English and Latin by the time he was 15. While still at school he also studied Sanskrit, an ancient language originating in India and influential in the development of European languages. The person credited with introducing Saussure to linguistics was Adolphe Picket, a philologist and family friend. Philology, the science that investigates historical and comparative aspects of languages, was the dominant school of linguistics in the nineteenth century.

Following in the footsteps of a family that had a strong tradition in the natural sciences, Saussure enrolled on courses in physics and chemistry when he entered the University of Geneva in 1875. But his passion for language studies induced him to take additional courses in Latin and Greek grammar. Unsatisfied with the academic offerings at that university, he succeeded in persuading his parents to allow him to enrol at the University of Leipzig, Germany, then developing into the world centre for neogrammarians, a group of historical linguists. A key figure at Leipzig was Karl *Brugmann, a neogrammarian who augmented the historical flavour of contemporary language study with a more scientific interest in phonetics and phonology, especially in the study of Indo-European languages.

Saussure received his doctorate *summa cum laude* (with high distinction) from the University of Leipzig in 1880. His doctoral thesis investigated the genitive case in Sanskrit. Shortly after earning his doctorate, he moved to Paris to join the faculty of the School of Advanced Studies, where he taught Sanskrit, Gothic and Indo-European philology. He was also an active member of the Linguistic Society of Paris. Despite his success there, Saussure couldn't resist returning to his home town when he was offered a professorship at the University of Geneva in 1891.

It was at this university that Saussure taught Indo-European and general linguistics, and that the ideas he had been pondering about language began to crystallise. These are expressed in his seminal book *Course in General Linguistics* (1916, often known simply as the *Course*), reconstructed by Charles Bally and Albert Sechehaye from the lecture notes of students who attended Saussure's lectures on linguistics at Geneva. The book was posthumously published in French in 1915 (though usually dated 1916) and translated and published in English in 1959. The publication of the *Course* is widely held to be the founding moment of modern linguistics: certainly the book has influenced a variety of disciplines that include structuralism, sociology, semiology, psychology and literary criticism.

The introduction of the *Course* is a critical overview of the history of linguistics. The first school Saussure discusses in this section is the 'gram-marians', whose main concern was to prescribe rules distinguishing correct linguistic forms from incorrect ones. This tradition was started by the Greeks and continued until around the middle of the eighteenth century. The most dominant group adhering to this approach were the 'Port-Royal grammarians'. They included Antoine *Arnauld (1612–94) and considered language as a reflection of thought, or a means to understanding logic. This view is evident in their rational classification of linguistic categories, or parts of speech. Although Saussure credited the Port-Royal grammarians with employing a synchronic perspective (studying language without reference to its historical antecedents), he strongly criticised their theoretical assumptions and methodological framework, in particular their claim that grammar could be given a logical explanation. Moreover, he objected to Port-Royal's prescriptivist approach, whose sole purpose was to formulate rules defining correct usage. Saussure then traces the shift in orientation in eighteenth-century language studies as philologists attempted to discover the basic elements of experience. Assuming language is a representational system of human thought, eighteenth-century language scholars focused their attention on the etymological aspects of language, assuming this would reveal the basic human sensations, or universal atoms of thought. Unlike their predecessors, nineteenth-century language scholars refuted the notion of language as a means to understanding the human mind: they considered the linguistic unit a formal entity. The philologists' main objective during that period was to compare these formal entities across different languages or trace their historical evolution.

Dissatisfied with the failure of his predecessors and contemporaries to define the subject matter of linguistics, Saussure set out to determine the object of linguistics, emphasising that 'without this elementary operation, a science cannot develop an appropriate method' (1916: 3). He argued that language is a system of arbitrary signs and that each sign is a marriage between signifier and signified. He believed this concept was essential to differentiate between meaningful human utterances, or signs, and non-linguistic strings of sounds that are mere noise. Having identified the sign, the basic linguistic unit, Saussure proceeded to explain its nature as an arbitrary union between the signifier (spoken or written form) and signified meaning or concept. This arbitrariness, he points out, is manifested by the fact that languages have different signifiers for the same concept. The concept 'HORSE', for instance, has the denoting signifiers 'horse', 'cheval' and 'caballo', for English, French and Spanish speakers respectively. None of these signifiers has an intrinsic relationship with the denoted concept. Any other sequence of sounds would have been appropriate as a signifier, provided that it had been accepted by a speech community. This arbitrariness, Saussure argued, is not restricted to the signifiers: the signifieds are also arbitrary, since speech communities divide up the conceptual domain differently. The signified denoted by the English verb 'to know', for example, includes two French signifieds, which are 'savoir' and 'connaître'. Hence languages are not sets of nomenclatures that assign names to pre-existing ideas. Rather, each language arbitrarily breaks down the conceptual domain and assigns signs, which are themselves arbitrary, to these concepts.

Key to the revolution in thought triggered by Saussure is the idea that signs are not positively definitive by virtue of their inherent characteristics, but instead are negatively significant as a result of their differentiation from other signs in the system. To explain this apparently paradoxical argument, Saussure uses a chess analogy. He asserts that each piece in a chess game derives its value from what it is not. A pawn, for instance, does not have to possess a specific shape or be made from a certain type of material to be a pawn. What distinguishes it from the other chess pieces is that it is different from them. If it were to be lost, a pawn, or any other piece for that matter, could be replaced by any object, of any shape or substance, provided that it could not be confused with the other pieces.

Having identified the sign, Saussure then proceeded to explain two types of relationships between linguistic units. The first type is a horizontal relationship, which he called 'syntagmatic'. This refers to the ability of linguistic units to combine with each other on a linear scale, a phenomenon which can occur at all levels. On the phonological level, for instance, [p] can occur with [i] and [n] to create 'pin'. On the morphological level, on the other hand, the prefix {un-} can enter into a syntagmatic relation with {happy}, {certain} and {aware} to create 'unhappy', 'uncertain' and 'unaware', respectively. Finally, words are also capable of syntagmatically combining with other words to create phrases, clauses and sentences. Jack + is + happy, for instance, produces the sentence 'Jack is happy.' The second type is the associative relationship, now widely known as 'paradigmatic'. This refers to the ability of linguistic units to contrast with their counterparts at all levels. In the above example, for instance, 'Jack' could be contrasted with or substituted by 'Mary', 'Bill' or 'John'; 'is' by 'looks', 'seems' or 'appears'; and 'happy' by 'anxious', 'worried' or 'sad'. These syntagmatic and paradigmatic relationships enable linguistic units to form a network of combinations and contrasts, making language a system of systems.

Another fundamental distinction proposed by Saussure is between the language system (*langue*) and speech (*parole*). For him, *langue* was a societal construct that exists in its entirety in the collective mind of the speech community. It includes the grammatical rules speakers use to combine the different linguistic forms into meaningful utterances. *Parole*, on the other hand, was the realisation of these combinations into spoken expressions of thought. Saussure argued that *langue* should be the object of linguistic studies because it is the faculty which makes the construction of language possible. *Parole* could be considered important only in that it acts as a trigger of the functionally significant signs it initiates. To demonstrate that *langue* is independent of *parole*, he cites physician Paul Broca's findings that aphasics exhibited a variety of speech malfunctions as a result of lesions in the brain despite the fact that their speech organs were intact.

After distinguishing between *langue* and *parole*, Saussure proposes a model of communication that explains the complex phenomenon of face-to-face verbal interaction. When two interlocutors engage in such an activity, he argues, a multi-faceted process is set into action. As an illustration, he gives the following example of a short exchange between two people:

A: Do you have the time?
B: Six-thirty.

He explains that in order for this communicative act to be successfully executed, a series of conditions have to be in place:

1. Speaker A has to have a concept, or idea, he or she wishes to convey to interlocutor B.
2. A signal is transmitted from the part of speaker A's brain in which the concept is situated to the organs of speech responsible for executing this command into the corresponding speech signal.
3. Upon the utterance of the question, sound waves travel from A's mouth to B's ears.
4. When heard by B, the sound signal triggers the corresponding concept in B's brain. When speaker B responds, the process is repeated in a reversed sequence.

Saussure explains that the first step is psychological, the second and fourth are physiological, and the third one is physical. Then he explains the location] of both *langue* and *parole* within his proposed circuit of communication. *Parole*, he claims is confined to the executive part, which transforms the psychological command from the brain into physical speech patterns. *Langue*, on the other hand, is situated in the section where these concepts are located.

This model of communication has been a contentious issue among Saussure's interpreters. It is criticised by some for locating *langue* within a speaker, notwithstanding Saussure's earlier assertion that it is a social phenomenon existing outside the individual. However, the model is commended by others who regard it a confirmation of the primacy of speech and an assertion of its central role as the premier means of communication. This group argues that Saussure never claimed individuals do not possess *langue*. For them, he merely emphasised the existence of *langue* in its totality in the collective mind of the speech community, while he acknowledged its partial existence in an individual speaker.

Another significant Saussurian contribution is the distinction between synchronic and diachronic studies. The former investigates the language system at a particular point of time, whereas the latter examines the historical evolution of language over a period of time. Saussure asserted the importance of the synchronic approach on the premise that both the 'signifier' and 'signified' aspects of the 'sign' are arbitrary; hence, the significance of linguistic units is dependent upon their relationship in a certain state and at a certain time. He criticised the methodological framework of the diachronic perspective, comparing their approach to someone trying to get a full view of a range of mountains by looking at one peak at a time. He proposed diachronic linguistics should not focus on historic

changes, but it should offer an explanation of these changes.

The Saussurian theory of language had an impact on all schools of linguistics. It is widely believed Saussure's identification of *langue* as the subject matter of linguistics, and his proposed synchronic approach as an alternative to the diachronic perspective, have resulted in the emergence of modern linguistics. As a result of his legacy, comparative and historic perspectives were supplanted by synchronic studies of individual languages, resulting in a tremendous growth in the fields of descriptive and theoretical linguistics. Both European and American schools of linguistics were influenced by Saussure. The distinction made by the Prague School of linguistics between 'phonetics' and 'phonology' is based on his *langue–parole* dichotomy. This was a direct influence on *Jakobson's 'distinctive feature analysis' theory, an approach that uses articulatory and acoustic features to describe phonemic contrasts. Saussure's impact is also evident in the 'phoneme' theory of the British linguist Daniel *Jones, who regarded the phoneme as an abstract family of sounds realised phonetically by allophones (variants of the same phoneme), an approach related to Saussure's distinction between *langue* and *parole*.

Major developments in semantics are also indebted to Saussure's theory of language. Charles Ogden and I. A. Richards's well-known 'semiotic triangle', which defines meaning in terms of the relationship between 'thought', 'symbol' and 'referent', is in a direct line of influence from Saussure's identification of the 'sign' as an arbitrary union between the 'signifier' and the 'signified'. Another major development in modern semantics that has its roots in Saussure's theory is the assertion that the meaning of a word is not its 'referent', but its 'sense', or the significance derived from its syntagmatic and paradigmatic relationships with other words in the system. The structural approach to semantics is yet another discipline impacted by Saussure. This approach defines the basic meaning unit as a 'lexeme' to avoid the mismatch between 'word' and 'meaning'. Structural semanticists realised, among other things, that idiomatic expressions, for instance, consist of more than one word referring to the same 'concept', thus they came up with this alternative term. In addition, this approach categorised lexemes and classified them according to their sense relations, for example 'synonyms', 'antonyms', 'hyponyms' and so on.

Saussure's theory of language has influenced anthropologists as well as linguists. For example, the first two decades of the twentieth century witnessed a keen interest in the study of Native American languages. The pioneers of this movement were Franz *Boas and Edward *Sapir. Realising that many of the Native American languages were disappearing, Boas and Sapir pioneered a detailed description of them. But since these languages did not have a writing system, researchers had to rely on their observation of how the languages were used in everyday spoken communication, a task for which the philological method of analysis was completely unsuitable. Although this approach is anchored in the anthropological paradigm of 'participant observation', its essence is purely Saussurian because it emphasises the primacy of speech. In fact Saussurian linguistics is a major influence on the so-called Sapir-Whorf hypothesis (devised by Sapir and his student Benjamin Lee *Whorf) that language influences thought. Saussure, for example, argues that thought itself depends on the presence of language.

Another major development in American linguistics that can be traced to Saussure was triggered by Leonard *Bloomfield, who published *Language* in 1933. This book, outlining 'structural linguistics', dominated the field in America until the 1950s. Although it has been claimed Bloomfield's approach is superior to Saussure's (see 'Bloomfield's Saussure' in Harris 1987), Saussure's influence is evident in Bloomfield's notion of arbitrariness and his emphasis on the social aspect of language. In addition to these, Saussure also inspired 'tagmemics', a theory of language developed by American linguist Kenneth *Pike in the 1950s. Tagmemics distinguished between two types of linguistic units, the 'emic' and the 'etic', the former referring to functionally contrastive units and the latter to the physical realisation of them. This distinction is based on Saussure's identification of 'form' and 'substance' and his notion of the 'sign' as a contrastive unit.

Saussure's 'circuit of communication' and his identification of a series of stages constituting verbal interaction have been instrumental in a number of advancements in psycholinguistics and phonetics. Psycholinguistic research in the last two decades of the twentieth century confirmed the existence of different processing stages during speech production. The consensus among researchers is that the four main stages during this process are: (1) the conceptual formation; (2) the formulation of concepts into linguistic units; (3) the issuance of a command to the organs of speech; and (4) the execution of that command into a verbal utterance. These stages correspond to the ones identified by Saussure in his account of face-to-face verbal interaction.

Yet another field benefiting from this distinction is phonetics, which has three distinct branches. These are articulatory phonetics, which describes the production of different speech sounds and classifies them according to their phonetic characteristics; acoustic phonetics, which examines the physical properties of speech sounds; and auditory phonetics, which investigates the decoding of speech sounds and explains how they are transformed into contrastive linguistic units. Each of these three disciplines closely corresponds to one of the phases in the Saussurian circuit: articulatory phonetics studies the physiological aspect; acoustic phonetics examines the physical aspect; while auditory phonetics investigates the psychological aspect.

Furthermore, Saussure's influence is not confined to linguistics. He is often credited with initiating the structuralist school of thought, an approach widely employed in a variety of social sciences, in philosophy and in literary theory. The scholar most closely associated with the term 'structuralism' is the French anthropologist

Claude Lévi-Strauss. Acknowledging Saussure's contribution to the development of phonology, Lévi-Strauss outlined a structuralist approach to the study of anthropology. The proposed approach employs the Saussurian principles to determine the societal significance of all actions and objects. Structuralism was also employed in the field of literary criticism. Literary analysts adhering to this approach argue that the literary text is autonomous, just like *langue*, and as a result no extraneous factor is required for its interpretation.

The huge significance of Saussure's contributions to the development of linguistics, the social sciences, and human thought in general during the twentieth century is undeniable. Yet Saussure himself was not satisfied with his work, or at least did not see its implications: he left very little written work behind when he died in 1913. The reasons why he chose not to publish are unknown, but as a result Saussure's reputation as one of the most original and influential thinkers in history rests on the reconstructed lecture notes taken by his students at the University of Geneva.

Primary works

(1916). *Course in General Linguistics* (*Cours de Linguistic Générale*).Wade Baskin (trans.). New York: McGraw-Hill, 1966.

Further reading

Aarsleff, Hans (1982). 'Taine and Saussure'. In *From Locke to Saussure: Essays on the Study of Language and Intellectual History*. Minneapolis: University of Minnesota Press.

Culler, Jonathan (1976). *Ferdinand de Saussure*. Ithaca, NY: Cornell University Press, 1986.

Harris, Roy (1987). *Reading Saussure*. La Salle, IL: Open Court.

Harris, Roy (2001). *Saussure and his Interpreters*. New York: New York University Press.

Holdcroft, David (1991). *Saussure: Signs, System, and Arbitrariness*. Cambridge: Cambridge University Press.

Koerner, E. F. K. (1973). *Ferdinand de Saussure: The Origin and Development of his Linguistic Thought in Western Studies of Language*. Braunschweig: Vieweg.

Yousif Elhindi

JOHN SEARLE

Searle, John (*b.* 1932; American), Mills professor of philosophy of mind and language at the University of California at Berkeley. An outspoken and reactionary analytical philosopher of language and mind; famous for his neo-*Russellian semantic theory for proper names, the 'Chinese Room' argument against artificial intelligence (AI), 'biological naturalism' regarding the nature and origins of consciousness, and his development of speech act theory to include 'indirect speech acts'. (*See also* Austin, J. L.; Russell, Bertrand.)

Searle was born in Denver, Colorado, and began his studies in philosophy in 1949 at the University of Wisconsin, moving to Oxford on a Rhodes scholarship in 1952. At Oxford he studied under J. L. *Austin, one of the founders of ordinary language philosophy. This sought to solve (or dissolve) traditional philosophical questions by examining how competent speakers use their language: if what we are willing to say in ordinary conversations does not settle a question one way or the other, then we should stop asking the question. Searle was never a full believer in ordinary language philosophy, but he shared its respect for common sense: 'If somebody tells you that we can never really know how things are in the real world, or that consciousness doesn't exist, or that we really can't communicate with each other, or that you can't mean "rabbit" when you say "rabbit", I know that's false' (Faigenbaum 2001: 29).

After completing a DPhil, Searle took a post as lecturer at Christ Church College, Oxford (1957–9). One of his first substantial contributions to philosophy of language focused on the meanings of proper names – linguistic expressions like 'Aristotle', 'Afghanistan' and 'the Eiffel Tower'. A popular view made famous by J. S. *Mill and later defended by Saul *Kripke, among others, is that the meaning of a proper name is the bearer of the name, in other words the referent, the thing the name refers to. The main historical alternative to this 'direct reference' theory of meaning traces back to Gottlob *Frege and, as developed by Bertrand Russell, holds that the meaning of a proper name is an associated description of the thing it refers to. In 'Proper names' (1958), Searle developed a version of Russell's theory designed to overcome some famous objections. One such was that Russell's theory would make the meaning of a name change from one person's usage to another, depending on which of a range of identifying descriptions those people believed to be true of the bearer.

Instead Searle identified the meaning of a proper name not with any single description, but rather with a cluster of descriptions (thus garnering the name 'cluster-theory'): the cluster remains constant even though anyone who correctly uses the name need have in mind only some minimal subset of descriptions.

After moving back to the United States to take a teaching position at the University of California, at Berkeley, Searle developed and elaborated Austin's seminal theory of how we use language in *Speech Acts* (1969). This work was important in part for developing in more detail, and resolving some problems inherent in, Austin's original theory. For instance, Searle's taxonomy of speech acts was larger than Austin's, and Searle offered more of a substantive theory behind the commonalities and differences among the different types of speech acts. He also introduced the idea of indirect speech acts, and primary and secondary speech acts. The most important aspect of Searle's theory, however, in terms of the impact it was to have on his future work, was the focus it placed on the psychological intention of the writer or speaker.

We have already seen how intention came into play in the phenomenon of reference. According to Searle, in order for a speech act to refer to someone or something, the speaker must have in mind some minimal set of identifying descriptions that succeed in picking out the referent. Searle saw this as a general feature of language: speech acts, and hence language as a whole, perform their designated function only by virtue of our intentions

that they do so. This theory differed from many others by de-emphasising the grammatical or syntactical contribution to semantics, and instead analysing semantic properties in intentional terms. A promise, for instance, is defined not so much by the words one uses to make it as by the intention one has in using those words.

It was natural, then, for Searle to turn his focus on the 'seat' of intentions – namely, the mind. One of his first forays into philosophy of mind (1980) resulted in what was to become one of his most famous and controversial arguments: the so-called 'Chinese Room' argument against artificial intelligence (AI). AI traditionally includes any of a variety of research programmes concerned with designing and building machines (primarily, digital computers) capable of seemingly intelligent behaviour; in other words, AI is the quest for a 'thinking machine'. Searle distinguished two sorts of AI: a 'weak' version, which claims that mental processes like thinking can be simulated by an appropriately programmed computer; and a 'strong' version, which claims that mental processes can be replicated by such computers. Strong AI, in other words, claims that appropriately programmed computers actually think: thinking is just the instantiating of an appropriate program. A famous instance of strong AI was endorsed by Alan Turing, and can be summed up by what has since been called the 'Turing Test'. In short, Turing argued that if a computer can answer questions typed into it in a convincing enough manner to fool any reasonable person into believing that those responses are coming from a live human being, then it passes the test and should be considered a thinking machine.

Against this version of strong AI, Searle asked us to imagine him trapped in a room containing a slot in the wall and several large books. Through the slot would come slips of paper with Chinese characters written on them, and for each input, the books would instruct Searle to write a particular series of Chinese characters on another slip of paper and pass it back out through the slot. Searle then argued as follows: understanding language is a paradigm case of thinking; hence if strong AI is right then understanding language should simply consist in instantiating an appropriate 'understanding' program, and hence passing the Turing Test should suffice for thinking. If the books in the imagined room were written ingeniously enough, furthermore, Searle himself could pass that test. Of course, since Searle is a live human being with intelligence it is not surprising he could pass the Turing Test; what is surprising is that he could pass it in Chinese using the books to produce appropriately convincing responses for any Chinese characters passed into the room that constituted meaningful sentences. But Searle argued he still would not actually understand Chinese in that case; he would simply be able to convince a reasonable person he did. Hence the Turing Test, and strong AI with it, is false. Instantiating an appropriate program from inputs to outputs does not suffice for language understanding, or, it turns out, for thinking.

Three years later Searle published *Intentionality* (1983), in which he transformed his work on speech acts into a full-blown theory of the mind. Franz Brentano had brought the term 'intentionality' into common philosophical usage, meaning aboutness or directedness of the sort exhibited by both language and thought: both the word 'Aristotle' and your belief that Aristotle was wise, for instance, exhibit intentional properties, since they are about or directed towards the ancient Greek philosopher. The central aim of Searle's book was to clarify the nature and genesis of both of these forms of intentionality – linguistic and mental – as well as the relationship between them.

At the heart of Searle's theory was the idea that linguistic intentionality is 'derived' from mental intentionality, which in contrast is 'intrinsic'. Language gets to be about things in the world as a result of bearing appropriate relations to thoughts of ours that are about those things. As Searle notes, this idea placed his theory squarely in the tradition of H. P. *Grice; the difference was that where Grice saw linguistic meaning as resulting from the effects we intend our words to have, Searle saw it as resulting from the thoughts to which we intend our words to be semantically similar. In other words, 'Aristotle was a philosopher' means that Aristotle was a philosopher because I intend it to have the same intentional content as my thought that Aristotle was a philosopher.

Searle's discussion led naturally into the hotly debated question of whether intentional content, of either the linguistic or mental variety, is 'in the head'. Is what I say or think, when I say or think that I am dumber than Aristotle, for instance, determined entirely by the state of my brain; or is it also partly determined by my surrounding environmental and historical context? 'Externalism' or 'anti-individualism', developed and defended by Hilary *Putnam and Tyler Burge in the 1970s, held that content is not in the head. Someone can have Aristotle-thoughts, for instance, only if they have been causally impacted in the right ways by Aristotle himself (for example, by hearing of him or reading some of his work). 'Internalism', in contrast, held that content is in the head – in the very strong sense that any two persons whose brains are micro-physically identical must be mentally identical as well. Any micro-physical duplicates of someone with an Aristotle-thought, for instance, must have that same thought.

Searle's own view was an interesting compromise. Although mental contents never depend on environmental or historical context, they will not in general be shared among micro-physical duplicates. Searle disagreed with externalists, first of all, that my thought that I am dumber than Aristotle requires Aristotle's existence at all. In keeping with his view about proper names, he analysed the content of my thought as being something like 'that the owner of this thought is dumber than the guy who wrote the Nicomachaean Ethics and who is often called "Aristotle"'. But he also disagreed with internalists that micro-physical duplicates will share my thought: any such duplicate will instead believe that the owner of her thought (namely, she) is dumber than the guy called 'Aristotle'.

In his next two major works, *Minds, Brains, and Science* (1984) and *The Rediscovery of the Mind* (1992), Searle delved yet further into the philosophy of mind, setting himself the task of explaining how our view of ourselves as conscious agents, with subjective perspectives and free will, can be reconciled with a scientific view of the world as consisting of unconscious, non-intentional and fully determined physical particles. First of all, Searle took very seriously, and at face value, the common-sense idea that consciousness and intentionality are phenomena that are on the one hand fully real, and on the other hand irreducible to physics. Searle rejected out of hand, for instance, so-called 'eliminative materialism', which sees science as showing us that mental phenomena simply do not, despite our common-sense belief to the contrary, exist. He similarly disposed of the other traditional theories of the mind–brain relation – including behaviorism (the view that mental states consist in dispositions to behave in certain characteristic ways), identity theory (the view that mental state-types or state-tokens are identical with types or tokens of brain states) and functionalism (the view that mental states consist in instantiation of appropriate functions from formal inputs to behavioral outputs) – by claiming that they too disrespect a basic belief in mental reality, albeit more subtly than eliminativism. The inner, subjective and perspectival nature of consciousness simply cannot be captured by any fully objective, third person theory.

On the other hand, Searle insisted, we should not opt for the main historical alternative to the above views, namely *Cartesian dualism (the idea that there are two sorts of substance in the world, mental and physical). For there is something terribly wrong with the very tradition of forcing a decision between monism (the view that mind in some sense 'just is', or is 'nothing over and above', something material) and dualism. Instead, he argued, we never should have started counting in the first place: mind is one thing and matter another, but there are many others as well, such as the economy, liquidity, digestion, and split-level ranch houses (all Searle's examples). In Searle's view we should see consciousness and intentionality as 'biological' phenomena relating to the brain as liquidity relates to water or, more aptly, as digestion relates to the stomach. In particular, the former in each case is 'caused by and realized in' the latter. The mind, for instance, is caused by the brain because neural processes beget conscious processes, and it is realised in the brain because there is no mental substance distinct from or floating above the neural stuff.

Following on from his Chinese Room argument, Searle attacked cognitive science as a whole by arguing against its fundamental tenet, championed by Noam *Chomsky, David Marr and Jerry *Fodor, that mental processes consist in the following of unconscious rules. These unconscious rules are analogous to the instructions in the code of a computer program, accounting for everything from our grasp of the grammatical structure of language to our interpretation of visual stimuli as representing famil-iar objects. Searle showed the same hostility to these unconscious rules, predictably, as he did to AI's computer model of the mind. In particular, Searle rejected the entire idea of 'deeply unconscious' mental states, states that govern reasoning and behaviour yet could not even in principle be consciously introspected. For a state can be considered 'mental', Searle's contentious 'Connection Principle' asserted, only if it is at least in principle accessible to consciousness. Contrary to what not only cognitive scientists, but also most philosophers and psychologists, take to have been one of the great achievements of the twentieth century – namely, Freud's notion of unconscious mentality – Searle argued that anything that you cannot possibly introspect cannot be part of your mind.

In 1997, Searle extended his philosophical ambitions yet further, taking on the question of how social or 'institutional' facts can be accommodated by his picture of the world. A paradigmatic social fact is that certain sorts of coloured paper such as dollar bills can be worth something: that value cannot be explained by the intrinsic physical properties of the paper alone. Certainly the value of money comes from our believing that it has value; but why cannot such a belief, like any other, be false? According to Searle, tradition has had a difficult time accommodating social facts because it ignored what he calls 'collective' intentionality: money has value not because each of us believes it does, nor because each of us believes that she herself believes it does; but rather because each of us believes that we (as a whole) believe it does. The recognition of a collective intentionality (the 'we believe') that cannot be reduced to 'individual' intentionality (the 'I believe' or the 'you believe'), Searle argues, lies at the root of an understanding of social reality.

One of the few places Searle ever admitted to being stumped in the face of a traditional philosophical problem was in chapter 8 of *Minds, Brains, and Science* (1984), concerning the problem of freedom of the will. But in *Rationality in Action* (2002), Searle set out to make headway on that problem by revealing flaws in traditional ways of conceiving the mental causation of behaviour. That tradition sees beliefs as combining with desires in something like a mechanistic way to result in behavior: when you believe that action A will lead to outcome B, and you desire outcome B, then, all other things being equal, you try to perform action A. What the tradition does not recognise, Searle now argued, is the existence of a 'gap' between believing and desiring on the one hand, and performing an action on the other. Instead of being an unstoppable mechanistic process, the route from mind to action is mediated by the agent's free will.

As Searle saw it, he had not previously seen how free will was possible because he had assumed that determinism goes hand in hand with the determination of mental states by brain states. That assumption, he now argued, was mistaken, for it is entirely possible, or at least conceivable, that mental states are determined 'bottom-up', as it were, by brain states, even though they are not determined by previous brain states. Determinism, in other words – the thesis that what is the case is determined by what used to be the case – can be false even if there is determination of what goes on in the mind by what goes on in the brain.

Searle has served on the editorial boards of several journals and has held many visiting professorships. Many books, essays and conferences have been devoted to his work and he has received honours and awards from around the world. Yet in many ways he has made a career out of being a thorn in the side of the philosophical establishment, dogmatically but carefully defending what he considers to be common sense in the face of academic confusion. That attitude was echoed by his personal life during the civil rights movement in Berkeley, California, during the 1960s, when he broke ranks with the faculty and sided with the rebelling students in favour of free speech. He has been interviewed in a number of PBS (Public Brodcasting Service) specials, speaking about both his philosophy and his experience with political activism, and delivered the BBC's prestigious and popular Reith Lectures in London in 1984.

Primary works

(1958). 'Proper names'. *Mind*. Vol. LXVII

(1969). *Speech Acts: An Essay in the Philosophy of Language*. Cambridge: Cambridge University Press.

(1980). 'Minds, brains, and programs'. *Behavioral and Brain Sciences*. Vol. 3.

(1983). *Intentionality: An Essay in the Philosophy of Mind*. Cambridge: Cambridge University Press

(1984). *Minds, Brains, and Science*. Cambridge, MA: Harvard University Press.

(1992). *The Rediscovery of the Mind*. Cambridge, MA: MIT Press.

(1997). *The Construction of Social Reality*. New York: Free Press
(2002). *Rationality in Action*. Cambridge, MA: MIT Press.

Further reading

Austin, J. L. (1962). *How to Do Things With Words*. Cambridge, MA: Harvard University Press.
Faigenbaum, Gustavo (2001). *Conversations with John Searle*. Libros En Red (Digital Publisher).
Fotion, Nick (2000). *On Searle*. Teddington: Acumen.
Lepore, Ernest and Van Gulick, Robert (eds) (1991). *John Searle and his Critics*. Cambridge, MA: Blackwell.

Anthony Newman

JOHN SINCLAIR

Sinclair, John (McHardy) (*b.* 1933; Scottish), professor of modern English language, University of Birmingham. John Sinclair is best known in applied linguistics for his multiple initiatives in starting new areas of growth, notably in discourse analysis and corpus linguistics. His major published work is *Corpus, Concordance, Collocation* (1991), but he has published numerous articles on topics ranging from classroom discourse to the human–computer interface and the principles of dictionary making. However, perhaps the greatest of Sinclair's contributions to our understanding of language was his setting up of the Cobuild project, which culminated in the Bank of English corpus and a series of dictionaries, grammars and books that made use of it. (*See also* Firth, John; Halliday, M. A. K.)

Sinclair was born and educated in Edinburgh, where he studied mainly English literature. After National Service, he returned to work in English language, becoming embroiled in the controversy about literary stylistics; he obtained a post as lecturer in the University of Edinburgh in 1959 at a time when Angus McIntosh, M. A. K. *Halliday, David Abercrombie and Peter Strevens were also lecturing there. This was a golden team and Edinburgh was the leading British university in applied linguistics in the 1960s. In 1965, Sinclair was appointed to a new chair at the University of Birmingham, where he remained until his retirement in 2000. Since then he has been at the Tuscan Word Centre in Italy, which he runs with his second wife, Elena Tognini Bonelli.

Under Sinclair's leadership, Birmingham became a leading centre for innovative research, ushering in an age of the study of discourse analysis largely stimulated by the partnership between Sinclair and Malcolm Coulthard. Prior to this, discourse analysis was not in the syllabus in most courses of applied linguistics; afterwards, it became a requirement.

Sinclair compiled the first-ever electronic corpus of spoken language in the period 1963–5 in Edinburgh, in parallel with the American initiative for written language at Brown University. The first report of research into a corpus was published in 1970, but in the 1970s Sinclair stepped back from direct corpus research because of problems with the hardware and software of the period. In 1980, he realised that computers could at last support extensive study of corpora, enabling concordancing and the study of collocation. He arranged a contract between publisher Harper-Collins and the University of Birmingham involving the collection of large amounts of written, printed and transcribed spoken text in electronic format, an initiative that culminated in the Bank of English corpus and numerous publications.

His book *Corpus, Concordance, Collocation* (1991) expresses his firm, long-held belief in the primacy of evidence over intuition; particularly notable in this work are his presentation of the Idiom Principle, which underlies collocation, in contrast to the Open Choice principle. His innovative analysis of items such as 'of' and 'back' has helped the community realise that 'the language looks rather different when you look at a lot of it at once' (1991: 100).

Sinclair is very widely quoted indeed and has been enormously influential. He has throughout his career always been one step ahead of his contemporaries, often two or three, in seeing possibilities and questioning accepted theories. He has acted as a sower of seeds and a catalyst.

Primary works

(1970) (with S. Jones and R. Daley). *English Lexical Collocations*. R. Krishnamurthy (ed.). London: Continuum, 1994.
(1975) (with Malcolm Coulthard). *Towards an Analysis of Discourse*. London: Oxford University Press.
(1991). *Corpus, Concordance, Collocation*. Oxford: Oxford University Press.

Further reading

Baker, Mona, Francis, Gill and Bonelli, Elena Tognini (1993). *Text and Technology: In Honour of John Sinclair*. Amsterdam: John Benjamins.

Mike Scott

B. F. SKINNER

Skinner, B. F. (Burrhus Frederic) (*b.* 1904, *d.* 1990; American), professor, Harvard University (1948–90). Psychologist, who argued that verbal behaviour could be accounted for in terms of stimulus–response-reinforcement conditioning. (*See also* Chomsky, Noam; Hockett, Charles; Pike, Kenneth; Quine, W. V. O.)

The son of a lawyer, B. F. Skinner was born in the small town of Susquehanna, Pennsylvania, in March 1904. Much of his boyhood was spent building various machines and devices, including a failed attempt to build a perpetual motion machine. However, upon leaving university his early career aspirations were literary, leading him to move to Greenwich Village in New York City in the late 1920s. He soon returned to education, studying psychology at Harvard University. He received a Masters degree in 1930 and a PhD in 1936.

Skinner's central insight was that in shaping behaviour, what followed the behaviour (that is, the reinforcement) was central, as opposed to what preceded the behaviour, as had been claimed by Pavlov and

Watson. Skinner referred to the shaping of behaviour through a 'stimulus–response–reinforcement' paradigm as 'operant conditioning'. As an experimental psychologist, his boyhood interest in constructing devices returned to stand him in good stead. In a typical experiment, an animal would be placed into a box and would have to press a bar in order to receive food. Gradually, the conditions under which the animal received food would become more varied and complex, and some quite involved behaviour could eventually be elicited. Such devices eventually became known as 'Skinner boxes'.

In his 1957 book *Verbal Behavior*, Skinner claimed that human language could be explained in terms of operant conditioning. Essentially, verbal behaviour consists of responses to objectively identifiable stimuli and these responses are the result of years of operant conditioning by other members of the speech community. Two years later a critical review by *Chomsky dealt a severe blow to the behaviourist approach to language within mainstream linguistics. However, the general view did continue to find some support, most notably from *Pike and *Hockett, but also from philosophers such as *Quine, and (perhaps) *Wittgenstein. In his later years, Skinner continued to feel that behaviourism was popularly misunderstood, as perhaps evinced by the persistent myth that he raised his daughter in a 'Skinner box' and that she suffered severe psychological damage as a result. This led to his 1974 work *About Behaviorism*.

Although Skinner's direct influence within mainstream linguistics was relatively short-lived, his work continues to be important in other areas. Interestingly, some of his students went on use the techniques he pioneered outside of academia, and became well known as trainers of dolphins and other animals. Skinner died of leukaemia in August 1990, and is buried in the Mount Auburn garden cemetery in Cambridge, Massachusetts.

Primary works

(1957). *Verbal Behavior*. New York: Appleton-Century-Crofts.
(1974). *About Behaviorism*. New York: Random House.

Further reading

Chomsky, Noam (1959). 'Review of Skinner (1957)'. *Language*. Vol. 35: 26–58.
MacCorquodale, Kenneth (1970). 'On Chomsky's review of Skinner's *Verbal Behavior*'. *Journal of the Experimental Analysis of Behavior*. Vol. 13: 83–99.

Geoffrey Poole

P. F. STRAWSON

Strawson, P. F. (Peter Frederick) (*b.* 1919; British), fellow in philosophy at University College (1948–68) and Waynflete professor of metaphysical philosophy (1968–87) at Oxford. Knighted 1977. A member of the school of 'ordinary language philosophy', who later worked on metaphysics and epistemology. In the philosophy of language, his most influential work is concerned with the relationship between logic and natural language, and in particular with the definition of 'presupposition'. (*See also* Austin, J. L.; Grice, H. P.; Kant, Immanuel; Quine, W. V. O.; Russell, Bertrand; Searle, John.)

Strawson was born on 23 November 1919 in Ealing, London, but his family moved soon after his birth to Finchley, another London suburb, where he was brought up. He was the second of four children. His father was a headmaster and his mother was a school teacher until her marriage. Strawson was educated at Finchley County School and then at Christ's College Finchley, from where he won an open scholarship in English to St John's College, Oxford, in 1937. He soon persuaded the college authorities to allow him to change his degree subject to philosophy, politics and economics (PPE); he has commented that he was not much interested by economics, but 'philosophy I found congenial and absorbing from the start' (Hahn 1998: 4).

After graduation, Strawson was called up to the army in the summer of 1940. He excelled in electronics, commanding a radar station on the Sussex coast and rising to the rank of captain, before being posted abroad to Italy and then Austria. In 1945 he married Grace Hall Martin, whom he always called Ann. On leaving the army in 1946, he became assistant lecturer in philosophy at University College of North Wales, Bangor, before returning to Oxford as college lecturer at University College in 1947 and being elected fellow the following year.

Soon after his return to Oxford, Strawson came into contact with the approach to philosophy being pioneered by Gilbert *Ryle and J. L. *Austin. Their approach emphasised both the importance of natural language as a focus of philosophical study in its own right, and the possibilities for the clarification of philosophical questions offered by suitably rigorous analysis of the ordinary use of language. Strawson became a prominent member of the group known as 'ordinary language philosophers' that collected around Austin; he was unusual among them in his active pursuit of publication for his ideas. In his 1950 paper 'On referring' (1971), he took issue with Bertrand *Russell's theory of descriptions, which had gone unchallenged for almost fifty years. Russell had argued that definite descriptions are not referring expressions at all, but complex symbols that have meaning only when they form part of a sentence. Furthermore, the grammatical form of such a sentence is a poor guide to its underlying logical form, which consists of a complex of propositions about existence and uniqueness. For example, the sentence 'the king of France is bald' is not logically of subject–predicate form, with a property being ascribed to an individual, but must be 'translated' into a logical form such as 'there is one entity that is the king of France, and that entity is unique, and that entity is bald'.

Strawson begins 'On referring' with an uncompromising challenge to Russell. He states that: 'We very commonly use expressions of certain kinds to mention or refer to some individual person or single object or particular event or place or process' (1971: 1), and makes a point of including definite descriptions such as 'the king of France' in this class of expressions. He is both insisting that philosophical discussion should focus on how speakers *use* expressions, rather than on expressions in isolation, and asserting that uses of definite descriptions do refer to individuals. Strawson's 'ordinary language' approach is even more apparent in the consequences he draws for the truth values of uses of sentences containing definite descriptions. For Russell, in the absence of a current and unique king of France, his example sentence is simply false. This can be explained by the fact that one part of its logical form (the proposition affirming the existence of the king of France) is false. Strawson argues that Russell is seriously missing the point by failing to take account of how an ordinary person would react to a use of the sentence. In a context where there is no current king of France, a use of Russell's sentence would not seem false, but objectionable or wrong-headed in some other way. Strawson accuses Russell of being obsessed with maintaining classical logic (in which every sentence must be either true or false) and of ignoring the fact that it may be possible for the use of a sentence to be neither true nor false. Strawson concludes 'On referring' with a pithy statement of this position: 'Neither Aristotelian nor Russellian rules give the exact logic of any expression of ordinary language; for ordinary language has no exact logic' (1971: 27).

For Strawson, the existence of the king of France is not a logical entailment of Russell's example sentence, but is implied in a 'special' manner by a use of that sentence, or a particular statement. In *Introduction to Logical Theory* (1952), Strawson gives a name to this special type of implication, labelling it 'presupposition' and defining it with reference to the observation that the same proposition is presupposed by both a statement and its denial ('there is a king of France' is a presupposition of both 'the king of France is bald' and 'the king of France is not bald'). Whereas a logical entailment is a precondition only for the truth of a statement that entails it, a presupposition is a precondition for the truth *or falsity* of a statement that presupposes it. Strawson's theory has formed the basis of a continuing debate about the nature and status of presupposition in philosophy and particularly in linguistics.

In *Introduction to Logical Theory*, Strawson also develops further his account of the differences between logic and language by considering the discrepancies in meaning between logical connectives and their apparent counterparts in natural language. In particular he discusses how natural language 'if ... then' differs from the logical conditional. Whereas the meaning of a logical conditional such as 'p → q' can be defined entirely in terms of a truth table, a natural language expression of the form 'if p then q' seems to convey at least two further elements of meaning: namely that there is some causal connection between p and q, and that there is some doubt about the truth of p. Strawson suggests that 'if p then q' entails 'p → q', but that there are further aspects of its meaning that are not explained by the logical conditional. H. P. *Grice took issue with Strawson's insistence on the semantic differences between logic and natural language when he developed his theory of conversational implicature, arguing that the apparent differences noticed by Strawson were differences not in 'what is said' but in 'what is implicated'. Strawson and Grice engaged in a long collaborative project in the 1950s on *Aristotle's categories. This remained unpublished, although Grice and Strawson did produce one joint paper, 'In defence of a dogma' (1956), in which they respond to W. V. O. *Quine's rejection of the distinction between analytic and synthetic sentences, urging both the long philosophical pedigree of the terms, and the currency of related expressions such as 'means the same as' in ordinary language.

Some of the collaborative project on categories fed into Strawson's *Individuals* (1959), in which he undertakes what he describes as 'descriptive metaphysics', analysing the language we use in describing the world and the conceptual categories this reflects. His later work, undertaken during and after the gradual demise of 'ordinary language philosophy', is less directly concerned with philosophy of language and therefore less well known in linguistics. It includes *The Bounds of Sense* (1966), which is a critical study of *Kant's *Critique of Pure Reason*,

and also work on theories of knowledge, freedom, action and identity.

Apart from his year in Bangor, Strawson spent his entire academic career at Oxford, succeeding Ryle to the Waynflete chair in 1968. A collection of his writings on the philosophy of language, including 'On referring', was published in 1971 as *Logico-Linguistic Papers*. He retired in 1987 but continues both his association with the university and his philosophical work.

Primary works

(1952). *Introduction to Logical Theory*. London: Methuen.
(1956) (with H. P. Grice) 'In defence of a dogma'. *Philosophical Review*. Vol. 65: 141–58.
(1959). *Individuals: An Essay in Descriptive Metaphysics*. London: Methuen.
(1966). *The Bounds of Sense*. London: Methuen.
(1971). *Logico-Linguistic Papers*. London: Methuen.

Further reading

Hahn, Lewis Edwin (ed.) (1998). *The Philosophy of P. F. Strawson*. Chicago: Open Court.
Magee, Bryan (1971). *Modern British Philosophy*. Oxford: Oxford University Press, 1986.
Neale, Stephen (1990). *Descriptions*. Cambridge, MA: MIT Press.
Sen, Pranab Kumar and Verma, Rop Rekha (eds) (1995). *The Philosophy of P. F. Strawson*. New Delhi: Indian Council of Philosophical Research.
(1981). *Philosophia*. Vol. 10: 141–328. Special journal issue.

Siobhan Chapman

DEBORAH TANNEN

Tannen, Deborah (*b.* 1945; American), professor of linguistics at Georgetown University. PhD in linguistics, University of California at Berkeley (1979). Discourse analyst best known for her popular works on language and gender. (*See also* Cameron, Deborah.)

Born in New York, Tannen was educated in the United States. After majoring in English and teaching English as a second language, in both Greece and the United States, she conducted her doctoral research in the tradition of interactional sociolinguistics. Since the publication of her book *You Just Don't Understand* in 1990, which was on the *New York Times* bestseller list for four years, she has been widely considered as one of the world's best-known linguists. Her work includes other titles that have found a wide audience outside academia and have been translated into numerous languages.

Tannen's research career began with her analysis of a dinner table conversation among friends for her PhD. There she developed the focus on the expression of interpersonal relationships that has characterised most of her work to date. In particular, she has worked on the expression of interpersonal relationships as related to gender, in both private and workplace contexts, and to cross-cultural communication. Her work on gender has made her well known as an exponent of work in the 'dual-culture' tradition, which claims that men and women speak differently because they belong to different cultures. Because as children boys and girls play in same-sex groups, they are said to develop gender-specific communication styles and to have trouble communicating with members of the opposite group in later life, be it in their private relationships or in the workplace. Feminist linguists such as Deborah *Cameron have been highly critical of work in the dual-culture tradition, and in particular Tannen's work, for failing to account for the differential access to power enjoyed by men and women. Cameron herself approaches the subject from a broadly poststructuralist viewpoint, and the debate between the dual-culture tradition and the 'patriarchal' argument about women's speech has in fact since been transcended in poststructuralist thinking on language and gender, a mode of thought that eschews the question of differences in female and male speech. Instead, these newer approaches seek to elucidate how gender is discursively constructed and how gender structures access to, and use of, linguistic resources. Even so, Tannen's work remains fundamental in the field, either as a point of departure to develop new work, or against which to define new work.

One of the reasons for the popularity of Tannen's work is her ear for the way people talk and the fact that many of the anecdotes she uses to illustrate her work ring true with the communicative experiences of her readers. Her ear for these anecdotes may well have been sharpened by her interest in literature: apart from her linguistic work, she has written poetry, short stories and plays.

Primary works

(1984). *Conversational Style: Analyzing Talk among Friends.* Norwood, NJ: Ablex.

(1986). *That's Not What I Meant! How Conversational Style Makes or Breaks Relationships.* New York: Ballantine.

(1990). *You Just Don't Understand: Women And Men in Conversation.* New York: Ballantine.

(1994). *Talking from 9 to 5: Women and Men in the Workplace: Language, Sex, and Power.* New York: Avon.

(1998). *The Argument Culture: Moving from Debate to Dialogue.* New York: Random House.

(2002). *I Only Say This Because I Love You: Talking To Your Parents, Partner, Sibs, and Kids When You're All Adults.* New York: Ballantine.

Web page of Deborah Tannen. [Online] www.georgetown.edu/faculty/tannend/index.htm (accessed 18 August 2003).

Ingrid Piller

ALFRED TARSKI

Tarski, Alfred (*b.* 1902, *d.* 1983; Polish, naturalised American 1945), lecturer in mathematics and logic University of Warsaw (1925–39), Harvard (1939–41), City College New York (1940) and Princeton (1941–42). In 1942 he joined the staff of the University of California at Berkeley, first as a lecturer and assistant professor, then as professor of mathematics (1949–68) and professor emeritus (1968–83). The leading figure of the Lvov-Warsaw School, he introduced the concept of truth in the languages of deductive sciences as the basis for the theory of logical semantics and model-theoretic semantics. In mathematics, his name is closely associated with logical deduction, universal algebra and metamathematical model theory. (*See also* Aristotle; Austin, J. L.; Ayer, A. J.; Carnap, Rudolf; Davidson, Donald; Frege, Gottlob; Montague, Richard; Popper, Karl; Wittgenstein, Ludwig.)

Tarski, or rather Alfred Teitelbaum, was born in Warsaw to Ignacy Teteilbaum, a wealthy Jewish businessman, and his wife Rosa Prussak. Though they were not an intellectual family, they considered education to be very important and sent their son to the Schola Mazowiecka, one of the best grammar schools. Tarski was a very good student and studied subjects such as Greek and Latin, Russian, French and German, as well as the natural sciences and mathematics. His main interests were in biology, and after some time in the Polish army, he enrolled at the University of Warsaw to study for a degree in biology. After taking a course on logic, Tarski realised where his real interest lay and changed to mathematics. He published his first paper at the age of 19, and two years later he submitted his doctoral thesis. It was clear to him that he wanted to follow an academic career. However, his Jewish background and his name would have made it nearly impossible for him to get a post at the university, and as he also had strong nationalist feelings for the new Poland, he decided to change his name to Tarski and to become a Roman Catholic. Whether these moves really helped is not clear, but in 1925 he was appointed lecturer in mathematics and logic at the University of Warsaw, and he held this post until 1939. Even so, he still had to teach full-time at a grammar school to earn his living.

At the beginning of his academic career Tarski continued his research on set theory, and he published his first results in 1924 in a joint paper with Stefan Banach. They proved that a sphere can be cut into a finite number of pieces and then be reassembled into a sphere of a larger size, or into two spheres of the original size. As this phenomenon is so counter-intuitive, it became known as the Banach-Tarski paradox. Both Banach and Tarski were members of the Lvov-Warsaw School, a group of Polish logicians who carried out important research in formal logic, the philosophy of mathematics and semantics in the 1920s and 1930s. Their close connection to the Vienna Circle of Logical Positivists gave them access to the International Congresses on Unified Science and thus provided them with a platform for the dissemination of their ideas.

In 1933 Tarski published 'Pojęcie prawdy w językach nauk dedukcyjnych' ('The concept of truth in the languages of deductive sciences'), which is considered to be among the most important papers written on mathematical logic, and whose impact resulted in the change from logic as calculus to logic as language. The presentation of his theory of truth at the Congress on Unified Science in Paris (1935) was a highlight of the conference. In his paper he laid the foundation for modern semantics, which hitherto was preoccupied with lexical meaning and its changes through time. Tarski stated that concepts such as satisfaction, denoting, truth, definability and so on all belong to the semantics of a language, as 'they give expression to certain relations between the expressions of language and the objects about which these expressions speak, or that by means of such relations they characterize certain classes of expressions or other objects' (1956: 252). It was due to Tarski that logical semantics (or model theory) became the central area in logic and the philosophy of language. This might be considered a semantic revolution.

An important principle in logical semantics is Tarski's clear distinction between the language to be interpreted, that is, the object language, and his new concept of metalanguage, the language used to analyse or describe the sentences or elements of the object language. The difference between object language and metalanguage can be best seen in Tarski's definition of truth: 'X is true if, and only if, p', in which p is a variable representing any sentence and X a variable representing the name, or unique description, of that sentence, as in '"Snow is white" is true if, and only if, snow is white'. X represents the name of that sentence in the object language, the language we use to talk about things in the world, whereas the whole statement is in the metalanguage, the language used to talk about things in the world as well as sentences of the object language. With the sentence 'This very sentence is false', Tarski proved further that no language can contain its own truth predicate, as it is only true if it is false, a paradox that shows that semantic predicates must belong to a language of a higher order.

Tarski clearly stated that his logical theory was restricted to formalised languages and never claimed that it could be applied to natural language, which is far more complex. Yet it had a great impact on linguistics, as it served as the input to different semantic and syntactic theories. *Montague (1970) thought that the inadequacies could be overcome by means of a universal, algebraically formulated language theory. He tried to establish a link between formalised and natural languages and to develop a system that accounted for both syntax and semantics of all languages, but in which syntactic rules were based on semantics which had to be truth-conditional. *Austin (1962), on the other hand, was intrigued by the fact that Tarski's theory only accounted for statements, whereas promises, requests, orders, performatives and so forth cannot be handled, although they also have meaning. Apart from truth, there are other dimensions in natural language, such as feasibility, utility or moral values. To account for these elements Austin, among others, developed speech act theory. For pragmatics the concept of truth was also a necessary prerequisite, since at least at the beginning everything that could not be handled by truth conditions was considered to belong to pragmatics rather than to semantics. Donald *Davidson also concentrated on the inability of Tarski's theory to explain natural language, and proposed an axiomatic account to address this issue.

The 1935 congress in Paris was a landmark in Tarski's academic career, and he soon gained an outstanding international reputation as an eminent logician. The 1939 Congress, on the other hand, probably saved his life: he was at Harvard when Hitler gave the order to invade Poland, and Tarski succeeded in getting permission to stay in the United States. His wife and his two children, however, had remained in Poland and could only join him in 1946. By that time, Tarski was a naturalised American citizen and had joined the staff of the University of California at Berkeley, where he became professor of mathematics in 1949. Although he remained there for the rest of his life, lecturing and carrying out research in logic, algebra, geometry and set theory, he took many opportunities to work in other places, such as University College London, the Henri-Poincaré Institute in Paris, the Miller Institute of Basic Research, UC Los Angeles and the Catholic University of Chile, where he was awarded an honorary doctorate.

Tarski is recognised as one of the great logicians of the twentieth century. He made many important contributions in different areas of mathematics, metamathematics and logic, and established the mathematical theory of models. However, he is best known for his concept of truth in formalised languages and for his proof that truth within a natural language cannot be defined comprehensibly. His work was seminal for all modern philosophical discussions of truth. In his later years at Berkeley he was responsible for influencing the careers of students in mathematics as well as in philosophy and linguistics. Tarski died in San Francisco on 26 October 1983.

Primary reading

(1924) (with Stefan Banach). 'Sur la décomposition des ensembles de points en parties respectivement congruentes'... *Fundamenta Mathematica.* Vol. 6: 244–77.

(1933). 'Pojęcie prawdy w językach nauk dedukcyjnych'. *Prace Towarzystwa Naukowego Warszwskiego.* Trans. in Tarski (1956).

(1936). *Introduction to Logic and to the Methodology of Deductive Sciences.* O. Helmer (trans.). New York: Oxford University Press, 1941.

(1943). 'The semantic concept of truth'. *Philosophy and Phenomenological Research.* Vol. 4: 341–75.

(1953) (with A. Mostowski and R. M. Robinson). *Undecidable Theories.* Amsterdam: North-Holland.

(1956). *Logic, Semantics, Metamathematics: Papers from 1923 to 1938.* J. H. Woodger (trans.). Oxford: Clarendon Press.

(1986). *Collected Papers.* Steven R. Givant and Ralph N. McKenzie (eds.). Basel: Birkhäuser.

Further reading

Austin, J. L. (1962). *How to Do Things With Words.* Oxford: Clarendon Press.

Montague, Richard (1970). 'Universal Grammar'. *Theoria.* Vol. 36: 373–98.

Woleński, Jan and Köhle, Eckehart (eds) (1999). *Alfred Tarski and the Vienna Circle: Austro-Polish Connections in Logical Empiricism.* Dordrecht: Kluwer Academic.

Jürg Strässler

TZVETAN TODOROV

Todorov, Tzvetan (*b.* 1939; Bulgarian, naturalised French), structuralist thinker, narratologist and historian.

Todorov was initially concerned with poetics as a scientific discipline and literary texts as semantic units. He was also interested in interpretation and the subjective nature of meaning. In his later works, Todorov's thinking has shifted towards ideas of otherness, in particular the realisation that authors do not determine the rules and structures that texts must obey; this poststructuralist turn deconstructs his own earlier work defining typologies of literary genres. (*See also* Bakhtin, Mikhail; Barthes, Roland; (Derrida, Jacques; Greimas, Algirdas.)

Todorov was born in Sofia, Bulgaria, and completed his first degree at the University of Sofia. In 1963, aged 24, he moved to Paris, hoping to study at the Sorbonne, but despite supporting letters from his Bulgarian tutors he was not allowed to begin his research there. Nevertheless he completed a doctoral thesis in 1966, studying with Roland *Barthes at the École des Hautes Études en Sciences Sociales. He went on to teach at the University of Paris and at various universities in the United States, including Yale, Columbia, NYU and Wisconsin. In 1970, the year he presented his doctorat d'État at the Centre National de Recherche Scientifiques (CNRS) in Paris, he helped found the journal *Poétique* along with Hélène Cixous and Gerard Genette. In 1996, he became director of research at the CNRS.

Throughout his career Todorov has concerned himself with the boundaries and links between literature, or belles-lettres, and popular forms of narrative. Arriving from a background in structuralism (see Barthes, *Saussure) and Russian formalism (see *Bakhtin), Todorov attempted to show how genres depend on the connections between texts, rather than the limitations of their internal structures. In this respect his approach follows on from that of Barthes, much of whose writing attempts to apply scientific principles to the process of reading and writing, while at the same time recognising the value of subjectivity and interpretation. Structural analysis of narratives, for Todorov, frees readers from the strict generic formulas established by *Aristotle, who ranks genres according to their merit. Todorov suggested instead that while individual texts can be described in terms of discrete internal structures, genres constantly respond to outside influences and cultural change. Far from being static, genres exist in a state of instability and flux; their value is arbitrary and imposed from outside.

Todorov's early poetics is deeply engaged with the 'scientific' principles of structuralism, yet as Robert Scholes points out in his introduction to The Fantastic (1970), Todorov is a poetician first and a structuralist second. While conventional linguistics – even in a structuralist framework – limits its scope to the semantic unit of the sentence or even the individual word, many structuralist thinkers after Barthes have attempted to apply linguistic principles to whole texts, narratives, even cultures. Such a view depends on the idea that a complex system of relationships exists between texts, and that such a system may be notated as a 'typology' that can be used to identify works within a particular genre. In this respect, Todorov began using linguistics to build a literary theory that could, in principle, analyse literary texts as semantic units in the same way as sentences are unpicked in traditional linguistics. Furthermore, he explored the idea that literary works have a syntax, be it mythological, where events in the narrative follow a logical order, or ideological, where the narrative lends itself to the support of an idea. The third part of his early poetics concerns the 'verbal' characteristics of the text, that is, the ways in which it deals with time, space and voice; the aspects readers use to construct imaginary worlds.

Much of Todorov's early thinking derives from his doctoral thesis, which analyses the eighteenth-century novel Les Liaisons Dangereuses in terms of its levels of narrative and the processes behind them. In Littérature et signification (Literature and Signification) (1967), developed from his thesis, he argues that novels are linguistic acts, and that as such they are built on a set of internal processes and structures. However, because his poetics can be applied to all narratives, not just novels, Todorov focuses on genres, rather than individual texts. Arguably his two most influential books from this early period are Introduction à la littérature fantastique (The Fantastic) (1970), and La Poétique de la prose (The Poetics of Prose) (1971). The extent to which he uses linguistics as the key to his poetics is evident in each of these books. The Fantastic discusses the reasons why a study of literary genres should consist of more than a list of features shared by a group of works. Todorov points out that in defining a typology by this inclusive

265

method – a common approach in the 1960s and 1970s – one would have to read all of the works even loosely connected with a genre; in the case of fantastic literature, this would run to many thousands of novels and stories. Instead, he proposes a more language-based method, identifying the three aspects of a literary work through which a scientific analysis should be possible; namely, 'the verbal, the syntactical, and the semantic'.

The Poetics of Prose is rather more explicit in its application of linguistics to texts and narrative, but it is also more wide ranging. While there are chapters such as 'Language and literature' and 'The grammar of literature', *The Poetics of Prose* also offers sections on Henry James, and an important essay on detective fiction. In this respect the book blurs the distinction between criticism and poetics, while at the same time keeping language to the fore. The act of reading, Todorov argues, presupposes a poetics; that is, it presupposes some kind of linguistic analysis.

By the late 1970s and early 1980s, Todorov began to move away from this text-centred approach and back to one that demanded the understanding of texts from the premise that the meaning of a literary work exists only in its relationship with other narratives. In other words, meaning derives from a narrative's intertextuality; it is relational, or 'dialogic' in a Bakhtinian sense. In 1977, Todorov published *Théorie du symbole* (*Theories of the Symbol*), a history of semiotics with an emphasis on historicity (the relationship of texts to their historical context), and by 1982 he had written an actual work of history, *The Conquest*

of America. This book, which analyses the interaction of Columbus's world-view with that of the native Americans, makes explicit Todorov's interest in alterity (otherness), in that it demonstrates how the arrival of Europeans both exposed and denied the differences between European culture and the cultures of the native North American people. While his earlier work on literary texts had suggested that the true subject of any text is its own creation, here Todorov's historical work depends on his own interaction with the object of his study. The historian enters a dialogue with his material in order to allow the previously silent voice of the other to be heard.

While Todorov has moved away from language as an explicit subject of his work, the idea of otherness raises issues of meaning in interaction – a difficult area for structuralist poetics – at the same time as it builds on structuralist foundations. His work as a whole represents a significant contribution to semiotics, literary theory and structuralist philosophy. Less directly, the typologies laid out in books such as *The Poetics of Prose* offer a rich source of material against which deconstructionist theorists such as *Derrida have been able to react in fomenting their own philosophical revolution.

Primary works

(1967). *Literature and Signification*. Paris: Larousse.
(1970). *The Fantastic: A Structural Approach to a Literary Genre*. Richard Howard (trans). Ithaca, NY: Cornell University Press, 1973.

(1971). *The Poetics of Prose*. Richard Howard (trans.). Ithaca, NY: Cornell University Press, 1977.

(1977). *Theories of the Symbol*. Catherine Porter (trans.). Ithaca, NY: Cornell University Press, 1982.

(1981). *Mikhail Bakhtin: The Dialogical Principle*. Wlad Godzich (trans.). Manchester: Manchester University Press, 1984.

(1982). *The Conquest of America: The Question of the Other*. Richard Howard (trans.). New York: Harper and Row, 1984.

(1984). *Literature and its Theorists: A Personal View of Twentieth Century Criticism*. Catherine Porter (trans.). London: Routledge and Kegan Paul, 1988.

Christopher Routledge

N. S. TRUBETZKOY

Trubetzkoy, N. S. (Nikolai Sergeevich) (*b*. 1890, *d*. 1938; Russian), lecturer at Moscow University (1915–16), Rostov-on-Don University (1918), Sofia University (1920–22), finally professor of Slavic linguistics at Vienna University (1922–38). One of the founding fathers of phonology and a key theorist of the Prague School. (*See also* Jakobson, Roman; Martinet, André; Saussure, Ferdinand de.)

Trubetzkoy's life was blighted by persecution. Born in Moscow of aristocratic, academic parents, Trubetzkoy (whose names have been transliterated variously) was a prince, and, after study and an immediate start to a university career in Moscow, he was forced to flee by the 1917 Bolshevik revolution; he subsequently also had to leave Rostov and Sofia. On settling in Vienna, he became a geographically distant member of the Prague Linguistic Circle.

It is at times difficult to tease his ideas apart from those of his friend *Jakobson, who ensured that Trubetzkoy's nearly finished *Grundzüge der Phonologie* (*Principles of Phonology*) (1939) was posthumously published. Trubetzkoy had previously published substantial work in several fields, but this was his *magnum opus*. It summarised his previous phonological work and stands now as the classic statement of Prague School phonology, setting out an array of phonological ideas, several of which still characterise debate on phonological representations. Through *Principles* and the publications that preceded it, as well as his work at conferences and general enthusiasm for making contacts, Trubetzkoy was crucial in the development of phonology as a discipline distinct from phonetics, and influential in the change in phonological focus from diachrony (the study of language over a long period of time) to synchrony (the study of language as it stands in a limited time frame). He argued that form (contrast, systemic patterning) must be studied separately from substance (acoustics, articulation), although he did not see the two as completely separate, unlike *Hjelmslev.

Trubetzkoy argued that phonology should deal with the linguistic function of sounds (their ability to signal differences in word-meaning), as members of phonemic oppositions. The phoneme was his smallest phonological unit, as for him 'oppositions' existed only within a language's system. They were not quite the autonomous segmental building blocks that they later became as the 'distinctive features' of Jakobson, and through him, generative phonology (originated by *Chomsky and Halle).

Trubetzkoy also investigated the neutralisation of contrast, which helped reveal segmental (un-)markedness, and was the first to consider these subsequently extremely important ideas. He introduced too the notion of 'functional load' (later developed by *Martinet). Trubetzkoy considered each system in its own right, but was also crucially concerned with establishing universal explanatory laws of phonological organisation (such as the symmetrical patterning in vowel systems), and his work involves the discussion of hundreds of languages, including their prosody.

Having fled persecution before, the Nazi annexation of Austria proved too much. A brutal Gestapo raid on his home aggravated a heart condition and he died of a heart attack in hospital. His legacy lives on in the thriving field of phonology.

Primary works

(1939). *Grundzüge der Phonologie.* English translation: *Principles of Phonology.* Christiane Baltaxe (trans.). Berkeley, CA: University of California Press, 1969.

Further reading

Anderson, Stephen (1985). *Phonology in the Twentieth Century.* Chicago: University of Chicago Press.
Jakobson, Roman (1939). 'Nécrologie Nikolaj Sergejevič Trubetzkoy'. *Acta Linguistica 1.* Reprinted in Thomas Sebeok (ed.), *Portraits of Linguists.* Bloomington: Indiana University Press, 1966.
Jakobson, Roman (ed.) (1958). 'Autobiographical notes on N. S. Trubetzkoy'. Appendix to second edition of Trubetzkoy's *Grundzüge*; also in Baltaxe's (1969) translation.

Patrick Honeybone

BENJAMIN LEE WHORF

Whorf, Benjamin Lee (*b.* 1897, *d.* 1941; American), fire prevention officer and linguist best known for the controversial and often misrepresented Sapir-Whorf hypothesis or, as he termed it, linguistic relativity. His major work in linguistics was *Language, Thought and Reality*, a collection of essays published posthumously, thanks to the editorship of John B. Carroll. (*See also:* Sapir, Edward.)

Whorf was born in a suburb of Boston, Massachusetts. After attending local schools, he entered the Massachusetts Institute of Technology in 1914, graduating with a BSc in chemical engineering in 1918, after an illness that delayed him for a year and without any especially high grades. Soon after, he started a career as a fire prevention officer with the Hartford Fire Insurance Company in Hartford, Connecticut. In 1920 he married; his wife and he had three children. For the rest of his relatively short life, he worked a normal eight-hour day preventing fires and rising within the company. He pursued his interest in linguistics in his spare time.

It was not until 1924 that Whorf began to study linguistics in a serious way. As a boy he had been interested in secret codes as well as in chemistry, but the key to his interest in language was religion. Whorf was a Methodist Episcopalian, for whom the Bible was fundamental. At the same time, as a chemical engineer and scientist, he was concerned by the problem of reconciling the Bible and contemporary science. In fact, in 1925 he wrote a 130,000-word book of religious philosophy, though it was rejected by publishers. For these reasons he began to study Hebrew, not just to learn the language but to attempt to get at the hidden roots of language and belief. From this he was led in 1926, via a local library, to a study of Nahuatl, the language of the Aztecs, and from there to Maya in 1928. Whorf's first academic publication concerned Aztec history and language. He began to work on other Mexican languages at around the same time. In 1928, around the time he first met Edward *Sapir, he decided to apply for a Social Science Research Council fellowship to study Mexican linguistics. His research application makes it clear that he planned to work out 'the primitive underlying basis of all speech behaviour' and that he expects this to manifest 'the deeper psychological, symbolic, and philosophical sense contained in the cosmology of the Bible'. Whorf's application was successful despite his complete lack of any qualifications in linguistics.

In 1931, Sapir took a job at Yale as professor of linguistics and anthropology. Whorf entered his first course in American Indian linguistics. Very soon thereafter, with the support and encouragement of his teacher, Whorf turned attention towards Hopi, a distant relative of Aztec. He learned the language with the help of linguistic informants near his home and during a short stay in the Hopi reservation in Arizona. From this time to the end of his life in 1941, there followed a number of articles on Hopi and related languages, and Whorf became established in linguistics as an expert on Hopi. He became increasingly aware that the Hopi language was structured in such a way that he believed the speaker of Hopi thought differently from the speaker of English. This is the cornerstone of his understanding of linguistic relativity.

What Whorf had realised as early as the late 1920s was that the different structure of the world's languages was likely to lead to different ways of perceiving the world. In 1936 he wrote:

linguistics is essentially the quest of MEANING. It may seem to the outsider to be inordinately absorbed in recording hairsplitting distinctions of sound, performing phonetic gymnastics, and writing complex grammars which only grammarians read. But the simple fact is that its real concern is to light up the thick darkness of the language, and thereby of much of the thought, the culture, and the outlook on life of a given community, with this transmuting principle of meaning. (1936: 133)

In 1939, Whorf reported that he first began to think of this problem of underlying meaning in relation to fires. In a certain wood distillation plant, nobody had paid much attention to fire risks connected with an insulation material called 'spun limestone', which 'because it ends in "-stone" implies non-combustibility'; in a second case a kettle of hot varnish was 'off' the fire, but ignited because it was not covered; in a third case a workman threw a match into a mix of water and animal matter with a wooden cover, which 'was evolving gas under the wood cover, so that the setup was the reverse of "watery"'. From this initial word-based realisation that there may be a connection between language and attitudes to fire risks, Whorf moves towards grammar.

He explicitly denies a correlation 'in the generally accepted sense of correlation' between language and culture. This denial seems to knock on the head any idea that Whorf regarded the linkage between language and thought as simply determined or deterministic. However, by reconsidering the grammatical categories of English thanks to his knowledge of Hopi and other indigenous North American languages, he was led, like Sapir before him, to a realisation that there is a covert connection all the same. Whorf's discussion of the difference between covert grammatical categories and overt ones is long and complex, but it can be summarised in the example of the distinction between count and mass nouns, which is grammatically overt in English. For example, there is a grammatical difference between 'many dollars' and 'much money', where 'dollars' are treated grammatically as countable (because they go with 'many') but 'money' is treated by English as if it were a substance (going with 'much'): we can say 'six dollars' but not 'six monies'. English solves the problem of counting the uncountable, such as 'soap' or 'chocolate', by requiring 'bar, or piece of'. Other languages such as Chinese

or Hopi have no such need: one can say 'sikwi' ('a meat') in Hopi, for example: that language 'deals with formlessness through other symbols than nouns'.

Another example is the simple present tense in English, which is used for lots of different meanings. These include 'oil floats on water' (timeless, it always has and always will), 'I see him' (now) and 'We see with our eyes' (habitual). The speaker of English, Whorf points out, can be brought to realise the differences between these meanings (for example, if learning to teach English as a foreign language), but is generally unlikely to become aware of them otherwise. In the same way, the speaker of Hopi, or Japanese, or any other language will tend to perceive the world in a way that is conditioned by the grammar of the language she or he speaks. This is the key to linguistic relativity: the speaker sees the world in terms of the categories of the language he or she speaks. Different languages therefore drive and are driven by different perceptions of the world.

It has often been claimed that there are two forms of the Sapir-Whorf hypothesis, the 'strong' and the 'weak': in the strong form a speaker is a prisoner of his or her language and quite unable to think in other terms. The weak form is as described above: the speaker can become aware of alternative possibilities, and indeed will almost certainly have to when learning a new language. It is not likely that either Sapir or Whorf ever held to the 'strong' form of linguistic relativity, and the term 'hypothesis' seems to have come from Carroll (1956: 27).

Whorf was the epitome of the self-taught man: for nearly two decades, he managed a regular job along alongside an apparently unrelated linguistic research output that would be the envy of many full-time academic researchers. And although he died of cancer in 1941, aged only 44, he made a name in linguistics that is hard to equal. It is to Whorf that we owe the terms 'allophone' in phonetics and 'SAE' (Standard Average European) languages, but he is best known as the explicit advocate of 'linguistic relativity'.

Primary works

(1936). 'A linguistic consideration of thinking in primitive communities'. In Hymes (1964).
(1956). *Language, Thought and Reality*. John B. Carroll (ed.). Cambridge, MA: MIT Press.

Further reading

Carroll, John B. (1956). 'Introduction'. In Whorf (1956).
Hayakawa, Samuel I. (1990). *Language in Thought and Action*. Fifth edition. San Diego: Harcourt Brace Jovanovich.
Hymes, Dell (ed.) (1964). *Language in Culture and Society: A Reader in Linguistics and Anthropology*. New York: Harper Row.

Mike Scott

LUDWIG WITTGENSTEIN

Wittgenstein, Ludwig (Josef Johann) (*b.* 1889, *d.* 1951; Austrian, naturalised British 1938), philosopher, engineer, teacher, architect, gardener, medical orderly, war prisoner. Fellow of Trinity College (1929); professor of philosophy, Cambridge (1939). Idiosyncratic philosopher in the analytic tradition who introduced the idea of language both as the source of error and delusion concerning philosophical problems and as the method of getting rid of such errors. Wittgenstein is a major influence on the study of language and academic discourses after World War II, not least because of his view of language as a collection of 'games'. (*See also*: Austin, J. L.; Grice, H. P.; Malinowski, Bronislaw; Moore, G. E.; Peirce, C. S.; Russell, Bertrand; Searle, John.)

Wittgenstein was born in Habsburg Vienna to one of Europe's wealthiest and most cultured families. His father Karl, who owned a large iron and steel company, made young Wittgenstein's childhood home a meeting place for artists, musicians and writers, including Gustav Klimt, Johannes Brahms, Gustav Mahler, Richard Strauss, Maurice Ravel and Arthur Schnitzler. All seven of Wittgenstein's older siblings were artistically and intellectually gifted, but three of his four brothers committed suicide. A contemporary of Adolf Hitler at a Realschule in Linz in 1904–5, Wittgenstein went on to study mechanical engineering in Berlin (1906), aeronautical engineering at the University of Manchester (1908) and mathematical logic and philosophy at Trinity College, Cambridge (1911–14). From 1929 until 1947 he was a member of faculty of Trinity College, with sabbaticals in Norway and Ireland. From 1941 to 1944 he was given leave of absence to work at Guy's Hospital, London, and at the Royal Victoria Infirmary, Newcastle-upon-Tyne. This was because he wanted to help in the war effort but was too old for active service.

Published in 1921 (English edition, 1922), his early work *Tractatus Logico-Philosophicus*, written in part in the trenches of World War I and sent to his instructor *Russell from an Italian prison camp in 1919, presented a lively argument for the interconnectedness of the logical structure of the world, language and thought. The work was submitted as his doctoral degree, defended at Cambridge in June 1929 and swiftly approved by Russell and *Moore. Written in 'bullet points' rather than sustained prose, the *Tractatus* consists of seven principal propositions divided into further sub-propositions. This accounts for the elaborate referencing system. For instance, Wittgenstein asserts in his characteristically terse style that the world is everything that is the case (§1); what is the case – a fact – is the existence of atomic facts (states of affairs) (§2); the facts consist of independent atomic facts (§2.061) and the atomic facts are connections of objects and things (§2.1). Set against the backdrop of Russell's theory of knowledge, these propositions present the idea of simple objects, which are given in direct experience and in immediate awareness of one's sense-data, and are represented in language by names.

In 1913, while still a student and while working on the *Tractatus*, Wittgenstein retreated from academic life and moved to Skjolden, where he lived as the reclusive – or frustrated – Mr Ludwig. But when war broke out shortly afterwards, he immediately volunteered. Soon after the war ended, he took a job as a primary school teacher in Trattenbach and in Ottenthal, lower Austria. Following this somewhat disastrous episode, he first worked as a gardener, and then in 1926–8 designed and built a brilliant but decidedly strange house for his sister Margaret Stoneborough-Wittgenstein. Meanwhile his *Tractatus* had become a subject of much interest in philosophical circles, especially in Vienna.

Only in 1928 did Wittgenstein return to academic life. Karl Menger, Friedrich Weissman and Herbert Feigl persuaded him to attend the Dutch mathematician L. E. J. Brouwer's lecturers for the Vienna Circle (see *Ayer and *Carnap). Even though Wittgenstein never entirely accepted Brouwer's original ideas about language, it is clear that he became preoccupied with them and with Brouwer. Wittgenstein's transition phase, as it has come to be known, may be viewed as a reaction to Brouwer's non-mathematical discussion on the interconnections between mathematics, science and language. The encounter with Brouwer encouraged Wittgenstein to step out from the shadow of the *Tractatus*, and to repudiate, for instance, the earlier importance he assigned to the logical independence of elementary propositions. During his transition phase, he quickly embraced the view that meaning is mediated not in motionless naming but in dynamic, goal-directed and purposeful activities, most conspicuously illustrated in the processes of customary, habitual and institutionalised ways of using language.

This new view is evidenced in the best known of his works, *Philosophical Investigations* (1953), published two years after his death. The earliest versions of part I go back to *The Blue and Brown Books* (1958) circulated at Cambridge in 1932–3, while the material in part II was selected by the editors, G. E. M. Anscombe and Rush Rhees, from manuscripts written in 1946–9. Both in substance and chronologically, the clippings included in the posthumously edited and organised *Zettel* (1967) may be regarded as representing an intermediate phase in his thought between the two parts of *Investigations*.

Wittgenstein's style of writing and dictating to a typist accords with his singular ineptitude in language, which was largely due to his dyslexic symptoms. His poor writing and reading skills did not deter him from attempting unified presentations and argumentative structures of his most remarkable and original philosophical ideas, even while these attempts were continuously frustrated not only by his extraordinary standards for philosophical rigour, intellectual honesty and self-criticism, but also by the difficulty of maintaining the complex network of his philosophical ideas in proper order and at easy recall.

Among his considerable innovations in philosophy was his view of language as a goal-directed and use-governed system of communication. In this context, he coined the idea of a 'language game' serving as the mediator between language and the world. The first pages of the *Investigations* show that the words of a text (or a complete primitive language) derive their meaning from the role they have in certain non-linguistic activities that Wittgenstein called games. The fundamental purpose of games was not something residing in logic or language. He considered games conceptually prior to such symbolic codes, activities from which logic and language derived their meaning. Through an analysis of the workings of a language one might hope to dissolve philosophical problems, or to show that they are pseudo-problems endlessly dissipating along further cycles of analysis. His *Nachlass* (1998–2000) has turned out to be invaluable in illuminating all aspects of his philosophy. For instance, it confirms that the notion of language game in his philosophy is not as ambiguous as often thought.

Perhaps the most influential field of study in advancing views on language games has been the theory of speech acts (see *Austin and *Searle), a major topic in pragmatics. Yet there are reasons to believe that the most intriguing forms of language games have little to do with speech acts or the related interpersonal communicative acts and modes of language in social contexts. The most interesting games that Wittgenstein advocated appear to be intra-linguistic. They work in the way they do because language has to function in a certain way, acquiring meaning from different but interrelated processes and procedures as one game transforms to another. The key to meaning is the contextual shift, by which an expression gains and loses its meaning as the old language game gains credit or loses its point, just as a position or a move in a game gains and loses its power in the context of the game in which it is situated.

This adoption of games was not accidental. *Nachlass* has revealed that game theory was not unknown to Wittgenstein: 'The theory of the game is *not* arbitrary although the game is' (2000: item 161, p. 15r, 1939). Apart from some isolated remarks concerning decisions and mathematical proofs, Wittgenstein did not show any particular interest in taking game-theoretic concepts further. This is not the end of the story, however. In 1937, two years before he made the statement above, he had drawn an intriguing analogy between an application of economic theory and communications consisting only of words and commands. The analogy was followed by an explication of the idea of language games. The impact of game theory on economics was in its early stages in 1937 when he drew this analogy, but it shows that his idea of language games was by no means isolated from advancements elsewhere. Wittgenstein's view of language marked a considerable step towards the science of pragmatics. To see the origins and growth of this view throughout his thinking, we nevertheless need to go back to his *Tractarian* era.

In 1914 (*Notebooks 14–16*, 1961), Wittgenstein was of the opinion that all propositions are unasserted, and assertions are merely psychological. His early conception of assertion revolved around this psychological view of assertions, as distinguished from strictly binary, truth-valued propositions. The idea of extracting assertory elements from statements was maintained until after the final revisions to the *Investigations*, by which time the idea had taken a linguistic turn towards what later developed into the theory of speech acts. He considered and rejected possibilities suggested by *Frege, whom he had met in 1911, that sentences contain an *annahme* (assumption) that is being asserted, or that there would be some special assertion signs, for instance question marks or signs pertaining to intonation, delineating the part of the sentence that is assigned a truth value.

Wittgenstein none the less repudiated the philosophical relevance of assertion signs. As the published version of the *Investigations* argues, what people say or assert is true or false, and they agree on what they say in that very same language, not some other language. Such language is an example of a life form of human beings, because any assertion turning out to be of contrary truth value to what was expected in intending it is an infringement of agreements made in the language. By uttering false assertions, or by committing a material breach of what soon after Wittgenstein were formulated as conversational maxims (see *Grice), one runs a risk of penalties. Looking beyond Wittgenstein on this point, such penalties may actually be implemented by imaginary quantities deducted from the pay-offs of a language game assigned to the overall conversational strategies of the parties engaged in communication.

The idea of language as a form of life provides us with what has often been referred to as the common ground of language users. Forms of life are ways of experiencing, and various ways of enjoying, shared events with others. This formed the arena for one of the most important activities of language games, according to Wittgenstein, namely the game of showing and saying what one sees to be the case in the context of the assertion. What Wittgenstein took use of language in ordinary life to presuppose is exactly these kinds of games. Language games function by way of roles in our ordinary life. One cannot call using language a game at all unless it is tied to what experience has provided, understood in the broad sense of encompassing all that can be communicated, given away or narrated by these games.

In nurturing the common ground, there needs to be a complex system of presuppositions and other related material in these forms of life. According to Wittgenstein, the moves in language games rest on tacit presuppositions, including the mutually agreed existence of the presuppositions themselves. Just how tacit these presuppositions and rules of language may be is shown by the fact that, under many circumstances, they are recognised and followed blindly, without the intervention of conscious or aware interpretation. Since Wittgenstein theorised this area, it has been witnessed to by such diverse issues as the implicit–explicit distinction uncovered in neuroscientific experiments and the habitual and non-consciously rational character of strategies ascribed to populations in evolutionary game theory. Further, it has turned out that spelling out the structure of mutually agreed presuppositions along with the system of propositional attitudes involved in presuppositions may be extremely difficult.

Though his ideas have had influence in the scientific arena, Wittgenstein was influenced by a number of linguistically minded philosophers, even though he referred to them sparingly. The difficulty of ascertaining particular influence is made more problematic by his habit of adopting the terminology of others for his own purposes, typically without acknowledgement. A good example of this is *Malinowski and his contextual theory of speech, which purported to show the essence of language by charting the invariants that are preserved through the range of linguistic variations, including linguistic forms influenced by physiological, mental, social and cultural elements. Malinowski thought that such an investigation would reveal the nature of the correspondence between meaning and form, a subject in which Wittgenstein had a strong interest. Yet even though he at one point played with thought experiments concerning what a tribe with a different culture might have meant by an expression that is recognised by us, Wittgenstein's philosophical concept of a language was not grounded on sociological, anthropological or ethnographic investigations as was Malinowski's. In fact, he showed little regard for such empirically established contexts of language use.

Perhaps because of his own difficulties in understanding language, Wittgenstein was led to the search for other media, such as pictures. Already in the *Tractatus*, he had argued that a picture has the same logical form of representation as what it represents (§2.2), and that the logical picture of facts is the thought (§3). This view morphed into the language game idea of meaning as action that is in constant flux, dispensing with the earlier claim that representations could sustain the logical forms of the facts by a picture-like interior of elementary propositions, while preserving the pictorial character of the structure of the thought. Among the earlier dichotomies that Wittgenstein no longer wished to maintain was the distinction between saying and showing. Whereas under the rule outlined in *Tractatus* the relations between simple objects and names were given not by attempting to define the objects but by pointing at them and using demonstratives, his later, more pragmatic account of meaning for complex propositions considered such relations across the varying contexts of assertions and shifting environments, including the intended meaning of the proposition possessed by the utterer.

Dealing with the implications of Wittgenstein's thought requires complex methodological tools that have only since been devised. For example, it is unfortunate that Wittgenstein did not have the analytic diagrammatic logic of *Peirce at his disposal to facilitate a precise logical analysis of the content of thought. The reason why Wittgenstein was not entirely happy with the picture theory of language was the imprecision and qualitatively imperfect character of pictures, which served badly the needs of understanding general assertions. By contrast, language games were conveniently subservient to those human activities that create such pictures, and hence the static link between pictures and the world came to be replaced by language games as the primary media of all communication. Among the precise analytic tools that Wittgenstein lacked but nevertheless recognised the need for were the tools for a geometrical account of negation, for dealing

with polarity in general assertions, for determining indefinite and vague pictures, and for interpreting non-literal meaning. All these residual problems would be amenable to a rigorous logical analysis in Peirce's diagrammatic system of logic.

In rejecting the view of naming relations as accounting for the meaning of objects, Wittgenstein took the idea of private language off the board. Understanding an utterance, he realised, is not equal to contemplating some mental entity not publicly accessible to anyone other than the interpreter of that utterance. Understanding language is something that the interpreter shares with the community of interpreters, but does not need to be ultimately judged against the opinions of the others.

Another of Wittgenstein's famous concepts was the idea of rule-following. In trying to find their way in their environment, humans are remarkable in learning, habituating and mastering all kinds of rules. These rules Wittgenstein took to stand for the many signs, including linguistic and mathematical symbols, that are presented to the learner. To act according to a rule does not presuppose its understanding, however, because such acts are simply what humans do.

During the last two years of his life, after retirement from Cambridge and having lived in Ireland, Wittgenstein worked incessantly on *On Certainty* (1969) and *Remarks on Colour* (1977), both unpublished until after his death. The former work serves to confirm that he did not espouse the notions of forms of life, or language games, as culturally or socially relative notions by which language is learned, used and cultivated. Rather, the only way to ascertain the reliability or certainty of linguistic assertions, or beliefs, must come from considerations internal to language or the network of interconnected beliefs. This view committed Wittgenstein to universalism, in other words to the view that language and its meaning relations with the world cannot be observed from an outside perspective (Hintikka 1996). But it did not lead to a relativistic and functional *Weltanschauung* of the Malinowskian kind, according to which such immutable meaning relations are viewed differently depending on the perspective and the purpose of a single language user or a society of language users (Gellner 1995). Moreover, recent research has unearthed evidence that Wittgenstein's later views of language were anticipated by, or are to some extent consistent with, some of the chief elements of American pragmatism (see Peirce) and the normative character of language espoused early on, among others, by Erik Ahlman (1892–1952) in 1926.

Beyond the influence of his work in language and meaning, Wittgenstein is also known as something of an eccentric. The philosopher A. J. *Ayer noted that Wittgenstein's austere habits led him to furnish his rooms at Cambridge with canvas deckchairs. Wittgenstein is also noted for his irascible temper and a tendency to take philosophical agreements personally. Nevertheless, the intellectual honesty that led him to abandon professional academic life at times when he felt he had nothing to contribute is greatly to his credit. He died of cancer on 29 April 1951, and is buried in Cambridge, England, in St Giles's churchyard, off Huntingdon Road.

Primary works

(1922). *Tractatus Logico-Philosophicus*. London: Kegan Paul. C. K. Ogden and F. P. Ramsey (eds), D. F. Pears and B. F. McGuinnes (trans.). London: Routledge, 1961.

(1953). *Philosophical Investigations*. G. E. M. Anscombe (ed. and trans.), R. Rhees (ed.). Oxford: Blackwell.

(1956). *Remarks on the Foundations of Mathematics*. G. H. von Wright, and R. Rhees (eds), G. E. M. Anscombe (ed. and trans.). Oxford: Blackwell.

(1958). *The Blue and Brown Books*. Oxford: Blackwell.

(1961). *Notebooks 14–16*. G. H. von Wright (ed.), G. E. M. Anscombe (ed. and trans.). Oxford: Blackwell.

(1967). *Zettel*. G. H. von Wright (ed.), G. E. M. Anscombe (ed. and trans.). Oxford: Blackwell.

(1969). *On Certainty*. G. H. von Wright (ed.), D. Paul (trans.), G. E. M. Anscombe (ed. and trans.). Oxford: Blackwell.

(1974). *Philosophical Grammar*. R. Rhees (ed.), A. Kenny (trans.). Oxford: Blackwell.

(1975). *Philosophical Remarks*. R. Rhees (ed.), R. Hargreaves and R. White (trans.). Oxford: Blackwell.

(1977). *Remarks on Colour*. G. E. M. Anscombe (ed.), L. L. McAlister and M. Schättle (trans.). Oxford: Blackwell.

(1980–92). *Remarks on the Philosophy of Psychology*. Vol. 1: G. E. M. Anscombe (ed. and trans.), G. H. von Wright (ed.), 1980. Vol. 2: G. H. von Wright and H. Nyman (eds), C. G. Luckhardt and M. A. E. Aue (trans.). Oxford: Blackwell.

(1998–2000). *Wittgenstein's Nachlass: The Bergen Electronic Edition*. Oxford, New York: Wittgenstein Trustees, University of Bergen and Oxford University Press.

Further reading

Ahlman, Erik (1926). *Das Normative Moment in Bedeutungsbegriff*. Helsingfors: Druckerei der Finnischen Littetaturgesellschaft.

Canfield, J. V. (ed.) (1986–88). *The Philosophy of Wittgenstein*. New York: Garland.

Gellner, Ernest (1995). *Language and Solitude: Wittgenstein, Malinowski and the Habsburg Dilemma*. Cambridge: Cambridge University Press.

Hintikka, Jaakko (1996). *Ludwig Wittgenstein: Half-Truths and One-and-a-Half-Truths*. Dordrecht: Kluwer.

Hintikka, Jaakko and Hintikka, Merrill B.

(1986). *Investigating Wittgenstein*. Oxford: Blackwell.

Kenny, Anthony (1973). *Wittgenstein*. London: Allen Lane.

Pears, David (1987). *The False Prison*. Oxford: Oxford University Press.

von Wright, Georg Henrik (1982). *Wittgenstein*. Oxford: Blackwell.

Ahti-Veikko Pietarinen

Index

Main entries are indicated in **bold**.